D1469397

ALCOHOL, TOBACCO, AND ILLICIT DRUGS

2 $48.80 #52

ISSN 1938-8896

2

ALCOHOL, TOBACCO, AND ILLICIT DRUGS

Sandra M. Alters

INFORMATION PLUS® REFERENCE SERIES
Formerly Published by Information Plus, Wylie, Texas

GALE
CENGAGE Learning™

Detroit • New York • San Francisco • New Haven, Conn • Waterville, Maine • London

Alcohol, Tobacco, and Illicit Drugs

Sandra M. Alters

Kepos Media, Inc., Paula Kepos and Janice Jorgensen, Series Editors

Project Editors: Kathleen J. Edgar, Elizabeth Manar, Kimberley A. McGrath

Rights Acquisition and Management: Robyn V. Young

Composition: Evi Abou-El-Seoud, Mary Beth Trimper

Manufacturing: Cynde Lentz

For product information and technology assistance, contact us at
Gale Customer Support, 1-800-877-4253.
For permission to use material from this text or product,
submit all requests online at **www.cengage.com/permissions.**
Further permissions questions can be e-mailed to
permissionrequest@cengage.com

Cover photograph: Image copyright Konstantin Yolshin, 2009. Used under license from Shutterstock.com.

Gale
27500 Drake Rd.
Farmington Hills, MI 48331-3535

ISBN-13: 978-0-7876-5103-9 (set)   ISBN-10: 0-7876-5103-6 (set)
ISBN-13: 978-1-4144-4853-4   ISBN-10: 1-4144-4853-8

ISSN 1938-8896

This title is also available as an e-book.
ISBN-13: 978-1-4144-7524-0 (set)
ISBN-10: 1-4144-7524-1 (set)
Contact your Gale sales representative for ordering information.

Printed in the United States of America
1 2 3 4 5 6 7 15 14 13 12 11

TABLE OF CONTENTS

PREFACE

Alcohol, Tobacco, and Illicit Drugs is part of the *Information Plus Reference Series*. The purpose of each volume of the series is to present the latest facts on a topic of pressing concern in modern American life. These topics include the most controversial and studied social issues of the 21st century: abortion, capital punishment, care of senior citizens, crime, the environment, health care, immigration, minorities, national security, social welfare, water, women, youth, and many more. Even though this series is written especially for high school and undergraduate students, it is an excellent resource for anyone in need of factual information on current affairs.

By presenting the facts, it is the intention of Gale, Cengage Learning to provide its readers with everything they need to reach an informed opinion on current issues. To that end, there is a particular emphasis in this series on the presentation of scientific studies, surveys, and statistics. These data are generally presented in the form of tables, charts, and other graphics placed within the text of each book. Every graphic is directly referred to and carefully explained in the text. The source of each graphic is presented within the graphic itself. The data used in these graphics are drawn from the most reputable and reliable sources, such as from the various branches of the U.S. government and from private organizations and associations. Every effort has been made to secure the most recent information available. Readers should bear in mind that many major studies take years to conduct and that additional years often pass before the data from these studies are made available to the public. Therefore, in many cases the most recent information available in 2011 is dated from 2008 or 2009. Older statistics are sometimes presented as well if they are landmark studies or of particular interest and no more-recent information exists.

Even though statistics are a major focus of the *Information Plus Reference Series*, they are by no means its only content. Each book also presents the widely held positions and important ideas that shape how the book's subject is discussed in the United States. These positions are explained in detail and, where possible, in the words of their proponents. Some of the other material to be found in these books includes historical background, descriptions of major events related to the subject, relevant laws and court cases, and examples of how these issues play out in American life. Some books also feature primary documents or have pro and con debate sections that provide the words and opinions of prominent Americans on both sides of a controversial topic. All material is presented in an evenhanded and unbiased manner; readers will never be encouraged to accept one view of an issue over another.

HOW TO USE THIS BOOK

Both legal and illicit drugs—substances that can affect a person's mood or physiology—are used by people from all segments of American society. Legal drugs include prescription medications as well as popular and widely available substances such as alcohol, tobacco, and caffeine. Illegal drugs are those with no currently accepted medical use in the United States, such as heroin, lysergic acid diethylamide, ecstasy, and inhalants. This book provides an overview of legal and illicit drugs, including their health impact, addictive nature, and potential for abuse. Also discussed are the political and economic ramifications of such substances; their use among youth; possible treatments; drug trafficking; and antidrug efforts and campaigns.

Alcohol, Tobacco, and Illicit Drugs consists of nine chapters and three appendixes. Each chapter is devoted to a particular aspect of alcohol, tobacco, and illicit drugs in the United States. For a summary of the information covered in each chapter, please see the synopses provided in the Table of Contents. Chapters generally begin with an overview of the basic facts and background information on the chapter's topic, then proceed to examine subtopics of particular interest. For example, Chapter 6: Drug Treatment, begins with definitions of drug abuse and addiction from various sources. It then gives an overview of an integrated approach to drug treatment. Next, the chapter presents two data sets to show how many people are being treated for substance abuse and describes characteristics of those who are admitted for treatment, such as age, race, ethnicity, and age. The types of treatment are then surveyed, followed by statistics on admitted patients. Included are admissions by substance, demographics by substance, type of treatment, and referring source. The effectiveness of treatment is discussed, with the inclusion of short descriptions of comprehensive studies on the topic. The chapter ends with a look at drug courts and where to go for help. Readers can find their way through a chapter by looking for the section and subsection headings, which are clearly set off from the text. They can also refer to the book's extensive index if they already know what they are looking for.

Statistical Information

The tables and figures featured throughout *Alcohol, Tobacco, and Illicit Drugs* will be of particular use to readers in learning about this issue. These tables and figures represent an extensive collection of the most recent and valuable statistics on alcohol, tobacco, illicit drugs, and related issues—for example, graphics cover the amount of alcoholic beverages consumed per capita by American citizens over the past several decades; alcohol's involvement in fatal automobile crashes; the diseases associated with tobacco use; the number of youth who use illicit drugs; and the prevalence rates of hallucinogen use among students. Gale, Cengage Learning believes that making this information available to readers is the most important way to fulfill the goal of this book: to help readers understand the issues and controversies surrounding alcohol, tobacco, and illicit drugs in the United States and to reach their own conclusions.

Each table or figure has a unique identifier appearing above it for ease of identification and reference. Titles for the tables and figures explain their purpose. At the end of each table or figure, the original source of the data is provided.

To help readers understand these often complicated statistics, all tables and figures are explained in the text. References in the text direct readers to the relevant statistics. Furthermore, the contents of all tables and figures are fully indexed. Please see the opening section of the index at the back of this volume for a description of how to find tables and figures within it.

Appendixes

Besides the main body text and images, *Alcohol, Tobacco, and Illicit Drugs* has three appendixes. The first is the Important Names and Addresses directory. Here, readers will find contact information for a number of government and private organizations that can provide further information on alcohol, tobacco, and/or illicit drugs. The second appendix is the Resources section, which can also assist readers in conducting their own research. In this section the author and editors of *Alcohol, Tobacco, and Illicit Drugs* describe some of the sources that were most useful during the compilation of this book. The final appendix is the index. It has been greatly expanded from previous editions and should make it even easier to find specific topics in this book.

ADVISORY BOARD CONTRIBUTIONS

The staff of Information Plus would like to extend its heartfelt appreciation to the Information Plus Advisory Board. This dedicated group of media professionals provides feedback on the series on an ongoing basis. Their comments allow the editorial staff who work on the project to make the series better and more user-friendly. The staff's top priority is to produce the highest-quality and most useful books possible, and the Information Plus Advisory Board's contributions to this process are invaluable.

The members of the Information Plus Advisory Board are:

- Kathleen R. Bonn, Librarian, Newbury Park High School, Newbury Park, California

- Madelyn Garner, Librarian, San Jacinto College, North Campus, Houston, Texas

- Anne Oxenrider, Media Specialist, Dundee High School, Dundee, Michigan

- Charles R. Rodgers, Director of Libraries, Pasco-Hernando Community College, Dade City, Florida

- James N. Zitzelsberger, Library Media Department Chairman, Oshkosh West High School, Oshkosh, Wisconsin

COMMENTS AND SUGGESTIONS

The editors of the *Information Plus Reference Series* welcome your feedback on *Alcohol, Tobacco, and Illicit Drugs*. Please direct all correspondence to:

Editors
Information Plus Reference Series
27500 Drake Rd.
Farmington Hills, MI 48331-3535

CHAPTER 1
DRUGS: A DEFINITION

Drugs are nonfood chemicals that alter the way a person thinks, feels, functions, or behaves. This includes everything from prescription medications, to illegal chemicals such as heroin, to popular and widely available substances such as alcohol, tobacco, and caffeine. A wide variety of laws, regulations, and government agencies exist to control the possession, sale, and use of drugs. Different drugs are held to different standards based on their perceived dangers and usefulness, a fact that sometimes leads to disagreement and controversy.

Illegal drugs are those with no currently accepted medical use in the United States, such as heroin, lysergic acid diethylamide (LSD), and marijuana. It is illegal to buy, sell, possess, and use these drugs except for research purposes. They are supplied only to registered, qualified researchers. (Some states and local jurisdictions have decriminalized certain uses of specific amounts of marijuana, but federal laws supersede these state and local marijuana decriminalization laws. For a more detailed discussion on the legalization of marijuana, see Chapter 9.)

By contrast, legal drugs are drugs whose sale, possession, and use as intended are not forbidden by law. Their use may be restricted, however. For example, the U.S. Drug Enforcement Administration (DEA) controls the use of legal psychoactive (mood- or mind-altering) drugs that have the potential for abuse. These drugs, which include narcotics, depressants, and stimulants, are available only with a prescription and are called controlled substances. The term *illicit drugs* is used by the Substance Abuse and Mental Health Services Administration to describe both controlled substances that are used in violation of the law and drugs that are completely illegal.

The goal of the DEA is to ensure that controlled substances are readily available for medical use or research purposes while preventing their illegal sale and abuse. The agency works toward accomplishing this goal by requiring people and businesses that manufacture, distribute, pre-scribe, and dispense controlled substances to register with the DEA. Registrants must abide by a series of requirements that relate to drug security, records accountability, and adherence to standards. The DEA also enforces the controlled substances laws and regulations of the United States by investigating and prosecuting those who violate these laws.

The U.S. Food and Drug Administration (FDA) also plays a role in drug control. This agency regulates the manufacture and marketing of prescription and nonprescription drugs. It also requires that the active ingredients in a product be safe and effective before allowing the drug to be sold.

Alcohol and tobacco are monitored and specially taxed by the Alcohol and Tobacco Tax and Trade Bureau (TTB). The TTB was formed in January 2003 as a provision of the Homeland Security Act of 2002, which split the Bureau of Alcohol, Tobacco, and Firearms (ATF) into two new agencies. One of these agencies, the TTB, took over the taxation duties for alcohol, tobacco, and firearms and remained a part of the U.S. Department of the Treasury. The TTB also ensures that alcohol and tobacco products are legally labeled, advertised, and marketed; regulates the qualification and operations of distilleries, wineries, and breweries; tests alcoholic beverages to ensure that their regulated ingredients are within legal limits; and screens applicants who wish to manufacture, import, or export tobacco products.

The other agency split from the former ATF is the reformed ATF: the Bureau of Alcohol, Tobacco, Firearms, and Explosives. The ATF has become a principal law enforcement agency within the U.S. Department of Justice, enforcing federal criminal laws and regulating the firearms and explosives industries. It also investigates illegal trafficking of alcohol and tobacco products.

In June 2009 Congress and President Barack Obama (1961–) enacted legislation that gave the FDA authority over the sale and advertising of tobacco. The legislation granted the FDA various liberties, including regulating the levels of nicotine and other ingredients in cigarettes, banning tobacco manufacturers from selling candy-flavored or menthol cigarettes, forcing larger warning signs on tobacco packaging, and preventing the sale of so-called mild or light cigarettes.

FIVE CATEGORIES OF SUBSTANCES

Drugs may be classified into five categories:

- Depressants, including alcohol and tranquilizers—these substances slow down the activity of the nervous system. They produce sedative (calming) and hypnotic (trancelike) effects as well as drowsiness. If taken in large doses, depressants can cause intoxication (drunkenness).

- Hallucinogens, including marijuana, phencyclidine, and LSD—hallucinogens produce abnormal and unreal sensations such as seeing distorted and vividly colored images. Hallucinogens can also produce frightening psychological responses such as anxiety, depression, and the feeling of losing control of one's mind.

- Narcotics, including heroin and opium, from which morphine and codeine are derived—narcotics are drugs that alter the perception of pain and induce sleep and euphoria (an intense feeling of well-being; a "high").

- Stimulants, including caffeine, nicotine, cocaine, amphetamine, and methamphetamine—these substances speed up the processing rate of the central nervous system. They can reduce fatigue, elevate mood, increase energy, and help people stay awake. In large doses stimulants can cause irritability, anxiety, sleeplessness, and even psychotic behavior. Caffeine is the most commonly used stimulant in the world.

- Other compounds, including anabolic steroids and inhalants—anabolic steroids are a group of synthetic substances that are chemically related to testosterone and are promoted for their muscle-building properties. Inhalants are solvents and aerosol products that produce vapors that have psychoactive effects. These substances dull pain and can produce euphoria.

Table 1.1 provides an overview of alcohol, nicotine, and other selected psychoactive substances. It includes the DEA schedule for each drug listed. Developed as part of the Controlled Substances Act (CSA) of 1970, the DEA drug schedules are categories into which controlled substances are placed depending on their characteristics such as medical use, potential for abuse, safety, and danger of dependence. The types of drugs categorized in each of the five schedules, with examples, are shown in Table 1.2.

DRUGS DISCUSSED IN THIS BOOK

This book focuses on substances that are widely used throughout the world: alcohol, tobacco, and illicit drugs. Not only are alcohol and tobacco legal, relatively affordable, and more or less socially acceptable (depending on time, place, and circumstance) but also they are important economic commodities. Industries exist to produce, distribute, and sell these products, creating jobs and income and contributing to economic well-being. Thus, whenever discussions of possible government regulation of alcohol and tobacco arise, the topic brings with it significant economic and political issues.

Illicit drugs are those that are unlawful to possess or distribute under the CSA. Some controlled substances can be taken under the supervision of health care professionals who are licensed by the DEA. The CSA provides penalties for the unlawful manufacture, distribution, and dispensing of controlled substances, based on the schedule of the drug or substance. Nonetheless, illicit drugs have fostered huge illicit drug marketing and drug trafficking (buying and selling) networks. (See Chapter 8.) Tobacco, beer, wine, and spirits are exempt from the CSA and the DEA drug schedules.

Figure 1.1, Figure 1.2, and Figure 1.3 show trends in cigarette, illicit drug, and alcohol use from 1900 to the first decade of the 21st century. They also provide an overview of the ebb and flow of the use and abuse of these substances in the United States. This chapter will take a historical look at the use and abuse of each substance, and the chapters that follow will present more up-to-date information.

WHAT ARE ABUSE AND ADDICTION?

Many drugs, both legal and illicit, have the potential for abuse and addiction. Research and treatment experts identify three general levels of interaction with drugs: use, abuse, and dependence (or addiction). In general, abuse involves a compulsive use of a substance and impaired social or occupational functioning. Dependence (addiction) includes these traits, plus evidence of physical tolerance (a need to take increasingly higher doses to achieve the same effect) or withdrawal symptoms when use of the drug is stopped.

The progression from use to dependence is complex, as are the abused substances themselves. Researchers find no standard boundaries between using a substance, abusing a substance, and being addicted to a substance. They believe these lines vary widely from substance to substance and from individual to individual.

In addition, scientists have been working to understand why some people who use addictive substances become addicted and why others do not or can more easily break the addiction. The results of many studies of identical and fraternal (nonidentical) twins and families with histories of

TABLE 1.1

Commonly abused drugs

Substance: category and name	Examples of *commercial* and street names	DEA Schedule[a]/how administered[b]	*Intoxication effects*/potential health consequences
Depressants			
Alcohol	Beer, wine, hard liquor	Not scheduled/swallowed	*Reduced anxiety; feeling of well-being; lowered inhibitions; slowed pulse and breathing; lowered blood pressure; poor concentration*/fatigue; confusion; impaired coordination, memory, judgment; addiction; respiratory depression and arrest, death
Barbiturates	*Amytal, Nembutal, Seconal, Phenobarbital;* barbs, reds, red birds, phennies, tooies, yellows, yellow jackets	II, III, V/injected, swallowed	*Also, for barbiturates—sedation, drowsiness*/depression, unusual excitement, fever, irritability, poor judgment, slurred speech, dizziness, life-threatening withdrawal.
Benzodiazepines (other than flunitrazepam)	*Ativan, Halcion, Librium, Valium, Xanax;* candy, downers, sleeping pills, tranks	IV/swallowed, injected	*For benzodiazepines—sedation, drowsiness*/dizziness
Flunitrazepam[c]	*Rohypnol;* forget-me pill, Mexican Valium, R2, Roche, roofies, roofinol, rope, rophies	IV/swallowed, snorted	*For flunitrazepam—visual and gastrointestinal disturbances, urinary retention, memory loss for the time under the drug's effects*
GHB[c]	*gamma-hydroxybutyrate;* G, Georgia home boy, grievous bodily harm, liquid ecstasy	I/swallowed	*For GHB—drowsiness, nausea*/vomiting, headache, loss of consciousness, loss of reflexes, seizures, coma, death
Methaqualone	*Quaalude, Sopor, Parest;* ludes, mandex, quad, quay	I/injected, swallowed	*For methaqualone—euphoria*/depression, poor reflexes, slurred speech, coma
Cannabinoids (hallucinogens)			
Hashish	Boom, chronic, gangster, hash, hash oil, hemp	I/swallowed, smoked	*Euphoria, slowed thinking and reaction time, confusion, impaired balance and coordination*/cough, frequent respiratory infections; impaired memory and learning; increased heart rate, anxiety; panic attacks; tolerance, addiction
Marijuana	Blunt, dope, ganja, grass, herb, joints, Mary Jane, pot, reefer, sinsemilla, skunk, weed	I/swallowed, smoked	
Dissociative anesthetics (hallucinogens)			
Ketamine	*Ketalar SV;* cat Valiums, K, Special K, vitamin K	III/injected, snorted, smoked	*Increased heart rate and blood pressure, impaired motor function/memory loss;* numbness; nausea/vomiting *Also, for ketamine—at high doses, delirium, depression, respiratory depression and arrest*
PCP and analogs	*phencyclidine;* angel dust, boat, hog, love boat, peace pill	I, II/injected, swallowed, smoked	*For PCP and analogs—possible decrease in blood pressure and heart rate, panic, aggression, violence*/loss of appetite, depression
Hallucinogens			*Altered states of perception and feeling; nausea; persisting perception disorder (flashbacks)*
LSD	*Lysergic acid diethylamide;* acid, blotter, boomers, cubes, microdot, yellow	I/swallowed, absorbed through mouth tissues	*Also, for LSD and mescaline—increased body temperature, heart rate, blood pressure; loss of appetite, sleeplessness, numbness, weakness, tremors*
Mescaline	Buttons, cactus, mesc, peyote	I/swallowed, smoked	*For LSD—persistent mental disorders*
Psilocybin	Magic mushroom, purple passion, shrooms	I/swallowed	*For psilocybin—nervousness, paranoia*
Opioids and morphine derivatives (narcotics)			
Codeine	*Empirin with Codeine, Fiorinal with Codeine, Robitussin A-C, Tylenol with Codeine;* Captain Cody, Cody, schoolboy; (with glutethimide) doors & fours, loads, pancakes and syrup	II, III, IV/injected, swallowed	*Pain relief, euphoria, drowsiness*/nausea, constipation, confusion, sedation, respiratory depression and arrest, tolerance, addiction, unconsciousness, coma, death
Fentanyl and fentanyl analogs	*Actiq, Duragesic, Sublimaze;* Apache, China girl, China white, dance fever, friend, goodfella, jackpot, murder 8, TNT, Tango and Cash	I, II/injected smoked, snorted	*Also, for codeine—less analgesia, sedation, and respiratory depression than morphine*
Heroin	*Diacetylmorphine;* brown sugar, dope, H, horse, junk, skag, skunk, smack, white horse	I/injected smoked, snorted	*For heroin—staggering gait*
Morphine	*Roxanol, Duramorph;* M, Miss Emma, monkey, white stuff	II, III/injected, swallowed, smoked	
Opium	*Laudanum, paregoric;* big O, black stuff, block, gum, hop	II, III, V/swallowed, smoked	
Oxycodone HCL	*Oxycontin;* Oxy, O.C., killer	II/swallowed, snorted, injected	
Hydrocodone bitartrate, acetaminophen	*Vicodin;* vike, Watson-387	II/swallowed	

substance abuse and addiction indicate that there is a genetic component to addiction. For example, in "Are There Genetic Influences on Addiction: Evidence from Family, Adoption, and Twin Studies" (*Addiction*, vol. 103, no. 7, July 2008), Arpana Agrawal and Michael T. Lynskey of the Washington University School of Medicine in St. Louis, Missouri, review studies that examined the genetic basis for addition. The researchers determine that inheritance accounts for a wide range of influence on addiction—from 30% to 70%. Other factors, such as gender, age, social

TABLE 1.1

Commonly abused drugs [CONTINUED]

Substance: category and name	Examples of *commercial* and street names	DEA Schedule[a]/how administered[b]	*Intoxication effects*/potential health consequences
Stimulants			*Increased heart rate, blood pressure, metabolism; feelings of exhilaration, energy, increased mental alertness*/rapid or irregular heart beat; reduced appetite, weight loss, heart failure, nervousness, insomnia
Amphetamine	*Biphetamine, Dexedrine;* bennies, black beauties, crosses, hearts, LA turnaround, speed, truck drivers, uppers	II/injected, swallowed, smoked, snorted	*Also, for amphetamine—rapid breathing*/tremor, loss of coordination; irritability, anxiousness, restlessness, delirium, panic, paranoia, impulsive behavior, aggressiveness, tolerance, addiction, psychosis
Cocaine	*Cocaine hydrochloride;* blow, bump, C, candy Charlie, coke, crack, flake, rock, snow, toot	II/injected, smoked, snorted	*For cocaine—increased temperature*/chest pain, respiratory failure, nausea, abdominal pain, strokes, seizures, headaches, malnutrition, panic attacks
MDMA (methylenedioxy-methamphetamine)	Adam, clarity, ecstasy, Eve, lover's speed, peace, STP, X, XTC	I/swallowed	*For MDMA—mild hallucinogenic effects, increased tactile sensitivity, empathic feelings*/impaired memory and learning, hyperthermia, cardiac toxicity, renal failure, liver toxicity
Methamphetamine	*Desoxyn;* chalk, crank, crystal, fire, glass, go fast, ice, meth, speed	II/injected, swallowed, smoked, snorted	*For methamphetamine—aggression, violence, psychotic behavior*/memory loss, cardiac and neurological damage; impaired memory and learning, tolerance, addiction
Methylphenidate (safe and effective for treatment of ADHD)	*Ritalin;* JIF, MPH, R-ball, Skippy, the smart drug, vitamin R	II/injected, swallowed, snorted	
Nicotine	Cigarettes, cigars, smokeless tobacco, snuff, spit tobacco, bidis, chew	Not scheduled/smoked, snorted, taken in snuff and spit	*For nicotine—additional effects attributable to tobacco exposure,* adverse pregnancy outcomes, chronic lung disease, cardiovascular disease, stroke, cancer, tolerance, addiction
Other compounds			
Anabolic steroids	*Anadrol, Oxandrin, Durabolin, Depo-Testosterone, Equipoise;* roids, juice	III/injected, swallowed, applied to skin	*No intoxication effects*/hypertension, blood clotting and cholesterol changes, liver cysts and cancer, kidney cancer, hostility and aggression, acne; in adolescents, premature stoppage of growth; in males, prostate cancer, reduced sperm production, shrunken testicles, breast enlargement; in females, menstrual irregularities, development of beard and other masculine characteristics
Dextromethorphan (DXM)	*Found in some cough and cold medications;* Robotripping, Robo, Triple C	Not scheduled/swallowed	*Dissociative effects, distortive visual perceptions to complete dissociative effects*
Inhalants	*Solvents (paint thinners, gasoline, glues), gases (butane, propane, aerosol propellants, nitrous oxide), nitrites (isoamyl, isobutyl, cyclohexyl);* laughing gas, poppers, snappers, whippets	Not scheduled/inhaled through nose or mouth	*Stimulation, loss of inhibition; headache; nausea or vomiting; slurred speech, loss of motor coordination; wheezing*/unconsciousness, cramps, weight loss, muscle weakness, depression, memory impairment, damage to cardiovascular and nervous systems, sudden death

[a]Schedule I and II drugs have a high potential for abuse. They require greater storage security and have a quota on manufacturing, among other restrictions. Schedule I drugs are available for research only and have no approved medical use; schedule II drugs are available only by prescription (unrefillable) and require a form for ordering. Schedule III and IV drugs are available by prescription, may have five refills in 6 months, and may be ordered orally. Some schedule V drugs are available over the counter.
[b]Taking drugs by injection can increase the risk of infection through needle contamination with staphylococci, HIV, hepatitis, and other organisms.
[c]Associated with sexual assaults.

SOURCE: Adapted from "Commonly Abused Drugs," National Institutes of Health, National Institute on Drug Abuse, February 2007, http://www.drugabuse.gov/PDF/CADChart.pdf (accessed November 7, 2010)

influences, and cultural characteristics, interact with one's genetics, resulting in an individual's susceptibility to addictive behavior.

Physiological, Psychological, and Sociocultural Factors

Some researchers maintain that the principal causes of substance use are external social influences, such as peer pressure, whereas the principal causes of substance abuse and/or dependence are psychological and physiological needs and pressures, including inherited tendencies. Additionally, psychoactive drug use at an early age may be a risk factor (a characteristic that increases likelihood) for subsequent dependence.

Physically, mood-altering substances affect brain processes. Most drugs that are abused stimulate the reward or pleasure centers of the brain by causing the release of dopamine, which is a neurotransmitter—a chemical in the brain that relays messages from one nerve cell to another.

Psychologically, a person may become dependent on a substance because it relieves pain, offers escape from real or perceived problems, or makes the user feel more relaxed or confident in certain social settings. A successful first use of a substance may reduce the user's fear of the drug and thus lead to continued use and even dependence.

TABLE 1.2

Drug schedules established by the Controlled Substances Act (CSA), 1970

Schedule I

- The drug or other substance has a high potential for abuse.
- The drug or other substance has no currently accepted medical use in treatment in the United States.
- There is a lack of accepted safety for use of the drug or other substance under medical supervision.
- Examples of Schedule I substances include heroin, lysergic acid diethylamide (LSD), marijuana, and methaqualone.

Schedule II

- The drug or other substance has a high potential for abuse.
- The drug or other substance has a currently accepted medical use in treatment in the United States or a currently accepted medical use with severe restrictions.
- Abuse of the drug or other substance may lead to severe psychological or physical dependence.
- Examples of Schedule II substances include morphine, phencyclidine (PCP), cocaine, methadone, and methamphetamine.

Schedule III

- The drug or other substance has less potential for abuse than the drugs or other substances in Schedules I and II.
- The drug or other substance has a currently accepted medical use in treatment in the United States.
- Abuse of the drug or other substance may lead to moderate or low physical dependence or high psychological dependence.
- Anabolic steroids, codeine and hydrocodone with aspirin or Tylenol, and some barbiturates are examples of Schedule III substances.

Schedule IV

- The drug or other substance has a low potential for abuse relative to the drugs or other substances in Schedule III.
- The drug or other substance has a currently accepted medical use in treatment in the United States.
- Abuse of the drug or other substance may lead to limited physical dependence or psychological dependence relative to the drugs or other substances in Schedule III.
- Examples of drugs included in Schedule IV are Darvon, Talwin, Equanil, Valium and Xanax.

Schedule V

- The drug or other substance has a low potential for abuse relative to the drugs or other substances in Schedule IV.
- The drug or other substance has a currently accepted medical use in treatment in the United States.
- Abuse of the drug or other substances may lead to limited physical dependence or psychological dependence relative to the drugs or other substances in Schedule IV.
- Cough medicines with codeine are examples of Schedule V drugs.

SOURCE: Adapted from *Drugs of Abuse, 2005 Edition*, U.S. Department of Justice, Drug Enforcement Administration, 2005, http://www.usdoj.gov/dea/pubs/abuse/doa-p.pdf (accessed November 7, 2010)

FIGURE 1.1

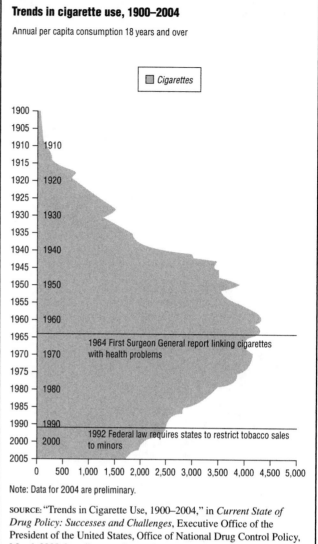

Trends in cigarette use, 1900–2004

Annual per capita consumption 18 years and over

Note: Data for 2004 are preliminary.

SOURCE: "Trends in Cigarette Use, 1900–2004," in *Current State of Drug Policy: Successes and Challenges*, Executive Office of the President of the United States, Office of National Drug Control Policy, March 2008, http://www.ncjrs.gov/ondcppubs/publications/pdf/successes_challenges.pdf (accessed November 9, 2010). Data from Miller, R. U.S. cigarette consumption 1900 to date. In Harr W. ed. Tobacco Yearbook. Bowling Green KY. Cockrel Corporation 1981.

Socially, substance use may be widespread in some groups or environments. The desire to belong to a special group is a strong human characteristic, and those who use one or more substances may become part of a subculture that encourages and promotes use. An individual may be influenced by one of these groups to start using a substance, or he or she may be drawn to such a group after starting use somewhere else. In addition, a person—especially a young person—may not have access to alternative rewarding or pleasurable groups or activities that do not include substance use.

Figure 1.4 illustrates some of the relationships between physiological, psychological, and cultural factors that influence drinking and drinking patterns. Constraints (inhibitory factors) and motivations influence drinking patterns. In turn, drinking patterns influence the relationship between routine activities that are related to drinking and acute (immediate) consequences of drinking.

Definitions of Abuse and Dependence

Two texts provide the most commonly used medical definitions of substance abuse and dependence. The *Diagnostic and Statistical Manual of Mental Disorders* (*DSM*) is published by the American Psychiatric Association. The *International Classification of Diseases* (*ICD*) is published by the World Health Organization (WHO). Even though the definitions of dependence in these two manuals are almost identical, the definitions of abuse are not.

THE *DSM* DEFINITION OF ABUSE. The text revision of the fourth edition of the *DSM*, *Diagnostic and Statistical Manual of Mental Disorders-IV Text Revision* (*DSM-IV-TR*),

FIGURE 1.2

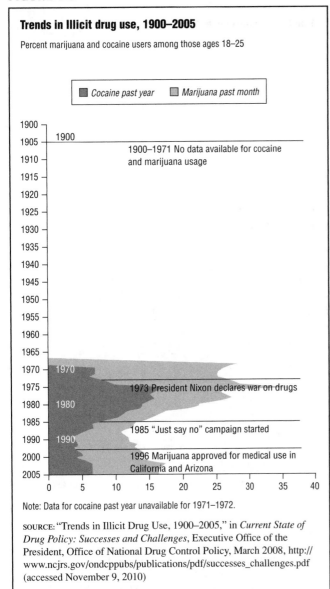

Trends in Illicit drug use, 1900–2005

Percent marijuana and cocaine users among those ages 18–25

Note: Data for cocaine past year unavailable for 1971–1972.

SOURCE: "Trends in Illicit Drug Use, 1900–2005," in *Current State of Drug Policy: Successes and Challenges*, Executive Office of the President, Office of National Drug Control Policy, March 2008, http://www.ncjrs.gov/ondcppubs/publications/pdf/successes_challenges.pdf (accessed November 9, 2010)

FIGURE 1.3

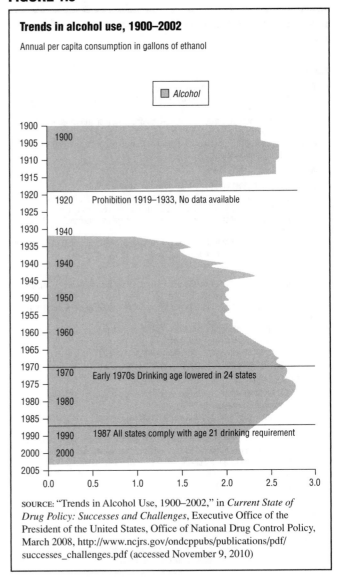

Trends in alcohol use, 1900–2002

Annual per capita consumption in gallons of ethanol

SOURCE: "Trends in Alcohol Use, 1900–2002," in *Current State of Drug Policy: Successes and Challenges*, Executive Office of the President of the United States, Office of National Drug Control Policy, March 2008, http://www.ncjrs.gov/ondcppubs/publications/pdf/successes_challenges.pdf (accessed November 9, 2010)

was published in 2000 and was the most recent revision available as of February 2011. (The publication of the *DSM-5* in its final form is expected in May 2013.) The *DSM-IV-TR* defines abuse as an abnormal pattern of recurring use that leads to "significant impairment or distress," marked by one or more of the following during a 12-month period:

- Failure to fulfill major obligations at home, school, or work (e.g., repeated absences, poor performance, or neglect)

- Use in hazardous or potentially hazardous situations, such as driving a car or operating a machine while impaired

- Legal problems, such as arrest for disorderly conduct while under the influence of the substance

- Continued use in spite of social or interpersonal problems caused by the use of the substance, such as fights or family arguments

THE *ICD* DEFINITION OF HARMFUL USE. The 10th and most recent revision (as of February 2011) of the *ICD* (*ICD-10*), which was endorsed by the 43rd World Health Assembly in May 1990 and has been used by WHO member states since 1994, uses the term *harmful use* rather than *abuse*. (The publication of the *ICD-11* in its final form is expected in 2015.) It defines harmful use as "a pattern of psychoactive substance use that is causing damage to health," either physical or mental.

Because the *ICD* manual is targeted toward international use, its definition must be broader than the *DSM* definition, which is intended for use in the United States. Cultural customs of substance use vary widely, sometimes even within the same country.

DEFINITIONS OF DEPENDENCE. In general, the *DSM-IV-TR* and the *ICD-10* manuals agree that dependence is present if three or more of the following occur during a 12-month period:

FIGURE 1.4

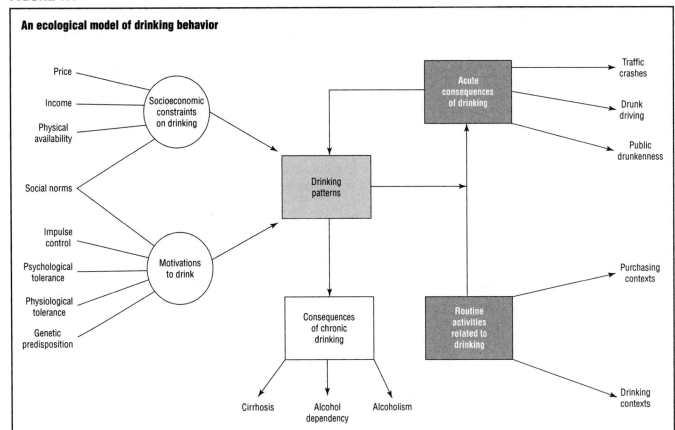

An ecological model of drinking behavior

SOURCE: Paul J. Gruenewald and Alex B. Millar, "An Ecological Model of Drinking Behavior," in "Alcohol Availability and the Ecology of Drinking Behavior," *Alcohol Health & Research World*, vol. 17, no. 1, 1993 (updated October 2000), http://www.niaaa.nih.gov/Resources/GraphicsGallery/TreatmentPrevention/gruen.htm (accessed February 16, 2011)

• Increasing need for more of the substance to achieve the same effect (occurs as the user builds up a tolerance to the substance), or a reduction in effect when using the same amount as used previously

• Withdrawal symptoms if use of the substance is stopped or reduced

• Progressive neglect of other pleasures and duties

• A strong desire to take the substance or a persistent but unsuccessful desire to control or reduce the use of the substance

• Continued use in spite of physical or mental health problems caused by the substance

• Use of the substance in larger amounts or over longer periods of time than originally intended, or difficulties in controlling the amount of the substance used or when trying to stop using it

• Considerable time spent in obtaining the substance, using it, or recovering from its effects

Progression from Use to Dependence

The rate at which individuals progress from drug use to drug abuse to drug dependence (or addiction) depends on many of the aforementioned factors. In general, each level is more dangerous, more invasive in the user's life, and more likely to cause social interventions, such as family pressure to enter treatment programs or prison sentences for drug offenses, than the previous level.

Figure 1.5 is a diagram of the progression from drug use to addiction. Notice that the intensification of use leads to abuse and that abuse leads to dependence. The right side of the diagram shows social interventions that are appropriate at various stages of drug use, abuse, and dependence. The dotted lines on the left side of the diagram show that relapse after recovery may lead to renewed drug use, abuse, or dependence.

THE HISTORY OF ALCOHOL USE

Ethyl alcohol (ethanol), the active ingredient in beer, wine, and other liquors, is the oldest known psychoactive drug. It is also the only type of alcohol that is used as a beverage. Other alcohols, such as methanol and isopropyl alcohol, when ingested even in small amounts, can produce severe negative health effects and often death.

The basic characteristics of alcoholic beverages have remained unchanged from early times. Beer and wine are created through the natural chemical process called fermentation. Fermentation can produce beverages with an

FIGURE 1.5

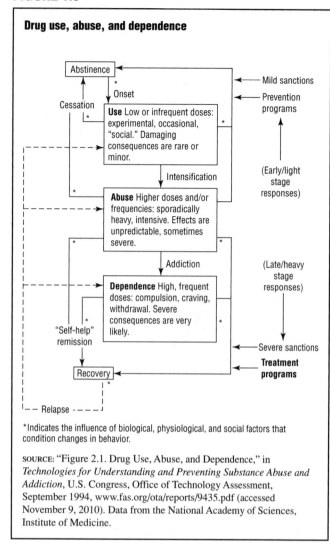

Drug use, abuse, and dependence

*Indicates the influence of biological, physiological, and social factors that condition changes in behavior.

SOURCE: "Figure 2.1. Drug Use, Abuse, and Dependence," in *Technologies for Understanding and Preventing Substance Abuse and Addiction*, U.S. Congress, Office of Technology Assessment, September 1994, www.fas.org/ota/reports/9435.pdf (accessed November 9, 2010). Data from the National Academy of Sciences, Institute of Medicine.

alcohol content of up to only 14%. More potent drinks, such as rum or vodka (known as spirits or liquors), can be produced through distillation. This is a process that involves using heat to separate and concentrate the alcohol found in fermented beverages and can result in drinks that have an alcoholic content of 50% or more.

Early Uses and Abuses of Alcohol

Beer and wine have been used since ancient times in religious rituals, celebrations of councils, coronations, war, peacemaking, festivals, hospitality, and the rites of birth, initiation, marriage, and death. In ancient times, just as in the 21st century, the use of beer and wine sometimes led to drunkenness. One of the earliest works on temperance (controlling one's drinking or not drinking at all) was written in Egypt nearly 3,000 years ago. These writings can be thought of as similar to present-day pamphlets that espouse moderation in alcohol consumption. Similar recommendations have been found in early Greek, Roman, Indian, Japanese, and Chinese writings, as well as in the Bible.

Drinking in Colonial America

In colonial America people drank much more alcohol than they do in the 21st century, with estimates ranging from three to seven times more alcohol per person per year. Liquor was used to ease the pain and discomfort of many illnesses and injuries such as the common cold, fever, broken bones, toothaches, frostbite, and the like. Parents often gave liquor to children to relieve their minor aches and pains or to help them sleep. Until 1842, when modern surgical anesthesia began with the use of ether, only heavy doses of alcohol were consistently effective to ease pain during operations.

As early as 1619 drunkenness was illegal in the Virginia Colony. It was punished in various ways: whipping, placement in the stocks, fines, and even wearing a red D (for "drunkard"). By the 18th century all classes of people were getting drunk with greater frequency, even though it was well known that alcohol affected the senses and motor skills and that drunkenness led to increased crime, violence, accidents, and death.

Temperance

In 1784 Benjamin Rush (1746–1813), a physician and signer of the Declaration of Independence, published the booklet *An Inquiry into the Effects of Ardent Spirits on the Mind and Body*. The pamphlet became popular among the growing number of people who were concerned about the excessive drinking of many Americans. Such concern gave rise to the temperance movement.

The temperance movement in the United States spanned the 19th and early 20th centuries. Initially, the goal of the movement was to promote moderation in the consumption of alcohol. By the 1850s large numbers of people were completely giving up alcohol, and by the 1870s the goal of the temperance movement was to promote abstinence from alcohol. Reformers were concerned about the effects of alcohol on the family, the labor force, and the nation, all of which needed sober participants if they were to remain healthy and productive. Temperance supporters also saw alcoholism as a problem of personal immorality.

Prohibition

Temperance organizations lobbied for the prohibition of alcohol in the United States during the early years of the 20th century. One of the leading temperance organizations was the Anti-Saloon League, which created print materials to convince the public that alcohol should be banned. Figure 1.6 is one of the league's flyers, which showed that families who drank alcohol had a higher rate of child death than families who abstained from alcohol. However, the Anti-Saloon League's research did not take into account other factors that might affect the rate of child death among families, such as poverty. In addition, the league

FIGURE 1.6

Anti-Saloon League flyer promoting alcohol abstinence, 1909

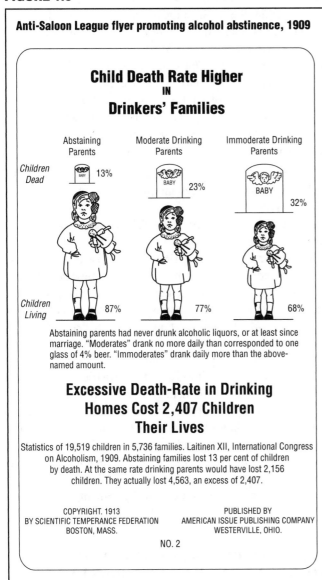

Child Death Rate Higher
IN
Drinkers' Families

Abstaining Parents

Moderate Drinking Parents

Immoderate Drinking Parents

Children Dead   13%   BABY 23%   BABY 32%

Children Living   87%   77%   68%

Abstaining parents had never drunk alcoholic liquors, or at least since marriage. "Moderates" drank no more daily than corresponded to one glass of 4% beer. "Immoderates" drank daily more than the above-named amount.

Excessive Death-Rate in Drinking Homes Cost 2,407 Children Their Lives

Statistics of 19,519 children in 5,736 families. Laitinen XII, International Congress on Alcoholism, 1909. Abstaining families lost 13 per cent of children by death. At the same rate drinking parents would have lost 2,156 children. They actually lost 4,563, an excess of 2,407.

COPYRIGHT. 1913
BY SCIENTIFIC TEMPERANCE FEDERATION
BOSTON, MASS.

PUBLISHED BY
AMERICAN ISSUE PUBLISHING COMPANY
WESTERVILLE, OHIO.

NO. 2

SOURCE: "Child Death Rate Higher in Drinkers' Families," Anti-Saloon League, 1909. c. Westerville Public Library. Reprinted courtesy of the Westerville Public Library, Westerville, OH.

used sensationalist images in its print materials, such as children with gravestones above their heads, to sway public opinion.

In 1919 reform efforts led to the passage of the 18th Amendment of the U.S. Constitution, which prohibited the "manufacture, sale, or transportation of intoxicating liquors" and their importation and exportation. The Volstead Act of 1919, which passed over President Woodrow Wilson's (1856–1924) veto, was the Prohibition law that enforced the 18th Amendment.

Outlawing alcohol did not stop most people from drinking; instead, alcohol was manufactured and sold illegally by gangsters, who organized themselves efficiently and gained considerable political influence from the money they earned. In addition, many individuals illegally brewed alcoholic beverages at home or smuggled alcohol from Canada and Mexico. Ultimately, the 18th Amendment was repealed in 1933 with the passage of the 21st Amendment.

Understanding the Dangers of Alcohol

As the decades passed, recognition of the dangers of alcohol increased. In 1956 the American Medical Association endorsed classifying and treating alcoholism as a disease. In 1970 Congress created the National Institute on Alcohol Abuse and Alcoholism, which established a public commitment to alcohol-related research. During the 1970s, however, many states lowered their drinking age to 18 when the legal voting age was lowered to this age.

Traffic fatalities rose after these laws took effect, and many such accidents involved people between the ages of 18 and 21 years who had been drinking and driving. Organizations such as Mothers against Drunk Driving and Students against Drunk Driving sought to educate the public about the great harm drunk drivers had done to others. As a result, and because of pressure from the federal government, by 1988 all states raised their minimum drinking age to 21. The National Highway Traffic Safety Administration of the U.S. Department of Transportation estimates in *Traffic Safety Facts, 2008 Data: Young Drivers* (October 2009, http://www-nrd.nhtsa.dot .gov/pubs/811169.pdf), the most recent publication on this topic as of February 2011, that laws making 21 the minimum drinking age saved an estimated 27,052 lives between 1975 and 2008. By 1989 warning labels noting the deleterious effects of alcohol on health were required on all retail containers of alcoholic beverages. Nonetheless, the misuse and abuse of alcohol remain major health and social problems in the 21st century.

THE HISTORY OF TOBACCO USE

Tobacco is a commercially grown plant that contains nicotine, an addictive drug. Tobacco is native to North America, where since ancient times it has played an important part in Native American social and religious customs. Additionally, Native Americans believed that tobacco had medicinal properties, so it was used to treat pain, epilepsy, colds, and headaches.

From Pipes to Cigarettes

As European explorers and settlers came to North America during the 15th and 16th centuries, Native Americans introduced them to tobacco. Its use soon spread among the settlers, and then throughout Europe and Asia, although some rulers and nations opposed it and sought to outlaw it. At this time tobacco was smoked in pipes, chewed, or taken as snuff. Snuff is finely powdered tobacco that can be chewed, rubbed on the gums, or inhaled through the nose.

Cigar smoking was introduced to the United States in about 1762. Cigars are tobacco leaves that are rolled and prepared for smoking. The U.S. consumption of cigars exceeded 4 billion in 1898, according to various tobacco-related websites. However, cigarettes (cut tobacco rolled in a paper tube) would soon become the choice of most smokers, thanks to the 1881 invention of a cigarette-making machine that allowed them to be mass produced and sold cheaply.

Early Antismoking Efforts in the United States

The first antismoking movement in the United States was organized during the 1830s (just as the temperance movement was growing in the country). Reformers characterized tobacco as an unhealthy and even fatal habit. Tobacco use was linked to increased alcohol use and lack of cleanliness. Antismoking reformers also suggested that tobacco exhausted the soil, wasted money, and promoted laziness, promiscuity, and profanity. Their efforts to limit or outlaw smoking were met with only small, temporary, successes until well into the 20th century.

A Boom in Smoking in the United States

The National Center for Chronic Disease Prevention and Health Promotion reports in "Consumption Data" (September 17, 2010, http://www.cdc.gov/tobacco/data _statistics/tables/economics/consumption/index.htm) that cigarette usage increased dramatically during the early 1900s, with the total consumption increasing from 2.5 billion cigarettes in 1901 to 13.2 billion cigarettes in 1912. In 1913 the R. J. Reynolds Company introduced Camel cigarettes, an event that is often called the birth of the modern cigarette. During World War I (1914–1918) cigarettes were shipped to U.S. troops fighting overseas (this also occurred during World War II [1939–1945]). They were included in soldiers' rations and were dispensed by groups such as the American Red Cross and the Young Men's Christian Association. Women began openly smoking in larger numbers as well, which was something that tobacco companies noticed; in 1919 the first advertisement featuring a woman smoking cigarettes appeared.

Cigarette smoking was very common and an accepted part of society, but doubts about its safety were growing. On July 12, 1957, following a joint report by the National Cancer Institute, the National Heart Institute, the American Cancer Society, and the American Heart Association, the U.S. surgeon general Leroy E. Burney (1906–1998), a smoker himself, delivered the official statement "Lung Cancer and Excessive Cigarette Smoking" (http://caonline.amcancersoc .org/cgi/reprint/8/2/44.pdf), in which he declared that "the weight of the evidence is increasingly pointing in one direction: that excessive smoking is one of the causative factors in lung cancer." Nevertheless, cigarette ads of the 1950s touted cigarette smoking as pleasurable, sexy, relaxing, flavorful, and fun. (See Figure 1.7.)

Health Risks Lead to Diminished Smoking

In 1964 the U.S. surgeon general Luther L. Terry (1911–1985) released *Smoking and Health: Report of the Advisory Committee to the Surgeon General of the Public Health Service* (http://profiles.nlm.nih.gov/NN/B/B/M/Q/ _/nnbbmq.pdf). This landmark document was the first widely publicized official recognition that cigarette smoking is a cause of lung cancer and laryngeal cancer in men, a probable cause of lung cancer in women, and the most important cause of chronic bronchitis.

Increased attention was paid to the potential health risks of smoking throughout the rest of the 1960s and 1970s. The first health warnings appeared on cigarette packages in 1966. In 1970 the WHO took a public stand against smoking. On January 2, 1971, the Public Health Cigarette Smoking Act of 1969 went into effect, removing cigarette advertising from radio and television in the United States. A growing number of individuals, cities, and states filed lawsuits against U.S. tobacco companies. Some individuals claimed they had been deceived about the potential harm of smoking. A few states filed lawsuits to recoup money spent on smokers' Medicaid bills. In 1998, 46 states, 5 territories, and the District of Columbia signed the Master Settlement Agreement (http://ag.ca.gov/ tobacco/msa.php) with the major tobacco companies to settle all state lawsuits for $206 billion. Excluded from the settlement were Florida, Minnesota, Mississippi, and Texas, which had already concluded previous settlements with the tobacco industry. Chapter 7 includes more information on the Master Settlement Agreement and its long-term effects.

THE EARLY HISTORY OF NARCOTIC, STIMULANT, AND HALLUCINOGEN USE

Humans have experimented with narcotic and hallucinogenic plants since before recorded history, discovering their properties as they tested plants for edibility or were attracted by the odors of some leaves when the leaves were burned. Ancient cultures used narcotic plants to relieve pain or to heighten pleasure and hallucinogenic plants to induce trancelike states during religious ceremonies. Natural substances, used directly or in refined extracts, have also served simply to increase or dull alertness, to invigorate the body, or to change the mood.

Narcotic Use through the 19th Century

As mentioned earlier, narcotics, including heroin and opium, are drugs that alter the perception of pain and induce sleep and euphoria. Opium is a dried powdered extract that is derived from the opium poppy plant *Papaver somniferum*. Morphine and heroin are made from opium, and all three of these addicting narcotics are called opiates.

Opium itself has been used as a pain reliever in Europe and Asia for thousands of years. In 1805 Friedrich

FIGURE 1.7

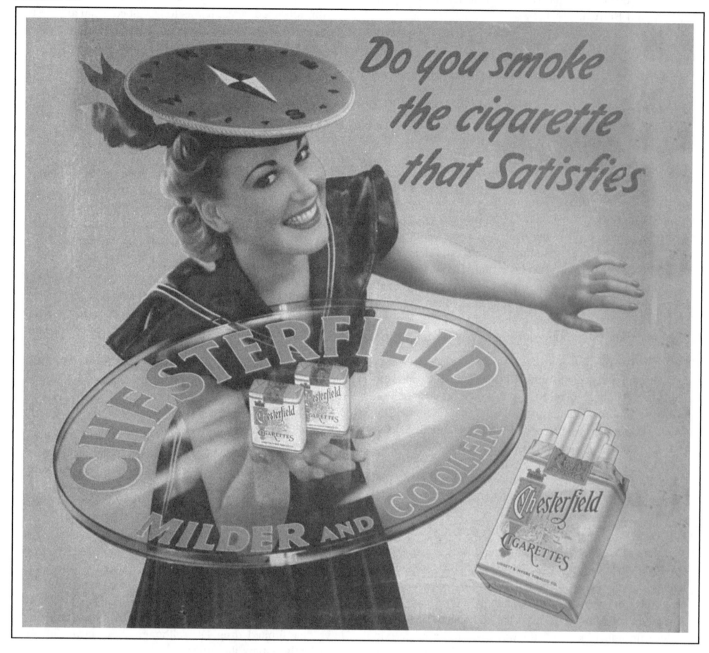

A cigarette advertisement from the 1950s. © *Robert Landau/Corbis.*

Sertürner (1793–1841), a German pharmacist, discovered how to isolate the highly potent morphine from opium. In 1832 the French chemist Pierre-Jean Robiquet (1780–1840) isolated codeine from opium, which is milder than morphine. It came to be used in cough remedies. The development of the hypodermic needle during the early 1850s made it easier to use morphine. It became a common medicine for treating severe pain, such as battlefield injuries. During the U.S. Civil War (1861–1865) so many soldiers became addicted to morphine that the addiction was later called soldier's disease.

The most potent narcotic that is derived from opium is heroin, which was first synthesized in 1874 by C. R. Alder Wright (1844–1894) at St. Mary's Hospital in London, England. In 1898 the Bayer Company of Elberfeld, Germany, began marketing the drug as a cough remedy and painkiller under the brand-name Heroin; the word was derived from the German word for "heroic," which was intended to convey the drug's power and potency. The drug was an instant success and was soon exported.

Stimulant Use through the 19th Century

The use of stimulants dates back to about 3000 BC with South American societies. Even then, the people of this region knew that cocaine, which was extracted from the leaves of the coca tree *Erythroxylon coca*, was capable of producing euphoria, hyperactivity, and hallucinations.

This small coca tree is native to tropical mountain regions in Peru and Bolivia.

After the Spanish conquest of the Incas during the early 1500s and the ensuing Spanish immigration into South America, coca was grown on plantations and used as wages to pay workers. The drug seemed to negate the effects of exhaustion and malnutrition, especially at high altitudes. Many South Americans still chew coca leaves to alleviate the effects of high altitudes.

The spread of the use of coca is attributed to Paolo Mantegazza (1831–1910), an Italian physician who came to value the restorative powers of coca while living in Lima, Peru, during the 1850s. He praised the drug, which led to interest in coca in the United States and Europe. In 1863 the French chemist Angelo Mariani (1838–1914) extracted cocaine from coca leaves and used it as the main ingredient in his coca wine, called Vin Mariani. Shortly thereafter, cough syrups and tonics holding drops of cocaine in solution became popular. Eventually, extracts from coca leaves not only appeared in wine but also in chewing gum, tea, and throat lozenges.

The temperance movement in the United States from 1800 to 1890 helped fuel the public's fondness for non-alcoholic products containing coca. During the mid-1880s Atlanta, Georgia, became one of the first major U.S. cities to forbid the sale of alcohol. It was there that the American inventor John Pemberton (1831–1888) first marketed Coca-Cola, a syrup that then contained extracts of both coca and the kola nut, as a "temperance drink."

Hallucinogen Use through the 19th Century

Naturally occurring hallucinogens, which are derived from plants, have been used by various cultures for magical, religious, recreational, and health-related purposes for thousands of years. For more than 2,000 years Native American societies often used hallucinogens, such as the psilocybin mushroom (*Psilocybe mexicana*) of Mexico and the peyote cactus (*Lophophora williamsii*) of the U.S. Southwest, in religious ceremonies. Even though scientists were slow to discover the medicinal possibilities of hallucinogens, by 1919 they had isolated mescaline from the peyote cactus and recognized its resemblance to the adrenal hormone epinephrine (adrenaline).

Cannabis, also a hallucinogen, is the term generally applied to the Himalayan hemp plant *Cannabis sativa* from which marijuana, bhang, and ganja (hashish) are derived. Bhang is equivalent to the U.S.-style marijuana, consisting of the leaves, fruits, and stems of the plant. Ganja, which is prepared by crushing the flowering tips of cannabis and collecting a resinous paste, is more potent than marijuana and bhang.

Cannabis dates back more than 5,000 years to Central Asia and China; from there it spread to India and the Near East. Cannabis was highly regarded as a medicinal plant used in folk medicines. It was long valued as an analgesic (painkiller), topical anesthetic, antispasmodic, antidepressant, appetite stimulant, antiasthmatic, and antibiotic.

NARCOTIC, STIMULANT, AND HALLUCINOGEN USE AT THE TURN OF THE 19TH CENTURY AND BEYOND

In late 19th-century America it was possible to buy, in a store or by mail order, many medicines (or alleged medicines) containing morphine, cocaine, and even heroin. Until 1903 the soft drink Coca-Cola contained cocaine. The cocaine was removed and more caffeine (which was already present in the drink from the kola nut) was added. Pharmacies sold cocaine in pure form, as well as many drugs made from opium, such as morphine and heroin.

Beginning in 1898 heroin became widely available when the Bayer Company marketed it as a powerful cough suppressant. According to the Office of Technology Assessment, in *Technologies for Understanding and Preventing Substance Abuse and Addiction* (September 1994, http://www.princeton.edu/~ota/disk1/1994/9435/9435.PDF), physician prescriptions of these drugs increased from 1% of all prescriptions in 1874 to between 20% and 25% in 1902. These drugs were available and widely used, with little concern for negative health consequences.

Soon, however, cocaine, heroin, and other drugs were taken off the market for a number of reasons. A growing awareness of the dangers of drug use and food contamination led to the passage of laws such as the Pure Food and Drug Act of 1906. Among other things, the act required the removal of false claims from patent medicines. Medical labels also had to state the amount of any narcotic ingredient the medicine contained and whether that medicine was habit-forming. A growing temperance movement, the development of safe painkillers (such as aspirin), and more alternative medical treatments contributed to the passage of laws that limited drug use, although these laws did not completely outlaw the drugs.

Besides health-related worries, by the mid- to late 1800s drug use had come to be associated with "undesirables." When drug users were thought to live only in the slums, drug use was considered solely a criminal problem; but when it was finally recognized in middle-class neighborhoods, it came to be seen as a mental health problem. By the turn of the 20th century the use of narcotics was considered an international problem. In 1909 the International Opium Commission met to discuss worldwide drug use. This meeting led to the signing of a treaty two years later in the Netherlands requiring all signatories to pass laws that limited the use of narcotics for medicinal purposes. After nearly three years of debate, Congress passed the Harrison Narcotic Act of 1914, which called for the strict control of opium and coca (although coca is a stimulant and not a narcotic).

Regulating Narcotics, Stimulants, and Hallucinogens

During the 1920s the federal government regulated drugs through the U.S. Department of the Treasury. In 1930 President Herbert Hoover (1874–1964) created the Federal Bureau of Narcotics and selected Harry J. Anslinger (1892–1975) to head it. Believing that all drug users were deviant criminals, Anslinger vigorously enforced the law for the next 32 years. Marijuana, for example, was presented as a "killer weed" that threatened the very fabric of American society.

Marijuana is thought to have been introduced to the United States by Mexican immigrants. Thus, according to the Office of Technology Assessment, in *Technologies for Understanding and Preventing Substance Abuse and Addiction*, it was widely believed that anti-Mexican attitudes, as well as Anslinger's considerable influence, prompted the passage of the Marijuana Tax Act of 1937. The act made the use or sale of marijuana without a tax stamp a federal offense. Because by this time the sale of marijuana was illegal in most states, buying a federal tax stamp would alert the authorities in a particular state to who was selling drugs. Naturally, no marijuana dealer wanted to buy a stamp and expose his or her identity to the authorities.

From the 1940s to the 1960s the FDA, based on the authority granted by the Food, Drug, and Cosmetic Act of 1938, began to police the sale of certain drugs. The act had required the FDA to stipulate if specific drugs, such as amphetamines and barbiturates, were safe for self-medication.

After studying most amphetamines (stimulants) and barbiturates (depressants), the agency concluded that it simply could not declare them safe for self-medication. (See Table 1.1 for listings of stimulants and depressants.) Therefore, it ruled that these drugs could only be used under medical supervision—that is, with a physician's prescription. For all pharmaceutical products other than narcotics, this marked the beginning of the distinction between prescription and over-the-counter (without a prescription) drugs.

For 25 years undercover FDA inspectors identified pharmacists who sold amphetamines and barbiturates without a prescription and doctors who wrote illegal prescriptions. During the 1950s, with the growing sale of amphetamines, barbiturates, and, eventually, LSD and other hallucinogens at cafés, truck stops, flophouses, and weight-reduction salons and by street-corner pushers, FDA authorities went after these other illegal dealers. In 1968 the drug-enforcement responsibilities of the FDA were transferred to the Department of Justice.

War on Drugs

From the mid-1960s to the late 1970s the demographic profile of drug users changed. Previously, drug use had generally been associated with minorities, lower classes, or young "hippies" and "beatniks." During this period drug use among middle-class whites became widespread and more generally accepted. Cocaine, an expensive drug, began to be used by middle- and upper-class whites, many of whom looked on it as a nonaddictive recreational drug and status symbol. In addition, drugs had become much more prevalent in the military because they were cheap and plentiful in Vietnam.

Whereas some circles viewed drug use with wider acceptance, other public sectors came to see drugs as a threat to their communities—much as, 40 years earlier, alcohol had acquired a negative image, leading to Prohibition. Drugs not only symbolized poverty but also were associated with protest movements against the Vietnam War (1955–1975) and the so-called Establishment. Many parents began to perceive the widespread availability of drugs as a threat to their children. By the end of the 1960s such views began to acquire a political expression.

When Richard M. Nixon (1913–1994) ran for president in 1968, he included a strong antidrug plank in his law-and-order platform, calling for a War on Drugs. After he was elected president, Nixon created the President's National Commission on Marihuana and Drug Abuse, which published its findings in *Marihuana: A Signal of Misunderstanding* (March 1972, http://www.druglibrary.org/Schaffer/Library/studies/nc/ncmenu.htm). Nixon ignored the commission's findings, which called for the legalization of marijuana. Since that time the U.S. government has been waging the War on Drugs. In 1973 Congress authorized the formation of the DEA to reduce the supply of drugs. A year later the National Institute on Drug Abuse (NIDA) was created to lead the effort to reduce the demand for drugs and to direct research, federal prevention, and treatment services.

Under the Nixon, Ford, and Carter administrations federal spending tended to emphasize the treatment of drug abusers. Meanwhile, a growing number of parents, fearing that their children were being exposed to drugs, began to pressure elected officials and government agencies to do more about the growing use of drugs. In response, the NIDA began widely publicizing the dangers of marijuana and other drugs once thought not to be particularly harmful.

President Ronald Reagan (1911–2004) favored a strict approach to drug use, popularized the phrase "War on Drugs," and increased enforcement efforts. In *Technologies for Understanding and Preventing Substance Abuse and Addiction*, the Office of Technology Assessment states that the budget to fight drugs rose from $1.5 billion in fiscal year (FY) 1981 to $4.2 billion in FY 1989. By the end of the Reagan administration two-thirds of all drug control funding went for law enforcement and one-third went for treatment and prevention. First Lady Nancy Reagan (1921–) vigorously campaigned against drug use, urging children to "just say no!" The Crime Control Act of

1984 dramatically increased the penalties for drug use and drug trafficking.

INTRODUCTION OF CRACK COCAINE. Cocaine use increased dramatically during the 1960s and 1970s, but the drug's high cost restricted its use to the more affluent. During the early 1980s cocaine dealers discovered a way to prepare cocaine so that it could be smoked in small and inexpensive but powerful and highly addictive amounts. The creation of this so-called crack cocaine meant that poor people could now afford to use the drug, and a new market opened. In addition, the acquired immunodeficiency syndrome (AIDS) epidemic caused some injection drug users to switch to smoking crack to avoid exposure to the human immunodeficiency virus (HIV), which can be contracted by sharing needles with an infected user.

Battles for control of the distribution and sale of the drug led to a violent black market. The easy availability of firearms and the huge amounts of money to be made selling crack and other drugs transformed many areas of the nation—but particularly the inner cities—into dangerous places.

The widespread fear of crack cocaine led to increasingly harsh laws and penalties. Authorities warned that crack was highly addictive and spreading rapidly, and they predicted a subsequent generation of "crack babies"—that is, babies born addicted to crack because their mothers were using it during pregnancy.

HEROIN GETS CHEAPER AND PURER. The dangers associated with crack cocaine caused changes in the use of heroin during the 1980s. Many reported deaths from heroin overdosing had lessened the drug's attraction. In addition, heroin had to be injected by syringe, and concerns regarding HIV infection contributed to the dangers of using the drug. During the 1990s an oversupply of heroin, innovations that produced a smokable variety of the drug, and the appearance of purer forms of the drug restored its attractiveness to the relatively small number of people who were addicted to so-called hard drugs. It was no longer necessary to take the drug intravenously— it could be sniffed like cocaine—although many users continued to use needles.

The War Continues: The Office of National Drug Control Policy

The Anti-drug Abuse Act of 1988 created the Office of National Drug Control Policy (ONDCP), to be headed by a director—popularly referred to as the drug czar—who would coordinate the nation's drug policy. The Office of Technology Assessment reports in *Technologies for Understanding and Preventing Substance Abuse and Addiction* that spending for drug control rose from $4.2 billion in FY 1989 under President Reagan to $12.7 billion in FY 1993 under President George H. W. Bush (1924–). As was the case during the Reagan administration, the

monetary split was roughly two-thirds for law enforcement and one-third for treatment and prevention. By 1990 every state that had once decriminalized the use of marijuana had repealed those laws.

The Office of Technology Assessment indicates that when President Bill Clinton (1946–) took office in 1993, he cut the ONDCP staff from 146 to 25, while at the same time raising the director of the ONDCP to cabinet status. Clinton called for 100,000 more police officers on the streets and advocated drug treatment on demand. According to the ONDCP, in *The National Drug Control Strategy, FY 2004 Budget Summary* (February 2003, http://www.ncjrs.gov/pdffiles1/ondcp/198157.pdf), drug control funding totaled $8.2 billion in FY 1998, with the split 52% for law enforcement and 48% for treatment and prevention. (It is important to note that during the mid-1990s changes were made in the list of expenditures included in this tally and that in 2003 the national drug control budget was restructured, thus making it difficult to analyze historical drug control spending trends before and after 1995. The FY 2004 budget summary provides a recalculation of historical tables from FYs 1995 to 2004.)

When he took office in 2001, President George W. Bush (1946–) promised to continue national efforts to eradicate illicit drugs in the United States and abroad. In May 2001 he appointed John P. Walters (1952?–) as the new drug czar. Together, they pledged to continue to reduce illicit drug use in the United States. Their proposed goals included increased spending on treatment, intensified work with foreign nations, and an adamant opposition to the legalization of any currently illicit drugs. The Bush administration also wove its antidrug message into its arguments for invading Afghanistan. Even though Bush's case was built primarily on the notion that Afghanistan's Taliban leaders were harboring the terrorist Osama bin Laden (1957?–2011), Bush regularly referred to Afghanistan's role as the world's biggest producer of opium poppies.

The ONDCP indicates that at the start of the Bush administration federal spending on drug control started at $10.4 billion in FY 2001 (as shown in the FY 2004 budget summary). By FY 2009 the ONDCP notes in *National Drug Control Strategy: FY 2009 Budget Summary* (February 2008, http://www.whitehousedrugpolicy.gov/publications/policy/09budget/fy09budget.pdf) that drug control grew to a requested $14.1 billion, with treatment accounting for 24.1% of the total in the requested budget.

Questioning the War on Drugs

By 2007 there was considerable controversy surrounding the necessity and effectiveness of the War on Drugs. Decades of effort had led to large numbers of people serving prison sentences for manufacturing, selling, or using drugs. Yet, the illicit drug trade continued to thrive.

Many critics argued that a different approach was necessary and questioned whether illicit drugs were an enemy worth waging war against, especially such a costly war during a time of rapidly rising federal budget deficits.

The American public also appeared to view the War on Drugs as a low priority. In *Economy Runaway Winner as Most Important Problem* (November 21, 2008, http://www.gallup.com/poll/112093/Economy-Runaway-Winner-Most-Important-Problem.aspx), Jeffrey M. Jones of the Gallup Organization notes that in 2008, 58% of adult Americans rated the economy as the top problem in the United States; drugs were not listed among the top 13 most important problems. Other problems seen as having a higher priority than drugs were the war in Iraq, unemployment, dissatisfaction with government leaders, national security, education, and terrorism.

In the fall of 2008 two reports were published that also documented inadequacies with the War on Drugs. In October 2008 the U.S. Government Accountability Office (GAO) released *Plan Colombia: Drug Reduction Goals Were Not Fully Met, but Security Has Improved; U.S. Agencies Need More Detailed Plans for Reducing Assistance* (http://www.gao.gov/new.items/d0971.pdf). The GAO examined progress made toward the Colombian government's strategy "Plan Colombia," the goals of which included reducing the production of illicit drugs by half between 2000 and 2006 (with a focus on cocaine) and improving security in areas of Colombia that were held by illegal armed groups. The United States supported this plan and provided nearly $6 billion for its implementation. The GAO found that security had been increased and that opium poppy cultivation and heroin production had decreased by about half. However, coca cultivation and cocaine production had increased.

In November 2008 the Partnership for the Americas Commission of the Brookings Institution released *Rethinking U.S.-Latin American Relations: A Hemispheric Partnership for a Turbulent World* (http://www.brookings.edu/reports/2008/~/media/Files/rc/reports/2008/1124_latin_america_partnership/1124_latin_america_partnership.pdf). The report noted that "current U.S. counternarcotics policies are failing by most objective measures" and that "the only long-run solution to the problem of illegal narcotics is to reduce the demand for drugs in the major consuming countries, including the United States." The report also suggested that the United States should work to reduce the flow of guns to Mexico, which would help curb the flow of drugs to the United States; expand drug prevention programs in schools, especially those that emphasize drugs' disfiguring attributes to young people; and promote drug courts, which merge treatment with incarceration.

In the months that followed President Obama's inauguration, his administration began to show signs of rethinking existing drug policy in the United States. Gil Kerlikowske (1949–), who was named the director of the ONDCP, called for an end to the War on Drugs and favored treatment over prison time for drug offenders. Certain federal drug policies began to change. For example, in 2009 Congress repealed the decades-old ban on federal funding for needle exchange programs. Nonetheless, the Obama administration firmly opposed the legalization of marijuana.

In 2009 the Transform Drug Policy Foundation, a United Kingdom–based organization that promotes drug regulation and control, released *After the War on Drugs: Blueprint for Regulation* (http://www.tdpf.org.uk/Transform_Drugs_Blueprint.pdf). The foundation recognized the failure of the War on Drugs and the increasing recognition of this failure around the world. It suggested that a major reason many countries have not changed their drug policies is deep concern of what might happen if drugs are legalized. To diminish this fear of the unknown, the foundation proposed models of legal drug regulation and control, along with rationales for each model, to control drug production, supply, and use.

Charles Shaw suggests in "European Blueprint Signals Way for America to End the War on Drugs" (*Guardian* [London, England], November 15, 2010) that the United States is addicted to the War on Drugs. He notes that no real drop in the use of or demand for drugs has occurred as a result of the war, yet the United States continues spending billions of dollars on this failed policy—culminating in a total of $1 trillion spent over 40 years. Shaw discusses the Transform Drug Policy Foundation's *Blueprint for Regulation* as well as *Drug Policy Guide* (March 2010, http://idpc.net/sites/default/files/library/IDPC%20Drug%20Policy%20Guide_Version%201.pdf) by the International Drug Policy Consortium, a worldwide group of nongovernmental organizations. The consortium notes that the approach of trying to eradicate the supply of illegal drugs has been ineffective. The consortium proposes that countries should focus on reducing the harmful consequences of drug use on individuals rather than on fighting drug use. Shaw agrees and suggests that "the primary drivers of this issue are economic: money and jobs." He calculates that the U.S. criminal justice system employs more workers than Wal-Mart and McDonald's combined. Shaw also explains, "And just like military spending, any attempts to cut criminal justice or prison budgets is considered political suicide."

Thus, at the end of 2010, continuing the War on Drugs was a growing question in the United States and around the world, but reasons for resistance to change and the approach that should be followed were growing questions as well.

ALCOHOL

Contrary to popular belief, ethanol (the alcohol in alcoholic beverages) is not a stimulant, but a depressant. Even though many of those who drink alcoholic beverages feel relaxation, pleasure, and stimulation, these feelings are caused by the depressant effects of alcohol on the brain.

WHAT CONSTITUTES A DRINK?

In the United States a standard drink contains about 0.5 ounces (14.8 mL) of pure alcohol. The following beverages contain nearly equal amounts of alcohol and are approximately standard drink equivalents:

- One shot (1.5 ounces, or 44.4 mL) of spirits (80-proof whiskey, vodka, gin, and so on)

- One 2.5-ounce (73.9-mL) glass of a cordial, liqueur, or aperitif

- One 5-ounce (147.9-mL) glass of table wine

- One 3- to 4-ounce (88.7- to 118.3-mL) glass of fortified wine, such as sherry or port

- One 12-ounce (354.9-mL) bottle or can of beer

- One 8- to 9-ounce (236.6- to 266.2-mL) bottle or can of malt liquor

ALCOHOL CONSUMPTION IN THE UNITED STATES

After caffeine, alcohol is the most commonly used drug in the United States. Even though researchers frequently count how many people are drinking and how often, the statistics do not necessarily reflect the true picture of alcohol consumption in the United States. People tend to under-report their drinking. Furthermore, survey interviewees are typically people living in households; therefore, the results of survey research may not include the homeless, a portion of the U.S. population that is traditionally at risk for alcoholism (alcohol dependence).

Per Capita Consumption of Alcohol

The yearly per capita (per person) consumption of alcoholic beverages peaked at 28.8 gallons (109 L) in 1981. (See Table 2.1.) Per capita consumption declined to 24.7 gallons (93.5 L) in 1995 and 1997 and has climbed only slightly since then. In 2008 the per capita consumption of alcoholic beverages was 25.7 gallons (97.3 L).

Beer remained the most popular alcoholic beverage in 2008, being consumed at a rate of 21.7 gallons (82.1 L) per person. Beer consumption peaked in 1981 at 24.6 gallons (93.1 L) per person, but its consumption declined steadily to its present relatively stable level by 1995. The per capita consumption of wine and spirits in the United States is much lower than that of beer. The 2008 per capita consumption of wine was 2.5 gallons (9.5 L) and of distilled spirits (liquor), 1.4 gallons (5.3 L).

A complex set of factors contributes to variations in alcohol use over people's life spans. Part of the decline in alcohol consumption is a result of population trends. During the 1980s and 1990s the number of people in their early 20s (the leading consumers of alcohol) declined fairly steadily. The United States is also seeing a growing number of residents in their 50s and 60s. This is a group that is, in general, unlikely to consume as much alcohol as younger people.

Individual Consumption of Alcohol

The data for alcohol consumption mentioned in the previous section are per capita figures, which are determined by taking the total consumption of alcohol per year and dividing by the total resident population, including children. This figure is useful to see how consumption changes from year to year because it takes into account changes in the size of the resident population. Nonetheless, babies and small children generally do not consume alcohol, so it is also useful to look at consumption figures that are based on U.S. residents aged 12 years and older.

TABLE 2.1

Per capita consumption of beer, wine, and distilled spirits, 1966–2008

Year	Beer	Wine[a]	Distilled spirits	Total[b]
		Gallons		
1966	16.5	1.0	1.6	19.0
1967	16.8	1.0	1.6	19.4
1968	17.3	1.1	1.7	20.1
1969	17.8	1.2	1.8	20.8
1970	18.5	1.3	1.8	21.6
1971	18.9	1.5	1.8	22.3
1972	19.3	1.6	1.9	22.8
1973	20.1	1.6	1.9	23.6
1974	20.9	1.6	2.0	24.5
1975	21.3	1.7	2.0	25.0
1976	21.5	1.7	2.0	25.2
1977	22.4	1.8	2.0	26.1
1978	23.0	2.0	2.0	26.9
1979	23.8	2.0	2.0	27.8
1980	24.3	2.1	2.0	28.3
1981	24.6	2.2	2.0	28.8
1982	24.4	2.2	1.9	28.5
1983	24.2	2.3	1.8	28.3
1984	24.0	2.4	1.8	28.1
1985	23.8	2.4	1.8	28.0
1986	24.1	2.4	1.6	28.2
1987	24.0	2.4	1.6	28.0
1988	23.8	2.3	1.5	27.6
1989	23.6	2.1	1.5	27.2
1990	23.9	2.0	1.5	27.5
1991	23.1	1.8	1.4	26.3
1992	22.7	1.9	1.4	25.9
1993	22.4	1.7	1.3	25.5
1994	22.3	1.7	1.3	25.3
1995	21.8	1.7	1.2	24.7
1996	21.7	1.9	1.2	24.8
1997	21.6	1.9	1.2	24.7
1998	21.7	1.9	1.2	24.8
1999	21.8	1.9	1.2	25.0
2000	21.7	2.0	1.3	25.0
2001	21.8	2.0	1.3	25.0
2002	21.8	2.1	1.3	25.3
2003	21.6	2.2	1.3	25.2
2004	21.7	2.3	1.4	25.3
2005	21.5	2.3	1.4	25.2
2006	21.8	2.4	1.4	25.6
2007	21.8	2.5	1.4	25.7
2008	21.7	2.5	1.4	25.7

Note: Alcoholic beverage per capita figures are calculated by ERS using industry data. Uses U.S. resident population, July.
[a]Beginning in 1983, includes wine coolers.
[b]Computed from unrounded data.

SOURCE: "Alcoholic Beverages: Per Capita Availability," U.S. Department of Agriculture, Economic Research Service, February 1, 2010, http://www.ers.usda.gov/data/foodconsumption/spreadsheets/beverage.xls (accessed November 8, 2010)

Table 2.2 shows the percentage of respondents aged 12 years and older who reported consuming alcohol in the past month in 2008 and 2009 when questioned for the annual National Survey on Drug Use and Health, which is conducted by the Substance Abuse and Mental Health Services Administration. In 2009, 51.9% of this total population had consumed alcohol in the month before the survey, as opposed to 51.6% of the total population in 2008. A higher percentage of males consumed alcoholic beverages in the past month than did females in both years. Table 2.2 also shows that alcohol consumption varies by race. A higher percentage of whites had used alcohol within the month before the survey than had African-Americans or Hispanics.

Prevalence of Problem Drinking

Table 2.2 also shows the percentages of Americans aged 12 years and older who engaged in binge drinking or heavy alcohol use in the month before the survey. Binge drinking means a person had five or more drinks on the same occasion, that is, within a few hours of each other. Heavy alcohol use means a person had five or more drinks on the same occasion on each of five or more days in the past 30 days. All heavy alcohol users are binge drinkers, but not all binge drinkers are heavy alcohol users.

In both 2008 and 2009 people aged 18 to 25 years were more likely than people in other age groups to be binge drinkers and heavy alcohol users. Much higher percentages of males binge drank and used alcohol heavily than females in the month before each of these surveys. In addition, Hispanics were the most likely to have engaged in binge drinking in 2008 and 2009. However, whites were more likely than all other groups to have engaged in heavy alcohol use in 2008. The percentage of Native Americans or Alaskan natives who engaged in heavy alcohol use rose from 2008 to 2009, giving them the highest percentage of heavy alcohol use among all groups shown in 2009.

DEFINING ALCOHOLISM

Most people consider an alcoholic to be someone who drinks too much alcohol and cannot control his or her drinking. Alcoholism, however, does not merely refer to heavy drinking or getting drunk a certain number of times. The diagnosis of alcoholism applies only to those who show specific symptoms of addiction, which the Institute of Medicine defines in *Dispelling the Myths about Addiction: Strategies to Increase Understanding and Strengthen Research* (1997) as a brain disease "manifested by a complex set of behaviors that are the result of genetic, biological, psychological, and environmental interactions."

In "The Definition of Alcoholism" (*Journal of the American Medical Association*, vol. 268, no. 8, August 26, 1992), Robert M. Morse and Daniel K. Flavin define alcoholism as "a primary, chronic disease with genetic, psychosocial, and environmental factors influencing its development and manifestations. The disease is often progressive and fatal. It is characterized by impaired control over drinking, preoccupation with the drug alcohol, use of alcohol despite adverse consequences, and distortions in thinking, most notably denial. Each of these symptoms may be continuous or periodic."

"Primary" refers to alcoholism as a disease independent from any other psychological disease (e.g., schizophrenia), rather than as a symptom of some other underlying disease.

TABLE 2.2

Percentage of past-month alcohol use, binge alcohol use, and heavy alcohol use among drinkers aged 12 and older, by demographic characteristics, 2008 and 2009

Demographic characteristic	Alcohol use (2008)	Alcohol use (2009)	Binge alcohol use (2008)	Binge alcohol use (2009)	Heavy alcohol use (2008)	Heavy alcohol use (2009)
Total	51.6	51.9	23.3	23.7	6.9	6.8
Age						
12–17	14.6	14.7	8.8	8.8	2.0	2.1
18–25	61.2	61.8	41.0	41.7	14.5	13.7
26 or Older	54.8	54.9	22.1	22.4	6.3	6.2
Gender						
Male	57.7	57.6	31.6	31.6	10.6	10.3
Female	45.9	46.5	15.4	16.1	3.4	3.5
Hispanic origin and race						
Not Hispanic or Latino	53.0	53.6	22.9	23.4	7.1	7.1
White	56.2	56.7	24.0	24.8	7.7	7.9
Black or African American	41.9	42.8	20.4	19.8	5.6	4.5
American Indian or Alaska Native	43.3	37.1	24.4	22.2	5.7	8.3
Native Hawaiian or other Pacific Islander	*	*	*	*	3.5	3.6
Asian	37.0	37.6	11.9	11.1	2.4	1.5
Two or more races	47.5	47.6	22.0	24.1	7.4	6.4
Hispanic or Latino	43.2	41.7	25.6	25.0	5.7	5.2

*Low precision; no estimate reported.

Note: Binge alcohol use is defined as drinking five or more drinks on the same occasion (i.e., at the same time or within a couple of hours of each other) on at least 1 day in the past 30 days. Heavy alcohol use is defined as drinking five or more drinks on the same occasion on each of 5 or more days in the past 30 days; all heavy alcohol users are also binge alcohol users.

SOURCE: "Table 2.42B. Alcohol Use, Binge Alcohol Use, and Heavy Alcohol Use in the Past Month among Persons Aged 12 or Older, by Demographic Characteristics: Percentages, 2008 and 2009," in *Results from the 2009 National Survey on Drug Use and Health: Detailed Tables*, U.S. Department of Health and Human Services, Substance Abuse and Mental Health Services Administration, Office of Applied Studies, September 2010, http://www.oas.samhsa.gov/NSDUH/2k9NSDUH/tabs/Sect2peTabs37to46.pdf (accessed November 8, 2010)

"Adverse consequences" for an alcoholic can include physical illness (such as liver disease or withdrawal symptoms), psychological problems, interpersonal difficulties (such as marital problems or domestic violence), and problems at work. "Denial" includes a number of psychological maneuvers by the drinker to avoid the fact that alcohol is the cause of his or her problems. Family and friends may reinforce an alcoholic's denial by covering up his or her drinking (e.g., calling an employer to say the alcoholic has the flu rather than a hangover). Such behavior is also known as enabling. In other words, the family and friends make excuses for the drinker and enable him or her to continue drinking as opposed to having to face the repercussions of his or her alcohol abuse. Denial is a major obstacle in recovery from alcoholism.

In "Alcoholism" (May 6, 2010, http://www.mayoclinic.com/print/alcoholism/DS00340/METHOD=print&DSECTION=all), the Mayo Clinic provides a very simple and straightforward definition of alcoholism: "Alcoholism is a chronic disease in which your body becomes dependent on alcohol. When you have alcoholism, you lose control over your drinking. You may not be able to control when you drink, how much you drink, or how long you drink on each occasion. If you have alcoholism, you continue to drink even though you know it's causing problems with your relationships, health, work or finances."

ALCOHOLISM AND ALCOHOL ABUSE

The American Psychiatric Association (APA), which publishes the *Diagnostic and Statistical Manual of Mental Disorders* (*DSM*), first defined alcoholism in 1952. *DSM-III*, the third edition of the APA's publication, renamed alcoholism as alcohol dependence and introduced the term *alcohol abuse*. According to *DSM-III*'s definitions of alcohol abuse, the condition involves a compulsive use of alcohol and impaired social or occupational functioning, whereas alcohol dependence includes physical tolerance and withdrawal symptoms when the drug is stopped. *DSM-IV-TR*, the most recent edition as of February 2011, refines these definitions further, but the basic definitions remain the same.

The World Health Organization publishes the *International Classification of Diseases* (*ICD*), which is designed to standardize health data collection throughout the world. The 10th edition (*ICD-10*) generally defines abuse and tolerance similarly to the *DSM-IV-TR*.

Alcoholism includes the following four symptoms: craving, loss of control, physical dependence, and tolerance. These symptoms are described in Table 2.3 and are a result of changes in the functioning of the brain and underlying changes in gene expression as its cells adapt to the chronic heavy use and abuse of alcohol.

TABLE 2.3

Four symptoms of alcoholism

Alcoholism, also known as "alcohol dependence," is a disease that includes four symptoms:

- Craving: A strong need, or compulsion, to drink.
- Loss of control: The inability to limit one's drinking on any given occasion.
- Physical dependence: Withdrawal symptoms, such as nausea, sweating, shakiness, and anxiety, occur when alcohol use is stopped after a period of heavy drinking.
- Tolerance: The need to drink greater amounts of alcohol in order to "get high."

SOURCE: Adapted from *FAQs for the General Public: 1. What Is Alcoholism?* U.S. Department of Health and Human Services, National Institutes of Health, National Institute on Alcohol Abuse and Alcoholism, February 2007, http://www.niaaa.nih.gov/FAQs/General-English/default.htm#whatis (accessed November 8, 2010)

TABLE 2.4

Four symptoms of alcohol abuse

Alcohol abuse is defined as a pattern of drinking that results in one or more of the following situations within a 12-month period:

- Failure to fulfill major work, school, or home responsibilities;
- Drinking in situations that are physically dangerous, such as while driving a car or operating machinery;
- Having recurring alcohol-related legal problems, such as being arrested for driving under the influence of alcohol or for physically hurting someone while drunk; and
- Continued drinking despite having ongoing relationship problems that are caused or worsened by the drinking.

SOURCE: Adapted from "Module 4. Screening and Assessment: Alcohol Use Disorders," in *The ABCs of Bullying: Addressing, Blocking, and Curbing School Aggression*, U.S. Department of Health and Human Services, Substance Abuse and Mental Health Services Administration, Center for Substance Abuse Prevention, May 19, 2004, http://pathwayscourses.samhsa.gov/bully/bully_4_pg18.htm (accessed November 8, 2010)

Those who are alcohol dependent—as well as those who are not—may manifest the symptoms of alcohol abuse. The primary symptoms of alcohol abuse are listed in Table 2.4. Other characteristics of alcohol abuse include the need to drink before facing certain situations, frequent drinking sprees, a steady increase in intake, solitary drinking, early morning drinking, and the occurrence of blackouts. For heavy drinkers, blackouts are not episodes of passing out, but are periods drinkers cannot remember later, even though they appeared to be functioning at the time.

Prevalence of Alcohol Dependence, Alcohol Abuse, Binge Drinking, and Heavy Drinking

The National Institute on Alcohol Abuse and Alcoholism (NIAAA) notes in *Five Year Strategic Plan FY09–14* (2008, http://pubs.niaaa.nih.gov/publications/StrategicPlan/StrategicPlan.doc) that 18 million Americans (8.5% of the population aged 18 years and older) have alcohol use disorders (AUD; alcohol abuse and alcohol dependence).

Figure 2.1 shows the percentages of people who engaged in alcohol use, binge drinking, and heavy alcohol use in 2009 by age group. The graph shows that people aged 21 to 25 years are more likely to engage in binge drinking and heavy alcohol use than those in younger or older age groups. The rate of binge drinking and heavy alcohol use in this age group was slightly over 46% in 2009. The graph also shows that as people grow older, the proportion of people who use alcohol without manifesting binge or heavy alcohol use increases.

Table 2.2 compares the rates of binge drinking and heavy alcohol use for males and females across all age groups. In 2008 and 2009 the rate of binge drinking in males was substantially higher than that of females. The percentage of males who binge drank in 2008 and 2009 was 31.6% in both years, whereas the percentage of females who binge drank was about half that, at 15.4% in 2008 and 16.1% in 2009. Heavy alcohol use was much more prevalent in males than in females. More than 10% of males were heavy alcohol users in 2008 and 2009, whereas only about 3.5% of females were.

ALCOHOL ABUSE AND ALCOHOLISM IN VARIOUS RACIAL AND ETHNIC GROUPS

The patterns of alcohol consumption vary across racial and ethnic groups. (See Table 2.2.) Low alcoholism rates occur in certain groups and individuals due to their customs or religion. Groups and individuals with multicultural backgrounds generally have fewer cultural or religious constraints regarding alcohol use and tend to have higher alcoholism rates. For example, alcohol is forbidden in Islam, so it is rare to find Muslims who engage in alcohol use. However, whites are a diverse population, both religiously and culturally. This group had the highest rate of alcohol use of all the groups listed in Table 2.2. Native Americans or Alaskan natives had the highest prevalence of heavy alcohol use in 2009.

Certain populations may be at a higher or lower risk for binge or heavy alcohol use because of the way their bodies metabolize (chemically process) alcohol. For example, many Asian-Americans have an inherited deficiency of aldehyde dehydrogenase, a chemical that breaks down ethyl alcohol in the body. Without it, toxic substances build up after drinking alcohol and rapidly lead to flushing, dizziness, and nausea. Therefore, many Asian-Americans experience warning signals very early on and are less likely to continue drinking. Conversely, research results suggest that Native Americans or Alaskan natives may lack these warning signals. They are less sensitive to the intoxicating effects of alcohol and are more likely to develop alcoholism. Table 2.2 shows that the prevalence of binge alcohol use and heavy alcohol use is low for Asian-Americans and high for Native Americans or Alaskan natives.

FIGURE 2.1

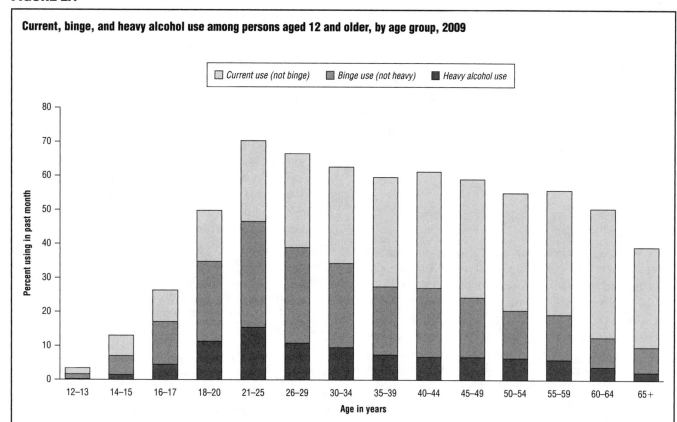

Current, binge, and heavy alcohol use among persons aged 12 and older, by age group, 2009

SOURCE: "Figure 3.1 Current, Binge, and Heavy Alcohol Use among Persons Aged 12 or Older, by Age: 2009," in *Results from the 2009 National Survey on Drug Use and Health: Volume I. Summary of National Findings*, U.S. Department of Health and Human Services, Substance Abuse and Mental Health Services Administration, Office of Applied Studies, September 2010, http://www.oas.samhsa.gov/NSDUH/2k9NSDUH/2k9ResultsP.pdf (accessed November 8, 2010)

RISK FACTORS OF ALCOHOL USE DISORDERS

The development of AUD is the result of a complex mix of biological, psychological, and social factors including genetics, alcohol reactivity (sensitivity), and psychosocial factors. Genetics and alcohol reactivity are biological factors. The rest are psychosocial factors. Table 2.5 lists the factors that are involved in the development of AUD, which are discussed in the following sections.

Biological Factors

GENETICS. A variety of studies investigating family history, adopted versus biological children living in the same families, and twins separated and living in different families all indicate that genetics play a substantial role in some forms of AUD. For example, R. Dayne Mayfield, R. Adron Harris, and Marc A. Schuckit indicate in "Genetic Factors Influencing Alcohol Dependence" (*British Journal of Pharmacology*, vol. 154, no. 2, May 2008) that relatives of alcoholics have four times the risk of developing alcohol dependence than do nonrelatives of alcoholics and that the identical twins of those dependent on alcohol have a higher risk of developing alcohol dependence than do fraternal twins or nontwin siblings. Most

TABLE 2.5

Factors involved in the development of alcohol use disorders

Biological
Genetics
Alcohol reactivity

Psychosocial

Social sanctions
Gender roles
Coping styles
Drinking motives and expectations
Depression
Sensation-seeking
Stress
Impulsivity
Interpersonal relationships
History of sexual assault or child abuse

SOURCE: Created by Sandra Alters for Gale, 2010

likely, many genes influence a range of characteristics that affect risk. Marc A. Schuckit of the University of California, San Diego, states in "An Overview of Genetic Influences in Alcoholism" (*Journal of Substance Abuse Treatment*, vol. 36, no. 1, January 2009) that "genes explain about 50% of the vulnerabilities leading to heavy drinking and associated problems."

ALCOHOL REACTIVITY. Alcohol reactivity refers to the sense of intoxication one has when drinking alcohol. Without early signals of intoxication, an individual may tend to drink more before feeling drunk and thus may develop a high physiological tolerance for alcohol. An individual with low alcohol reactivity to moderate doses of alcohol may be more likely to become an alcoholic over time than an individual with greater reactivity. Typically, the sons of alcoholics report a lower sense of intoxication and show fewer signs of intoxication when given moderate amounts of alcohol, compared with the sons of nonalcoholics, showing a likely genetic link to alcoholism as Schuckit describes.

Psychosocial Factors

SOCIAL SANCTIONS, GENDER ROLES, BIOLOGICAL DIFFERENCES, AND CULTURAL FACTORS. Social sanctions are a mechanism of social control for enforcing a society's standards. Social sanctions may be one factor explaining why men drink more alcohol than women. Besides social sanctions against women drinking as heavily as men, American culture appears to identify alcohol consumption as more of a part of the male gender role than of the female gender role. However, gender differences in alcohol consumption are seen not only in the United States but also around the world.

Richard W. Wilsnack et al. explain in "Gender and Alcohol Consumption: Patterns from the Multinational GENACIS Project" (*Addiction*, vol. 104, no. 9, September 2009) that:

> gender differences in alcohol consumption remain universal [among countries], although the sizes of gender differences vary. More drinking and heavy drinking occur among men, more long-term abstention occurs among women, and no cultural differences or historical changes have entirely erased these differences. As there are relatively few universals in human social behavior, these findings suggest that biological differences play some role in how men and women drink. However, because the gender differences vary in magnitude across cultures and across different drinking patterns, it is also very likely that gender differences in drinking behavior are modified by cultural and not just biological factors.

DRINKING MOTIVES, EXPECTATIONS, AND DEPRESSION/DISTRESS. People consume alcohol for various reasons: as part of a meal, to celebrate certain occasions, and to reduce anxiety in social situations. People also consume alcohol to cope with distress or depression or to escape from negative feelings. Those who have positive expectations for their drinking, such as the belief that alcohol will reduce distress, tend to drink more than those who have negative expectations, such as the belief that alcohol will interfere with the ability to cope with distress. In general, Shelly F. Greenfield et al. note in "Substance Abuse in Women" (*Psychiatric Clinics of North America*, vol. 33, no. 2, June 2010) that

men have more positive expectations concerning alcohol consumption than women. In addition, women are more likely than men to drink alcohol in response to distress and negative emotions. The researchers note, however, that even though these generalizations can be made, the relationships among depression, general distress, and alcohol consumption are quite complex.

IMPULSIVITY, SENSATION-SEEKING, BEHAVIORAL UNDERCONTROL, AND ANTISOCIALITY. In "Sex Difference in Alcoholism: Who Is at a Greater Risk for Development of Alcoholic Complication?" (*Life Sciences*, vol. 87, nos. 5–6, July 31, 2010), Asli F. Ceylan-Isik, Shawna M. McBride, and Jun Ren of the University of Wyoming, Laramie, indicate that impulsivity, sensation-seeking, and behavioral undercontrol (not controlling one's behavior well) are consistently associated with alcohol use and problems in men rather than in women. The researchers suggest this may occur because "women perceive greater social and health sanctions for drinking while alcohol and alcoholism may counter desirable feminine traits."

Antisociality is a personality disorder that includes a chronic disregard for the rights of others and an absence of remorse for the harmful effects of these behaviors on others. People with this disorder are usually involved in aggressive and illegal activities. They are often impulsive and reckless and are more likely to become alcohol dependent. Males are more likely than females to demonstrate antisociality.

INTERPERSONAL RELATIONSHIPS, SEXUAL ASSAULT, AND CHILD ABUSE. Married couples often have strongly similar levels of drinking. It is unclear whether men and women with problem drinking patterns seek out partners with similar drinking patterns or whether either is influenced by the other to drink during the marriage. However, marital discord is often present when spouses' drinking patterns differ significantly.

Being a victim of sexual assault and/or child abuse is a risk factor for AUD. Women who have been sexually assaulted, whether during childhood or as an adult, are at an increased risk for problem drinking and alcohol abuse. According to Karen A. Kalmakis of the University of Massachusetts, Amherst, in "Cycle of Sexual Assault and Women's Alcohol Misuse" (*Journal of the American Academy of Nurse Practitioners*, vol. 22, no. 12, December 2010), over half of the individuals who enter substance abuse treatment programs report a history of physical or sexual abuse. She adds that these individuals are primarily women and that they mostly abuse alcohol. Kalmakis adds that women who experienced sexual abuse and then misuse alcohol are more likely to experience subsequent sexual assault as an adult than are women who do not misuse alcohol. She concludes, "The psychological impact of women's childhood sexual abuse, combined with their alcohol misuse, makes them vulnerable to further victimization, creating a cycle of alcohol misuse and victimization."

Daniel F. Becker and Carlos M. Grilo, in investigating the psychosocial factors of drug and alcohol abuse in adolescents, note that women are not the only victims of this abuse/misuse cycle. The researchers suggest in "Prediction of Drug and Alcohol Abuse in Hospitalized Adolescents: Comparisons by Gender and Substance Type" (*Behaviour Research and Therapy*, vol. 44, no. 10, October 2006) that a history of child abuse is a risk factor for drug and alcohol abuse in both males and females.

EFFECTS OF PARENTAL ALCOHOLISM ON CHILDREN

Living with someone who has an alcohol problem affects every member of the family. Children often suffer many problems as a result. In the fact sheet "Children of Addicted Parents: Important Facts" (2008, http://www.nacoa.net/pdfs/addicted.pdf), the National Association for Children of Alcoholics (NACoA) estimates that there are over 28 million children of alcoholics in the United States, including 11 million under the age of 18 years.

As mentioned earlier, relatives of alcoholics have four times the risk of alcoholism than do nonrelatives. Jodi M. Gilman, James M. Bjork, and Daniel W. Hommer of the NIAAA note in "Parental Alcohol Use and Brain Volumes in Early and Late-Onset Alcoholics" (*Biological Psychiatry*, vol. 62, no. 6, September 15, 2007) that many factors contribute to this increased risk. Some of these contributing factors are a genetic predisposition to alcoholism as well as a poor diet, unstable parental relationships, and alcohol exposure in the womb. Their research adds another factor, however: the effect of a family history of heavy drinking on brain volume. Gilman, Bjork, and Hommer find that alcoholic patients who had a family history of heavy drinking had significantly smaller brain volumes than did alcoholic patients with no family history of heavy drinking. The researchers conclude that "parental alcohol use may increase risk for alcoholism in offspring in part by a genetic and/or environmental effect that may be related to reduced brain growth."

The NACoA also notes that children of alcoholics are more likely to suffer from attention-deficit hyperactivity disorder, behavioral problems, and anxiety disorders. They tend to score lower on tests that measure cognitive and verbal skills. Furthermore, children of alcoholics are more likely to be truant, repeat grades, drop out of school, or be referred to a school counselor or psychologist.

SHORT-TERM EFFECTS OF ALCOHOL ON THE BODY

When most people think about how alcohol affects them, they think of a temporary light-headedness or a hangover the next morning. Many are also aware of the serious damage that continuous, excessive alcohol use can do to the liver. Alcohol, however, affects many organs of the body and has been linked to cancer, mental and/or physical retardation in newborns, heart disease, and other health problems.

Low to moderate doses of alcohol produce a slight, brief increase in heartbeat and blood pressure. Large doses can reduce the pumping power of the heart and produce irregular heartbeats. In addition, blood vessels within muscles constrict, but those at the surface expand, causing rapid heat loss from the skin and a flushing or reddening. Thus, large doses of alcohol decrease body temperature and, additionally, may cause numbness of the skin, legs, and arms, creating a false feeling of warmth. Figure 2.2 illustrates and describes in more detail the path that alcohol takes through the body after it is consumed.

Alcohol affects the endocrine system (a group of glands that produce hormones) in several ways. One effect is increased urination. Urination increases not only because of fluid intake but also because alcohol stops the release of vasopressin (an antidiuretic hormone) from the pituitary gland. This hormone controls how much water the kidneys reabsorb from the urine as it is being produced and how much water the kidneys excrete. Therefore, heavy alcohol intake can result in both dehydration and an imbalance in electrolytes, which are chemicals dissolved in body fluids that conduct electrical currents. Both of these conditions are serious health hazards.

Alcohol is sometimes believed to be an aphrodisiac (sexual stimulant). Whereas low to moderate amounts of alcohol can reduce fear and decrease sexual inhibitions, larger doses tend to impair sexual performance. Alcoholics sometimes report difficulties in their sex life.

Intoxication

The speed of alcohol absorption affects the rate at which one becomes intoxicated. Intoxication occurs when alcohol is absorbed into the blood faster than the liver can oxidize it (or break it down into water, carbon dioxide, and energy). In a 160-pound (72.6-kg) man, alcohol is metabolized (absorbed and processed by the body) at a rate of about one drink every two hours. The absorption of alcohol is influenced by several factors:

- Body weight—heavier people are less affected than lighter people by the same amount of alcohol because there is more blood and water in their system to dilute the alcohol intake. In addition, the greater the body muscle weight, the lower the blood alcohol concentration (BAC) for a given amount of alcohol.

- Speed of drinking—the faster alcohol is drunk, the faster the BAC level rises.

FIGURE 2.2

The path alcohol takes after consumption

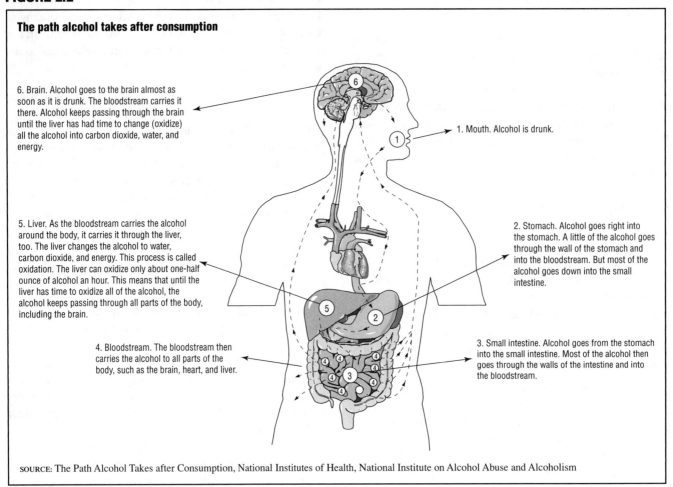

6. Brain. Alcohol goes to the brain almost as soon as it is drunk. The bloodstream carries it there. Alcohol keeps passing through the brain until the liver has had time to change (oxidize) all the alcohol into carbon dioxide, water, and energy.

1. Mouth. Alcohol is drunk.

5. Liver. As the bloodstream carries the alcohol around the body, it carries it through the liver, too. The liver changes the alcohol to water, carbon dioxide, and energy. This process is called oxidation. The liver can oxidize only about one-half ounce of alcohol an hour. This means that until the liver has time to oxidize all of the alcohol, the alcohol keeps passing through all parts of the body, including the brain.

2. Stomach. Alcohol goes right into the stomach. A little of the alcohol goes through the wall of the stomach and into the bloodstream. But most of the alcohol goes down into the small intestine.

4. Bloodstream. The bloodstream then carries the alcohol to all parts of the body, such as the brain, heart, and liver.

3. Small intestine. Alcohol goes from the stomach into the small intestine. Most of the alcohol then goes through the walls of the intestine and into the bloodstream.

SOURCE: The Path Alcohol Takes after Consumption, National Institutes of Health, National Institute on Alcohol Abuse and Alcoholism

- Presence of food in the stomach—eating while drinking slows down the absorption of alcohol by increasing the amount of time it takes the alcohol to get from the stomach to the small intestine.

- Drinking history and body chemistry—the longer a person has been drinking, the greater his or her tolerance (in other words, the more alcohol it takes him or her to get drunk). An individual's physiological functioning or "body chemistry" may also affect his or her reactions to alcohol. Women are more easily affected by alcohol regardless of weight because women metabolize alcohol differently than men. Women are known to have less body water than men of the same body weight, so equivalent amounts of alcohol result in higher concentrations of alcohol in the blood of women than men.

As a person's BAC rises, there are somewhat predictable responses in behavior.

- At a BAC of about 0.05 grams (g) of alcohol per 1 deciliter (dL) of blood, thought processes, judgment, and restraint are more lax. The person may feel more at ease socially. Also, reaction time to visual or auditory stimuli slows down as the BAC rises. (It should be noted that a measurement of g/dL—a mass/volume measure—is approximately equal to a volume/volume—or a percentage—measurement when calculating BAC, and that the two are often used interchangeably; so a BAC of 0.05 g/dL can also mean a BAC of 0.05%.)

- At 0.10 g/dL, voluntary motor actions become noticeably clumsy. (It is illegal to drive with a BAC of 0.08 g/dL or higher.)

- At 0.20 g/dL, the entire motor area of the brain becomes significantly depressed. The person staggers, may want to lie down, may be easily angered, or may shout or weep.

- At 0.30 g/dL, the person generally acts confused or may be in a stupor.

- At 0.40 g/dL, the person usually falls into a coma.

- At 0.50 g/dL or more, the medulla is severely depressed, and death generally occurs within several hours, usually from respiratory failure. The medulla is the portion of the brainstem that regulates many involuntary processes, such as breathing.

Without immediate medical attention, a person whose BAC reaches 0.50 g/dL will almost certainly die.

Death may even occur at a BAC of 0.40 g/dL if the alcohol is consumed quickly and in a large amount, causing the BAC to rise rapidly.

Sobering Up

Time is the only way to rid the body of alcohol. The more slowly a person drinks, the more time the body has to process the alcohol, so less alcohol accumulates in the bloodstream. In addition, having food in the stomach slows the absorption of alcohol there. Drinking slowly while eating and alternating nonalcoholic beverages with alcoholic beverages helps keep the BAC at lower levels than drinking more quickly on an empty stomach.

According to Brown University, in "Alcohol and Your Body" (2011, http://brown.edu/Student_Services/Health_Services/Health_Education/alcohol,_tobacco,_&_other_drugs/alcohol/alcohol_&_your_body.php), five drinks consumed in quick succession by a 175-pound (79.4-kg) man will produce a BAC of 0.125 g/dL. In a 150-pound (68-kg) man this intake will produce a higher BAC of 0.145 g/dL. In a 125-pound (56.7-kg) woman it will produce an even higher BAC of 0.202 g/dL. It will take six hours for the BAC level of the 125-pound woman to drop to 0.112, which is still high above the legal driving limit of 0.08 g/dL.

Hangovers

Hangovers cause a great deal of misery as well as absenteeism and loss of productivity at school or work. A person with a hangover experiences two or more physical symptoms after drinking and fully metabolizing alcohol. The major symptoms of a hangover are listed in Table 2.6, but the causes of these symptoms are not well known. Gemma Prat, Ana Adan, and Miquel Sánchez-Turet of the University of Barcelona review explanations of hangovers in "Alcohol Hangover: A Critical Review of Explanatory Factors" (*Human Psychopharmacology: Clinical and Experimental*, vol. 24, no. 4, June 2009). The primary hypotheses as to the causes of hangovers are that they are a physiological response to withdrawal from alcohol, impurities produced during fermentation that are present in alcoholic beverages, or by-products that are produced by the body during the metabolism of alcohol. Fluctuations

TABLE 2.6

Symptoms of a hangover

Body aches
Diarrhea
Dizziness/lightheadedness
Dry mouth/thirst
Fatigue
Headache
Irritability
Lack of alertness/difficulty concentrating
Nausea

SOURCE: Created by Sandra Alters for Gale, 2010

in body hormones and dehydration intensify hangover symptoms.

There is no scientific evidence to support popular hangover cures, such as black coffee, raw egg, chili pepper, steak sauce, "alkalizers," and vitamins. To treat a hangover, health care practitioners usually prescribe bed rest as well as eating food and drinking nonalcoholic fluids.

LONG-TERM EFFECTS OF ALCOHOL ON THE BODY

The results of scientific research help health care practitioners and the general public understand both the positive and negative health consequences of drinking alcohol. Robin Room, Thomas Babor, and Jürgen Rehm summarize in "Alcohol and Public Health" (*Lancet*, vol. 365, no. 9458, February 2005) the major diseases and injury conditions related to alcohol use and the proportions attributable to alcohol worldwide. They note that about one-fifth of mouth and throat cancers are related to drinking alcohol. Nearly one-third of cancers of the esophagus (food tube) and one-fourth of cancers of the liver are linked to alcohol consumption as well. Alcohol consumption is also related to heart disease and stroke and is associated with cirrhosis of the liver, a condition in which the liver becomes scarred and dysfunctional. In addition, one-fifth of motor vehicle accidents are related to alcohol consumption.

Not all the effects of alcohol consumption are harmful to health, however. In "Alcohol on Trial: The Evidence" (*Southern Medical Journal*, vol. 98, no. 1, January 2005), Ronald C. Hamdy and Melissa McManama Aukerman list levels of alcohol consumption and the relative risk for total mortality (death) for a variety of diseases and conditions. Their data show that men aged 40 to 85 years who drank up to, and possibly slightly over, two drinks per day had a lower total mortality risk than those who did not drink. That is, this level of drinking was good for the men's overall health and life expectancy.

Benjamin Taylor et al. compare in "Alcohol and Hypertension: Gender Differences in Dose-Response Relationships Determined through Systematic Review and Meta-Analysis" (*Addiction*, vol. 104, no 12, December 2009) alcohol consumption versus relative risk of hypertension (chronic high blood pressure) in women versus men. Alcohol consumption of between two and four drinks per week, with only one drink per day on any occasion, lowered the risk of hypertension in women. Once that level of alcohol consumption was reached, however, the risk of hypertension in women rose as their alcohol consumption rose. With men, low levels of alcohol consumption were not protective against hypertension as in women. Furthermore, the more men drank, the higher their risk of hypertension.

In "Effects of Beer, Wine, and Liquor Intakes on Bone Mineral Density in Older Men and Women" (*American Journal of Clinical Nutrition*, February 25, 2009), Katherine L. Tucker et al. of Tufts University indicate that bone density can also benefit from alcohol consumption. In reporting on Tucker et al.'s study, Anne Harding explains in "Moderate Drinking May Help Bone Density" (Reuters, March 20, 2009) that "people who enjoy a glass or two of wine or beer every day could be helping to keep their bones strong." However, Harding cautions that "drinking more—and choosing hard liquor instead of wine or beer—may actually weaken bones."

The studies mentioned in this section provide only a small sample of the wide variety and large number of studies that have been conducted on the long-term effects of alcohol consumption on health. With so many studies and so many health-related factors to take into account, how does a person know how much alcohol is beneficial and how much is too much? The World Cancer Research Fund and the American Institute for Cancer Research state in *Food, Nutrition, Physical Activity, and the Prevention of Cancer: A Global Perspective* (2007, http://www.dietandcancerreport.org/downloads/summary/english.pdf): "If alcoholic drinks are consumed, limit consumption to no more than two drinks a day for men and one drink a day for women." Their justification for this statement is as follows: "The evidence on cancer justifies a recommendation not to drink alcoholic drinks. Other evidence shows that modest amounts of alcoholic drinks are likely to reduce the risk of coronary heart disease."

In "Alcohol, Wine, and Cardiovascular Disease" (2011, http://www.americanheart.org/presenter.jhtml?identifier=4422), the American Heart Association states that "if you drink alcohol, do so in moderation. This means an average of one to two drinks per day for men and one drink per day for women. . . . Drinking more alcohol increases such dangers as alcoholism, high blood pressure, obesity, stroke, breast cancer, suicide and accidents. Also, it's not possible to predict in which people alcoholism will become a problem. Given these and other risks, the American Heart Association cautions people NOT to start drinking ... if they do not already drink alcohol. Consult your doctor on the benefits and risks of consuming alcohol in moderation."

EFFECTS OF ALCOHOL ON SEX AND REPRODUCTION

Alcohol consumption can affect sexual response and reproduction in profound ways. Many alcoholics suffer from erectile dysfunction (impotence) and/or reduced sexual drive. Valentina Boddi et al. suggest in "Priapus Is Happier with Venus Than with Bacchus" (*Journal of Sexual Medicine*, vol. 7, no. 8, August 2010) that male alcohol consumption of four or more drinks per day was associated with a greater risk of erectile dysfunction as shown by a reduction in penile blood flow. The researchers also note that this level of alcohol consumption "was associated with low perceived partner's sexual desire, worse couple relationship, and smoking abuse." Many alcoholics suffer from depression, which may further impair their sexual function. In addition, Jerrold S. Greenberg, Clint E. Bruess, and Sarah C. Conklin report in *Exploring the Dimensions of Human Sexuality* (2011) that alcohol use is associated with poor sperm quality in men.

In premenopausal women chronic heavy drinking can contribute to a variety of reproductive disorders. According to Greenberg, Bruess, and Conklin, these disorders include the cessation of menstruation, irregular menstrual cycles, failure to ovulate, early menopause, increased risk of spontaneous miscarriages, and lower rates of conception. Some of these disorders can be caused directly by the interference of alcohol with the hormonal regulation of the reproductive system. They may also be caused indirectly through other disorders that are associated with alcohol abuse, such as liver disease, pancreatic disease, malnutrition, or fetal abnormalities.

Fetal Alcohol Spectrum Disorders

Alcohol consumption during pregnancy can result in severe harm to the fetus (unborn child). The development of such defects can begin early in pregnancy when the mother-to-be may not even know she is pregnant, and such defects are likely to be exacerbated by binge drinking. For example, Lisa A. DeRoo et al. reveal in "First-Trimester Maternal Alcohol Consumption and the Risk of Infant Oral Clefts in Norway: A Population-Based Case-Control Study" (*American Journal of Epidemiology*, vol. 168, no. 6, September 15, 2008) that women who binge drank during their first trimester of pregnancy were twice as likely as nondrinkers to give birth to an infant having a cleft lip, cleft palate, or both. Other alcohol-related birth defects include malformations and abnormal development of the heart, bones, and kidneys.

It should be noted that drinking during pregnancy can cause more than physical alcohol-related birth defects. Exposure to alcohol in the womb can cause a variety of conditions that are collectively called fetal alcohol spectrum disorders (FASD). Alcohol-related birth defects is only one FASD. Children with FASDs can exhibit not only physical birth defects but also a complex pattern of behavioral and cognitive dysfunctions, which are listed in Table 2.7. Together, FASDs include effects that are physical, cognitive, and behavioral; cannot be cured; and last throughout the life of the affected individual.

Fetal alcohol syndrome (FAS) is the most severe FASD. An individual with FAS has characteristic facial anomalies, growth deficiency, and central nervous system abnormalities. The key facial characteristics of a child with FAS are shown in Figure 2.3. Children with these

TABLE 2.7

Characteristics typical of fetal alcohol spectrum disorders (FASD)

Characteristic facial features (fetal alcohol syndrome only)
Delayed motor development
Difficulties in learning and in abstract thinking
Disregard for authority
Disruptive and impulsive behavior
Growth deficiency
Hyperactivity
Low birth weight
Low IQ
Poor social skills
Short attention span
Slow reaction time

SOURCE: Created by Sandra Alters for Gale, 2010

FIGURE 2.3

Characteristic facial features in children with Fetal Alcohol Syndrome (FAS)

Skin folds at the corner of the eye
Low nasal bridge (flattening of top part of the nose)
Short nose
Indistinct philtrum (groove between nose and upper lip)

Small head circumference
Small eye opening
Small midface
Thin upper lip

SOURCE: Jennifer D. Thomas, Kenneth R. Warren, and Brenda G. Hewitt, "Figure 1. Facial features of FAS," in "Fetal Alcohol Spectrum Disorders: From Research to Policy," in "Celebrating 40 Years of Alcohol Research," *Alcohol Research and Health*, vol. 33, nos. 1 & 2, 2010, http://pubs.niaaa.nih.gov/publications/arh40/118-126 .htm (accessed November 8, 2010)

TABLE 2.8

Key points in the U.S. Surgeon General's advisory on alcohol use during pregnancy, 2005

Based on the current, best science available we now know the following:

• Alcohol consumed during pregnancy increases the risk of alcohol related birth defects, including growth deficiencies, facial abnormalities, central nervous system impairment, behavioral disorders, and impaired intellectual development.
• No amount of alcohol consumption can be considered safe during pregnancy.
• Alcohol can damage a fetus at any stage of pregnancy. Damage can occur in the earliest weeks of pregnancy, even before a woman knows that she is pregnant.
• The cognitive deficits and behavioral problems resulting from prenatal alcohol exposure are lifelong.
• Alcohol-related birth defects are completely preventable.

For these reasons:

1. A pregnant woman should not drink alcohol during pregnancy.
2. A pregnant woman who has already consumed alcohol during her pregnancy should stop in order to minimize further risk.
3. A woman who is considering becoming pregnant should abstain from alcohol.
4. Recognizing that nearly half of all births in the United States are unplanned, women of childbearing age should consult their physician and take steps to reduce the possibility of prenatal alcohol exposure.
5. Health professionals should inquire routinely about alcohol consumption by women of childbearing age, inform them of the risks of alcohol consumption during pregnancy, and advise them not to drink alcoholic beverages during pregnancy.

SOURCE: Adapted from "Surgeon General's Advisory on Alcohol Use in Pregnancy," in *News Release: U.S. Surgeon General Releases Advisory on Alcohol Use in Pregnancy*, U.S. Department of Health and Human Services, February 21, 2005, http://www.surgeongeneral.gov/pressreleases/ sg02222005.html (accessed November 9, 2010)

fasd/data.html), the Centers for Disease Control and Prevention (CDC) notes that FAS rates range from 0.2 to 1.5 per 1,000 live births in results of CDC studies, and from 0.5 to 2 per 1,000 live births in results from other studies. In addition, the CDC reports that other prenatal alcohol-related conditions that are less severe than FAS, such as ARND and alcohol-related birth defects (ARBD), occur approximately three times as often as FAS. ARND and ARBD were formerly and collectively known as fetal alcohol effects. In the 21st century all prenatal alcohol-related conditions are collectively known as FASD.

In February 2005 the U.S. surgeon general Richard Carmona (1949–) issued an advisory on alcohol use during pregnancy. Key points of the advisory are listed in Table 2.8. As noted in the advisory, there is no known safe level of alcohol consumption during pregnancy. The CDC emphasizes, along with the surgeon general, that FAS and other prenatal alcohol-related disorders are 100% preventable if a woman does not drink alcohol while she is pregnant or if she is of reproductive age and is not using birth control. Yet, data show that some women who might become pregnant, or who are pregnant, consume alcohol and put themselves at risk for having a child with FASD.

Table 2.9 shows that 10.6% of pregnant women consumed alcohol in the past month in 2007–08 when questioned for the annual National Survey on Drug Use and Health. This figure was down from 11.8% in 2005–06. In 2005–06 and 2007–08 approximately one-sixth (15.7%)

facial anomalies and the central nervous system abnormalities of FAS but who have normal growth patterns, are said to have partial FAS. Children exposed to alcohol before birth who do not have the facial characteristics typical of FAS, but who have severe central nervous system dysfunction have the FASD called alcohol-related neurodevelopmental disorder (ARND).

In "Fetal Alcohol Spectrum Disorders: Data and Statistics" (October 6, 2010, http://www.cdc.gov/ncbddd/

TABLE 2.9

Percentage of past-month alcohol use among females aged 15–44, by pregnancy status, 2005–06 and 2007–08

| Demographic/pregnancy characteristic | Total[a] | | | Pregnancy status | | |
| | | | Pregnant | | Not pregnant | |
	2005–2006	2007–2008	2005–2006	2007–2008	2005–2006	2007–2008
Total	**51.3**	**52.1**	**11.8**	**10.6**	**53.0**	**54.0**
Age						
15–17	26.4	23.8	16.4	16.0	26.6	23.9
18–25	56.7	57.5	8.5	10.9	59.7	60.4
26–44	53.1	54.5	13.7	10.1	54.6	56.4
Hispanic origin and race						
Not Hispanic or Latino	53.9	54.8	14.2	11.7	55.4	56.6
White	59.0	59.0	15.2	11.0	60.6	60.9
Black or African American	41.3	44.7	11.6	19.1	42.5	46.0
American Indian or Alaska Native	35.7	51.6	*	*	36.5	53.3
Native Hawaiian or other Pacific Islander	*	*	*	*	*	*
Asian	30.8	33.4	*	*	31.7	35.0
Two or more races	56.3	53.2	*	*	57.4	55.4
Hispanic or Latino	37.7	39.3	3.4	6.4	39.8	41.0
Trimester[b]						
First	N/A	N/A	15.7	20.7	N/A	N/A
Second	N/A	N/A	9.0	7.8	N/A	N/A
Third	N/A	N/A	10.4[b]	3.5	N/A	N/A

*Low precision; no estimate reported.
N/A: Not applicable.
[a]Estimates in the total column are for all females aged 15 to 44, including those with unknown pregnancy status.
[b]Pregnant females aged 15 to 44 not reporting trimester were excluded.

SOURCE: "Table 7.76B. Alcohol Use in the Past Month among Females Aged 15 to 44, by Pregnancy and Demographic Characteristics: Percentages, Annual Averages Based on 2005–2006 and 2007–2008," in *Results from the 2008 National Survey on Drug Use and Health: Detailed Tables*, U.S. Department of Health and Human Services, Substance Abuse and Mental Health Services Administration, Office of Applied Studies, September 2010, http://oas.samhsa.gov/NSDUH/2K8NSDUH/tabs/Sect7peTabs71to78.pdf (accessed November 8, 2010)

and one-fifth (20.7%), respectively, of pregnant women drank during their first trimester of pregnancy, a time when all the organ systems of the fetus are developing. Fewer women drank during their second and third trimesters.

ALCOHOL'S INTERACTION WITH OTHER DRUGS

Because alcohol is easily available and such an accepted part of American social life, people often forget that it is a drug. When someone takes a medication while drinking alcohol, he or she is taking two drugs. Alcohol consumed with other drugs—for example, an illegal drug such as cocaine, an over-the-counter (without a prescription) drug such as cough medicine, or a prescription drug such as an antibiotic—may make the combination harmful or even deadly or may counteract the effectiveness of a prescribed medication.

To promote the desired chemical or physical effects, a medication must be absorbed into the body and must reach its site of action. Alcohol may prevent an appropriate amount of the medication from reaching its site of action. In other cases alcohol can alter the drug's effects once it reaches the site. Alcohol interacts negatively with more than 150 medications. Table 2.10 shows some possible interactions when combining alcohol and other types of drugs.

TABLE 2.10

Interactions between alcohol and medications

Medications	Interactions when taken with alcohol.
Antidepressants	Increase in the sedative effects of some antidepressants.
Antibiotics	Nausea, vomiting, headache, and possibly convulsions may occur with some antibiotics. Effectiveness of antibiotics may be reduced.
Antihistamines	Increase in the sedative effects of some antihistamines Dizziness and excessive sedation may occur in the elderly.
Cardiovascular medications	Dizziness or fainting upon standing may occur. Effect of some cardiovascular medications may be reduced.
Narcotic pain relievers (e.g. morphine, codeine, Darvon, Demerol)	Increase in the sedative effects of both alcohol and narcotics. Risk of death increased from overdose.
Non-narcotic pain relievers (e.g. Aspirin, acetominaphen [Tylenol], ibuprophen	Stomach bleeding and liver damage may occur. Blood clotting may be inhibited. Alcohol effects may be increased.
Sedatives/hypnotics (e.g. sleeping pills)	Great increase in the sedative effects of both drugs. May result in reduced heartbeat and breathing rates. May lead to coma and death.

SOURCE: Created by Sandra Alters for Gale, 2010

The U.S. Food and Drug Administration recommends that anyone who regularly has three alcoholic drinks per day should check with a physician before taking aspirin, acetaminophen, or any other over-the-counter painkiller. Combining alcohol with aspirin, ibuprofen, or related pain relievers may promote stomach bleeding. Combining alcohol with acetaminophen may promote liver damage.

ALCOHOL-RELATED DEATHS

Jiaquan Xu et al. of the CDC report in "Deaths: Final Data for 2007" (*National Vital Statistics Reports*, vol. 58, no. 19, May 20, 2010) that 23,199 people in the United States died of alcohol-induced causes in 2007. This category includes deaths from dependent use of alcohol, nondependent use of alcohol, and accidental alcohol poisoning. It excludes accidents, homicides, and other causes indirectly related to alcohol use, as well as deaths because of fetal alcohol syndrome. The age-adjusted death rate for males was 3.2 times the rate for females. In 2007, 14,406 people died from alcoholic liver disease.

MOTOR VEHICLE AND PEDESTRIAN ACCIDENTS

In *Traffic Safety Facts, 2008* (March 2010, http://www-nrd.nhtsa.dot.gov/Pubs/811170.pdf), the National Highway Traffic Safety Administration (NHTSA) of the U.S. Department of Transportation defines a fatal traffic crash as alcohol related if either the driver or an involved pedestrian has a BAC of 0.01 g/dL or greater. If either the driver or an involved pedestrian has a BAC of 0.08 g/dL

or greater, the individual is considered to be intoxicated and the crash is classified as alcohol impaired. However, neither definition means that alcohol is necessarily the cause of the accident.

The NHTSA reports that 37,261 people were killed in traffic accidents in 2008, with 13,846 of them in alcohol-related crashes. (See Table 2.11.) These alcohol-related traffic deaths represented 37% of all car crash fatalities in 2008. The percentage of alcohol-related traffic fatalities has declined somewhat steadily from a high of 55% in 1982, and leveled out from about the mid-1990s to 2008. The peak number of fatalities occurred in 1988, when 47,087 traffic accident deaths, including both alcohol-related accidents (46%) and nonalcohol-related accidents (53%), were recorded.

A number of important factors have contributed to the decline of drunk driving fatalities. Mothers against Drunk Driving was founded in 1980. This organization's most significant achievement was lobbying to get the legal drinking age raised to 21 in all states, which occurred in 1988. There were also successful campaigns such as "Friends Don't Let Friends Drive Drunk." The use of seat belts has also helped reduce deaths in motor vehicle accidents.

TABLE 2.11

Fatalities in motor vehicle accidents, by blood alcohol concentration (BAC) at time of crash, 1982 and 1985–2008

Year	BAC=.00 alcohol not consumed		BAC=.01–.07 impaired		Alcohol-impaired driving fatalities (BAC=.08+) intoxicated		BAC=.01+		Total fatalities	
	Number	Percent	Number	Percent	Number	Percent	Number	Percent	Number	Percent
1982	19,771	45	2,912	7	21,113	48	24,025	55	43,945	100
1985	22,589	52	2,974	7	18,125	41	21,098	48	43,825	100
1986	22,896	50	3,487	8	19,554	42	23,041	50	46,087	100
1987	24,186	52	3,238	7	18,813	41	22,051	48	46,390	100
1988	25,164	53	3,156	7	18,611	40	21,767	46	47,087	100
1989	25,152	55	2,793	6	17,521	38	20,314	45	45,582	100
1990	23,823	53	2,901	7	17,705	40	20,607	46	44,599	100
1991	23,025	55	2,480	6	15,827	38	18,307	44	41,508	100
1992	22,726	58	2,352	6	14,049	36	16,401	42	39,250	100
1993	23,979	60	2,300	6	13,739	34	16,039	40	40,150	100
1994	24,948	61	2,236	5	13,390	33	15,626	38	40,716	100
1995	25,768	62	2,416	6	13,478	32	15,893	38	41,817	100
1996	26,052	62	2,415	6	13,451	32	15,866	38	42,065	100
1997	26,902	64	2,216	5	12,757	30	14,973	36	42,013	100
1998	26,477	64	2,353	6	12,546	30	14,899	36	41,501	100
1999	26,798	64	2,235	5	12,555	30	14,790	35	41,717	100
2000	26,082	62	2,422	6	13,324	32	15,746	38	41,945	100
2001	26,334	62	2,441	6	13,290	31	15,731	37	42,196	100
2002	27,080	63	2,321	5	13,472	31	15,793	37	43,005	100
2003	27,328	64	2,327	5	13,096	31	15,423	36	42,884	100
2004	27,413	64	2,212	5	13,099	31	15,311	36	42,836	100
2005	27,423	63	2,404	6	13,582	31	15,985	37	43,510	100
2006	26,633	62	2,479	6	13,491	32	15,970	37	42,708	100
2007	25,611	62	2,494	6	13,041	32	15,534	38	41,259	100
2008	23,317	63	2,072	6	11,773	32	13,846	37	37,261	100

Notes: Total fatalities include those in which there was no driver or motorcycle rider present.
The National Highway Traffic Safety Administration estimates alcohol involvement when alcohol test results are unknown.

SOURCE: "Table 13. Persons Killed, by Highest Blood Alcohol Concentration (BAC) in the Crash, 1982–2008," in *Traffic Safety Facts 2008: A Compilation of Motor Vehicle Crash Data from the Fatality Analysis Reporting System and the General Estimates System*, U.S. Department of Transportation, National Highway Traffic Safety Administration, National Center for Statistics and Analysis, 2009, http://www-nrd.nhtsa.dot.gov/Pubs/811170.pdf (accessed November 9, 2010)

By August 2005 all 50 states, the District of Columbia, and Puerto Rico had lowered the BAC limit for drunk driving from 0.1 g/dL to 0.08 g/dL. According to the Insurance Institute for Highway Safety, in "DUI/DWI Laws" (http://www.iihs.org/laws/dui.aspx), as of February 2011, 41 states and the District of Columbia also had administrative license revocation laws, which require prompt, mandatory suspension of driver's licenses when drivers fail or refuse to take the BAC test. This immediate suspension, before conviction and independent of criminal procedures, is invoked immediately after arrest.

In both 1998 and 2008 drivers aged 21 to 44 years were the most likely to be involved in fatal crashes in which the driver had a BAC of 0.08 g/dL or higher, and their percentages have risen. (See Table 2.12.) The percentage of drivers within the 21- to 24-year-old age group increased from 32% in 1998 to 34% in 2008, the percentage of drivers in the 25- to 34-year-old age group increased from 28% to 31%, and the percentage of drivers in the 35- to 44-year-old group increased from 24% to 25%. Those in the 45- to 54-year-old group accounted for 18% of fatal crashes in which the driver had a BAC of 0.08 g/dL or higher in 1998; this percentage increased to 21% in 2008.

In 2008 the percentage of male drivers (25%) involved in fatal crashes who had a BAC of 0.08 g/dL or greater was 12 percentage points higher than female

drivers (13%) involved in fatal crashes. (See Table 2.12.) When compared with 1998, the percentage of drunk male and female drivers in fatal accidents in 2008 increased by two percentage points for males, from 23% to 25%, and increased by one percentage point for females, from 12% to 13%; thus the gap between the two groups remained nearly the same over the decade.

Alcohol was related to a higher percentage of fatal crashes by motorcycles (29%) in 2008 than for crashes involving automobiles and light trucks (23% each). (See Table 2.12.) Fatal crashes involving large trucks were very unlikely to be alcohol related (2%).

In 1998 over half of all pedestrians aged 21 to 44 years who were killed in a traffic accident had a BAC of 0.08 g/dL or greater. (See Table 2.13.) In 2008 the percentages within the age subgroups of this group had not changed by more than two percentage points.

ALCOHOL-RELATED OFFENSES

Table 2.14 shows arrest trends for alcohol-related offenses and driving under the influence between 1970 and 2008. Arrests were the highest for alcohol-related offenses from 1975 to 1992, with 1981 being the peak year. Arrests for driving under the influence were the highest from 1977 to 1996, with 1983 being the peak

TABLE 2.12

Drivers with a blood alcohol concentration (BAC) of 0.08 or higher involved in motor vehicle crashes, by age, gender, and vehicle type, 1998 and 2008

	Total drivers						Change in percentage with BAC=.08+ 1998–2008
	1998			2008			
		BAC=.08+			BAC=.08+		
Drivers involved in fatal crashes	Total number of drivers	Number	Percent of total	Total number of drivers	Number	Percent of total	
Total	56,604	11,561	20%	50,186	10,946	22%	+10%
Drivers by age group (years)							
16–20	7,767	1,295	17%	5,729	996	17%	0%
21–24	5,613	1,776	32%	5,312	1,829	34%	+6%
25–34	11,925	3,285	28%	9,745	2,997	31%	+11%
35–44	11,241	2,717	24%	8,762	2,221	25%	+4%
45–54	7,690	1,355	18%	8,313	1,724	21%	+17%
55–64	4,478	494	11%	5,695	708	12%	+9%
65–74	3,399	236	7%	2,913	198	7%	0%
75+	3,291	132	4%	2,656	106	4%	0%
Drivers by gender							
Male	40,816	9,548	23%	36,881	9,175	25%	+2%
Female	15,089	1,822	12%	12,568	1,650	13%	+1%
Drivers by vehicle type							
Passenger cars	28,907	6,155	21%	20,284	4,692	23%	+2%
Light trucks	19,247	4,271	22%	18,989	4,307	23%	+1%
Large trucks	4,905	72	1%	4,017	68	2%	+1%
Motorcycles	2,333	803	34%	5,383	1,564	29%	−5%

Note: Numbers shown for groups of drivers do not add to the total number of drivers due to unknown or other data not included.

SOURCE: "Table 3. Drivers in Fatal Crashes with a BAC of 0.08 or Higher, by Age, Gender, and Vehicle Type, 1998 and 2008," in *Traffic Safety Facts 2008 Data: Alcohol-Impaired Driving*, U.S. Department of Transportation, National Highway Traffic Safety Administration, National Center for Statistics and Analysis, 2009, http://www-nrd.nhtsa.dot.gov/Pubs/811155.pdf (accessed November 9, 2010)

TABLE 2.13

Pedestrians killed in motor vehicle crashes, by age group and percent BAC, 1998 and 2008

Age (years)	1998					2008				
	Number of fatalities	% with BAC=.00	% with BAC=.01–.07	% with BAC=.08+	% with BAC=.01+	Number of fatalities	% with BAC=.00	% with BAC=.01–.07	% with BAC=.08+	% with BAC=.01+
16–20	301	65	6	29	35	286	66	4	30	34
21–24	255	41	7	52	59	272	43	4	53	57
25–34	676	43	6	51	57	580	46	5	49	54
35–44	938	40	7	53	60	670	45	4	51	55
45–54	729	48	6	45	52	872	49	5	47	51
55–64	522	65	4	31	35	547	61	5	35	39
65–74	462	80	4	16	20	360	82	5	13	18
75–84	530	88	4	8	12	297	92	3	6	8
85+	184	92	1	7	8	146	96	2	2	4
Total*	4,597	58	5	37	42	4,030	58	4	38	42

*Excludes pedestrians under 16 years old and pedestrians of unknown age.

SOURCE: "Table 4. Alcohol Involvement for Pedestrians Killed in Fatal Crashes by Age, 1998 and 2008," in *Traffic Safety Facts 2008 Data: Pedestrians*, U.S. Department of Transportation, National Highway Traffic Safety Administration, National Center for Statistics and Analysis, 2009, http://www-nrd.nhtsa.dot .gov/Pubs/811163.pdf (accessed November 9, 2010)

year. In 2008 there were 2.6 million alcohol-related arrests; more than 1.1 million of those arrests were for driving under the influence.

Doris J. James of the Bureau of Justice Statistics (BJS) mentions in *Profile of Jail Inmates, 2002* (July 2004, http://bjs.ojp.usdoj.gov/content/pub/pdf/pji02.pdf) that in 2002, 33.4% of convicted jail inmates reported that they had been under the influence of alcohol alone (not in combination with any other drug) when they committed their offenses. This figure had decreased since 1996. A higher percentage of jail inmates used alcohol when committing a violent offense than did those committing other types of crimes, such as property or drug offenses. As of February 2011, these data were the most recent from the BJS.

TABLE 2.14

Arrests for alcohol-related offenses and driving under the influence, 1970–2008

United States, 1970–2008

[In thousands]

	Alcohol-related offenses	Driving under the influence
1970	2,849	424
1971	2,914	490
1972	2,835	604
1973	2,539	654
1974	2,297	617
1975	3,044	909
1976	2,790	838
1977	3,303	1,104
1978	3,406	1,205
1979	3,455	1,232
1980	3,535	1,304
1981	3,745	1,422
1982	3,640	1,405
1983	3,729	1,613
1984	3,153	1,347
1985	3,418	1,503
1986	3,325	1,459
1987	3,248	1,410
1988	2,995	1,294
1989	3,180	1,333
1990	3,270	1,391
1991	3,000	1,289
1992	3,061	1,320
1993	2,886	1,229
1994	2,698	1,080
1995	2,578	1,033
1996	2,677	1,014
1997	2,510	986
1998	2,451	969
1999	2,238	931
2000	2,218	916
2001	2,224	947
2002	2,401	1,020
2003	2,301	1,006
2004	2,373	1,014
2005	2,374	997
2006	2,463	1,039
2007	2,552	1,056
2008	2,620	1,110

Note: These data were compiled by the Federal Bureau of Investigation through the Uniform Crime Reporting (UCR) Program. On a monthly basis, law enforcement agencies report the number of offenses that become known to them in the following crime categories: murder and nonnegligent manslaughter, forcible rape, robbery, aggravated assault, burglary, larceny-theft, motor vehicle theft, and arson. Arrest statistics are compiled as part of this monthly data collection effort. Participating law enforcement agencies are instructed to count one arrest each time a person is taken into custody, notified, or cited for criminal infractions other than traffic violations. Annual arrest figures do not measure the number of individuals taken into custody because one person may be arrested several times during the year for the same type of offense or for different offenses. A juvenile is counted as a person arrested when he/she commits an act that would be a criminal offense if committed by an adult.
The number of agencies reporting and the populations represented vary from year to year. Due to National Incident-Based Reporting System conversion efforts beginning in 1991 as well as other reporting problems, complete arrest data were not available for a small number of jurisdictions for certain years.
This table presents data from all law enforcement agencies submitting complete reports for 12 months. Alcohol-related offenses include driving under the influence, liquor law violations, drunkenness, disorderly conduct, and vagrancy.

SOURCE: Kathleen Maguire, ed. "Table 4.27.2008. Arrests for Alcohol-Related Offenses and Driving under the Influence, United States, 1970–2008," in *Sourcebook of Criminal Justice Statistics Online*, U.S. Department of Justice, Bureau of Justice Statistics, University at Albany School of Criminal Justice, Hindelang Criminal Justice Research Center, 2010, http://www.albany.edu/sourcebook/pdf/t4272008.pdf (accessed November 9, 2010)

CHAPTER 3
TOBACCO

During the mid-20th century smoking in the United States was often associated with adventure, relaxation, and romance; movie stars oozed glamour on screen while smoking, and movie tough guys were never more masculine than when lighting up. Songs such as "Smoke Gets in Your Eyes" topped the list of most popular songs. Smoking became a rite of passage for young males and a sign of increasing independence for young females.

Since the 1990s, however, there has been an increase in opposition to tobacco use. Health authorities warn of the dangers of smoking and chewing tobacco, and nonsmokers object to secondhand smoke—because of both the smell and the health dangers of breathing smoke from other people's cigarettes. In the 21st century a smoker is more likely to ask for permission before lighting up, and the answer is often "no." Because of health concerns, smoking has been banned on airplanes, in hospitals, and in many workplaces, restaurants, and bars. In 2008, 82% of respondents to a Gallup poll believed that cigarette smoking was very harmful to adults who smoke. (See Figure 3.1.)

PHYSICAL PROPERTIES OF NICOTINE

Tobacco is a plant native to the Western Hemisphere. It contains nicotine, a drug that is classified as a stimulant, although it has some depressive effects as well. Nicotine is a poisonous alkaloid that is the major psychoactive (mood-altering) ingredient in tobacco. Alkaloids are carbon- and nitrogen-containing compounds that are found in some families of plants. They have both poisonous and medicinal properties.

Nicotine's effects on the body are complex. The drug affects the brain and central nervous system as well as the hypothalamus and pituitary glands of the endocrine (hormone) system. Nicotine easily crosses the blood-brain barrier—a series of capillaries and cells that control the flow of substances from the blood to the brain. It accumulates in the brain faster than caffeine or heroin but slower than Valium, a sedative medicine that is used to treat anxiety. In the brain nicotine imitates the actions of the hormone epinephrine (adrenaline) and the neurotransmitter acetylcholine, both of which heighten awareness. Nicotine also triggers the release of dopamine, which enhances feelings of pleasure, and endorphins, which have a calming effect.

As noted earlier, nicotine acts as both a stimulant and a depressant. By stimulating certain nerve cells in the spinal cord, nicotine relaxes the nerves and slows some reactions, such as the knee-jerk reflex. Small amounts of nicotine stimulate some nerve cells, but these cells are depressed by large amounts of nicotine. In addition, nicotine stimulates the brain cortex (the outer layer of the brain) and affects the functions of the heart and lungs.

TRENDS IN TOBACCO USE
Cigarettes

CONSUMPTION DATA. According to the Centers for Disease Control and Prevention (CDC), in "The National Tobacco Control Program" (*Chronic Disease Notes and Reports*, vol. 14, no. 3, fall 2001), the consumption of cigarettes, the most widely used tobacco product, has decreased over the past generation among adults. After increasing rather consistently for 60 years, the per capita (per person) consumption of cigarettes peaked during the 1960s at well over 4,000 cigarettes per year. The steady decline in smoking came shortly after 1964, when *Smoking and Health: Report of the Advisory Committee to the Surgeon General of the Public Health Service* (1964, http://profiles.nlm.nih.gov/NN/B/B/M/Q/_/nnbbmq.pdf) concluded that cigarette smoking is a cause of lung and laryngeal cancer in men, a probable cause of lung cancer in women, and the most important cause of chronic bronchitis in both genders.

FIGURE 3.1

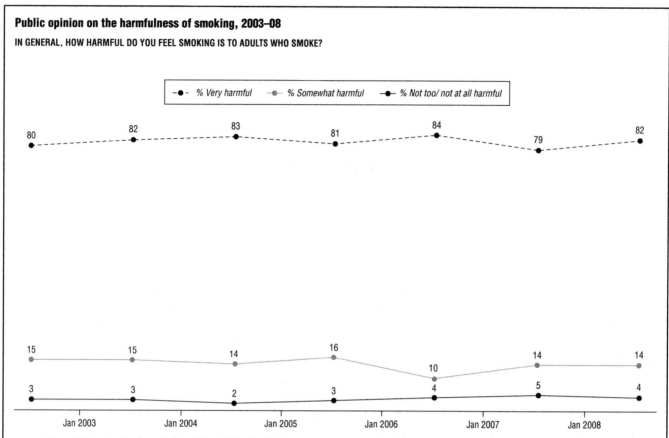

Public opinion on the harmfulness of smoking, 2003–08

IN GENERAL, HOW HARMFUL DO YOU FEEL SMOKING IS TO ADULTS WHO SMOKE?

SOURCE: Lymari Morales, "In General, How Harmful Do You Feel Smoking Is to Adults Who Smoke?" in *Most Americans Consider Smoking Very Harmful*, The Gallup Organization, July 28, 2008, http://www.gallup.com/poll/109129/Most-Americans-Consider-Smoking-Very-Harmful. aspx?version= print (accessed November 9, 2010). Copyright © 2008 by The Gallup Organization. Reproduced by permission of The Gallup Organization.

By 2006 the annual per capita consumption of cigarettes for those aged 18 years and older was 1,691. These data are taken from *Tobacco Outlook* (September 26, 2006, http://usda.mannlib.cornell.edu/usda/ers/TBS//2000s/2006/TBS-09-26-2006.pdf) by Tom Capehart of the Economic Research Service (ERS). This was the final report provided by the ERS on this topic because the ERS discontinued this publication along with another tobacco-related publication, the *Tobacco Briefing Room*, after a tobacco buyout was formalized by the U.S. Department of Agriculture (USDA) in February 2005. The tobacco buyout is a part of the Fair and Equitable Tobacco Reform Act of 2004 and is formally known as the Tobacco Transition Payment Program. (See Chapter 7.) Several USDA agencies discontinued their tobacco programs after the buyout. As of February 2011, none of the programs had been reinstituted nor were any governmental agencies collecting these data.

Each year the Substance Abuse and Mental Health Services Administration surveys U.S. households on drug use for the National Survey on Drug Use and Health (NSDUH). According to the NSDUH, in *Results from the 2009 National Survey on Drug Use and Health: Detailed Tables* (September 2010, http://oas.samhsa.gov/NSDUH/2k9NSDUH/tabs/Sect2peTabs22to26.pdf),

64.6% of the U.S. population in 2009 had smoked cigarettes at some point during their lifetime and 23.3% were current smokers (meaning they had smoked within the month before the survey). (See Table 3.1.)

In 2009 men (25.3%) were more likely than women (21.4%) to be current smokers. (See Table 3.1.) Additionally, whites (24.5%) were more likely to be current smokers than African-Americans (22.8%), Hispanics (21.2%), or Asian-Americans (10.9%). Those aged 18 to 25 years had the highest rate of current smoking at 35.8%, compared with 8.9% for those aged 12 to 17 years and 23% for those aged 26 years and older. Rates of current cigarette smoking declined overall from 23.9% in 2008 to 23.3% in 2009.

The National Health Interview Survey (NHIS), which is conducted annually by the National Center for Health Statistics, reports findings similar to those of the NSDUH. In *Early Release of Selected Estimates Based on Data from the 2009 National Health Interview Survey* (June 2010, http://www.cdc.gov/nchs/data/nhis/earlyrelease/201006_08.pdf), the NHIS indicates that 20.6% of adults in the United States were current smokers in 2009, down from 24.7% in 1997. (See Figure 3.2.) Like the NSDUH, the NHIS finds that men are more likely than women to

TABLE 3.1

Percentage of lifetime, past-year, and past-month cigarette users, by age group, gender, and ethnicity, 2008 and 2009

Demographic characteristic	Lifetime (2008)	Lifetime (2009)	Past year (2008)	Past year (2009)	Past month (2008)	Past month (2009)
Total	65.1	64.6	28.0	27.5	23.9	23.3
Age						
12–17	22.9	22.2	15.0	15.0	9.1	8.9
18–25	64.2	63.7	45.0	45.2	35.7	35.8
26 or older	70.7	70.1	26.8	26.0	23.8	23.0
Gender						
Male	69.6	69.3	30.9	30.1	26.3	25.3
Female	60.8	60.2	25.3	25.0	21.7	21.4
Hispanic origin and race						
Not Hispanic or Latino	67.0	66.6	28.6[a]	27.6	24.7[a]	23.6
White	71.4	71.2	29.4	28.7	25.2	24.5
Black or African American	53.4	52.1	28.0	25.9	24.8	22.8
American Indian or Alaska Native	73.1	74.3	49.2	37.6	44.1	33.0
Native Hawaiian or other Pacific Islander	*	*	*	*	*	15.4
Asian	34.9	35.6	15.0	13.3	11.9	10.9
Two or more races	71.1	66.8	35.6	34.0	32.2	30.7
Hispanic or Latino	53.2	52.4	24.2[a]	26.6	19.4	21.2

*Low precision; no estimate reported

SOURCE: "Table 2.22B. Cigarette Use in Lifetime, Past Year, and Past Month among Persons Aged 12 or Older, by Demographic Characteristics: Percentages, 2008 and 2009," in *Results from the 2009 National Survey on Drug Use and Health: Detailed Tables*, U.S. Department of Health and Human Services, Substance Abuse and Mental Health Services Administration, Office of Applied Studies, September 2010, http://oas.samhsa.gov/NSDUH/2k9NSDUH/tabs/Sect2peTabs22to26.pdf (accessed November 8, 2010)

smoke. Of adult men, 23.4% were current smokers in 2009. Of adult women, 17.9% were current smokers. (See Figure 3.3.) Women were more likely than men to have never smoked.

Even though the NHIS uses different age groups than the NHSDA, the results of both surveys show that younger people smoked at a higher rate than older people in 2009. Figure 3.4 shows that those aged 18 to 44 years were slightly more likely to smoke than those aged 45 to 64 years. The rate of smoking in the 65-and-older age group was dramatically lower than in either of the two younger groups. Men in all age categories except in the 65-and-older category were more likely than women in the same age group to smoke.

Furthermore, the NHIS finds that the prevalence of current smoking among various races and ethnicities was highest for non-Hispanic whites (22.8%) in 2009. (See Figure 3.5.) Non-Hispanic African-Americans (21%) were less likely to smoke than non-Hispanic whites, whereas Hispanics (13.5%) were the least likely to smoke among the three groups.

In 2009 the Gallup Organization looked at smoking by state to determine which states had the highest and which states had lowest percentage of smokers. The results are shown in Table 3.2. The states with the highest percentage of smokers were clustered in the central and southeastern portion of the United States. The two states with the highest percentage of smokers were Kentucky (31%) and West

Virginia (31%), followed by Oklahoma (28%), Tennessee (28%), and Indiana (27%). The states with the lowest percentage of smokers were scattered around the United States. The state with the lowest percentage of smokers was Utah (13%), followed by California (16%), Idaho (18%), Montana (18%), the District of Columbia (18%), and New Jersey (18%).

Cigars, Pipes, and Other Forms of Tobacco

According to the NSDUH, 3.4% of those aged 12 years and older were current users of smokeless tobacco (chewing tobacco and/or snuff) and 5.3% were current users of cigars in 2009. (See Figure 3.6.) Only 0.8% smoked pipes. These percentages remained relatively constant between 2002 and 2009.

However, the overall use of tobacco products has declined modestly since 2002, from 30.4% of people aged 12 years and older using tobacco products in that year to 27.7% in 2009. (See Figure 3.6.) The current use of cigarettes by people aged 12 years and older has declined as well, from 26% in 2002 to 23.3% in 2009.

ADDICTIVE NATURE OF NICOTINE

Is tobacco addictive? In *The Health Consequences of Smoking—Nicotine Addiction: A Report of the Surgeon General* (1988, http://profiles.nlm.nih.gov/NN/B/B/Z/D/_/nnbbzd.pdf), researchers first examined this question. They determined that the pharmacological (chemical and physical) effects and behavioral processes that contribute

FIGURE 3.2

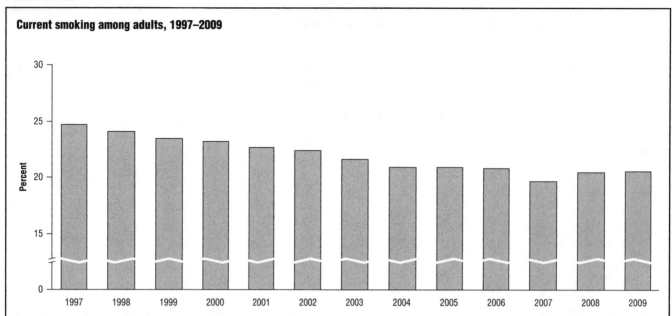

Current smoking among adults, 1997–2009

Notes: Current smokers were defined as those who had smoked more than 100 cigarettes in their lifetime and now smoke every day or some days. The analyses excluded persons with unknown smoking status (about 2% of respondents each year). Beginning with the 2003 data, the National Health Interview Survey transitioned to weights derived from the 2000 census. In this Early Release, estimates for 2000–2002 were recalculated using weights derived from the 2000 census.

SOURCE: P. M. Barnes et al., "Figure 8.1. Prevalence of Current Smoking among Adults Aged 18 Years and over: United States, 1997–2009," in *Early Release of Selected Estimates Based on Data from the 2009 National Health Interview Survey*, U.S. Department of Health and Human Services, Centers for Disease Control and Prevention, National Center for Health Statistics, June 2010, http://www.cdc.gov/nchs/data/nhis/earlyrelease/201006_08.pdf (accessed November 9, 2010)

FIGURE 3.3

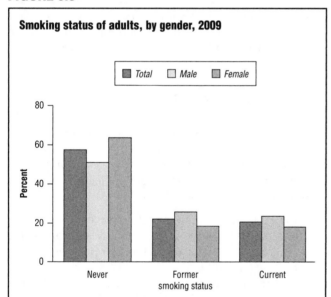

Smoking status of adults, by gender, 2009

Notes: Current smokers were defined as those who had smoked more than 100 cigarettes in their lifetime and now smoke every day or some days. The analyses excluded 130 persons (0.5%) with unknown smoking status.

SOURCE: P. M. Barnes et al., "Figure 8.2. Percent Distribution of Smoking Status among Adults Aged 18 Years and over, by Sex: United States, 2009," in *Early Release of Selected Estimates Based on Data from the 2009 National Health Interview Survey*, U.S. Department of Health and Human Services, Centers for Disease Control and Prevention, National Center for Health Statistics, June 2010, http://www.cdc.gov/nchs/data/nhis/earlyrelease/201006_08.pdf (accessed November 9, 2010)

FIGURE 3.4

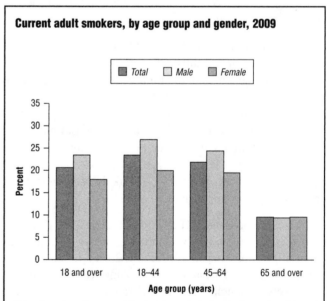

Current adult smokers, by age group and gender, 2009

Notes: Current smokers were defined as those who had smoked more than 100 cigarettes in their lifetime and now smoke every day or some days. The analyses excluded 130 persons (0.5%) with unknown smoking status.

SOURCE: P. M. Barnes et al., "Figure 8.3. Prevalence of Current Smoking among Adults Aged 18 Years and over, by Age Group and Sex: United States, 2009," in *Early Release of Selected Estimates Based on Data from the 2009 National Health Interview Survey*, U.S. Department of Health and Human Services, Centers for Disease Control and Prevention, National Center for Health Statistics, June 2010, http://www.cdc.gov/nchs/data/nhis/earlyrelease/201006_08.pdf (accessed November 9, 2010)

FIGURE 3.5

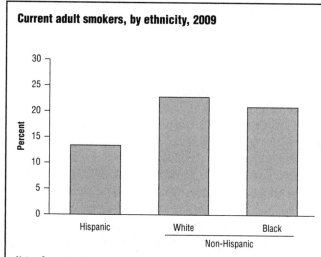

Current adult smokers, by ethnicity, 2009

Notes: Current smokers were defined as those who had smoked more than 100 cigarettes in their lifetime and now smoke every day or some days. The analyses excluded 130 persons (0.5%) with unknown smoking status. Estimates are age-sex adjusted using the projected 2000 U.S. population as the standard population and using five age groups: 18–24 years, 25–34 years, 35–44 years, 45–64 years, and 65 years and over.

SOURCE: P. M. Barnes et al., "Figure 8.4. Age-Sex-Adjusted Prevalence of Current Smoking among Adults Aged 18 Years and over, by Race/Ethnicity: United States, 2009," in *Early Release of Selected Estimates Based on Data from the 2009 National Health Interview Survey*, U.S. Department of Health and Human Services, Centers for Disease Control and Prevention, National Center for Health Statistics, June 2010, http://www.cdc.gov/nchs/data/nhis/earlyrelease/201006_08.pdf (accessed November 9, 2010)

TABLE 3.2

States with highest and lowest percentages of smokers, 2009

States with highest percentage of smokers

Percentage who smoke is 25% or more	% smoke
Kentucky	31
West Virginia	31
Oklahoma	28
Tennessee	28
Indiana	27
Arkansas	26
Missouri	26
Ohio	26
Louisiana	26
South Carolina	26
Alabama	25

States with lowest percentage of smokers

Percentage who smoke is below 20%	% smoke
Utah	13
California	16
Idaho	18
Montana	18
District of Columbia	18
New Jersey	18
Minnesota	19
Hawaii	19
Massachusetts	19
Arizona	19
Maryland	19

SOURCE: Lydia Saad, "States with Highest Percentage of Smokers, States with Lowest Percentage of Smokers," in *Adult Smoking Ranges from 13% to 31% across U.S. States*, The Gallup Organization, August 26, 2010, http://www.gallup.com/poll/142694/Adult-Smoking-Ranges-Across-States.aspx (accessed December 2, 2010). Copyright © 2010 by The Gallup Organization. Reproduced by permission of The Gallup Organization.

to tobacco addiction are similar to those that contribute in the addiction to drugs such as heroin and cocaine. Many researchers consider nicotine to be as potentially addictive as cocaine and heroin and note that it can create dependence quickly in some users. After more than 20 years since the surgeon general's report—with study after study confirming the addictive nature of nicotine while also zeroing in on characteristics that increase the likelihood for addiction, such as genetics, ethnicity, and even tobacco additives such as menthol—the National Institute on Drug Abuse states conclusively in "Tobacco/Nicotine" (February 2011, http://www.drugabuse.gov/drugpages/nicotine.html) that nicotine is not only "highly addictive" but also "one of the most heavily used addictive drugs" in the United States.

Cigarette smoking results in the rapid distribution of nicotine throughout the body, reaching the brain within 10 seconds of inhalation. However, the intense effects of nicotine disappear in a few minutes, causing smokers to continue smoking frequently throughout the day to maintain its pleasurable effects and to prevent withdrawal. Tolerance develops after repeated exposure to nicotine, and higher doses are required to produce the same initial stimulation. Because nicotine is metabolized (chemically processed) fairly quickly, disappearing from the body in a few hours, some tolerance is lost overnight. Smokers often report that the first cigarette of the day is the most satisfying. The more cigarettes smoked during the day, the more tolerance develops, and the less effect subsequent cigarettes have.

Is There a Genetic Basis for Nicotine Addiction?

Smoking is influenced by both environment and genetics, as are all addictions. (See Chapter 1.) The results of many scientific studies, such as M. K. Ho and Rachel F. Tyndale's "Overview of the Pharmacogenomics of Cigarette Smoking" (*Pharmacogenomics Journal*, vol. 7, no. 2, April 2007), show that between 11% and 78% of the initiation of smoking and between 28% and 84% of the maintenance of dependent smoking behavior are genetically influenced. In addition, 28% to 84% of the number of cigarettes an individual smokes is genetically influenced as is 31% to 75% of nicotine dependence. The ranges in these data are due to the variations in the results of numerous studies. Ho and Tyndale conclude that "taken together, these studies suggest a substantial genetic contribution to most aspects of smoking."

Nicotine May Not Be the Only Substance in Cigarettes Linked to Addiction

Research results suggest that nicotine may not be the only ingredient in tobacco involved with addiction. Various compounds called monoamine oxidase (MAO) inhibitors

FIGURE 3.6

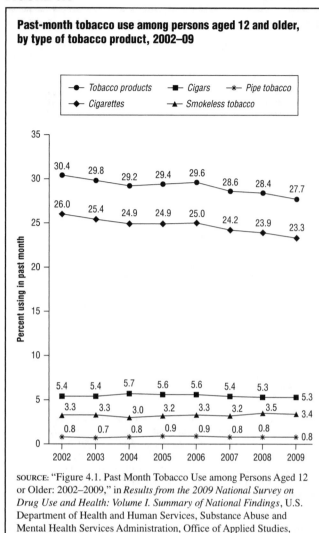

Past-month tobacco use among persons aged 12 and older, by type of tobacco product, 2002–09

SOURCE: "Figure 4.1. Past Month Tobacco Use among Persons Aged 12 or Older: 2002–2009," in *Results from the 2009 National Survey on Drug Use and Health: Volume I. Summary of National Findings*, U.S. Department of Health and Human Services, Substance Abuse and Mental Health Services Administration, Office of Applied Studies, September 2010, http://www.oas.samhsa.gov/NSDUH/2k9NSDUH/2k9ResultsP.pdf (accessed November 8, 2010)

are found in high concentrations in cigarette smoke. MAO is an enzyme that is responsible for breaking down the brain chemical dopamine. The decrease in MAO results in higher dopamine levels and may be another reason that smokers continue to smoke—to sustain the high dopamine levels that result in pleasurable effects and the desire for repeated cigarette use.

One issue that complicates any efforts by a longtime smoker to quit is nicotine withdrawal, which is often referred to as craving. This urge for nicotine is not well understood by researchers. Withdrawal may begin within a few hours after the last cigarette. According to the National Institute on Drug Abuse, high levels of craving may persist six months or longer. Besides craving, withdrawal can include irritability, attention deficits, interruption of thought processes, sleep disturbances, and increased appetite.

Some researchers also point out the behavioral aspects that are involved in smoking. The purchasing, handling, and lighting of cigarettes may be just as pleasing

psychologically to the user as the chemical properties of the tobacco itself.

HEALTH CONSEQUENCES OF TOBACCO USE
Respiratory System Effects

Cigarette smoke contains almost 4,000 different chemical compounds, many of which are toxic, mutagenic (capable of increasing the frequency of mutation, or change, in the genetic material), and carcinogenic (cancer causing). At least 43 carcinogens have been identified in tobacco smoke. Besides nicotine, the most damaging substances are tar and carbon monoxide (CO). Smoke also contains hydrogen cyanide and other chemicals that can damage the respiratory system. These substances and nicotine are absorbed into the body through the linings of the mouth, nose, throat, and lungs. About 10 seconds later they are delivered by the bloodstream to the brain.

Tar, which adds to the flavor of cigarettes, is released by the burning of tobacco. As it is inhaled, it enters the alveoli (air cells) of the lungs. There, the tar hampers the action of cilia (small, hairlike extensions of cells that clean foreign substances from the lungs), allowing the substances in cigarette smoke to accumulate.

CO affects the blood's ability to distribute oxygen throughout the body. CO is chemically similar to carbon dioxide (CO_2), which bonds with the hemoglobin in blood so that the CO_2 can be carried to the lungs for elimination. Hemoglobin has two primary functions: to carry oxygen to all parts of the body and to remove excess CO_2 from the body's tissues. CO bonds to hemoglobin more tightly than CO_2 and leaves the body more slowly, which allows CO to build up in the hemoglobin, in turn reducing the amount of oxygen the blood can carry. The lack of adequate oxygen is damaging to most of the body's organs, including the heart and brain.

Diseases and Conditions Linked to Tobacco Use

The results of medical research show an association between smoking and cancer, as well as heart and circulatory disease, fetal growth retardation, and low birth weight babies. The 1983 *Health Consequences of Smoking—Cardiovascular Disease: Report of the Surgeon General* (http://profiles.nlm.nih.gov/NN/B/B/T/D/_/nnbbtd.pdf) linked cigarette smoking to cerebrovascular disease (strokes) and associated it with cancer of the uterine cervix. Two 1992 studies showed that people who smoke double their risk of forming cataracts, the leading cause of blindness. Several other studies linked smoking to unsuccessful pregnancies, increased infant mortality, and peptic ulcer disease. In 2004 the U.S. surgeon general Richard Carmona (1949–) released *The Health Consequences of Smoking: A Report of the Surgeon General* (http://www.cdc.gov/tobacco/data_statistics/sgr/2004/), which revealed for the first time that cigarette smoking causes diseases in nearly every organ of the body. In December

2010 the U.S. surgeon general Regina Benjamin (1956–) released *How Tobacco Smoke Causes Disease: The Biology and Behavioral Basis for Smoking-Attributable Disease: A Report of the Surgeon General* (http://www.surgeongeneral.gov/library/tobaccosmoke/report/full_report.pdf). This report pictorially shows the long list of health consequences and diseases that are caused by smoking. (See Figure 3.7.)

The National Cancer Institute notes in "Cigar Smoking and Cancer" (October 27, 2010, http://www.cancer.gov/cancertopics/factsheet/Tobacco/cigars) that cigar smoking is associated with cancers of the lip, tongue, mouth, throat, larynx (voice box), lungs, esophagus (food tube), and possibly the pancreas. Those who smoke cigars daily and inhale the smoke have an increased risk for developing heart and lung disease.

Smokeless tobacco, which includes chewing tobacco and snuff, also creates health hazards for its users. The National Cancer Institute explains that smokeless tobacco is associated with cancers of the lip, gum, mouth, esophagus, and pancreas. It can also cause heart disease, gum disease, and precancerous white patches in the mouth. It is not a safer alternative to smoking. In addition, smokeless tobacco use can lead to nicotine addiction and may, therefore, lead to smoking.

Premature Aging

Smoking cigarettes contributes to premature aging in a variety of ways. The results of research conducted over nearly four decades, such as Akimichi Morita et al.'s "Molecular Basis of Tobacco Smoke-Induced Premature Skin Aging" (*Journal of Investigative Dermatology Symposium Proceedings*, vol. 14, no. 1, August 2009), show that smoking enhances facial aging and skin wrinkling. The researchers also note that cigarette smoking results in "smoker's face," which consists of a gray pallor and deep wrinkles. Cigarette smoking is also associated with the development of gray hair, cataracts, diabetes, weak bones, and atherosclerosis (a hardening of the walls of the arteries caused by the buildup of fatty deposits on the inner walls of the arteries that interferes with blood flow).

Why do these changes occur? The University of Alabama Health System explains in "Smoking (Premature Aging)" (2008, http://www.health.uab.edu/17863/) that nicotine tightens blood vessels, which decreases blood flow to the body's organs, depriving them of the proper amount of oxygen and nutrients that they need for good health. The skin, which is the body's largest organ, also receives less oxygen and nutrients than it needs, especially vitamin A. This vitamin is critical to regenerating new skin cells, which are essential to healthy, youthful-looking skin. In addition, the lack of proper skin nutrition damages structural proteins within the skin, resulting in skin sagging and wrinkling. Morita et al. state a startling fact: "Because many people begin smoking during their teenage years, a 30-year-old woman may have the face of a 50 year old."

In "Cigarette Smoke Induces Cellular Senescence via Werner's Syndrome Protein Down-Regulation" (*American Journal of Respiratory and Critical Care Medicine*, vol. 179, no. 4, February 15, 2009), Toru Nyunoya et al. report that cigarette smokers have the same cell defect as individuals with the genetic premature aging disease Werner's syndrome. Research results show that both cigarette smokers and individuals with Werner's syndrome do not produce enough of a protein called WRN, which protects and repairs genetic material in the body. In addition, an extract of cigarette smoke is found to reduce WRN production in cultured lung cells in the laboratory. Not enough of WRN leads to premature aging. This information may help researchers develop a treatment for premature aging in smokers.

FIGURE 3.7

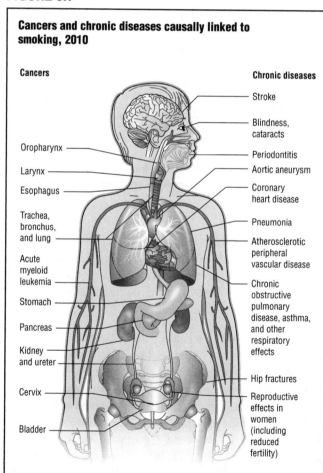

Cancers and chronic diseases causally linked to smoking, 2010

Cancers

- Oropharynx
- Larynx
- Esophagus
- Trachea, bronchus, and lung
- Acute myeloid leukemia
- Stomach
- Pancreas
- Kidney and ureter
- Cervix
- Bladder

Chronic diseases

- Stroke
- Blindness, cataracts
- Periodontitis
- Aortic aneurysm
- Coronary heart disease
- Pneumonia
- Atherosclerotic peripheral vascular disease
- Chronic obstructive pulmonary disease, asthma, and other respiratory effects
- Hip fractures
- Reproductive effects in women (including reduced fertility)

SOURCE: Adapted from "Figure 1.1. The Health Consequences Causally Linked to Smoking and Exposure to Secondhand Smoke," in *How Tobacco Smoke Causes Disease: The Biology and Behavioral Basis for Smoking-Attributable Disease: A Report of the Surgeon General*, U.S. Department of Health and Human Services, Office on Smoking and Health, December 9, 2010, http://www.cdc.gov/tobacco/data_statistics/sgr/2010/index.htm (accessed December 13, 2010)

Interactions with Other Drugs

Smoking can have adverse effects when combined with over-the-counter (without a prescription) and prescription medications that a smoker may be taking. In many cases smoking reduces the effectiveness of medications, such as pain relievers (acetaminophen), antidepressants, tranquilizers, sedatives, ulcer medications, and insulin. With estrogen and oral contraceptives, smoking may increase the risk of heart and blood vessel disease and can cause strokes and blood clots.

Robert G. Smith notes in "An Appraisal of Potential Drug Interactions in Cigarette Smokers and Alcohol Drinkers" (*Journal of the American Podiatric Medical Association*, vol. 99, no. 1, January–February 2009) that many drug interactions with smoking have been identified, and therefore smokers should be screened by their physicians for potential harmful drug interactions. In addition, individuals may need to take higher doses of some medications while they are current smokers and may need to reduce dosages when they quit.

SMOKING AND PUBLIC HEALTH

A study during the 1920s found that men who smoked two or more packs of cigarettes per day were 22 times more likely than nonsmokers to die of lung cancer. At the time, these results surprised researchers and medical authorities alike. Some 40 years ago, the U.S. government first officially recognized the negative health consequences of smoking. In 1964 the Advisory Committee to the Surgeon General released a groundbreaking survey of studies on tobacco use. In *Smoking and Health: Report of the Advisory Committee to the Surgeon General of the Public Health Service*, the U.S. surgeon general Luther L. Terry (1911–1985) reported that cigarette smoking increased overall mortality in men and caused lung and laryngeal cancer, as well as chronic bronchitis. Terry concluded, "Cigarette smoking is a health hazard of sufficient importance in the United States to warrant appropriate remedial action," but what action should be taken was left unspecified at that time.

Later surgeons general issued additional reports on the health effects of smoking and the dangers to nonsmokers of secondhand smoke. Besides general health concerns, the reports addressed specific health consequences and populations. Table 3.3 shows a listing of reports of the surgeons general and the years in which they were published. The later reports concluded that smoking increases the morbidity (proportion of diseased people in a particular population) and mortality (proportion of deaths in a particular population) of both men and women.

In 1965 Congress passed the Federal Cigarette Labeling and Advertising Act, which required the following health warning on all cigarette packages: "Caution: Cigarette smoking may be hazardous to your health." The

TABLE 3.3

Surgeon General's reports on smoking and health, 1964–2010

1964	Smoking and Health: Report of the Advisory Committee to the Surgeon General of the Public Health Service
1967	The Health Consequences of Smoking: A Public Health Service Review
1968	The Health Consequences of Smoking: 1968 Supplement to the 1967 Public Health Service Review
1969	The Health Consequences of Smoking: 1969 Supplement to the 1967 Public Health Service Review
1971	The Health Consequences of Smoking
1972	The Health Consequences of Smoking
1973	The Health Consequences of Smoking
1974	The Health Consequences of Smoking
1975	The Health Consequences of Smoking
1976	The Health Consequences of Smoking: A Reference Edition
1979	The Health Consequences of Smoking, 1977–1978
1979	Smoking and Health
1980	The Health Consequences of Smoking for Women
1981	The Health Consequences of Smoking: The Changing Cigarette
1982	The Health Consequences of Smoking: Cancer
1983	The Health Consequences of Smoking: Cardiovascular Disease
1984	The Health Consequences of Smoking: Chronic Obstructive Lung Disease
1985	The Health Consequences of Smoking: Cancer and Chronic Lung Disease in the Workplace
1986	The Health Consequences of Involuntary Smoking
1988	The Health Consequences of Smoking: Nicotine Addiction
1989	Reducing the Health Consequences of Smoking: 25 Years of Progress
1990	Smoking and Health: A National Status Report
1990	The Health Benefits of Smoking Cessation
1992	Smoking and Health in the Americas
1994	SGR 4 KIDS: The Surgeon General's Report for Kids About Smoking
1995	Preventing Tobacco Use among Young People
1998	Tobacco Use among U.S. Racial/Ethnic Minority Groups
2000	Reducing Tobacco Use
2001	Women and Smoking
2004	The Health Consequences of Smoking
2006	The Health Consequences of Involuntary Exposure to Tobacco Smoke
2007	Children and Secondhand Smoke Exposure: Excerpts from the Health Consequences of Involuntary Exposure to Tobacco Smoke
2008	Treating Tobacco Use and Dependence: 2008 Update
2010	How Tobacco Smoke Causes Disease: The Biology and Behavioral Basis for Smoking-Attributable Disease

SOURCE: Created by Sandra Alters for Gale, 2010

Public Health Cigarette Smoking Act of 1969 strengthened the warning to read: "Warning: The Surgeon General has determined that cigarette smoking is dangerous to your health." Still later acts resulted in four different health warnings to be used in rotation.

In June 2009 President Barack Obama (1961–) signed the Family Smoking Prevention and Tobacco Control Act. The act gave the U.S. Food and Drug Administration (FDA) regulatory authority over tobacco products and required that cigarette packages and advertisements have larger and more visible graphic health warnings. The FDA explains in "Proposed Cigarette Product Warning Labels" (February 23, 2011, http://www.fda.gov/Tobacco Products/Labeling/CigaretteProductWarningLabels/ucm 2024177.htm) that two of the proposed warnings were "Smoking can kill you," with an accompanying photo of a dead person, and "Cigarettes cause cancer," with an accompanying photo of an emaciated person near death lying in a hospital bed. The FDA was expected to issue final regulations on the graphics in June 2011 and the new warnings would begin appearing on cigarette packages in late 2012.

DEATHS ATTRIBUTED TO TOBACCO USE

According to the 2010 surgeon general's report *How Tobacco Smoke Causes Disease*, cigarette smoking is the leading cause of preventable death and disability in the United States and produces substantial health-related economic costs to society. The report notes that smoking causes an estimated 443,000 deaths in the United States annually. Nationwide, smoking kills more people each year than alcohol, drug abuse, car crashes, murders, suicides, fires, and acquired immunodeficiency syndrome (AIDS) combined.

In 2007 diseases linked to smoking accounted for four of the top five causes of death in the United States. (See Table 3.4.) The CDC shows in "QuickStats from the National Center for Health Statistics" (*Morbidity and Mortality Weekly Report*, vol. 57, no. 24, June 20, 2008) that this fact has remained the same since 2001. The death rates for heart disease, cancer, and cerebrovascular disease declined from 2001 to 2006, whereas the rates for chronic lower respiratory diseases, such as emphysema and chronic bronchitis, stayed about the same. For example, heart disease death rates declined from 247.8 deaths per 100,000 people in 2001 to 190.9 deaths per 100,000 people in 2007, a drop of 23%. Cancer death rates declined from 196 deaths per 100,000 people to 178.4 deaths per 100,000 people during this period, a drop of 9%.

TABLE 3.4

Death rates for the five leading causes of death, 2007, and percent change, 2006–07

Rank*	Cause of death	Percent of total deaths	Age-adjusted death rate 2007	Percent change 2006 to 2007
. . .	All causes	100.0	760.2	−2.1
1	Diseases of heart	25.4	190.9	−4.6
2	Malignant neoplasms	23.2	178.4	−1.3
3	Cerebrovascular diseases	5.6	42.2	−3.2
4	Chronidower respiratory diseases	5.3	40.8	0.7
5	Accidents (unintentional injuries)	5.1	40.0	0.5

*Rank is based on number of deaths

SOURCE: Adapted from Jiaquan Xu et al., "Table B. Percentage of Total Deaths, Death Rates, Age-Adjusted Death Rates for 2007, Percentage Change in Age-Adjusted Death Rates in 2007 from 2006, and Ratio of Age-Adjusted Death Rates, by Race and Sex for the 15 Leading Causes of Death for the Total Population in 2007: United States," in "Deaths: Final Data for 2007," *National Vital Statistics Reports*, vol. 58, no. 19, May 20, 2010, http://www.cdc.gov/nchs/data/nvsr/nvsr58/nvsr58_19.pdf (accessed November 9, 2010)

In *Cancer Facts and Figures, 2010* (2010, http://www.cancer.org/acs/groups/content/@epidemiologysurveilance/documents/document/acspc-026238.pdf), the American Cancer Society estimates that 157,300 Americans died of lung and bronchus cancer in 2010. Even though not all lung and bronchus cancer deaths are directly attributable to smoking, a large proportion of them are. Lung cancer is the leading cause of cancer mortality in both men and women in the United States. It has been the leading cause of cancer deaths among men since the early 1950s and, in 1987, it surpassed breast cancer to become the leading cause of cancer deaths in women.

SECONDHAND SMOKE

Secondhand smoke, also known as environmental tobacco smoke or passive smoke, is a health hazard for nonsmokers who live or work with smokers. In the fact sheet "Secondhand Smoke and Cancer" (January 12, 2011, http://www.cancer.gov/cancertopics/factsheet/Tobacco/ETS), the National Cancer Institute defines secondhand smoke as "the smoke given off by a burning tobacco product and the smoke exhaled by a smoker."

The article "Non-smoking Wives of Heavy Smokers Have a Higher Risk of Lung Cancer: A Study from Japan" (*British Medical Journal*, vol. 282, no. 6259, January 17, 1981) by Takeshi Hirayama of the National Cancer Centre Research Institute was the first scientific paper on the harmful effects of secondhand smoke. Hirayama studied 91,540 nonsmoking wives of smoking husbands and a similarly sized group of nonsmoking women who were married to nonsmokers. He discovered that nonsmoking wives of husbands who smoked faced a 40% to 90% elevated risk of lung cancer (depending on how frequently their husband smoked) compared with the wives of nonsmoking husbands.

Other studies followed. The U.S. Environmental Protection Agency (EPA) concluded in *Respiratory Health Effects of Passive Smoking: Lung Cancer and Other Disorders* (December 1992, http://cfpub2.epa.gov/ncea/cfm/recordisplay.cfm?deid=2835) that the "widespread exposure to environmental tobacco smoke (ETS) in the United States presents a serious and substantial public health impact." In "Environmental Tobacco Smoke and Lung Cancer in Nonsmoking Women: A Multicenter Study" (*Journal of the American Medical Association*, vol. 271, no. 22, June 8, 1994), a large case-control study on secondhand smoke, Elizabeth T. H. Fontham et al. found compelling links between passive smoke and lung cancer. In 2000 the Environmental Health Information Service's *Ninth Report on Carcinogens* classified secondhand smoke as a Group A (human) carcinogen. According to the EPA, there is no safe level of exposure to such Group A toxins.

In 2005 more evidence accumulated on the risks of secondhand smoking. In "Environmental Tobacco Smoke and Risk of Respiratory Cancer and Chronic Obstructive Pulmonary Disease in Former Smokers and Never Smokers in the EPIC Prospective Study" (*British Medical Journal*, vol. 330, no. 7486, February 5, 2005), Paolo Vineis et al. revealed that those who had been exposed to secondhand smoke during childhood for many hours each day had more than triple the risk of developing lung cancer compared with people who were not exposed. In addition, Sarah M. McGhee et al. showed in "Mortality Associated with Passive Smoking in Hong Kong" (*British Medical Journal*, vol. 330, no. 7486, February 5, 2005) that there is a correlation between an increased risk of dying from various causes (including lung cancer and other lung diseases, heart disease, and stroke) and the number of smokers in the home. The risk increased by 24% when one smoker lived in the home and by 74% with two smokers in the household.

In 2006 the 31st report of the surgeon general on smoking—*The Health Consequences of Involuntary Exposure to Tobacco Smoke* (http://www.surgeongeneral.gov/library/secondhandsmoke/report/fullreport.pdf)—was published. The report noted that:

> With regard to the involuntary exposure of nonsmokers to tobacco smoke, the scientific evidence now supports the following major conclusions:
>
> 1. Secondhand smoke causes premature death and disease in children and in adults who do not smoke.
>
> 2. Children exposed to secondhand smoke are at an increased risk for sudden infant death syndrome (SIDS), acute respiratory infections, ear problems, and more severe asthma. Smoking by parents causes respiratory symptoms and slows lung growth in their children.
>
> 3. Exposure of adults to secondhand smoke has immediate adverse effects on the cardiovascular system and causes coronary heart disease and lung cancer.
>
> 4. The scientific evidence indicates that there is no risk-free level of exposure to secondhand smoke.
>
> 5. Many millions of Americans, both children and adults, are still exposed to secondhand smoke in their homes and workplaces despite substantial progress in tobacco control.
>
> 6. Eliminating smoking in indoor spaces fully protects nonsmokers from exposure to secondhand smoke. Separating smokers from nonsmokers, cleaning the air, and ventilating buildings cannot eliminate exposures of nonsmokers to secondhand smoke.

In 2007 an excerpt of this report was published: *Children and Secondhand Smoke Exposure: Excerpts from the Health Consequences of Involuntary Exposure to Tobacco Smoke* (http://www.surgeongeneral.gov/library/smokeexposure/report/fullreport.pdf). The purpose of the publication was to highlight the serious consequences of secondhand

FIGURE 3.8

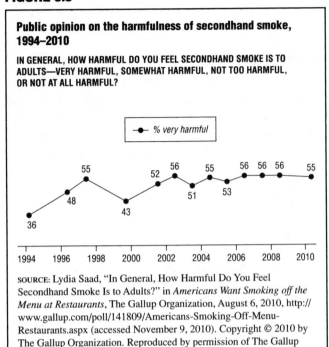

Public opinion on the harmfulness of secondhand smoke, 1994–2010

IN GENERAL, HOW HARMFUL DO YOU FEEL SECONDHAND SMOKE IS TO ADULTS—VERY HARMFUL, SOMEWHAT HARMFUL, NOT TOO HARMFUL, OR NOT AT ALL HARMFUL?

SOURCE: Lydia Saad, "In General, How Harmful Do You Feel Secondhand Smoke Is to Adults?" in *Americans Want Smoking off the Menu at Restaurants*, The Gallup Organization, August 6, 2010, http://www.gallup.com/poll/141809/Americans-Smoking-Off-Menu-Restaurants.aspx (accessed November 9, 2010). Copyright © 2010 by The Gallup Organization. Reproduced by permission of The Gallup Organization.

smoke exposure on the health of children, to emphasize that they are more heavily exposed to secondhand smoke than are adults, and to urge that children be protected from this unnecessary threat to their health.

The 2010 surgeon general's report *How Tobacco Smoke Causes Disease* emphasizes the dangers of secondhand smoke and notes that secondhand smoke exposure causes middle ear disease, impaired lung function, lower respiratory illness, and SIDS in children. In adults, secondhand smoke can cause lung cancer and coronary heart disease. Also, pregnant women who are exposed to secondhand smoke have an increased risk of giving birth to low birth weight babies.

Even though the percentage of those who perceive secondhand smoke to be very harmful has increased since 1994, this percentage has not increased in recent years. (See Figure 3.8.) In 2010, 55% of people said secondhand smoke is very harmful, which was down slightly from 56% in 2008.

THIRDHAND SMOKE

According to Jonathan P. Winickoff et al., in "Beliefs about the Health Effects of 'Thirdhand' Smoke and Home Smoking Bans" (*Pediatrics*, vol. 123, no. 1, January 2009), "thirdhand smoke is residual tobacco smoke contamination that remains after the cigarette is extinguished." The researchers find an association between parents believing that thirdhand smoke harms children and their banning smoking in the home.

Discussions and research results regarding thirdhand smoke have appeared in the medical literature only since 2009. Just a few studies on the existence and harmfulness of thirdhand smoke were available as of February 2011. For example, Marie-Hélène Becquemin et al. were the first to show that particles from cigarette smoke that fall onto furniture and other surfaces can become airborne long after a cigarette is extinguished. Once airborne, these potentially harmful particles can be inhaled and enter the lungs. The researchers published their findings in "Third-Hand Smoking: Indoor Measurements of Concentration and Sizes of Cigarette Smoke Particles after Resuspension" (*Tobacco Control*, vol. 19, no. 4, August 2010).

A MOVEMENT TO BAN SMOKING

Many efforts have been initiated over the years to control public smoking or to separate smokers and non-smokers. In 1975 Minnesota became the first state in the nation to require the separation of smokers and nonsmokers following passage of the Clean Indoor Air Act. The purpose of the law was to protect public health, public comfort, and the environment by banning smoking in public places and at public meetings, except in designated smoking areas.

Other states soon followed. In 1977 Berkeley became the first community in California to limit smoking in restaurants and other public places. In 1990 San Luis Obispo, California, became the first city to ban smoking in all public buildings, bars, and restaurants. In 1994 smoking was restricted in many government buildings in California. That same year the fast-food giant McDonald's banned smoking in all of its establishments. In 1995 New York City banned smoking in the dining areas of all restaurants with more than 35 seats. As of July 2003, all public and private workplaces in New York City became smoke-free, including bars and restaurants. Laws vary from state to state and from city to city, but by 2005 smoking was banned in most workplaces, hospitals, government buildings, museums, schools, theaters, and restaurants throughout the United States.

As shown in Figure 3.9, support for banning smoking in public places has risen steadily since 1987. In 1987, only 17% of those surveyed by the Gallup Organization thought that smoking should be banned in restaurants and workplaces. By 2009, 59% thought that smoking should be banned in restaurants and 44% in workplaces.

STOPPING SMOKING

In "Vital Signs: Cigarette Smoking among Adults Aged ≥18 Years—United States, 2009" (*Morbidity and Mortality Weekly Report*, vol. 59, no. 35, September 10, 2010), the CDC estimates that there were 46.6 million current smokers in 2009. This number was high, but the CDC notes that "the enactment of the 2009 Family Smoking Prevention and Tobacco Control Act has provided new opportunities for reductions in tobacco use. The Act gives the Food and Drug Administration authority to regulate the manufacturing, marketing, and distribution of tobacco products. Full implementation of comprehensive tobacco control policies and programs at CDC-recommended levels of funding would resume progress toward reducing the prevalence of smoking in the population."

FIGURE 3.9

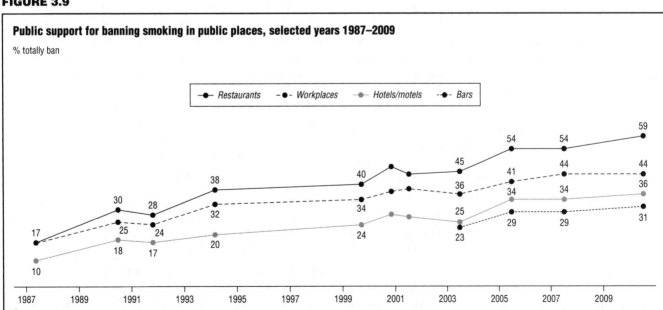

Public support for banning smoking in public places, selected years 1987–2009

% totally ban

Legend: Restaurants · Workplaces · Hotels/motels · Bars

SOURCE: Lydia Saad, "Support for Banning Smoking in Public Venues" in *Americans Want Smoking Off the Menu at Restaurants*, The Gallup Organization, August 6, 2010, http://www.gallup.com/poll/141809/Americans-Smoking-Off-Menu-Restaurants.aspx (accessed November 9, 2010). Copyright © 2010 by The Gallup Organization. Reproduced by permission of The Gallup Organization.

FIGURE 3.10

Percentage of cigarette smokers and nonsmokers who approve or disapprove of a new law allowing the government to regulate the manufacture and marketing of tobacco products, 2009

DO YOU APPROVE OR DISAPPROVE OF A NEW LAW THAT GIVES THE FEDERAL GOVERNMENT POWER TO REGULATE THE MANUFACTURING AND MARKETING OF CIGARETTES AND OTHER TOBACCO PRODUCTS?

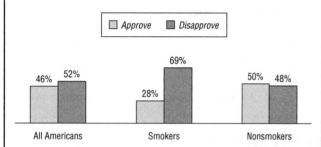

SOURCE: Jeffrey M. Jones, "Do you approve or disapprove of a new law that gives the federal government power to regulate the manufacturing and marketing of cigarettes and other tobacco products?" in *Majority Disapproves of New Law Regulating Tobacco*, The Gallup Organization, June 22, 2009, http://www.gallup.com/poll/121079/Majority-Disapproves-New-Law-Regulating-Tobacco.aspx (accessed November 9, 2010). Copyright © 2010 by The Gallup Organization. Reproduced by permission of The Gallup Organization.

Many current cigarette smokers report they are trying to stop smoking—or would like to. In *Tobacco and Smoking* (2010, http://www.gallup.com/poll/1717/Tobacco-Smoking .aspx), the Gallup Organization asked smokers in July 2010 if they would like to give up smoking. Seventy-four percent answered yes. This figure was down from 82% in 2004 but up from 63% in 1989.

Regardless, not all Americans approve of the new law regulating tobacco. Figure 3.10 shows that in 2009 only 46% approved of the power given to the FDA to regulate tobacco products. Among smokers, only 28% approved. Even though a high percentage of smokers wanted to give up smoking, only a small percentage wanted their smoking to be regulated by the government.

Global Efforts to Reduce Tobacco Use

According to the World Health Organization (WHO), in *WHO Report on the Global Tobacco Epidemic, 2009: Implementing Smoke-Free Environments* (2009, http://whqlibdoc .who.int/publications/2009/9789241563918_eng_full.pdf), tobacco use kills approximately 5 million people worldwide annually and by 2030 it is expected to kill 8 million annually. Most deaths occur in low- and middle-income countries.

The WHO is working diligently to curb smoking around the world. In May 2003 member states of the WHO adopted the world's first international public health treaty for global cooperation in reducing the negative health consequences of tobacco use. The WHO Framework Convention on Tobacco

Control (2005, http://www.who.int/tobacco/framework/ WHO_FCTC_english.pdf) was designed to reduce tobacco-related deaths and disease worldwide. In February 2005 the treaty came into force after 40 member countries had ratified it (become bound by it). Each of the other 128 countries that signed the treaty but did not ratify it was to work toward this goal in their country. The WHO notes in "Parties to the WHO Framework Convention on Tobacco Control" (January 20, 2011, http://www.who.int/fctc/ signatories_parties/en/index.html) that the United States signed the treaty in May 2004, indicating its general acceptance, but as of January 2011 it had not yet ratified the treaty. The treaty has many measures, which include requiring countries to impose restrictions on tobacco advertising, sponsorship, and promotion; creating new packaging and labeling of tobacco products; establishing clean indoor air controls; and promoting taxation as a way to cut consumption and fight smuggling.

In *WHO Report on the Global Tobacco Epidemic, 2008: The MPOWER Package* (2008, http://www.who.int/ tobacco/mpower/mpower_report_full_2008.pdf), the WHO configures the primary measures of the treaty into the acronym MPOWER, which stands for:

- Monitor tobacco use and prevention policies
- Protect people from tobacco smoke
- Offer help to quit tobacco use
- Warn about the dangers of tobacco
- Enforce bans on tobacco advertising, promotion and sponsorship
- Raise taxes on tobacco

The WHO indicates that young females are being targeted by tobacco companies, especially in developing countries and in many countries in which women traditionally do not smoke. The WHO suggests that tobacco companies are working to weaken this cultural taboo in their "advertising, promotion and sponsorship, including charitable donations to women's causes." It also notes that many poorer nations, in which tobacco controls are weak, rely on income from the tobacco business for revenue. The state-owned China National Tobacco Corporation is given as one example of this fiscal reliance.

In *WHO Report on the Global Tobacco Epidemic, 2009*, the WHO focuses on smoke-free legislation that has taken place worldwide as a result of the treaty and notes that "154 million people, mostly in low- and middle-income countries, became newly covered by comprehensive smoke-free laws in 2008." The WHO adds, however, that "with nearly 400 million people newly covered by at least one complete measure during 2008, there is still considerable work to be done. Less than 10% of the world's population is covered by any one of the measures."

Benefits of Stopping

The 1990 *Health Benefits of Smoking Cessation: A Report of the Surgeon General* (http://profiles.nlm.nih.gov/NN/B/B/C/T/_/nnbbct.pdf) noted that quitting offers major and immediate health benefits for both sexes and for all ages. This first comprehensive report on the benefits of quitting showed that many of the ill effects of smoking can be reversed. The subsequent 2004 surgeon general's report *Health Consequences of Smoking* revealed that deaths attributable to smoking can be reduced dramatically if the prevalence of smoking is cut.

The 2010 surgeon general's report *How Tobacco Smoke Causes Disease* states that of smokers who try to quit at any one time, less than 5% are successful. However, the report notes that the U.S. Lung Health Study, a 10-week intensive smoking cessation program, had a smoking cessation rate of nearly 22%.

According to the 2010 surgeon general's report, smokers who quit early in life (aged 25 to 34 years) reduce their risk of dying from all causes to that of lifetime nonsmokers. Those who quit slightly later in life (aged 35 to 44 years) reduce their risk of dying from all causes to nearly that of nonsmokers. Even those who quit after the age of 45 years reduce their risk of dying to a level in between that of nonsmokers and smokers. Nonetheless, for lung cancer alone, "there is a persistent elevated risk in former smokers compared with lifetime nonsmokers of the same age even after a long abstinence." The report adds, "Evidence indicates that lung cancer risk increases far more strongly with each additional year of smoking than it increases for a higher average number of cigarettes smoked per day."

Quitting and Pregnancy

In *Results from the 2009 National Survey on Drug Use and Health*, the NSDUH finds that in 2008–09, 15.3% of pregnant women smoked cigarettes in the month before the survey. (See Figure 3.11.) This percentage of smokers was lower than among women who were not pregnant (27.4%) and down from 18% in 2003–04. The report also notes that in the 15- to 17-year-old age group a higher percentage of pregnant girls smoked than nonpregnant girls (20.6% versus 13.9%, respectively).

Smoking during pregnancy can compromise the health of the developing fetus (unborn child). According to the 2010 surgeon general's report, evidence suggests the possibility of a causal relationship between maternal smoking and ectopic pregnancy, a situation in which the fertilized egg implants in the fallopian tube rather than in the uterus. This situation is quite serious and is life-threatening to the mother. Smoking by pregnant women is also linked to an increased risk of miscarriage, stillbirth, premature delivery, and SIDS and is a cause of low birth weight in infants. A woman who stops smoking before pregnancy or during

her first trimester (three months) of pregnancy significantly reduces her chances of having a low birth weight baby. Additionally, it takes smokers longer to get pregnant than nonsmokers; some smokers are unable to become pregnant. In general, however, women who quit are as likely to get pregnant as those who have never smoked.

Complaints about Quitting

A major side effect of smoking cessation is nicotine withdrawal. The short-term consequences of nicotine withdrawal may include anxiety, irritability, frustration, anger, difficulty concentrating, and restlessness. Possible long-term consequences are urges to smoke and increased appetite. Nicotine withdrawal symptoms peak in the first few days after quitting and subside during the following weeks. Improved self-esteem and an increased sense of control often accompany long-term abstinence.

One of the most common complaints among former smokers is that they gain weight when they stop smoking. Many reasons explain this weight gain, but two primary reasons are the metabolism changes when nicotine is withdrawn from the body and the use of food by many former smokers in attempts to manage their withdrawal cravings. To combat weight gain, some former smokers start exercise programs.

FIGURE 3.11

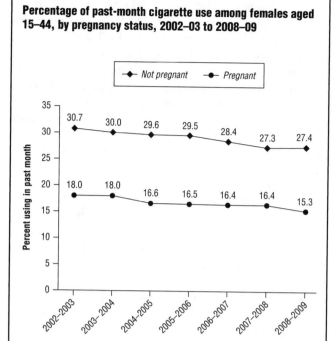

Percentage of past-month cigarette use among females aged 15–44, by pregnancy status, 2002–03 to 2008–09

SOURCE: "Figure 4.5. Past Month Cigarette Use among Women Aged 15 to 44, by Pregnancy Status: Combined Years 2002–2003 to 2008–2009," in *Results from the 2009 National Survey on Drug Use and Health: Volume I. Summary of National Findings*, U.S. Department of Health and Human Services, Substance Abuse and Mental Health Services Administration, Office of Applied Studies, September 2010, http://www.oas.samhsa.gov/NSDUH/2k9NSDUH/2k9ResultsP.pdf (accessed November 8, 2010)

Ways to Stop Smoking

Nicotine replacement treatments can be effective for many smokers. Nicotine patches and gum are two types of nicotine replacement therapy (NRT). The nicotine in a patch is absorbed through the skin, and the nicotine in the gum is absorbed through the mouth and throat. NRT helps a smoker cope with nicotine withdrawal symptoms that discourage many smokers from trying to stop. Nicotine patches and gum are available over the counter. Other NRT products are the nicotine nasal spray and the nicotine inhaler, which are available by prescription.

Another product marketed to combat the use of cigarettes—electronic cigarettes (e-cigarettes; plastic devices that are fashioned to look like cigarettes)—drew serious criticism from the FDA in 2010. E-cigarettes contain liquid nicotine. When the user inhales through the device, the battery heats up the nicotine into a vapor. In September 2010 the FDA sent warning letters to five e-cigarette distributors for violations of the Federal Food, Drug, and Cosmetic Act. The violations included poor manufacturing practices and unsubstantiated claims that the devices can help smokers quit their addiction. In the press release "FDA Acts against 5 Electronic Cigarette Distributors" (http://www.fda.gov/NewsEvents/News room/PressAnnouncements/ucm225224.htm), the FDA states that "a company cannot claim that its drug can treat or mitigate a disease, such as nicotine addiction, unless the drug's safety and effectiveness have been proven. Yet all five companies claim without FDA review of relevant evidence that the products help users quit smoking cigarettes."

The nonnicotine therapy bupropion (an antidepressant drug) is also available by prescription for the relief of nicotine withdrawal symptoms. In addition, behavioral treatments, such as smoking-cessation programs, are useful for some smokers who want to quit. Behavioral methods are designed to create an aversion to smoking, develop self-monitoring of smoking behavior, and establish alternative coping responses.

Quitting smoking is not an easy task, and many smokers try and fail. However, the FDA (February 9, 2011, http://www.fda.gov/TobaccoProducts/Labeling/Cigarette ProductWarningLabels/ucm231360.htm) notes in one of its proposed cigarette package warnings, which were being reviewed in early 2011, that "quitting smoking now greatly reduces serious risks to your health." In addition, quitting smoking releases the smoker from drug dependence and from the possibility of harming the health of others with their habit.

CHAPTER 4
ILLICIT DRUGS

Illegal drugs are those with no currently accepted medical use in the United States, such as heroin, lysergic acid diethylamide (LSD), and marijuana. (Some states and local jurisdictions have decriminalized certain uses of specific amounts of marijuana, but federal laws supersede these state and local marijuana decriminalization laws. For a more detailed discussion on the legalization of marijuana, see Chapter 9.) Controlled substances are legal drugs whose sale, possession, and use are restricted because they are psychoactive (mood- or mind-altering) drugs that have the potential for abuse. These drugs are medications, such as certain narcotics, depressants, and stimulants, that physicians prescribe for various conditions. The term *illicit drugs* is used by the Substance Abuse and Mental Health Services Administration (SAMHSA) to mean both illegal drugs and controlled substances that are used illegally.

WHO USES ILLICIT DRUGS?

The National Survey on Drug Use and Health (NSDUH) is an annual survey that is conducted by SAMHSA, and its 2009 survey results are published in *Results from the 2009 National Survey on Drug Use and Health: Volume I. Summary of National Findings* (September 2010, http://www.oas.samhsa.gov/NSDUH/2k9 NSDUH/2k9ResultsP.pdf). The NSDUH reveals that an estimated 21.8 million Americans aged 12 years and older were current illicit drug users in 2009, a number that was 8% higher than in 2008. By "current" SAMHSA means the people who were surveyed about their drug use and who had taken an illicit drug during the month before participating in the survey. (Current users are "past month" users.) This figure represented 8.7% of the U.S. population in 2009.

Table 4.1 presents a demographic profile of this population of drug users. In 2009, 21.2% of those aged 18 to 25 years and 10% of those aged 12 to 17 years were current illicit drug users. In contrast, only 6.3% of those aged 26 years and older were current illicit drug users.

Figure 4.1 shows a more detailed look at current illicit drug use by age. In 2009, 18- to 20-year-olds accounted for the highest percentage of illicit drug users. At 22.2% of their population, over one out of every five young people aged 18 to 20 years was a current illicit drug user in that year. Twenty-one- to 25-year-olds (20.5%) were the second-highest current illicit drug users, followed by 16- and 17-year-olds (16.7%).

Regarding other demographics of illicit drug use, Table 4.1 shows that a higher proportion of males than females were current, past-year, or lifetime illicit drug users in both 2008 and 2009. (Past-year users took a specific drug during the 12 months before taking the SAMHSA survey and lifetime users took a specific drug at least once during their lifetime.) Those of Native American or Alaskan native heritage had the highest percentage of current illicit drug users in their population in 2009 (18.3%). Those of two or more races were next (14.3%), followed by African-Americans (9.6%). Asian-Americans (3.7%) had the lowest percentage of current illicit drug users in their population.

WHICH ILLICIT DRUGS ARE USED MOST FREQUENTLY?

Figure 4.2 shows the types of illicit drugs that were used in 2009 and how many people used those drugs in that year. Over three-quarters (76.6%) of current illicit drug users used marijuana—16.7 million people of the 21.8 million illicit drug users. According to the NSDUH, those who used only marijuana made up 58% of the population of current illicit drug users in 2009.

Between 2002 and 2009, 5.8% to 6.6% of people aged 12 years and older had used marijuana in the month prior to being surveyed. (See Figure 4.3.) Psychotherapeutics

TABLE 4.1

Use of illicit drugs among persons aged 12 and older, by time of use and demographic characteristics, 2008–09

Demographic characteristic	Lifetime (2008)	Lifetime (2009)	Past year (2008)	Past year (2009)	Past month (2008)	Past month (2009)
Total	**47.0**	**47.1**	**14.2**	**15.1**	**8.0**	**8.7**
Age						
12–17	26.2	26.8	19.0	19.5	9.3	10.0
18–25	56.6	58.1	33.5	36.0	19.6	21.2
26 or older	48.0	47.8	10.3	10.9	5.9	6.3
Gender						
Male	51.3	51.9	16.4	17.9	9.9	10.8
Female	42.9	42.6	12.2	12.4	6.3	6.6
Hispanic origin and race						
Not Hispanic or Latino	48.7	48.7	14.5	15.1	8.3	8.8
White	50.7	51.2	14.4	15.3	8.2	8.8
Black or African American	46.1	43.5	16.9	15.9	10.1	9.6
American Indian or Alaska Native	57.6	64.8	19.5	27.1	9.5	18.3
Native Hawaiian or other Pacific Islander	*	*	*	*	7.3	*
Asian	21.2	20.1	7.4	6.2	3.6	3.7
Two or more races	56.1	55.8	21.2	23.4	14.7	14.3
Hispanic or Latino	36.4	37.6	12.3	14.9	6.2	7.9

*Low precision; no estimate reported.

Note: Illicit drugs include marijuana/hashish, cocaine (including crack), heroin, hallucinogens, inhalants, or prescription-type psychotherapeutics used nonmedically, based on data from original questions not including methamphetamine items added in 2005 and 2006.

SOURCE: "Table 1.19B. Illicit Drug Use in Lifetime, Past Year, and Past Month among Persons Aged 12 or Older, by Demographic Characteristics: Percentages, 2008 and 2009," in *Results from the 2009 National Survey on Drug Use and Health: Detailed Tables*, U.S. Department of Health and Human Services, Substance Abuse and Mental Health Services Administration, Office of Applied Studies, September 2010, http://oas.samhsa.gov/NSDUH/2k9NSDUH/tabs/Sect1peTabs19to23.pdf (accessed November 8, 2010)

FIGURE 4.1

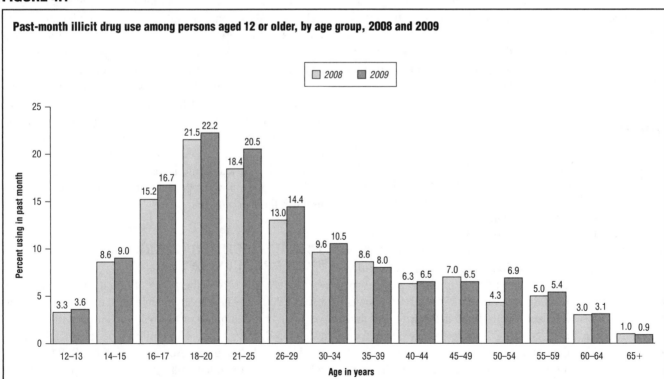

Past-month illicit drug use among persons aged 12 or older, by age group, 2008 and 2009

SOURCE: "Figure 2.4. Past Month Illicit Drug Use among Persons Aged 12 or Older, by Age: 2008 and 2009," in *Results from the 2009 National Survey on Drug Use and Health: Volume I. Summary of National Findings*, U.S. Department of Health and Human Services, Substance Abuse and Mental Health Services Administration, Office of Applied Studies, September 2010, http://www.oas.samhsa.gov/NSDUH/2k9NSDUH/2k9ResultsP.pdf (accessed November 8, 2010)

FIGURE 4.2

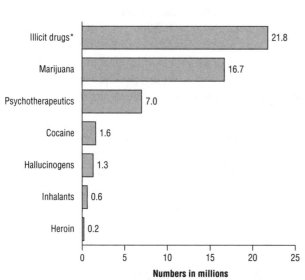

Drugs of choice for past-month users aged 12 and over, 2009

*Illicit drugs include marijuana/hashish, cocaine (including crack), heroin, hallucinogens, inhalants, or prescription-type psychotherapeutics used nonmedically.

SOURCE: "Figure 2.1. Past Month Illicit Drug Use among Persons Aged 12 or Older: 2009," in *Results from the 2009 National Survey on Drug Use and Health: Volume I. Summary of National Findings*, U.S. Department of Health and Human Services, Substance Abuse and Mental Health Services Administration, Office of Applied Studies, September 2010, http://www.oas.samhsa.gov/NSDUH/2k9NSDUH/2k9ResultsP.pdf (accessed November 8, 2010).

was the next most used group of illicit drugs, ranging from 2.5% to 2.9% of the population between 2002 and 2009. Psychotherapeutics is a group of drugs that include pain relievers, tranquilizers, stimulants (including methamphetamine), and sedatives. This group does not include over-the-counter (without a prescription) drugs. The next most used illicit drugs were cocaine and hallucinogens, ranging from 0.7% to 1% and from 0.4% to 0.5% of the population, respectively.

DRUG-RELATED DEATHS

Sherry L. Murphy of the Centers for Disease Control and Prevention (CDC) reports in "Deaths: Final Data for 1998" (*National Vital Statistics Reports*, vol. 48, no. 11, July 24, 2000) that there were 16,926 drug-related deaths in 1998, or 6.3 deaths per 1,000 population. Jiaquan Xu et al. of the CDC note in "Deaths: Final Data for 2007" (*National Vital Statistics Reports*, vol. 58, no. 19, May 20, 2010) that by 2007 the number of drug-related deaths more than doubled to 38,371. The rate doubled as well, reaching 12.7 deaths per 1,000 population. In this annual CDC report, drug-related deaths include those due directly to the use of either legal or illegal drugs but exclude deaths due indirectly to drug use, such as unintentional injuries or homicides.

FIGURE 4.3

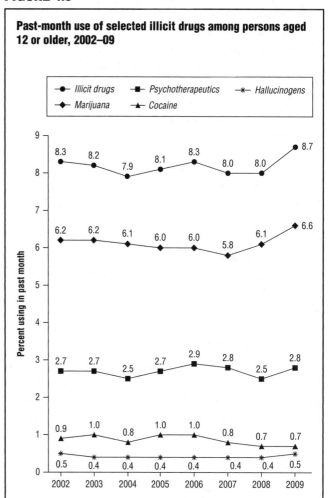

Past-month use of selected illicit drugs among persons aged 12 or older, 2002–09

SOURCE: "Figure 2.2. Past Month Use of Selected Illicit Drugs among Persons Aged 12 or Older: 2002–2009," in *Results from the 2009 National Survey on Drug Use and Health: Volume I. Summary of National Findings*, U.S. Department of Health and Human Services, Substance Abuse and Mental Health Services Administration, Office of Applied Studies, September 2010, http://www.oas.samhsa.gov/NSDUH/2k9NSDUH/2k9ResultsP.pdf (accessed November 8, 2010).

CANNABIS AND MARIJUANA

Cannabis sativa, the hemp plant from which marijuana is made, grows wild throughout most of the world's tropic and temperate regions, including Mexico, the Middle East, Africa, and India. For centuries its therapeutic potential has been explored, including uses as an analgesic (painkiller) and anticonvulsant. However, with the advent of new, synthetic drugs and the passage of the Marijuana Tax Act of 1937, interest in marijuana—even for medicinal purposes—faded. In 1970 the Controlled Substances Act (CSA) classified marijuana as a Schedule I drug because it has "no currently accepted medical use in treatment in the United States," though this classification is debated by those in favor of using it for medical and recreational purposes. (See Chapter 9.)

Besides regular marijuana, there are two alternate forms: ditchweed and sinsemilla. All three are tobacco-like substances that are produced by drying the leaves and flowery tops of the cannabis plants. The Office of National Drug Control Policy (ONDCP) shows in *National Drug Control Strategy: Data Supplement 2010* (2010, http://www.whitehousedrugpolicy.gov/publications/policy/ndcs10/ndcs10_data_supl/10datasupplement.pdf) that potency varies considerably among the three. The potency of the drug depends on how much of the chemical THC (delta-9-tetrahydrocannabinol) is present. Ditchweed, or wild U.S. marijuana, is the least potent form of marijuana and generally has a THC content of less than 0.5%. Sinsemilla is the most potent form of marijuana. The name is Spanish for "without seed" and refers to the unpollinated, and therefore seedless, female cannabis plant. The potency of sinsemilla ranges from about 7% to 14% THC. Generally, the marijuana cultivated in the United States has a THC content of about 2% to 3%, whereas the marijuana from other countries has a higher potency, in recent years ranging from about 6% to 7%.

Effects of Marijuana

Marijuana is usually smoked in the form of loosely rolled cigarettes called joints, in hollowed-out commercial cigars called blunts, or in water pipes called bongs. Sometimes it is ingested. The effects are felt within minutes, usually peaking in 10 to 30 minutes and lingering for two to three hours. Low doses induce restlessness and an increasing sense of well-being, followed by a dreamy state of relaxation and, frequently, hunger. Changes in sensory perception—a more vivid sense of sight, smell, touch, taste, and hearing—may occur, with subtle alterations in thought formation and expression. However, the National Institute on Drug Abuse reports in *NIDA InfoFacts: Marijuana* (November 2010, http://drugabuse.gov/infofacts/marijuana.html) that along with the pleasant side effects of smoking marijuana come some not-so-pleasant effects that include short-term memory loss, possible abnormalities in heart rhythm and an increased risk of heart attack, and lung damage.

The immediate physical effects of marijuana include a faster heartbeat (by as much as 50%), bloodshot eyes, and a dry mouth and throat. It can alter one's sense of time and reduce concentration and coordination. Some users experience lightheadedness and giddiness, whereas others feel depressed and sad. Many users have also reported experiencing severe anxiety attacks.

Even though the immediate effects of marijuana usually disappear in about four to six hours, it takes about three days for 50% of the drug to be broken down and eliminated from the body. It takes three weeks to completely excrete the THC from one marijuana cigarette. If a user smokes two joints per week, it takes months for all traces of the THC to disappear from the body.

Hashish and Hash Oil

Two other drugs besides marijuana come from the cannabis plant: hashish and hash oil. Hashish is made from the THC-rich, tar-like material that can be collected from the cannabis plant. This resin is dried and compressed into a variety of forms, including balls and cakes. Larger pieces are broken into smaller pieces and smoked. Most hashish comes from the Middle East, North Africa, Pakistan, and Afghanistan. Demand in the United States is limited.

Despite its name, hash oil is not directly related to hashish. It is produced by extracting the cannabinoids from the cannabis plant with a solvent. The color and odor of hash oil depend on the solvent that is used. Hash oil ranges from amber to dark brown and has a potency of about 15% THC. In terms of effect, a drop or two of hash oil on a cigarette is equal to a single marijuana joint.

Prevalence of Use of Marijuana

Figure 4.4 shows the lifetime, annual, and 30-day (current) use of marijuana among 18- to 50-year-olds in 2009. Current and annual use generally drops with age—younger people are more likely to have used marijuana during the past month or past year than older people. However, by the age of 50, 78% of Americans in 2009 had tried marijuana at some point during their lifetime.

In 2009, 21% of 18-year-olds were current users of marijuana. (See Figure 4.4.) Use rates dropped to 20% each for 19- to 20-year-olds and 21- to 22-year-olds. By the age of 30, 12% were current users of marijuana, and by the age of 50 this figure had dropped to 6%.

For each year between 2002 and 2009 approximately 2 million people over the age of 12 years tried marijuana for the first time. (See Figure 4.5.) The average age of those first-timers ranged from 16.8 years in 2003 to 17.8 years in 2008, indicating in general that the average age at which people tried marijuana for the first time is about 17.

PSYCHOTHERAPEUTICS

Psychotherapeutics, a group of drugs that includes pain relievers, tranquilizers, stimulants (including methamphetamine), and sedatives, was the second-most used group of illicit drugs between 2002 and 2009. (See Figure 4.3.) During those years the use of psychotherapeutics among people aged 12 years and older ranged from 2.5% to 2.9% of this population.

Figure 4.3 shows that 2.8% of the population aged 12 years and older were current users of prescription-type psychotherapeutic drugs for nonmedical reasons in 2009. Use was up from 2.5% in 2008. According to the NSDUH, in 2009 pain relievers were the most used and sedatives were the least used psychotherapeutics.

FIGURE 4.4

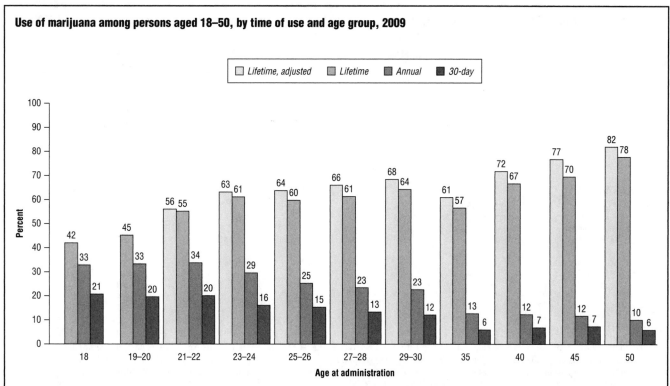

Use of marijuana among persons aged 18–50, by time of use and age group, 2009

Note: Lifetime prevalence estimates were adjusted for inconsistency in self-reports of drug use over time.

SOURCE: Lloyd D. Johnston et al., "Figure 4-3. Marijuana: Lifetime, Annual, and 30-Day Prevalence among Respondents of Modal Ages 18 through 50 by Age Group, 2009," in *Monitoring the Future National Survey Results on Drug Use, 1975–2009: Volume II, College Students and Adults Ages 19–50*, National Institute on Drug Abuse, 2010, http://monitoringthefuture.org/pubs/monographs/vol2_2009.pdf (accessed December 2, 2010)

FIGURE 4.5

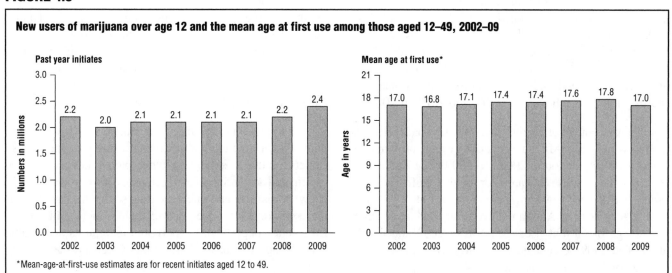

New users of marijuana over age 12 and the mean age at first use among those aged 12–49, 2002–09

*Mean-age-at-first-use estimates are for recent initiates aged 12 to 49.

SOURCE: "Figure 5.4. Past Year Marijuana Initiates among Persons Aged 12 or Older and Mean Age at First Use of Marijuana among Past Year Marijuana Initiates Aged 12 to 49: 2002–2009," in *Results from the 2009 National Survey on Drug Use and Health: Volume I. Summary of National Findings*, U.S. Department of Health and Human Services, Substance Abuse and Mental Health Services Administration, Office of Applied Studies, September 2010, http://www.oas.samhsa.gov/NSDUH/2k9NSDUH/2k9ResultsP.pdf (accessed November 8, 2010)

Pain Relievers

Table 4.2 shows the percentages of people aged 12 years and older who used prescription pain relievers for nonmedical reasons during their lifetime, during the past year, and during the past month in 2008 and 2009. Current users made up 2.1% of the population in 2009 and 1.9% in 2008. Approximately 5% of people had used painkillers for nonmedical reasons in 2008 and 2009,

TABLE 4.2

Nonmedical use of pain relievers among persons aged 12 and older, by time of use and demographic characteristics, 2008 and 2009

Demographic characteristic	Lifetime (2008)	Lifetime (2009)	Past year (2008)	Past year (2009)	Past month (2008)	Past month (2009)
Total	**14.0**	**13.9**	**4.8**	**4.9**	**1.9**	**2.1**
Age						
12–17	9.4	9.7	6.5	6.6	2.3	2.7
18–25	24.4	24.3	12.0	11.9	4.6	4.8
26 or older	12.7	12.7	3.3	3.5	1.4	1.6
Gender						
Male	15.6	15.8	5.3	5.6	2.0	2.4
Female	12.4	12.1	4.3	4.3	1.8	1.8
Hispanic origin and race						
Not Hispanic or Latino	14.4	14.4	4.9	5.0	2.0	2.1
White	15.6	15.8	5.2	5.3	2.1	2.2
Black or African American	10.1	9.0	3.9	3.5	1.6	1.6
American Indian or Alaska Native	13.3	26.7	5.8	10.2	2.5	6.0
Native Hawaiian or other Pacific Islander	15.2	*	*	*	1.3	*
Asian	6.5	5.4	2.5	2.3	0.9	1.3
Two or more races	16.0	18.2	5.1	6.0	2.4	2.8
Hispanic or Latino	11.3	11.1	3.9	4.7	1.4	1.8

*Low precision; no estimate reported

SOURCE: "Table 1.54B. Nonmedical Use of Pain Relievers in Lifetime, Past Year, and Past Month among Persons Aged 12 or Older, by Demographic Characteristics: Percentages, 2008 and 2009," in *Results from the 2009 National Survey on Drug Use and Health: Detailed Tables*, U.S. Department of Health and Human Services, Substance Abuse and Mental Health Services Administration, Office of Applied Studies, September 2010, http://oas.samhsa.gov/NSDUH/2k9NSDUH/tabs/Sect1peTabs54to58.pdf (accessed November 8, 2010)

and about 14% had tried them at least once during their lifetime.

Most current users of illicit pain relievers in 2008 and 2009 were young adults aged 18 to 25 years (4.6% in 2008 and 4.8% in 2009). (See Table 4.2.) Those aged 12 to 17 years were the next most likely to take these drugs (2.3% in 2008 and 2.7% in 2009). Only 1.4% of those aged 26 years and older were current illicit users of prescription pain relievers in 2008, and 1.6% in 2009.

The percentage of current users of illicit pain relievers among whites and African-Americans was approximately 2% of each population in 2008 and 2009. (See Table 4.2.) In 2008 the Native Hawaiian or other Pacific Islander group had a very low current rate of use at 1.3%. The Native American or Alaskan native group had a very high percentage of current users at 2.5% in 2008 and 6% in 2009. The 2009 percentage was nearly triple the national average of 2.1% in that year.

NARCOTICS: OXYCODONE, HYDROCODONE, AND MORPHINE. Two prescription pain relievers that have been popular with users of illicit prescription drugs are oxycodone and hydrocodone, both of which are strong narcotic pain relievers. Narcotics are addictive drugs, such as morphine, codeine, and opium, that reduce pain, alter mood and behavior, and usually induce sleep. Whereas morphine, codeine, and opium are natural narcotics extracted from the juice of the opium poppy, oxycodone and hydrocodone

are semisynthetic narcotics; that is, they are made in the laboratory from codeine.

Oxycodone and hydrocodone are two of the most commonly prescribed narcotic painkillers in the United States. Even though they are designed to have a less euphoric effect than morphine, they are still highly sought after by recreational users and addicts. Like morphine, these drugs have enough potential for abuse that they are classified as Schedule II substances.

Oxycodone is the active ingredient in many narcotic pain relievers, including those manufactured as time-release caplets or those containing other pain relievers such as aspirin and acetaminophen. Illicit users of oxycodone crush, chew, or dissolve and inject the drug so that they receive all the oxycodone at once, giving them a heroin-like high. Emergency departments report serious injuries and deaths from the abuse of oxycodone, often by teenagers and young adults.

According to the NSDUH, in 2009 there were 584,000 new nonmedical users of oxycodone aged 12 years and older. In *Monitoring the Future: National Survey Results on Drug Use, 1975–2009, Volume I: Secondary School Students* (September 2010, http://monitoringthefuture.org/pubs/monographs/vol1_2009.pdf), Lloyd D. Johnston et al. of the University of Michigan report that 4.9% of high school seniors had tried oxycodone at least once during the past year. The less dangerous drug, hydrocodone, showed an annual rate of use of 9.7% for high school seniors in 2009.

Morphine is extracted from opium and is one of the most effective drugs known for pain relief. It is marketed in the form of oral solutions, sustained-release tablets, and injectable preparations. Morphine is used legally only in hospitals or hospice care, usually to control the severe pain that results from illnesses such as cancer. Tolerance and dependence develop rapidly in the morphine abuser. According to Johnston et al., the annual prevalence rate of morphine use for high school seniors in 2009 was 1.5%.

Tranquilizers

A tranquilizer is a calming medication that relieves tension and anxiety. Tranquilizers are central nervous system depressants and include a group of drugs called benzodiazepines. They are also known as sleeping pills, downers, or tranks. Benzodiazepines have a relatively slow onset but long duration of action. They also have a greater margin of safety than other depressants. According to the U.S. Drug Enforcement Administration (DEA), in *Drugs of Abuse* (2005, http://www.usdoj.gov/dea/pubs/abuse/doa-p.pdf), benzodiazepines account for 20% of prescriptions in the United States.

Johnston et al. note that most illicit tranquilizer use reported in recent years involved the drugs Valium and Xanax. In 2009, 1.9% of high school seniors had taken Valium during the previous year and 3.6% had taken Xanax.

Prolonged use of excessive doses of tranquilizers may result in physical and psychological dependence. Because benzodiazepines are eliminated from the body slowly, withdrawal symptoms generally develop slowly, usually seven to 10 days after continued high doses are stopped. When these drugs are used illicitly, they are often taken with alcohol or marijuana to achieve a euphoric high.

ROHYPNOL: THE DATE RAPE DRUG. Rohypnol, another benzodiazepine, has become increasingly popular among young people. Manufactured as a short-term treatment for severe sleeping disorders, the drug is not marketed legally in the United States and must be smuggled in. It is widely known as a date rape drug because would-be rapists have been known to drop it secretly into a victim's drink to facilitate sexual assault. In a sufficiently large dose it can leave a victim physically incapacitated and cause amnesia that may prevent him or her from recalling an assault. Responding to pressure from the U.S. government, Roche, the Mexican producer of Rohypnol, began putting a blue dye in the pill so that it can be seen when dissolved in a drink. Johnston et al. indicate that in 2009, 1% of high school seniors used Rohypnol at least once during the previous year.

Synthetic Stimulants

Stimulants (uppers) are drugs that produce a sense of euphoria or wakefulness. They are used to increase alertness, boost endurance and productivity, and suppress the appetite. Examples of stimulants are caffeine, nicotine, amphetamine, methamphetamine, and cocaine.

Potent stimulants, such as amphetamine and methamphetamine, make users feel stronger, more decisive, and self-possessed. Chronic users often develop a pattern of using uppers in the morning and depressants (downers), such as alcohol or sleeping pills, at night. Such manipulation interferes with normal body processes and can lead to mental and physical illness.

Large doses of stimulants can produce paranoia and auditory and visual hallucinations. Overdoses can also produce dizziness, tremors, agitation, hostility, panic, headaches, flushed skin, chest pain with palpitations, excessive sweating, vomiting, and abdominal cramps. When withdrawing from stimulants, chronic high-dose users exhibit depression, apathy, fatigue, and disturbed sleep.

AMPHETAMINE AND METHAMPHETAMINE. Amphetamine has been used to treat sleeping disorders and during World War II (1939–1945) it was used to keep soldiers awake. Abuse of amphetamine was noticed during the 1960s. It was used by truckers to help them stay alert during long hauls, by athletes to help them train longer, and by many people to lose weight. An intravenous form of amphetamine, methamphetamine, was abused by a subculture of people dubbed "speed freaks."

In 1965 the federal government realized that amphetamine products had tremendous potential for abuse, so it amended food and drug laws to place stricter controls on their distribution and use. All amphetamines are now Schedule II drugs, in the same category as morphine and cocaine.

Methamphetamine is a powerful stimulant that is relatively easy for drug traffickers to synthesize in homemade labs, so its illegal synthesis, distribution, and sale developed after new laws made amphetamine more difficult to get. Two products that come out of these clandestine labs are the injectable form of methamphetamine (meth) and the crystallized form (crystal meth or ice) that is smoked. Both forms are highly addictive and toxic. Chronic abuse results in a schizophrenic-like mental illness that is characterized by paranoia, picking at the skin, and hallucinations.

Figure 4.6 shows data on new users of methamphetamine during the past year between 2002 and 2009. In 2009, 154,000 people aged 12 years and older began using methamphetamine. The number of methamphetamine initiates declined from 2002, but the downward trend had a zigzag pattern. The 2009 figure was up from 95,000 methamphetamine initiates in 2008. In addition,

FIGURE 4.6

New users of methamphetamine over age 12 and the mean age at first use among those aged 12–49, 2002–09

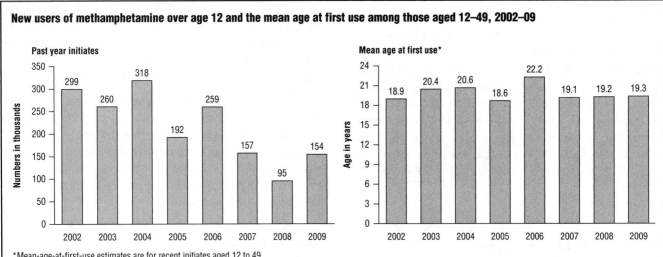

*Mean-age-at-first-use estimates are for recent initiates aged 12 to 49.

SOURCE: "Figure 5.6. Past Year Methamphetamine Initiates among Persons Aged 12 or Older and Mean Age at First Use of Methamphetamine among Past Year Methamphetamine Initiates Aged 12 to 49: 2002–2009," in *Results from the 2009 National Survey on Drug Use and Health: Volume I. Summary of National Findings*, U.S. Department of Health and Human Services, Substance Abuse and Mental Health Services Administration, Office of Applied Studies, September 2010, http://www.oas.samhsa.gov/NSDUH/2k9NSDUH/2k9ResultsP.pdf (accessed November 8, 2010)

FIGURE 4.7

Use of methamphetamine among persons aged 18–30, by time of use and age group, 2009

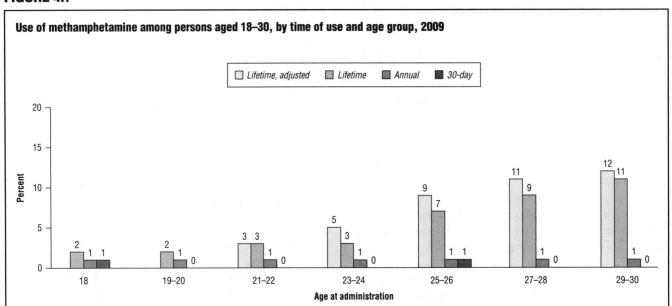

Note: Lifetime prevalence estimates were adjusted for inconsistency in self-reports of drug use over time.

SOURCE: Lloyd D. Johnston et al., "Figure 4-5. Methamphetamine: Lifetime, Annual, and 30-Day Prevalence among Respondents of Modal Ages 18 through 30 by Age Group, 2009," in *Monitoring the Future National Survey Results on Drug Use, 1975–2009: Volume II, College Students and Adults Ages 19–50*, National Institute on Drug Abuse, 2010, http://monitoringthefuture.org/pubs/monographs/vol2_2009.pdf (accessed December 2, 2010)

Figure 4.6 shows that the average age at which methamphetamine users first used the drug ranged from 18.6 years in 2005 to 22.2 years in 2006. However, between 2007 and 2009 the age at first use stabilized at approximately 19 years. Johnston et al. note that in 2009 annual methamphetamine use was approximately 1% for all age subgroups within the 18- to 30-year-old span. (See Figure 4.7.)

Sedatives

Like tranquilizers, sedatives are calming, soothing drugs. They relieve tension and anxiety. Also, like tranquilizers, sedatives are central nervous system depressants, but they include a group of drugs called barbiturates, which are generally stronger than tranquilizers. Barbiturates have many street names, including barbs, yellows, and reds.

Small therapeutic doses of sedatives calm nervous conditions; larger doses cause sleep within a short period. A feeling of excitement precedes the sedation. The primary danger of sedatives is that too large a dose can bring a person through stages of sedation, sleep, and coma and ultimately cause death via respiratory failure and cardiovascular complications. According to Johnston et al., the past-year use of sedatives by high school seniors gradually rose from 2.8% in 1992 to 7.2% in 2005, then slowly fell to 5.2% in 2009.

COCAINE

After marijuana and psychotherapeutics, cocaine was the next most used illicit drug in 2009. (See Figure 4.3.) Cocaine, a powerful stimulant, is extracted from the leaves of the coca plant (*Erythroxylon coca*). The plant has been cultivated in the Andean highlands of South America since prehistoric times. In these regions of South America, coca leaves are frequently chewed for refreshment and relief from fatigue—in much the same way some North Americans chew tobacco.

Pure cocaine was first used during the 1880s as a local anesthetic in eye, nose, and throat surgeries. It was also used in dental procedures. Since then, other drugs, such as lidocaine and novocaine, have replaced it as an anesthetic.

Illicit cocaine is distributed as a white crystalline powder and is often contaminated (cut) with sugars or local anesthetics. The drug is commonly snorted through the nasal passages. Less commonly, it is mixed with water and injected, which brings a more intense high because the drug reaches the brain more rapidly.

Cocaine produces a short but extremely powerful rush of energy and confidence. Because the pleasurable effects are so intense, cocaine can lead to severe mental dependency, destroying a person's life as the need for the drug supersedes any other considerations. Physically, cocaine users risk permanent damage to their nose by exposing the cartilage and dissolving the nasal septum (membrane), resulting in a collapsed nose. Cocaine significantly increases the risk of a heart attack in the first hour after use. Heavy use (0.1 of an ounce [2 g] or more per week) impairs memory, decision making, and manual dexterity.

Freebasing is the smoking of purified cocaine prepared using a method that frees the cocaine base from impurities. Freebase is prepared by mixing cocaine with ether and sodium hydroxide or baking powder (sodium bicarbonate). The salt base dissolves, leaving granules of pure cocaine. Next, these granules are collected, dried, and heated in a pipe that is filled with water or rum until they vaporize. The vapor is inhaled directly into the lungs, causing an immediate high that lasts about 10 minutes.

There is a danger of being badly burned if the open flame gets too close to the ether or the rum, causing it to flare up as it burns. After the late actor-comedian Richard Pryor (1940–2005) set himself on fire while freebasing in 1980, many users started to search for a safer way to achieve the same high. The dangers inherent in freebasing may have been the catalyst for the development of crack cocaine.

Crack Cocaine

Cocaine hydrochloride, the powdered form of cocaine, is soluble in water, can be injected, and is fairly insensitive to heat. Crack cocaine is processed by mixing cocaine with baking soda and heating it to remove the hydrochloride. The resultant chips or rocks of pure cocaine are usually smoked in a pipe or added to a cigarette or marijuana joint. The name comes from the crackling sound that is made when the mixture is smoked.

Inhaling the cocaine fumes produces a rapid, intense, and short-lived high. This incredible intensity is followed within minutes by an abnormally disconcerting and anxious crash, which leads almost inevitably to the need for more of the drug—and a great likelihood of addiction.

Prevalence of Cocaine Use

Figure 4.3 shows that about 1% of the population aged 12 years and older were current users of cocaine between 2002 and 2009. Narrowing the survey population from 18 to 50 years gives a clearer picture of actual use because most users are within this age range. Figure 4.8 shows that in 2009 between 2% and 3% of 21- through 30-year-olds were current users and between 4% and 7% were annual users. For 35- to 50-year-olds, 1% to 2% were current users and 2% to 3% were annual users.

HALLUCINOGENS

According to the NSDUH, after marijuana, psychotherapeutics, and cocaine, hallucinogenic drugs were the next most used illicit drugs in 2009. (See Figure 4.3.) Hallucinogens, also known as psychedelics, are natural or synthetic substances that distort the perceptions of reality. They cause excitation, which can vary from a sense of well-being to severe depression. Time may appear to stand still, and forms and colors seem to change and take on new meaning. Typically, the heart rate increases, blood pressure rises, and the pupils dilate. The experience may be pleasurable or extremely frightening. The effects of hallucinogens vary from use to use and cannot be predicted.

The most common danger of using hallucinogens is impaired judgment, which can lead to rash decisions and accidents. Long after hallucinogens have been eliminated from the body, users may experience flashbacks, in the form of perceived intensity of color, the apparent motion of fixed objects, or illusions that present one object when

FIGURE 4.8

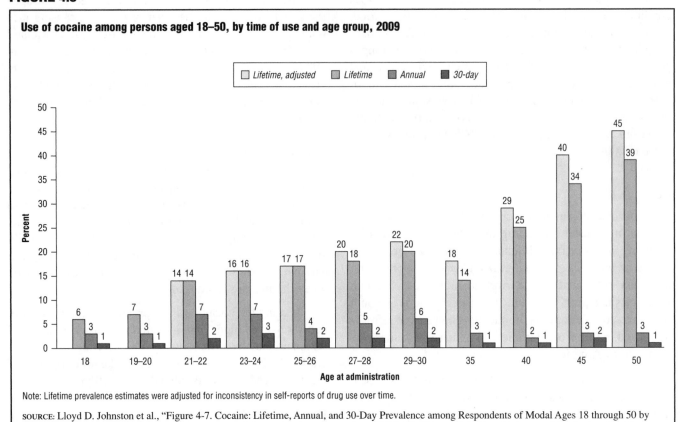

Use of cocaine among persons aged 18–50, by time of use and age group, 2009

Note: Lifetime prevalence estimates were adjusted for inconsistency in self-reports of drug use over time.

SOURCE: Lloyd D. Johnston et al., "Figure 4-7. Cocaine: Lifetime, Annual, and 30-Day Prevalence among Respondents of Modal Ages 18 through 50 by Age Group, 2009," in *Monitoring the Future National Survey Results on Drug Use, 1975–2009: Volume II, College Students and Adults Ages 19–50*, National Institute on Drug Abuse, 2010, http://monitoringthefuture.org/pubs/monographs/vol2_2009.pdf (accessed December 2, 2010)

another one is present. Some hallucinogens are present in plants (e.g., mescaline in the peyote cactus), whereas others (e.g., LSD) are synthetic.

Mescaline and Peyote

Mescaline is a psychoactive chemical that is found naturally in the peyote cactus (*Lophophora williamsii*), which is a small, spineless plant native to Mexico and the U.S. Southwest. The top of the cactus, often called the crown, consists of disk-shaped buttons that can be cut off and dried. These buttons are generally chewed or soaked in water to produce an intoxicating liquid. A dose of 0.01 to 0.02 of an ounce (350 to 500 mg) produces hallucinations lasting from five to 12 hours. Mescaline can be extracted from peyote or produced synthetically.

Mescaline and peyote have long been used by Native Americans in religious ceremonies. The legality of the use of peyote in these ceremonies is decided by individual states.

MDMA and Other Designer Drugs

Designer drugs are those that are produced in a laboratory by making minor modifications to the chemical structure of existing drugs, resulting in new substances with similar effects. DOM (4-methyl-2,5-dimethoxyamphetamine),

DOB (4-bromo-2,5-dimethoxyamphetamine), MDA (3,4-methylenedioxyamphetamine), MDMA (3,4-methylenedioxymethamphetamine), and other designer drugs are chemical variations of mescaline and amphetamine that have been synthesized in the laboratory. Designer drugs differ from one another in speed of onset, duration of action, and potency. They are usually taken orally, but they can also be snorted or injected intravenously. Because they are produced illegally, designer drugs are seldom pure. Dosage quantity and quality vary considerably.

The most noted designer drug is MDMA (also called ecstasy). It acts as both a stimulant and a psychedelic and is known for enhancing a user's sense of touch. It was first banned by the DEA in 1985. The Anti-drug Abuse Act of 1986 made all designer drugs illegal. Widespread abuse placed MDMA in Schedule I of the CSA.

Designer drugs such as MDMA are often used at raves (large, all-night dance parties that are held in unusual places such as warehouses or railroad yards). Even though many raves have become mainstream events that are professionally organized and held at public venues, the underground culture of raves remains an alluring draw to many teenagers. Part of the allure is drug use. For this reason, such drugs are also called club drugs. (Club drugs include MDMA, Rohypnol, LSD, and methamphetamine, among others.)

Users of MDMA have been known to suffer serious psychological effects—including confusion, depression, sleep problems, drug craving, severe anxiety, and paranoia—both during and sometimes weeks after taking the drug. Physical symptoms include muscle tension, involuntary teeth clenching, nausea, blurred vision, rapid eye movement, faintness, and chills or sweating. MDMA can also interfere with the body's ability to regulate temperature, and severe dehydration, particularly among users who dance for hours while under the drug's influence, is a serious hazard.

According to Johnston et al., past-year MDMA use by high school seniors rose from 3.6% in 1998 to 9.2% in 2001. Since then a dramatic decline in MDMA use in this group occurred. By 2009 only 4.3% of high school seniors used MDMA in the past year. Similar declines occurred among college students and young adults. Johnston et al. suggest this decline is due in large part to educational campaigns on the adverse effects of MDMA and the decreasing novelty of all-night raves.

LSD

LSD is one of the most potent mood-changing chemicals in existence. Odorless, colorless, and tasteless, it is produced from a substance derived from ergot fungus or from a chemical found in morning glory seeds. Both chemicals are found in Schedule III of the CSA, whereas LSD itself is a Schedule I substance.

LSD is usually sold in tablets, thin squares of gelatin, or impregnated paper. It can also be taken in a liquid form that is dropped on the tongue or in the eyes with an eye dropper. The effects of doses higher than 30 to 50 micrograms can persist for 10 to 12 hours, severely impairing judgment and decision making. Tolerance develops rapidly, and more of the drug is needed to achieve the desired effect. It is, however, nonaddictive.

Because of its structural similarity to a chemical that is present in the brain, LSD was originally used as a research tool to study the mechanism of mental illness. It was later adopted by the drug culture of the 1960s. LSD use dropped during the 1980s, showed a resurgence during the 1990s, and then dropped again through 2009. Johnston et al. note that the past-year use of LSD in 2009 was 1.9% for high school seniors, 2% for college students, and 1.7% for young adults.

Phencyclidine and Related Drugs

Many drug-treatment professionals believe that phencyclidine (PCP) poses greater risks to the user than any other drug. In the United States most PCP is manufactured in clandestine laboratories and sold on the black market. This drug is sold under at least 50 different names, many of which reflect its bizarre and volatile effects. It is often sold to users who think they are buying mescaline or LSD.

PCP is an anesthetic, so it produces an inability to feel pain, which can lead to serious bodily injury. Unlike other hallucinogens, PCP produces depression in some individuals. Regular use often impairs memory, perception, concentration, motor movement, and judgment. PCP can also produce a psychotic state that is in many ways indistinguishable from schizophrenia, or it can lead to hallucinations, mood swings, paranoia, and amnesia.

Because of the extreme psychic disorders that are associated with repeated use, or even with one dose, of PCP and related drugs, Congress passed the Psychotropic Substances Act of 1978. The penalties imposed for the manufacture or possession of these chemicals are the stiffest of any nonnarcotic violation under the CSA.

In its pure form PCP is a white crystalline powder that readily dissolves in water. It can also be taken in tablet or capsule form. It can be swallowed, snorted, smoked, or injected. It is commonly applied to a leafy material, such as parsley, mint, oregano, or marijuana, and smoked. According to Johnston et al., the past-year use of PCP in 2009 was 1% for high school seniors. For young adults the annual prevalence has historically fluctuated between 0.1% and 0.6%. No figure was available for college students.

Prevalence of Hallucinogen Use

According to the NSDUH, 1.3 million people aged 12 years and older used hallucinogens in the past month in 2009. (See Figure 4.2.) In 2009 current users were concentrated among 18- to 24-year-olds, while annual use persisted through age 40. (See Figure 4.9.) Johnston et al. indicate that the annual prevalence for hallucinogen use other than LSD in 2009 was 4.2% for high school seniors, 4.1% for college students, and 3.3% for young adults.

INHALANTS

Inhalants were the least used group of illicit drugs in 2009, with the exception of heroin. (See Figure 4.2.) Inhalants are volatile liquids, such as cleaning fluids, glue, gasoline, paint, and turpentine, the vapors of which are inhaled. Sometimes the sprays of aerosols are inhaled, such as those of spray paints, spray deodorants, hair spray, or fabric protector spray. According to the NSDUH, an estimated 813,000 people tried inhalants for the first time in 2009. As in past years, this group was dominated by those aged 18 years and younger, representing 67.9% of new users. The NSDUH also reports that in 2009, 1% of people aged 12 to 17 years were current inhalant users. By the age of 26, only 0.1% were inhalant users.

FIGURE 4.9

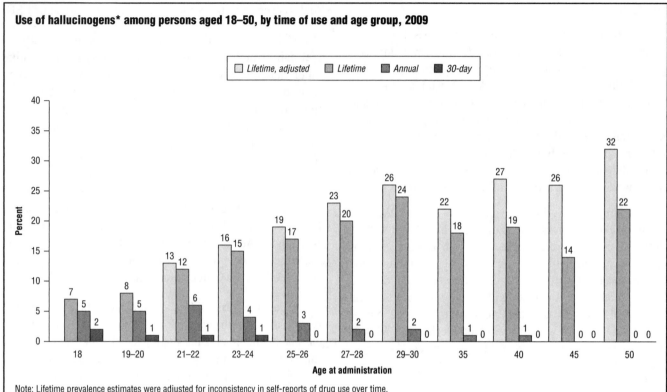

Use of hallucinogens* among persons aged 18–50, by time of use and age group, 2009

Note: Lifetime prevalence estimates were adjusted for inconsistency in self-reports of drug use over time.
*Unadjusted for the possible underreporting of PCP.

SOURCE: Lloyd D. Johnston et al., "Figure 4-10. Hallucinogens: Lifetime, Annual, and 30-Day Prevalence among Respondents of Modal Ages 18 through 50 by Age Group, 2009," in *Monitoring the Future National Survey Results on Drug Use, 1975–2009: Volume II, College Students and Adults Ages 19–50*, National Institute on Drug Abuse, 2010, http://monitoringthefuture.org/pubs/monographs/vol2_2009.pdf (accessed December 2, 2010)

OTHER ILLICIT DRUGS

Heroin

Heroin is a narcotic, as are oxycodone, hydrocodone, and morphine. Heroin, however, is not used as a medicine, so it is not included with the psychotherapeutics.

Heroin is extracted from morphine, which is extracted from opium. This drug was not used extensively until the Bayer Company of Elberfeld, Germany, began commercial production in 1898. It was widely used as a cough remedy and painkiller for years, with the medical profession largely unaware of its potential for addiction. However, by 1914 the Harrison Narcotic Act established control of heroin in the United States.

Pure heroin, a bitter white powder, is usually dissolved and injected. Street-quality heroin may vary in color from white to dark brown, depending on the amount of impurities left from the extraction process or the presence of additives, such as food coloring, cocoa, or brown sugar.

Black tar heroin is popular in the western United States. A crudely processed form of heroin, black tar is manufactured illegally in Mexico and derives its name from its sticky, dark brown or black appearance. Black tar is often sold on the street in its tar-like state and can be diluted with substances such as burned cornstarch or converted into a powder.

In the past heroin was usually injected—intravenously (the preferred method), subcutaneously (directly under the skin), or intramuscularly (directly into the muscle). However, the increased availability of high-purity heroin meant that users could snort or smoke the drug, which contributed to an increase in heroin use. Snorting or smoking is more appealing to users who fear contracting the human immunodeficiency virus (HIV) and hepatitis through needles that are shared with potentially infected users. Users who smoke or snort heroin also avoid the stigma that is attached to heroin use: the needle marks that are left on the user's skin. Once hooked, however, many abusers who started snorting or smoking heroin eventually shift to intravenous use.

Symptoms and signs of heroin use include euphoria, drowsiness, respiratory depression, constricted pupils, and nausea. Withdrawal symptoms include watery eyes, runny nose, yawning, loss of appetite, tremors, panic, chills, sweating, nausea, diarrhea, muscle cramps, and insomnia. Elevations in blood pressure, pulse, respiratory rate, and temperature occur as withdrawal progresses. Because heroin abusers are often unaware of the actual strength of the drug and its true contents, they are at risk of overdose. Symptoms of overdose, which may result in death, include shallow breathing, clammy skin, convulsions, and coma. The NSDUH reports that 200,000 Americans aged 12 years and older were current heroin users in 2009. (See Figure 4.2.)

Anabolic Steroids

Anabolic steroids are drugs that are derived from the male sex hormone testosterone. They are used illegally by some athletes, including weight lifters, bodybuilders, long-distance runners, cyclists, and others who believe these drugs can give them a competitive advantage or improve their physical appearance. When used in combination with exercise training and a high-protein diet, anabolic steroids can lead to increased size and strength of muscles, improved endurance, and shorter recovery time between workouts.

Steroids are taken orally or by intramuscular injection. Most are smuggled into the United States and sold at gyms and competitions or sold by mail-order companies. In 1991 concerns about anabolic steroids led Congress to place them into Schedule III of the CSA.

There is growing evidence that using anabolic steroids can result in serious health problems, including cardiovascular and liver damage and harm to reproductive organs. The U.S. Department of Justice and the DEA's Diversion Control Program list the effects of anabolic steroids in "Anabolic Steroids: Hidden Dangers" (March 2008, http://www.deadiversion.usdoj.gov/pubs/brochures/steroids/hidden/hiddendangers.pdf). There are many types of physical side effects, including elevated LDL (bad) cholesterol levels and reduced HDL (good) cholesterol levels, severe acne, premature balding, mood swings, and atrophying of the testicles. Males may develop breasts, whereas females may experience a deepening of the voice, increased body-hair growth, fewer menstrual cycles, and diminished breast size. Some of these effects are irreversible. In adolescents, bone development may stop, causing stunted growth. Some users become violently aggressive.

By the turn of the 21st century a few professional sports agencies had begun to acknowledge that widespread steroid use was taking place in their ranks. For example, in 2005 Major League Baseball (MLB) initiated regular testing of players for steroid use. In 2009 New York Yankees third baseman Alex Rodriguez (1975–) was accused of using steroids back in 2003, when he played for the Texas Rangers. Rodriguez joined a long list of other record-breaking, award-winning MLB players who have been implicated in the use of performance-enhancing drugs, including Roger Clemens (1962–), Mark McGwire (1963–), and Barry Bonds (1964–).

According to Amy Brittain and Mark Mueller, in "N.J. Doctor Supplied Steroids to Hundreds of Law Enforcement

Officers, Firefighters" (*Star-Ledger* [Newark, New Jersey], December 12, 2010), a seven-month-long investigation by the *Star-Ledger* revealed in December 2010 that over 200 police officers and firefighters had been using steroids. Brittain and Mueller note that the investigation implicates Joseph Colao, a Jersey City, New Jersey, physician, who died in 2007, and state that "in just over a year, records show, at least 248 officers and firefighters from 53 agencies used Colao's fraudulent practice to obtain muscle-building drugs, some of which have been linked to increased aggression, confusion and reckless behavior." Taxpayer dollars were allegedly used to fill the prescriptions. As of February 2011, an investigation was ongoing.

Steroid use is not limited to professional athletes and other public figures, however. Danice K. Eaton et al. of the CDC report in "Youth Risk Behavior Surveillance—United States, 2009" (*Morbidity and Mortality Weekly Report*, vol. 59, no. SS-05, June 4, 2010) that in 2009, 4.6% of male high school students and 1.6% of female students had used illegal steroids by the time they were seniors. Johnston et al. determine the annual prevalence rates for androstenedione, a precursor to anabolic steroids, which was available over the counter until early 2005: among male students, annual prevalence rates of this drug in 2009 were 1%, 1.2%, and 2.5% in eighth, 10th, and 12th grades, respectively. The rates among female students in 2009 were lower than among male students: 0.5%, 0.4%, and 0.4% in eighth, 10th, and 12th grades, respectively.

ILLICIT DRUG USE DURING PREGNANCY

Illicit drug use during pregnancy places both the mother and the fetus (unborn child) at risk for serious health problems. For example, a fetus may become addicted to heroin in its mother's womb—provided the fetus reaches full term and is born (fetal death is a possibility). Cocaine use by the pregnant mother carries similar risks to the fetus and may kill the mother as well. LSD use may lead to birth defects. PCP users may have smaller-than-normal babies who later turn out to have poor muscle control. Learning disabilities are associated with children born to women using cocaine and MDMA while pregnant. Smoking marijuana may prevent an embryo from attaching to the uterine wall and halt pregnancy.

The NSDUH surveyed women regarding their illicit drug use. A smaller percentage of pregnant women took illicit drugs than did women who were not pregnant. However, illicit drug use among pregnant women did occur. In 2007–08, 5.1% of pregnant women took illicit drugs. (See Table 4.3.) The most prevalent illicit drug use during pregnancy was smoking marijuana and hashish: 3.8% in 2007–08, up from 3% in 2005–06. Even though smoking marijuana may seem safe to some pregnant women, it is not. In "Neurobiological Consequences of Maternal Cannabis on Human Fetal Development and Its

TABLE 4.3

Percentage of past-month illicit drug use among females aged 15–44, by pregnancy status, 2005–06 and 2007–08

Drug	Total[a]		Pregnancy status			
			Pregnant		Not pregnant	
	2005–2006	2007–2008	2005–2006	2007–2008	2005–2006	2007–2008
Illicit drugs[b]	9.8	9.6	4.0	5.1	10.0	9.8
Marijuana and hashish	6.8	7.0	3.0	3.8	7.0	7.1
Cocaine	1.1	0.8	0.2	0.4	1.2	0.8
Crack	0.3	0.2	0.1	0.3	0.3	0.1
Heroin	0.1	0.1	0.1	*	0.1	0.1
Hallucinogens	0.6	0.5	0.3	0.4	0.6	0.5
LSD	0.1	0.1	0.1	0.0	0.1	0.1
PCP	0.0	0.0	0.0	0.0	0.0	0.0
Ecstasy	0.4	0.3	0.2	*	0.4	0.3
Inhalants	0.2	0.2	0.1	0.2	0.2	0.2
Nonmedical use of Psychotherapeutics[c, d]	3.9	3.6	1.3	1.0	4.0	3.7
Pain relievers	2.7	2.6	1.0	0.7	2.8	2.7
OxyContin®	0.2	0.2	0.0	0.1	0.2	0.2
Tranquilizers	1.1	1.2	0.4	0.2	1.2	1.2
Stimulants[d]	0.9	0.7	0.1	0.3	0.9	0.7
Methamphetamine[d]	0.4	0.2	0.1	*	0.4	0.2
Sedatives	0.2	0.2	0.0	*	0.2	0.2
Illicit drugs other than marijuana[b]	5.0[a]	4.5	1.5	2.0	5.1	4.6

*Low precision; no estimate reported.

[a]Estimates in the total column are for all females aged 15 to 44, including those with unknown pregnancy status.

[b]Illicit drugs include marijuana/hashish, cocaine (including crack), heroin, hallucinogens, inhalants, or prescription-type psychotherapeutics used nonmedically. Illicit drugs other than marijuana include cocaine (including crack), heroin, hallucinogens, inhalants, or prescription-type psychotherapeutics used nonmedically. The estimates for nonmedical use of psychotherapeutics, stimulants, and methamphetamine incorporated in these summary estimates do not include data from the methamphetamine items added in 2005 and 2006.

[c]Nonmedical use of prescription-type psychotherapeutics includes the nonmedical use of pain relievers, tranquilizers, stimulants, or sedatives and does not include over-the-counter drugs.

[d]Estimates of nonmedical use of psychotherapeutics, stimulants, and methamphetamine in the designated rows include data from methamphetamine items added in 2005 and 2006 and are not comparable with estimates presented in National Survey of Drug Abuse and Health (NSDUH) reports prior to the 2007 National Findings report.

SOURCE: "Table 7.71B. Types of Illicit Drug Use in the Past Month among Females Aged 15 to 44, by Pregnancy Status: Percentages, Annual Averages Based on 2005–2006 and 2007–2008," in *Results from the 2008 National Survey on Drug Use and Health: Detailed Tables*, U.S. Department of Health and Human Services, Substance Abuse and Mental Health Services Administration, Office of Applied Studies, September 2010, http://oas.samhsa.gov/NSDUH/2K8NSDUH/tabs/Sect7peTabs71to78.pdf (accessed November 8, 2010)

Neuropsychiatric Outcome" (*European Archives of Psychiatry and Clinical Neuroscience*, vol. 259, no. 7, October 2009), Didier Jutras-Aswad et al. note that there is growing scientific evidence that smoking marijuana during pregnancy has a long-term influence on the developing brain and other parts of the nervous system of the fetus, which affects behavior and mental health.

The next most used illicit drugs during pregnancy were psychotherapeutics, which were taken for nonmedical reasons. (See Table 4.3.) Over 1% of pregnant women in 2005–06 and 1% of pregnant women in 2007–08 took these prescription drugs, such as pain relievers, tranquilizers, stimulants, and sedatives. Of the psychotherapeutics, pain relievers were taken the most often. The percentage of pregnant women who used heroin, hallucinogens, or inhalants during their pregnancy was low.

DRUG ABUSE ARRESTS

Tina L. Dorsey and Priscilla Middleton of the Bureau of Justice Statistics (BJS) estimate in *Drugs and Crime Facts* (2011, http://www.whitehousedrugpolicy.gov/publi cations/pdf/adam2009.pdf) that there were over 1.8 million arrests for drug abuse violations in 2007. The estimated number of arrests for drug abuse violations increased rather steadily since the early 1990s, peaked at 1.9 million in 2006, and decreased slightly to 1.8 million in 2007. (See Figure 4.10.) The researchers also note that drug arrests increased as a percentage of all arrests, from 7.4% in 1987 to 13% in 2007. Drug abuse violations topped the list of the seven-leading arrest offenses in the United States in 2007. That year more people were arrested for drug abuse violations (1.8 million) than were arrested for driving under the influence (1.4 million), simple assault (1.3 million), larceny/theft (1.2 million), disorderly conduct (709,100), liquor laws (634,600), or drunkenness (589,400).

Possession versus Sale

Most people arrested for drug offenses are charged with possession (carrying some kind of drug) rather than with trafficking (the sale or manufacture of drugs). Dorsey and Middleton indicate that in 2007 more than four-fifths (82.5% or 1.5 million) of those arrested for drug law violations were for possession.

FIGURE 4.10

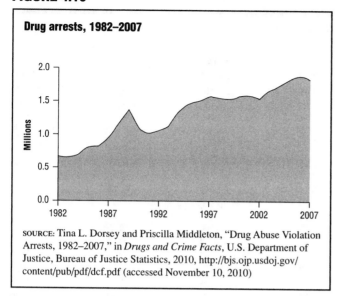

Drug arrests, 1982–2007

SOURCE: Tina L. Dorsey and Priscilla Middleton, "Drug Abuse Violation Arrests, 1982–2007," in *Drugs and Crime Facts*, U.S. Department of Justice, Bureau of Justice Statistics, 2010, http://bjs.ojp.usdoj.gov/content/pub/pdf/dcf.pdf (accessed November 10, 2010)

FIGURE 4.11

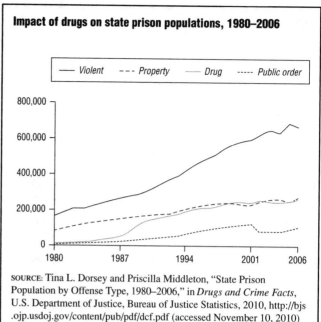

Impact of drugs on state prison populations, 1980–2006

SOURCE: Tina L. Dorsey and Priscilla Middleton, "State Prison Population by Offense Type, 1980–2006," in *Drugs and Crime Facts*, U.S. Department of Justice, Bureau of Justice Statistics, 2010, http://bjs.ojp.usdoj.gov/content/pub/pdf/dcf.pdf (accessed November 10, 2010)

ARRESTEE DRUG USE

The National Institute of Justice operated the Arrestee Drug Abuse Monitoring (ADAM) Program from 1987 to 2004 and published an annual report that summarized the previous year's data. The ADAM Program ended in 2004 in response to budgetary considerations and resumed in 2007 under the ONDCP.

In 2009 the ADAM Program surveyed arrestees in 10 urban sites about drug use in the past year and conducted urinalyses to determine if any of 10 drugs (amphetamines, barbiturates, benzodiazepines, cocaine, marijuana, methadone, opiates, oxycodone, PCP, and propoxyphene) had been used recently. According to the *ADAM II 2009 Annual Report* (June 2010, http://www.whitehousedrugpolicy.gov/publications/pdf/adam2009.pdf), in nine out of the 10 sites surveyed, urinalysis revealed that 60% or more of adult male arrestees in 2009 had used at least one of the 10 drugs. Over all sites, use ranged from a low of 56% of arrestees in Charlotte, North Carolina, to a high of 82% in Chicago, Illinois. Many had used multiple drugs, ranging from 12% in Charlotte to 28% in Chicago.

Arrests and Race

Enforcing the official public policy on drugs has a significant impact on the nation's justice system: local policing, the courts, and the state and federal corrections systems. A relatively small percentage of total users are arrested, but at increasing rates. Sentencing policies have changed to require mandatory incarceration of those who possess, not just those who sell, drugs. As a consequence, prison populations have swollen, thereby putting pressure on prison capacities. The number of people in state correctional facilities for drug offenses escalated from 19,000 in 1980 to 265,800 in 2006. (See Figure 4.11.) Table 4.4 shows the sentenced prisoners by offense under state jurisdiction in

2006 alone. The 265,800 people who were incarcerated for drug offenses made up 20% of the total state prison population of 1.3 million.

The proportion of state prison inmates incarcerated on drug charges differ for whites, African-Americans, and Hispanics. In 2006, 72,100 (out of 265,800, or 27.1%) of state drug offense arrestees were white, 117,600 (44.2%) were African-American, and 55,700 (21%) were Hispanic. (See Table 4.4.) The remainder were people of other races and ethnicities.

CONVICTION AND SENTENCING TRENDS

According to Dorsey and Middleton, drug prosecutions account for an increasing proportion of the federal criminal caseload, growing from 21% of defendants in 1982 to 33% in 2008. Similarly, the number of convictions of drug defendants increased from 76% in 1981 to 93% in 2006. Along with higher conviction rates came more and longer prison sentences for drug offenses. The proportion of drug offenders sentenced to federal prison rose from 79% in 1988 to 93% in 2006. Table 4.5 shows that the duration of sentences fluctuated in the years between 1988 and 2009, increasing from 78 months in 1988 to 95.7 months in 1991, then generally decreasing to a low of 73.8 months in 2001, then steadily increasing again to 88.9 months in 2007, and finally dropping to 83.7 months in 2009.

Convictions and Race

Dorsey and Middleton note that of the 282,590 adults arrested at the state level for drug trafficking in 2004, 201,760 were convicted. Of those convicted, 83% were

TABLE 4.4

Number of sentenced offenders in state prisons, by race, gender, and offense, 2006

Offense	All inmates	Male	Female	White[a]	Black[a]	Hispanic
Total	1,331,100	1,238,900	92,200	474,200	508,700	248,900
Violent	**667,900**	**638,100**	**29,800**	**217,100**	**256,400**	**145,300**
Murder[b]	144,500	135,700	8,800	34,700	61,400	36,800
Manslaughter	16,700	14,900	1,800	6,900	6,100	2,400
Rape	54,800	54,400	400	26,600	16,900	7,400
Other sexual assault	105,500	104,100	1,400	56,800	20,600	23,900
Robbery	179,500	172,400	7,100	37,500	91,500	33,900
Assault	136,600	128,800	7,900	42,800	49,800	34,700
Other violent	30,300	27,800	2,400	11,800	10,100	6,100
Property	**277,900**	**251,200**	**26,700**	**135,300**	**96,000**	**25,000**
Burglary	138,000	132,300	5,700	68,700	53,600	2,800
Larceny	51,600	43,800	7,800	23,300	17,600	7,200
Motor vehicle theft	27,100	25,500	1,600	10,900	7,100	7,900
Fraud	34,400	25,000	9,400	19,200	10,000	2,900
Other property	26,800	24,700	2,100	13,300	7,600	4,200
Drug offenses	**265,800**	**240,500**	**25,400**	**72,100**	**117,600**	**55,700**
Public-order offenses[c]	**112,300**	**106,100**	**6,200**	**48,200**	**35,400**	**21,000**
Other/unspecified[d]	**7,200**	**2,900**	**4,300**	**1,400**	**3,300**	**1,900**

Note: Totals based on prisoners with a sentence of more than 1 year. Detail may not add to total due to rounding.
[a]Excludes Hispanics and persons identifying two or more races.
[b]Includes negligent manslaughter.
[c]Includes weapons, drunk driving, court offenses, commercialized vice, morals and decency offenses, liquor law violations, and other public-order offenses.
[d]Includes juvenile offenses and other unspecified offense categories.

SOURCE: William J. Sabol, Heather C. West, and Matthew Cooper, "Appendix Table 15. Estimated Number of Sentenced Prisoners under State Jurisdiction, by Offense, Gender, Race, and Hispanic Origin, Yearend 2006," in *Prisoners in 2008*, U.S. Department of Justice, Office of Justice Programs, Bureau of Justice Statistics, December 2009 (revised June 30, 2010), http://bjs.ojp.usdoj.gov/zzcontent/pub/pdf/p08.pdf (accessed November 10, 2010)

male, 51% were white, and 47% were African-American. In absolute numbers, more whites were arrested and convicted for drug violations than African-Americans, but African-Americans were much more likely not only to be arrested but also to be convicted in proportion to their representation in the population. According the U.S. Census Bureau (August 11, 2005, http://www.census.gov/popest/ states/asrh/SC-EST2004-04.html), in 2004 the U.S. population was 80.4% (236.1 million of 293.7 million) white and 12.8% (37.5 million) African-American.

The Human Rights Watch (HRW), an independent and nongovernmental organization that is dedicated to protecting the human rights of people around the world, documents racial disparities in the incarceration of state drug offenders. The HRW considers crime rates, law enforcement priorities, and sentencing legislation as factors that contribute to creating racial disparities in incarceration. It contends that African-Americans have been disproportionately affected by the War on Drugs, which largely aims to arrest, prosecute, and imprison street-level drug offenders from inner-city areas. Bolstering its claims, the HRW discusses in "Race, Drugs, and Law Enforcement in the United States" (June 19, 2009, http://www.hrw.org/en/news/2009/06/19/ race-drugs-and-law-enforcement-united-states) these racial disparities and notes that African-American males are arrested and jailed on drug charges at "significantly higher rates" than that of white males and that these "rates bear no relationship to rates of offending."

THE BROADER RELATIONSHIP BETWEEN ILLICIT DRUGS AND CRIME

The relationship between illicit drugs and crime goes beyond the fact that illicit drug use is illegal. There are strong correlations between drug use and a variety of nondrug crimes. There are usually three reasons given for this correlation:

- Drugs may reduce inhibitions or stimulate aggression and interfere with the ability to earn a legitimate income.

- People who develop a dependence on an illegal drug need a substantial income to pay for it and may commit crimes to fund their habit.

- Drug trafficking may lead to crimes such as extortion, aggravated assault, and homicide.

In *Drug Use and Dependence, State and Federal Prisoners, 2004* (October 2006, http://bjs.ojp.usdoj.gov/ content/pub/pdf/dudsfp04.pdf), Christopher J. Mumola and Jennifer C. Karberg of the BJS discuss the drug use of state and federal prisoners by the type of offense they committed in 2004. (The next report on this topic is tentatively scheduled to be released by the BJS in the spring of 2011.) Overall, more than half of state and federal prisoners (56% and 50.2%, respectively) reported using illicit drugs in the month before their offense. Unsurprisingly, a high percentage of those in state prison for drug offenses (71.9%) had used drugs in the month

TABLE 4.5

Sentences for violation of drug laws, by type and length of sentence, U.S. District Courts, 1945–2009

		Type of sentence									Average sentence to imprisonment (in months)[d]	Average sentence to probation (in months)[e]
		Imprisonment										
		Regular sentences[a]										
	Total	Total regular	1 through 12 months	13 through 35 months	36 through 60 months	Over 60 months	Life sentences	Other[b]	Probation	Fine and other[c]		
1945	861	X	308	360	140	53	NA	X	287	37	22.2	NA
1946	949	X	430	377	108	34	NA	X	369	20	18.7	NA
1947	1,128	X	471	452	161	44	NA	X	504	38	19.7	NA
1948	1,048	X	488	408	122	30	NA	X	411	23	18.6	NA
1949	1,187	X	541	451	152	43	NA	X	398	13	18.9	NA
1950	1,654	X	595	736	218	105	NA	X	471	11	21.9	NA
1951	1,659	X	473	671	328	187	NA	X	345	24	27.1	NA
1952	1,551	X	221	652	402	276	NA	X	312	6	35.2	NA
1953	1,586	X	108	789	358	331	NA	X	403	14	38.4	NA
1954	1,483	X	72	681	360	370	NA	X	411	16	41.3	NA
1955	1,457	X	47	648	360	402	NA	X	329	17	43.5	NA
1956	1,258	X	30	511	341	376	NA	X	250	13	45.8	NA
1957	1,432	X	16	326	248	842	NA	X	220	2	66.0	NA
1958	1,351	X	25	167	141	1,018	NA	X	282	8	69.4	NA
1959	1,151	X	43	126	95	887	NA	X	224	3	74.2	NA
1960	1,232	X	33	145	148	906	NA	X	271	3	72.8	NA
1961	1,258	X	42	126	105	985	NA	X	252	5	74.0	NA
1962	1,173	X	38	129	106	900	NA	X	217	13	70.5	NA
1963	1,085	X	39	144	113	789	NA	X	304	17	70.1	NA
1964	1,076	X	28	142	157	749	NA	X	309	23	63.7	NA
1965	1,257	X	53	186	197	821	NA	X	480	18	60.3	NA
1966	1,272	X	85	154	276	757	NA	X	589	13	61.3	NA
1967	1,180	X	83	139	245	713	NA	X	620	22	62.0	NA
1968	1,368	X	93	141	293	841	NA	X	728	33	64.4	NA
1969	1,581	X	110	179	500	892	NA	X	1,110	18	63.7	NA
1970	1,283	X	101	166	276	740	NA	X	1,156	22	64.8	NA
1971	1,834	X	249	300	428	857	NA	X	1,258	70	58.5	NA
1972	3,050	X	882	396	789	983	NA	X	2,068	130	46.4	NA
1973	5,097	X	1,445	744	1,343	1,565	NA	X	2,591	126	45.5	NA
1974	5,125	X	1,547	792	1,390	1,396	NA	X	3,039	81	43.7	NA
1975	4,887	X	1,366	706	1,441	1,374	NA	X	3,209	55	45.3	NA
1976	5,039	X	1,221	790	1,544	1,484	NA	X	2,927	75	47.6	NA
1977	5,223	X	1,505	886	1,366	1,466	NA	X	2,324	88	47.3	NA
1978	4,119	3,605	885	623	956	1,141	NA	514	1,630	68	51.3	38.6
1979	3,641	2,820	369	614	868	969	NA	821	1,379	47	50.8	37.8
1980	3,479	2,547	281	565	792	909	NA	932	1,232	38	54.5	38.7
1981	3,856	2,865	403	578	748	1,136	NA	991	1,371	119	55.5	36.6
1982	4,586	3,516	383	729	966	1,438	NA	1,070	1,617	133	61.4	34.1
1983	5,449	4,150	447	890	1,011	1,802	NA	1,299	1,893	148	63.8	33.7
1984	5,756	4,306	354	845	1,173	1,934	NA	1,450	1,584	119	65.7	43.2
1985	6,786	5,207	411	1,103	1,459	2,234	NA	1,579	2,039	238	64.8	36.2
1986	8,152	6,601	506	1,271	1,808	3,016	NA	1,551	2,353	259	70.0	38.7
1987	9,907	8,188	613	1,491	2,049	4,035	NA	1,719	2,680	112	73.0	39.9
1988	9,983	8,560	708	1,466	1,577	4,809	NA	1,423	3,042	137	78.0	33.4
1989	11,626	10,838	1,270	2,343	1,844	5,381	NA	788	2,358	155	73.8	32.8
1990	13,838	13,462	1,490	3,047	1,801	7,124	NA	376	2,135	215	79.3	32.3
1991	14,382[f]	14,286	1,687	2,828	3,063	6,708	34	61	1,896	68	95.7	53.4
1992	16,040	15,775	1,810	3,423	3,397	7,145	80	185	2,011	194	87.8	38.7
1993	16,995[f]	16,639	2,097	3,383	4,128	7,031	186	169	1,943	310	83.2	35.8
1994	15,623	15,130	1,836	3,074	3,798	6,422	238	255	1,908	73	84.3	34.4
1995	14,157	13,734	1,606	2,716	3,311	6,101	150	273	1,597	107	88.7	33.6
1996	18,333	16,684	1,643	3,334	4,025	7,113	197	372	1,534	112	82.5	35.0
1997	18,231[f]	17,456	1,687	4,166	4,445	7,158	228	546	1,523	79	79.3	34.9
1998	19,809	19,062	2,100	4,443	4,517	8,002	180	567	1,629	91	78.0	34.9
1999	22,443[f]	21,513	2,670	5,074	5,240	8,529	205	724	1,719	85	74.6	34.2

before their offense. The correlation between drug use and nondrug crimes can be seen, however, in the fact that 64% of state prisoners who committed property offenses and 49.6% of those who committed violent offenses had used drugs in the month before their offense. The percentages for federal prisoners were lower but still substantial, with 57.3% of drug offenders, 49.1% of violent offenders, and 27.7% of property offenders reporting drug use in the month before their offense. Furthermore, more than a

quarter of state and federal prisoners (32.1% and 26.4%, respectively) reported they were using illicit drugs at the time of their offense.

Table 4.6 shows drug use in the month before the offense by selected characteristics of state and federal prisoners, comparing results from 1997 and 2004. For state prisoners the likelihood that they used drugs in the month before the offense stayed the same from 1997 to

TABLE 4.5

Sentences for violation of drug laws, by type and length of sentence, U.S. District Courts, 1945–2009 [CONTINUED]

		Type of sentence									Average sentence to imprisonment (in months)[d]	Average sentence to probation (in months)[e]
		Imprisonment										
		Regular sentences[a]										
	Total	Total regular	1 through 12 months	13 through 35 months	36 through 60 months	Over 60 months	Life sentences	Other[b]	Probation	Fine and other[c]		
2000	23,120	22,207	2,523	5,095	5,452	9,137	148	765	1,591	75	75.7	35.1
2001	24,011	23,127	2,780	5,350	5,670	9,327	122	762	1,671	133	73.8	34.5
2002	25,031	23,838	2,825	5,250	5,727	10,036	168	1,025	1,947	148	75.9	33.4
2003	25,060	23,937	2,632	4,781	5,967	10,557	157	966	1,781	145	80.2	32.2
2004	23,920	22,984	2,581	4,181	5,553	10,669	146	790	1,598	184	82.5	28.4
2005	24,786	23,831	2,389	4,296	5,719	11,427	151	804	1,508	294	85.7	32.7
2006	26,488[g]	25,437	2,035	4,438	6,159	12,805	195	853	1,548	275	87.9	31.8
2007	25,520	24,439	2,132	4,017	5,962	12,328	171	910	1,344	250	88.9	31.0
2008	25,305[f]	24,055	2,131	4,124	5,940	11,860	157	1,092	1,389	226	86.0	34.5
2009	24,929	23,396	2,304	4,150	5,822	11,120	183	1,350	1,420	263	83.7	36.2

Note: Data for 1945–91 are reported for the 12-month period ending June 30. Beginning in 1992, data are reported for the Federal fiscal year, which is the 12-month period ending September 30. Between 1991 and 2004, defendants charged in two or more cases that were terminated during the year are counted only once. Beginning in 2005, defendants charged in two or more cases that were terminated during the year are counted separately for each case.

[a]Includes sentences of more than 6 months that are to be followed by a term of probation (mixed sentences). Beginning in 1991, includes sentences of at least 1 month that may be followed by a term of probation.

[b]From 1978–88, "other" includes split sentences, indeterminate sentences, and Youth Corrections Act and youthful offender sentences. In 1989 and 1990, the category includes split sentences and indeterminate sentences. Beginning in 1991, "other" includes deportation, suspended and sealed sentences, imprisonment of 4 days or less, and no sentence.

[c]Includes supervised release, probation of 4 days or less, suspended sentences, sealed sentences, and no sentence.

[d]From 1978–90, split sentences, Youth Corrections Act and youthful offender sentences, and life sentences were not included in computing average sentence. Beginning in 1991, life sentences, death sentences, deportation, suspended and sealed sentences, imprisonment of 4 days or less, and no sentence also are not included in computing average sentence.

[e]From 1986–90, split sentences, indeterminate sentences, and Youth Corrections Act and youthful offender sentences were not included in computing average sentence. Beginning in 1991, supervised release, probation of 4 days or less, suspended sentences, sealed sentences, and no sentence also are not included in computing average sentence.

[f]Includes one death sentence.

[g]Includes three death sentences.

SOURCE: Kathleen Maguire, ed., "Table 5.38.2009. Defendants Sentenced for Violation of Drug Laws in U.S. District Courts, by Type and Length of Sentence, 1945–2009," in *Sourcebook of Criminal Justice Statistics Online*, U.S. Department of Justice, Bureau of Justice Statistics, University at Albany School of Criminal Justice, Hindelang Criminal Justice Research Center, 2010, http://www.albany.edu/sourcebook/pdf/t5382009.pdf (accessed November 10, 2010)

TABLE 4.6

Drug use among state and federal prisoners in the month before their offense, by demographic characteristics, 1997 and 2004

	State		Federal	
Characteristic	2004	1997	2004	1997
All prisoners	56.0%	56.5%	50.2%	44.8%
Gender				
Male	55.7%	56.1%	50.4%	45.4%
Female	59.3	62.4	47.6	36.7
Race/Hispanic origin				
White[a]	57.7%	55.2%	58.2%	49.4%
Black[a]	56.0	58.3	52.7	47.2
Hispanic	53.5	55.0	38.4	37.5
Other[a, b]	52.9	52.7	48.4	38.5
Age				
24 or younger	66.2%	63.2%	62.0%	57.2%
25–34	60.9	60.0	56.7	48.5
35–44	54.9	56.5	47.9	46.8
45–54	47.4	40.4	44.9	35.2
55 or older	19.2	18.4	20.9	24.3

[a]Excludes persons of Hispanic origin.

[b]Includes Asians, American Indians, Alaska Natives, Native Hawaiians, other Pacific Islanders, and inmates who specified more than one race.

SOURCE: Christopher J. Mumola and Jennifer C. Karberg, "Table 3. Drug Use in the Month before the Offense, by Selected Characteristics of State and Federal Prisoners, 1997 and 2004," in *Drug Use and Dependence, State and Federal Prisoners, 2004*, U.S. Department of Justice, Office of Justice Programs, Bureau of Justice Statistics, October 2006, http://www.ojp.usdoj.gov/bjs/pub/pdf/dudsfp04.pdf (accessed December 10, 2008)

2004, at approximately 56%. The likelihood that federal prisoners used drugs in the month before their offense rose from 44.8% in 1997 to 50.2% in 2004. For state prisoners, women were more likely than men to have used drugs in the month before their offense in both years. Federal prisoners showed the opposite trend—men were more likely than women to have used drugs in the month before their offense in both years.

For both state and federal prisoners, people aged 24 years and younger were the most likely to have used drugs in the month before the offense in both years. (See Table 4.6.) The likelihood of drug use fell with age in both years and for both sets of prisoners. In general, whites were slightly more likely than African-Americans to have used drugs in the month before their offense in both years. Hispanics were the least likely of the three racial groups to have used drugs in the month before their offense. In 2004 the incidence of drug use was over half for whites (58.2%) and African-Americans (52.7%) in federal prison. Only 38.4% of Hispanic federal prisoners used drugs in the month before their offense.

CHAPTER 5
ALCOHOL, TOBACCO, ILLICIT DRUGS, AND YOUTH

In 2009, when teens were asked, "What is the most important problem facing people your age?" the most frequent answer was "drugs," which included tobacco and alcohol. The National Center on Addiction and Substance Abuse (CASA) at Columbia University has been asking this question in its national survey for many years. In *National Survey of American Attitudes on Substance Abuse XV: Teens and Parents* (August 2010, http://www.casacolumbia.org/upload/2010/20100819teensurvey.pdf), CASA states that "as in past years, teens continue to cite drugs as their top concern."

According to CASA, 26% of teen respondents said that drugs (including alcohol and tobacco) are the most important problem facing them. The second-most important problem was social pressure (22%). CASA adds that "the pressure to drink or use drugs is often mentioned as one of the social pressures teens face."

PROBLEM BEHAVIORS BEGIN EARLY IN LIFE
Risk and Protective Factors

Figure 5.1 shows the risk factors that are associated with drug addiction. The figure points out that drug addiction is not due to a single factor but to a variety of interacting factors. A person's heredity and environment act together to influence his or her behavior. More specifically, the National Institute on Drug Abuse (NIDA) explains in *Drugs, Brains, and Behavior: The Science of Addiction* (February 2008, http://www.drugabuse.gov/ScienceofAddiction/scifaddiction.pdf) that genetic factors account for about half of an individual's risk for addiction. In addition, certain environmental factors, such as having parents or close friends who use drugs, being a victim of abuse, or being an underachiever in school, raise the risk that an individual will use and become addicted to drugs. Figure 5.1 notes that early use of drugs is also a risk factor for drug addiction.

Protective factors are those that lower the risk for drug addiction. According to the NIDA, these factors include positive relationships with peers and parents, success in schoolwork, self-control, and a strong neighborhood attachment.

Early Use of Alcohol, Tobacco, and Marijuana

Danice K. Eaton et al. of the Centers for Disease Control and Prevention indicate in "Youth Risk Behavior Surveillance—United States, 2009" (*Morbidity and Mortality Weekly Report*, vol. 59, no. SS-05, June 4, 2010) that high school students were asked if they had smoked a whole cigarette, had drunk alcohol, or had tried marijuana before the age of 13 years. The results are shown in Table 5.1 and Table 5.2.

A higher percentage of younger students than older students reported having initiated cigarette, alcohol, or marijuana use before the age of 13 years. The most frequently reported behavior in 2009 was drinking alcohol before the age of 13 years. Over one-quarter (28.1%) of ninth graders reported they had done so, as had nearly one-quarter (22.2%) of 10th graders, over one-sixth (17.9%) of 11th graders, and one-seventh (14.2%) of 12th graders. (See Table 5.1.) Males (23.7%) throughout all grades were more likely to report having had a drink before the age of 13 years than females (18.1%). Hispanics (27.1%) were the most likely ethnic group to report having an alcoholic drink before the age of 13 years, followed by non-Hispanic African-Americans (24.9%) and non-Hispanic whites (18.1%).

Table 5.1 shows that the next most frequently reported behavior in 2009 was smoking an entire cigarette before the age of 13 years. Once again, males (11.8%) throughout all grades were more likely than females (9.4%) to report having smoked a cigarette before the age of 13 years. Hispanics (12.6%) were the most likely to report having smoked before their teens. Non-Hispanic whites (10.3%) and non-Hispanic African-Americans (9.1%) reported this behavior slightly less frequently.

The same pattern between males (9.7%) and females (5%) emerged with the least frequently reported behavior in 2009 of trying marijuana before the age of 13 years. (See Table 5.2.) Hispanics (10.3%) and non-Hispanic African Americans (10.2%) were the most likely to report this early behavior, followed by non-Hispanic whites (5.7%).

ALCOHOL AND YOUTH

Age of First Use

The data in the previous section clearly show that the use of alcohol, tobacco, and marijuana often begins early in life, especially alcohol use. In *National Survey of American*

Attitudes on Substance Abuse XV, CASA notes that teens who attend schools in which drugs are used, kept, or sold (what the center calls "drug-infected" schools) are three times more likely to have used alcohol than students who attend drug-free schools. CASA also reveals that the percent of children attending middle schools (usually 12- to 13-year-olds) in which drugs are used, kept, or sold increased from 23% in 2008 to 32% in 2009. According to CASA, attending drug-infected schools places students at risk for early alcohol use.

The Substance Abuse and Mental Health Services Administration conducts the annual National Survey on Drug Use and Health (NSDUH), and its 2009 survey results are published in *Results from the 2009 National Survey on Drug Use and Health: Volume I. Summary of National Findings* (September 2010, http://www.oas.samhsa.gov/NSDUH/2k9NSDUH/2k9ResultsP.pdf). According to the NSDUH, 4.6 million people used alcohol for the first time in 2009. Approximately 85.5% of the 4.6 million alcohol initiates in 2009 were younger than the age of 21 years when they took their first drink.

Influences on the Decision to Drink

According to the *GfK Roper Youth Report, 2009* (February 18, 2010, http://www.alcoholstats.com/mm/docs/8052.pdf), a nationwide survey of eight- to 17-year-olds, 68% of respondents cited parents as the most influential factor in their decision to drink. Best friends (11%) were the second-most important factor influencing a young person's decision to drink. The attitudes of teachers, siblings, the media, and ads can hold sway over a young person's alcohol choices, though parents seem to exert the most influence by a large margin.

FIGURE 5.1

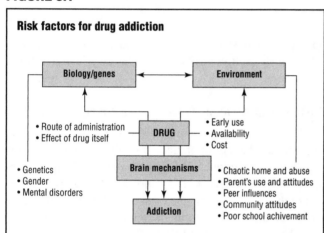

Risk factors for drug addiction

SOURCE: "Risk Factors," in *Drugs, Brains, and Behavior: The Science of Addiction*, National Institutes of Health, U.S. Department of Health and Human Services, National Institute on Drug Abuse, revised August 2010, http://www.drugabuse.gov/ScienceofAddiction/sciofaddiction.pdf (accessed November 10, 2010)

TABLE 5.1

Percentage of high school students who drank alcohol and smoked cigarettes before age 13, by gender, ethnicity, and grade, 2009

	Smoked a whole cigarette before age 13 years			Drank alcohol before age 13 years		
	Female	Male	Total	Female	Male	Total
Category	%	%	%	%	%	%
Race/ethnicity						
White*	9.8	10.8	10.3	15.5	20.3	18.1
Black*	6.9	11.2	9.1	21.9	27.6	24.9
Hispanic	10.5	14.7	12.6	23.2	31.0	27.1
Grade						
9	11.1	13.0	12.1	26.6	29.5	28.1
10	9.3	12.7	11.2	18.5	25.4	22.2
11	9.0	11.6	10.3	14.9	20.7	17.9
12	7.9	9.2	8.6	10.9	17.3	14.2
Total	**9.4**	**11.8**	**10.7**	**18.1**	**23.7**	**21.1**

Note: "Drank alcohol" is defined by other than a few sips.
*Non-Hispanic.

SOURCE: Adapted from Danice K. Eaton et. al, "Table 51. Percentage of High School Students Who Smoked a Whole Cigarette for the First Time before Age 13 Years and Who Drank Alcohol for the First Time before Age 13 Years, by Sex, Race/Ethnicity, and Grade—United States, Youth Risk Behavior Survey, 2009," in "Youth Risk Behavior Surveillance—United States, 2009," *Morbidity & Mortality Weekly Report*, vol. 59, no. SS-5, June 4, 2010, http://www.cdc.gov/mmwr/pdf/ss/ss5905.pdf (accessed November 10, 2010)

TABLE 5.2

Percentage of high school students who tried marijuana before age 13, by gender, ethnicity, and grade, 2009

Category	Female %	Male %	Total %
Race/ethnicity			
White*	4.0	7.1	5.7
Black*	4.1	16.1	10.2
Hispanic	7.8	12.9	10.3
Grade			
9	6.8	11.1	9.1
10	5.6	10.6	8.3
11	4.3	8.6	6.5
12	2.6	7.8	5.2
Total	**5.0**	**9.7**	**7.5**

*Non-Hispanic.

SOURCE: Adapted from Danice K. Eaton et. al, "Table 53. Percentage of High School Students Who Tried Marijuana for the First Time before Age 13 Years, by Sex, Race/Ethnicity, and Grade—United States, Youth Risk Behavior Survey, 2009," in "Youth Risk Behavior Surveillance—UnitedStates, 2009," *Morbidity & Mortality Weekly Report*, vol. 59, no. SS-5, June 4, 2010, http://www.cdc.gov/mmwr/pdf/ss/ss5905.pdf (accessed November 10, 2010)

How Do Adolescents Obtain Alcohol?

In "Youth Risk Behavior Surveillance—United States, 2009," Eaton et al. indicate that of high school students who drank alcohol in 2009, 42.2% were given the alcohol. The Century Council (2011, http://www.centurycouncil.org/stop-underage-drinking/initiatives/65percentcampaign), a nonprofit organization that works against drunk driving and underage drinking but that is funded by the distilling industry, reports an even higher percentage. Its data show that in 2003, 65% of underage drinkers said they get their alcohol from family and friends and only 7% said they obtain alcohol from retailers who do not check identification. Other ways in which teens obtain alcohol are by getting an adult to purchase it for them or by stealing it. In *National Survey of American Attitudes on Substance Abuse XV*, CASA indicates that it supports the idea that alcohol is easy for youth to obtain. When asked by researchers "Which is easiest to get: cigarettes, beer, marijuana, or prescription drugs?" teens responded that beer was easiest to get after cigarettes.

The Century Council notes in "We Don't Serve Teens" (2011, http://www.centurycouncil.org/stop-under age-drinking/initiatives/wedontserveteens) that 17% of adults think that it is acceptable for parents to provide their teens with alcohol in their own home, whereas 98% of parents do not think it is acceptable for another adult to provide alcohol to underage teens. However, many adults do not know that they can be held liable if they serve alcohol to a minor and if the minor is then killed or injured or kills or injures another person while under the influence of the alcohol that they served. Such laws vary from state to state and are called social liability laws. CASA reports that 86% of parents support social liability laws. Data from the survey also reveal that teens whose parents allow them to attend parties where alcohol is served are over twice as likely to have tried alcohol than teens whose parents do not allow them to attend such parties.

Current Use of Alcohol in High School Students

It is illegal for high school students to purchase alcoholic beverages, yet Eaton et al. indicate in "Youth Risk Behavior Surveillance—United States, 2009" that in 2009, 41.8% of high school students had consumed alcohol at least once in the 30 days before being surveyed. (See Table 5.3.) These students are considered current users. Lloyd D. Johnston et al. of the University of Michigan, in *Monitoring the Future National Survey Results on Drug Use, 1975–2009, Volume 1: Secondary School Students* (September 2010, http://monitoringthefuture.org/pubs/monographs/vol1_2009.pdf), provide data on current alcohol use among eighth, 10th, and 12th graders. Data from Johnston et al.'s survey and Eaton et al.'s survey overlap in current drinking data for 10th and 12th graders. Comparing the "total" figures in Table 5.3 and Table 5.4 for these grades, Eaton et al. show a higher prevalence of current drinking for 12th graders (51.7% compared with 43.5% by Johnston et al.) and for 10th graders (40.6% compared with 30.4% by Johnston et al.).

The NSDUH also collected data on alcohol use in 2009. It reports that an estimated 10.4 million people aged 12 to 20 years (27.2% of this age group) used alcohol in the month before the survey. The NSDUH presents rates of current alcohol use in 2009 among various age groups: 3.5% among 12- to 13-year-olds (seventh and eighth grades), 13% of 14- to 15-year-olds (ninth and 10th grades), 26.3% of 16- to 17-year-olds (11th and 12th grades), and 49.7% of 18- to 20-year-olds. The peak age of current alcohol use was 21 to 25 years at 70.2% of this population.

What can be gleaned from all these studies? Looking at all the data presented here, each study shows 2009 current rates of alcohol use in high school students rising with grade level. As students grew older, they drank more. Looking at the studies together, the percentage of 10th graders who were current alcohol users in 2009 ranged from about 13% to 41%. The percentage of 12th graders who were current alcohol users in 2009 ranged from about 44% to 52%. Taken separately or together, data from these surveys present a picture of a high percentage of teens who use alcohol, which can cause bodily harm, serious diseases, and possibly death. (See Chapter 2.) Concerning the teens who reported to survey researchers that alcohol was one of the most important problems facing young people today, they appear to understand the state of current alcohol use of high school students.

TABLE 5.3

Percentage of high school students who drank alcohol, by gender, ethnicity, and grade, 2009

	Ever drank alcohol[a]			Current alcohol use[b]		
	Female	Male	Total	Female	Male	Total
Category	%	%	%	%	%	%
Race/ethnicity						
White[c]	75.6	72.2	73.8	45.9	43.6	44.7
Black[c]	70.2	64.9	67.6	35.6	31.2	33.4
Hispanic	78.5	74.8	76.6	43.5	42.4	42.9
Grade						
9	66.4	60.8	63.4	35.3	28.4	31.5
10	72.5	69.9	71.1	41.2	40.1	40.6
11	79.0	76.5	77.8	45.6	45.7	45.7
12	80.3	79.0	79.7	50.7	52.6	51.7
Total	**74.2**	**70.8**	**72.5**	**42.9**	**40.8**	**41.8**

[a]Had at least one drink of alcohol on at least 1 day during their life.
[b]Had at least one drink of alcohol on at least 1 day during the 30 days before the survey.
[c]Non-Hispanic.

SOURCE: Adapted from Danice K. Eaton et. al, "Table 36. Percentage of High School Students Who Drank Alcohol, by Sex, Race/Ethnicity, and Grade—United States, Youth Risk Behavior Survey, 2009," in "Youth Risk Behavior Surveillance—United States, 2009," *Morbidity & Mortality Weekly Report*, vol. 59, no. SS-5, June 4, 2010, http://www.cdc.gov/mmwr/pdf/ss/ss5905.pdf (accessed November 10, 2010)

TABLE 5.4

Past-month use of alcohol by eighth, tenth, and twelfth graders, 2009

[Entries are percentages]

	Alcohol			Been drunk			Flavored alcoholic beverages		
Grade:	8th	10th	12th	8th	10th	12th	8th	10th	12th
Total	**14.9**	**30.4**	**43.5**	**5.4**	**15.5**	**27.4**	**9.5**	**19.0**	**27.4**
Gender									
Male	14.7	31.0	47.8	5.3	16.4	32.7	9.1	17.0	27.3
Female	14.9	29.8	38.9	5.3	14.8	22.5	9.7	20.9	27.1
College plans									
None or under 4 years	31.7	45.5	51.0	14.9	26.8	31.0	18.3	30.0	35.6
Complete 4 years	13.5	28.8	41.6	4.6	14.4	25.9	8.7	17.8	25.9
Region									
Northeast	15.3	30.5	48.4	4.7	14.6	36.3	8.8	18.6	34.0
Midwest	13.0	28.9	45.0	5.0	15.0	29.4	9.1	17.6	26.7
South	17.4	32.2	42.0	6.5	16.6	23.6	11.8	21.1	27.2
West	12.5	29.0	39.2	4.4	15.5	23.5	6.7	17.9	23.2
Population density									
Large MSA	12.9	30.3	46.7	4.0	15.3	29.8	7.2	17.6	27.0
Other MSA	15.9	29.7	41.5	5.8	15.3	25.9	9.7	19.6	28.8
Non-MSA	15.5	31.9	43.7	6.3	16.4	27.8	12.0	19.7	24.7
Parental education*									
1.0–2.0 (Low)	22.8	37.4	39.8	10.1	19.7	19.8	14.7	23.5	26.8
2.5–3.0	18.3	32.9	43.4	6.3	17.6	29.0	13.1	23.3	28.2
3.5–4.0	16.8	31.3	46.9	5.4	16.4	28.2	11.4	18.8	28.7
4.5–5.0	11.5	28.2	42.0	4.4	13.8	27.0	7.4	18.2	24.4
5.5–6.0 (High)	10.4	27.4	43.3	3.4	14.6	29.0	4.7	14.3	28.4
Race/ethnicity (2-year average)									
White	15.4	31.5	47.2	5.5	17.0	31.8	9.8	20.0	29.9
African American	12.3	20.2	30.5	3.6	8.4	15.1	8.5	14.2	19.3
Hispanic	19.2	34.1	40.1	6.2	14.9	21.7	11.8	23.0	25.2

MSA = Metropolitan statistical areas.
*Parental education is an average score of mother's education and father's education reported on the following scale: (1) completed grade school or less, (2) some high school, (3) completed high school, (4) some college, (5) completed college, (6) graduate or professional school after college. Missing data were allowed on one of the two variables.

SOURCE: Adapted from Lloyd D. Johnston et al., "Table 4-7. Thirty-Day Prevalence of Use of Various Drugs by Subgroups for 8th, 10th, and 12th Graders, 2009," in *Monitoring the Future National Survey Results on Drug Use, 1975–2009: Volume 1, Secondary School Students*, National Institute on Drug Abuse, 2010, http://monitoringthefuture.org/pubs/monographs/vol1_2009.pdf (accessed November 9, 2010)

Alcohol Use among College Students and Other Young Adults

The NSDUH indicates that 49.7% of 18- to 20-year-olds and 70.2% of 21- to 25-year-olds (the peak age group) were current alcohol users in 2009. These college-aged students and recent graduates are using a potentially dangerous drug, and those under the age of 21 years are using it illegally.

In *Monitoring the Future National Survey Results on Drug Use, 1975–2009, Volume 2: College Students and Adults Ages 19–50* (November 2010, http://monitoringthefuture.org/pubs/monographs/vol2_2009.pdf), Johnston et al. report the drug use results for college students and adults. Table 5.5 shows the annual prevalence of alcohol use by college students and other young adults who are one to four years beyond high school. The results indicate that both groups had a high annual prevalence of alcohol use in 2009 (79.4% for full-time college students and 75.5% for other young adults of the same age), but that college students had the higher rate of use. Male college students were more likely to have consumed alcohol during the past year (82.1%) than female college students (77.6%). The same is not true for other young adults one to four years beyond high school; females (76.5%) were slightly more likely than males (74%) to have consumed alcohol during the past year.

Table 5.6 shows the trend of lifetime prevalence of alcohol use between 1989 and 2009 among those aged 19 to 28 years. Between 1989 and 1991 the annual prevalence of alcohol use for this group remained relatively steady at slightly above 94%. Throughout the rest of the 1990s the annual prevalence fell slightly; by 1999 the annual prevalence of alcohol use for this group was 90.2%. In 2007 and 2009 the lifetime prevalence reached a low of 87.9%. The lifetime prevalence of drinking flavored alcoholic beverages (the data for which have only recently been gathered) among 19- to 28-year-olds remained about 84% in 2005 and 2007. In 2009 the lifetime prevalence decreased slightly to 83.5%.

Table 5.7 shows the trend of lifetime prevalence of alcohol use among college students one to four years beyond high school. The lifetime prevalence of alcohol use in this group (82.6% in 2009) was lower than that for the 19- to 28-year-old group (87.9% in 2009).

Heavy Drinking, Binge Drinking, and Drunkenness

Merriam-Webster's Collegiate Dictionary defines the term *drunk* as "having the faculties impaired by alcohol."

TABLE 5.5

Annual prevalence of alcohol use by full-time college students vs. other young adults 1–4 years beyond high school, by sex, 2009

[Entries are percentages]

	Total		Males		Females	
	Full-time College	Others	Full-time College	Others	Full-time College	Others
Alcohol	79.4	75.5	82.1	74.0	77.6	76.5
Been drunk	61.5	60.5	66.2	61.8	58.1	59.6
Flavored alcoholic beverage	66.1	62.2	62.7	55.2	67.9	67.3

SOURCE: Adapted from Lloyd D. Johnston et al., "Table 8-2. Annual Prevalence of Use for Various Types of Drugs, 2009: Full-Time College Students vs. Others among Respondents 1 to 4 Years beyond High School, by Gender," in *Monitoring the Future National Survey Results on Drug Use, 1975–2009: Volume II, College Students and Adults Ages 19–50*, National Institute on Drug Abuse, 2010, http://monitoringthefuture.org/pubs/monographs/vol2_2009.pdf (accessed December 2, 2010)

TABLE 5.6

Trends in lifetime prevalence of alcohol use among young adults aged 19–28, selected years 1989–2009

[Entries are percentages]

	1989	1991	1993	1995	1997	1999	2001	2003	2005	2007	2009	2008–2009 change
Alcohol	94.5	94.1	92.1	91.6	90.7	90.2	89.9	89.3	89.1	87.9	87.9	−0.4
Been drunk	NA	82.9	81.4	82.1	81.4	81.6	81.1	80.9	79.9	80.1	78.2	−1.9
Flavored alcoholic beverage	NA	NA	NA	NA	NA	NA	NA	NA	84.6	84.0	83.5	+0.9

Note: Any apparent inconsistency between the change estimate and the prevelance estimates for the two most recent years is due to rounding.
NA indicates data not available.

SOURCE: Adapted from Lloyd D. Johnston et al., "Table 5-1. Trends in Lifetime Prevalence of Various Types of Drugs among Respondents of Modal Ages 19–28," in *Monitoring the Future National Survey Results on Drug Use, 1975–2009: Volume II, College Students and Adults Ages 19–50*, National Institute on Drug Abuse, 2010, http://monitoringthefuture.org/pubs/monographs/vol2_2009.pdf (accessed December 2, 2010)

TABLE 5.7

Trends in lifetime prevalence of alcohol use among college students 1–4 years beyond high school, selected years 1989–2009

[Entries are percentages]

	1989	1991	1993	1995	1997	1999	2001	2003	2005	2007	2009	2008–2009 change
Alcohol	93.7	93.6	89.3	88.5	87.3	88.0	86.1	86.2	86.6	83.1	82.6	−2.7
Been drunk	NA	79.6	76.4	76.6	77.0	75.1	76.1	74.9	72.9	71.6	69.1	−3.4
Flavored alcoholic beverage	NA	NA	NA	NA	NA	NA	NA	NA	84.5	80.6	78.1	−0.5

Note: Any apparent inconsistency between the change estimate and the prevalence estimates for the two most recent years is due to rounding. NA indicates data not available.

SOURCE: Adapted from Lloyd D. Johnston et al., "Table 9-1. Trends in Lifetime Prevalence of Various Types of Drugs among College Students 1 to 4 Years beyond High School," in *Monitoring the Future National Survey Results on Drug Use, 1975–2009: Volume II, College Students and Adults Ages 19–50*, National Institute on Drug Abuse, 2010, http://monitoringthefuture.org/pubs/monographs/vol2_2009.pdf (accessed December 2, 2010)

TABLE 5.8

Percentage of high school students who had five or more drinks in a row and who usually obtained their alcohol by someone giving it to them, by gender, ethnicity, and grade, 2009

	Binge drinking			Someone gave alcohol to them		
	Female	Male	Total	Female	Male	Total
Category	%	%	%	%	%	%
Race/ethnicity						
White*	27.5	28.0	27.8	47.9	34.2	40.8
Black*	12.1	15.3	13.7	52.2	37.9	45.4
Hispanic	23.3	25.1	24.1	53.4	35.3	44.4
Grade						
9	17.2	13.6	15.3	53.2	39.6	46.5
10	21.1	23.3	22.3	48.2	35.5	41.6
11	26.4	30.0	28.3	47.9	34.9	41.3
12	30.4	36.6	33.5	50.3	31.5	40.6
Total	**23.4**	**25.0**	**24.2**	**49.8**	**35.0**	**42.2**

Notes: "Drinks in a row" is defined by alcohol taken within a couple of hours on at least 1 day during the 30 days before the survey. Among the 41.8% of students nationwide who currently drank alcohol during the 30 days before the survey.
*Non-Hispanic.

SOURCE: Adapted from Danice K. Eaton et. al, "Table 38. Percentage of High School Students Who Had Five or More Drinks of Alcohol in a Row and Who Usually Obtained the Alcohol They Drank by Someone Giving It to Them, by Sex, Race/Ethnicity, and Grade—United States, Youth Risk Behavior Survey, 2009," in "Youth Risk Behavior Surveillance—United States, 2009," *Morbidity & Mortality Weekly Report*, vol. 59, no. SS-5, June 4, 2010, http://www.cdc.gov/mmwr/pdf/ss/ss5905.pdf (accessed November 10, 2010)

According to Johnston et al., in *Monitoring the Future National Survey Results on Drug Use, 1975–2009, Volume 1*, the rates of occurrences of drunkenness within the past 30 days among high school students generally declined between 2000 and 2009 after having increased during the 1990s. The highest rate for eighth graders occurred in 1996, when 9.6% reported having been drunk in the past 30 days. The highest rate for 10th graders came in 2000, when the rate hit 23.5%. The highest rate for 12th graders was 34.2% in 1997. In 2009, 5.4% of eighth graders, 15.5% of 10th graders, and 27.4% of 12th graders reported being drunk during the previous month. (See Table 5.4.)

The National Institute on Alcohol Abuse and Alcoholism defines binge drinking as the consumption of five or more drinks of alcoholic beverages on at least one occasion during the past month. Heavy drinking is an average of more than one drink per day for women and more than two drinks per day for men. (There is a male-female difference because the same amount of alcohol affects women more than it does men. Women's bodies have less water than men's bodies, so a given amount of alcohol becomes more highly concentrated in a woman's body than in a man's.)

According to Eaton et al., in "Youth Risk Behavior Surveillance—United States, 2009," 24.2% of high school students were current binge drinkers in 2009. The incidence of binge drinking increased with grade level: 15.3% in ninth grade, 22.3% in 10th grade, 28.3% in 11th grade, and 33.5% in 12th grade. (See Table 5.8.)

Demographic Factors in Youth Alcohol Use

GENDER, RACIAL, AND ETHNIC DIFFERENCES. In 2009 high school males (40.8%) were slightly less likely to be current alcohol users than females (42.9%). (See Table 5.3.) However, males (25%) were slightly more likely than females (23.4%) to engage in binge drinking. (See Table 5.8.)

Similarly, Johnston et al. show in *Monitoring the Future National Survey Results on Drug Use, 1975–2009, Volume 1* close percentages of current alcohol use for males and females in grades eight and 10 in 2009. (See Table 5.4.) However, the data indicate that 12th-grade males (47.8%) were more likely to have been current drinkers in 2009 than females (38.9%). The results that Johnston et al. report for being drunk are similar to the results that Eaton et al. report in "Youth Risk Behavior Surveillance—United States, 2009" for binge drinking: males in grades 10 (16.4%) and 12 (32.7%) were more likely than females in these grades (14.8% and 22.5%, respectively) to have been drunk. Nonetheless, the data for eighth grade show that males and females were just as likely (5.3%) to have been drunk.

Johnston et al. also provide data for males and females among full-time college students and other young adults one to four years beyond high school. (See Table 5.5.) The 2009 annual prevalence rates for alcohol use show gender differences. Males of both groups were more likely than females to have been drunk. Full-time college females (67.9%) were more likely to drink flavored alcoholic beverages than full-time college males (62.7%). The same was true for other young adults in the same age group: females (67.3%) were more likely than males (55.2%) to drink flavored alcoholic beverages. A female preference for these drinks was also seen among eighth and 10th graders, but 12th-grade males (27.3%) and females (27.1%) each were as likely to drink flavored alcoholic beverages. (See Table 5.4.)

Table 5.3 also shows that in 2009 Hispanic (76.6%) high school students were more likely than non-Hispanic white (73.8%) or non-Hispanic African-American (67.6%) high school students to have consumed alcohol during their lifetime. However, non-Hispanic whites (27.8%) were more likely to have engaged in binge drinking than Hispanics (24.1%) or non-Hispanic African-Americans (13.7%). (See Table 5.8.) Non-Hispanic white (44.7%) high school students were slightly more likely than Hispanic (42.9%) high school students to be current drinkers in 2009, and non-Hispanic African-American (33.4%) high school students were much less likely than both to be current drinkers. (See Table 5.3.)

WHERE STUDENTS LIVE. In *Monitoring the Future National Survey Results on Drug Use, 1975–2009, Volume 1*, Johnston et al. look at population density as a factor in student drinking patterns. (See Table 5.4.) They use the category metropolitan statistical area (MSA), which means the area contains at least one town that has more than 50,000 inhabitants. Large MSAs are the biggest cities in the United States, such as New York City, New York; Los Angeles, California; Chicago, Illinois; Philadelphia, Pennsylvania; and Boston, Massachusetts. A smaller proportion of eighth graders who lived in large MSAs were current drinkers (12.9%) than were eighth graders who lived in other MSAs (15.9%) or non-MSAs (15.5%). By 10th grade, there was little difference in the proportion of students who were current drinkers in any of these three population density areas. The proportion was approximately 30%. Twelfth graders in large MSAs had the greatest proportion of current drinkers at 46.7%, followed by 12th graders who lived in non-MSAs (43.7%) and those who lived in other MSAs (41.5%). Senior high school students who lived in the Northeast were more likely to be current alcohol users than same-aged students who lived in other parts of the country, while eighth and 10th graders who lived in the South were more likely to be current alcohol users than their peers in other parts of the country.

PARENTAL EDUCATION. Table 5.4 shows an inverse relationship between current alcohol use in eighth and 10th graders and parental education: the less parental education, the more likely eighth and 10th graders were to drink. This relationship was not evident in 12th graders. In addition, students in all three grades who had no college plans were more likely to be current drinkers, to have been drunk in the past 30 days, and to drink flavored alcoholic beverages than those with plans to complete four years of college.

Perception of Harmfulness of Alcohol Use

The Pride Survey also asks adolescents and teenagers questions about drug and alcohol use. Figure 5.2 shows the results from the *Pride Surveys Questionnaire Report for Grades 6 to 12, National Summary Statistics for 2009–10* (September 27, 2010, http://www.pridesurveys.com/customercenter/us09ns.pdf). The report reveals that 48.1% of sixth graders perceived alcohol as having "great risk" with regular use. The perception of regular alcohol use having "great risk" decreased with increasing grade level. Only 34.6% of 12th graders perceived regular alcohol use as having "great risk." Thus, when the perception of risk decreased, the use of alcohol increased. (See Table 5.3 and Table 5.4.)

The Pride Survey also notes that easy access to alcohol increases the probability that adolescents and teenagers will drink. The survey results show that access to alcohol increased as the grade level increased. However, Eaton et al. show in "Youth Risk Behavior Surveillance—United States, 2009" that as the grade

FIGURE 5.2

Harmfulness of alcohol use as perceived by students in grades 6–12, 2009–10

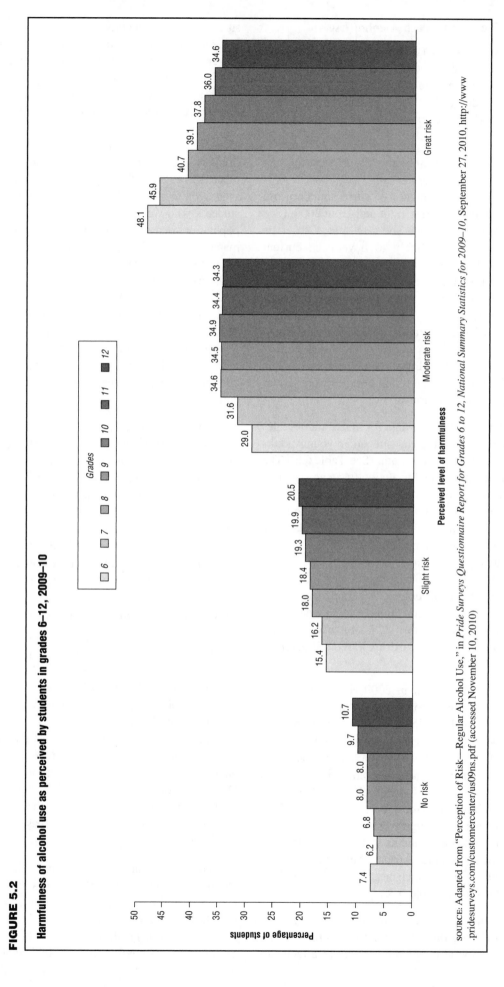

SOURCE: Adapted from "Perception of Risk—Regular Alcohol Use," in *Pride Surveys Questionnaire Report for Grades 6 to 12, National Summary Statistics for 2009–10*, September 27, 2010, http://www .pridesurveys.com/customercenter/us09ns.pdf (accessed November 10, 2010)

level increased the percentage of students who said that someone gave alcohol to them decreased. (See Table 5.8.) Conversely, Eaton et al. note in "Youth Risk Behavior Surveillance—United States, 2007" (*Morbidity and Mortality Weekly Report*, vol. 57, no. SS-04, June 6, 2008) that as the grade level increased from grade nine to grade 12, the percentage of students who purchased alcohol in a store in 2007 increased from 3.1% to 8%. Thus, it appears that older high school students have access to alcohol in ways that are not available to younger students, such as looking old enough to purchase alcohol from retailers who do not check for identification.

Drinking and Young Drivers

In *Traffic Safety Facts, 2008 Data: Young Drivers* (October 2009, http://www-nrd.nhtsa.dot.gov/Pubs/811169 .pdf), the National Highway Traffic Safety Administration (NHTSA) reports that a total of 5,864 drivers aged 15 to 20 years were involved in fatal crashes in 2008, which was a 27% decrease from the 7,987 drivers involved in fatal crashes in 1998. Twenty-five percent of the drivers aged 15 to 20 years who were killed in crashes were intoxicated (had a blood alcohol level of 0.08 grams per deciliter [g/dL] or higher). For young male drivers aged 15 to 20 years, fatalities dropped 26% between 1998 and 2008, compared with a 28% decrease for females.

As of July 2004, all 50 states, the District of Columbia, and Puerto Rico had lowered the legal blood alcohol concentration (BAC) limit for driving to 0.08 g/dL. The NHTSA estimates that between 1975 and 2008 the minimum drinking age laws reduced traffic fatalities involving drivers aged 18 to 20 years by 13%, saving approximately 27,052 lives. All 50 states and the District of Columbia have zero-tolerance laws for drinking drivers under the age of 21 years. It is illegal for drivers under the age of 21 years to drive with BAC levels of 0.02 g/dl or greater.

TOBACCO AND YOUTH

Health Consequences of Early Tobacco Use

In "Polyphenol Associated-DNA Adducts in Lung and Blood Mononuclear Cells from Lung Cancer Patients" (*Cancer Letters*, vol. 236, no. 1, May 8, 2006), Andrea Várkonyi et al. indicate that the age at which smoking is initiated is a significant factor in the risk of developing lung cancer. Smoking during the teen years appears to cause permanent genetic changes in the lungs, increasing the risk of lung cancer—even if the smoker quits. The younger a person starts smoking, the more lasting damage is done to his or her lungs. Such damage is less likely among smokers who start in their 20s.

Preventing Tobacco Use among Young People: A Report of the Surgeon General (1994, http://profiles.nlm .nih.gov/NN/B/C/L/Q/_/nnbclq.pdf) indicates that cigarette smoking during adolescence seems to retard lung growth and reduce maximum lung function. As a result, young smokers are less likely than their nonsmoking peers to be physically fit and more likely to experience shortness of breath, coughing spells, wheezing, and overall poorer health. These health problems pose a clear risk for developing other chronic conditions in adulthood, such as chronic obstructive pulmonary disease, including emphysema and chronic bronchitis. Early smoking is also linked to an increased risk of cardiovascular diseases, such as high cholesterol and triglyceride levels, atherosclerosis (a hardening of the walls of the arteries caused by the buildup of fatty deposits on the inner walls of the arteries that interferes with blood flow), and early onset of heart disease.

The surgeon general's report also points out that the use of smokeless tobacco has undesirable health effects on young users. Adolescent use is linked to the development of periodontal disease, soft-tissue damage, and oral cancers. In addition, young people who use smokeless tobacco are more likely than their nonusing peers to become cigarette smokers.

Tobacco Regulation and Youth

In June 2009 President Barack Obama (1961–) signed the Family Smoking Prevention and Tobacco Control Act, which granted the U.S. Food and Drug Administration (FDA) the power to regulate the production and marketing of tobacco products. In the fact sheet "The Family Smoking Prevention and Tobacco Control Act of 2009" (June 22, 2009, http://www.whitehouse.gov/the_press_office/Fact-sheet-and-expected-attendees-for-todays-Rose-Garden-bill-signing/), the White House lists key points of the new law. After October 2009 cigarette manufacturers were no longer allowed to produce fruit- and candy-flavored cigarettes, which appealed to adolescents and teens. In June 2010 provisions went into effect that banned marketing tactics that appealed to young smokers, such as advertising cigarettes at sporting events, giving away clothing with cigarette company logos, and distributing free samples of tobacco products to youth.

Age of First Use

Even though the health effects of early tobacco use are known, most cigarette smokers begin their habit early in life. According to Johnston et al., in *Monitoring the Future National Survey Results on Drug Use, 1975–2009, Volume 1*, 10.2% of the eighth graders surveyed in 2009 said they had their first cigarette in the sixth and seventh grades, and 6.9% said they had their first cigarette by the fifth grade. Slightly over 7% percent of the 12th graders who were surveyed said they had their first cigarette by the sixth grade.

Johnston et al. reveal that smokeless tobacco use begins early in life as well. Smokeless tobacco is chewing tobacco or finer-cut tobacco that is inhaled (snuff). The highest rates of initiation in smokeless tobacco use are in grades seven to 11. In 2009, 4.3% of the eighth graders surveyed reported they began using smokeless tobacco by the sixth grade, and 5.3% started by the eighth grade.

Current Use of Tobacco by High School Students

The NSDUH indicates that in 2009, 11.6% of students aged 12 to 17 years used various tobacco products in the month before the survey; that is, they were current users. The use of tobacco products among this age group declined from 15.2% in 2002. This decline was due primarily to the decrease in the use of cigarettes. In 2002, 13% of students aged 12 to 17 years were current cigarette smokers, and by 2009, 8.9% were. Use of other tobacco products (cigars, smokeless tobacco, and pipe tobacco) remained relatively steady. In 2009, 4% of students aged 12 to 17 years were current cigar smokers, 2.3% were smokeless tobacco users, and 0.9% were pipe tobacco users.

In "Youth Risk Behavior Surveillance—United States, 2009," Eaton et al. focus on students in grades nine to 12, not on students aged 12 to 17 years as the NSDUH does. The researchers note that 26% of high school students in 2009 reported current tobacco use. (See Table 5.9.) The NSDUH results are lower (11.6% of 12- to 17-year-olds), but it includes younger students, who are less likely to use tobacco, and it does not include 18-year-olds, who are more likely to use tobacco and who are likely present in Eaton et al.'s cohort of high school seniors. Eaton et al. find that 14% of high school students in 2009 were current cigar smokers (the NSDUH reports 4%) and that 8.9% were current smokeless tobacco users (the NSDUH reports 2.3%). (See Table 5.9 and Table 5.10.) Eaton et al.'s results also show that, in general, tobacco use increases with grade level.

Trends in Prevalence of Cigarette Use in High School Students

In "Youth Risk Behavior Surveillance—United States, 2009," Eaton et al. look for trends in the prevalence of cigarette smoking by high school students between 1991 and 2009. Their results reveal that in 2009, 19.5% of high school students were current cigarette smokers. This rate was down from 27.5% in 1991. Current cigarette smoking rates rose from 1991 to 1997, however, to a high of 36.4% in 1997 before falling in ensuing years to the 2009 level.

What are the causes of the general decrease in current smoking rates among high school students after 1997? In *Monitoring the Future National Survey Results on Drug Use, 1975–2009, Volume 1*, Johnston et al. provide a possible answer to this question: "We think that the extensive adverse publicity generated by the state attorneys general, the President, and Congress in the debate over a possible legal settlement with the tobacco companies contributed importantly to this turnaround by influencing youth attitudes toward cigarette companies and their products. Substantial price increases, the removal of some forms of advertising (such as billboard advertising and the Joe Camel campaign), the implementation of vigorous anti-smoking advertising (particularly that launched by the American Legacy Foundation and some of the states), and strong prevention programs in some states all may have contributed."

According to Eaton et al., lifetime cigarette use among high school students was also lower in 2009 (46.3%) than

TABLE 5.9

Percentage of high school students who smoked cigars and who used tobacco, by gender, ethnicity, and grade, 2009

	Current cigar use			Current tobacco use		
	Female	Male	Total	Female	Male	Total
Category	%	%	%	%	%	%
Race/ethnicity						
White*	8.0	21.0	14.9	24.9	35.1	30.3
Black*	11.5	13.9	12.8	14.5	17.8	16.2
Hispanic	9.5	15.8	12.7	18.1	23.6	20.8
Grade						
9	7.6	11.3	9.6	17.6	20.2	19.0
10	9.5	16.6	13.2	21.9	26.8	24.5
11	8.6	22.4	15.8	22.9	35.4	29.3
12	9.7	26.8	18.5	25.7	40.4	33.1
Total	**8.8**	**18.6**	**14.0**	**21.8**	**29.8**	**26.0**

*Non-Hispanic.
Note: "Smoked" is defined by students who smoked cigars, cigarillos, or little cigars on at least 1 day during the 30 days before the survey. "Used tobacco" is defined by current cigarette use, current smokeless tobacco use, or current cigar use.

SOURCE: Adapted from Danice K. Eaton et. al, "Table 34. Percentage of High School Students Who Currently Smoked Cigars and Who Currently Used Tobacco, by Sex, Race/Ethnicity, and Grade—United States, Youth Risk Behavior Survey, 2009," in "Youth Risk Behavior Surveillance—United States, 2009," *Morbidity & Mortality Weekly Report*, vol. 59, no. SS-5, June 4, 2010, http://www.cdc.gov/mmwr/pdf/ss/ss5905.pdf (accessed November 10, 2010)

TABLE 5.10

Percentage of high school students who used smokeless tobacco and who usually bought cigarettes at a store or gas station, by gender, ethnicity, and grade, 2009

	Bought cigarettes in a store or gas station			Current smokeless tobacco use		
	Female	Male	Total	Female	Male	Total
Category	%	%	%	%	%	%
Race/ethnicity						
White*	8.8	19.0	14.1	2.3	20.1	11.9
Black*	NA	24.8	19.7	1.3	5.2	3.3
Hispanic	11.5	15.0	13.3	2.6	7.5	5.1
Grade						
9	3.5	11.0	7.1	3.2	10.7	7.2
10	9.8	16.8	13.4	1.8	13.9	8.1
11	12.0	18.8	15.8	2.0	18.9	10.7
12	14.9	32.7	23.8	1.7	18.1	10.0
Total	**9.6**	**18.3**	**14.1**	**2.2**	**15.0**	**8.9**

*Non-Hispanic.
NA = Not available.
Notes: "Percentage of students who used smokeless tobacco" is defined by students who during the 30 days before the survey, were among the 15.7% of students nationwide who currently smoked cigarettes and who were under 18 years of age. Tobacco use also includes chewing tobacco, snuff, or dip on at least 1 day during the 30 days before the survey.

SOURCE: Adapted from Danice K. Eaton et. al, "Table 32. Percentage of High School Students Who Usually Obtained Their Own Cigarettes by Buying Them in a Store or Gas Station and Who Currently Used Smokeless Tobacco, by Sex, Race/Ethnicity, and Grade—United States, Youth Risk Behavior Survey, 2009," in "Youth Risk Behavior Surveillance—United States, 2009," *Morbidity & Mortality Weekly Report*, vol. 59, no. SS-5, June 4, 2010, http://www.cdc.gov/mmwr/pdf/ss/ss5905.pdf (accessed November 10, 2010)

in 1991. In 1991, 70.1% of all high school students had tried smoking. The lifetime rates did not begin to fall, however, until 2000. The percentage of high school students who were current, frequent users of cigarettes in 2009 was also down from 1991 (12.7% versus 7.3%), as was the percentage of students who smoked more than 10 cigarettes per day (18% versus 7.8%).

Tobacco Use among College Students and Other Young Adults

In *Monitoring the Future National Survey Results on Drug Use, 1975–2009, Volume 2*, Johnston et al. report on the prevalence of drug use for college students and adults aged 19 to 50 years. In 2009 the rates of current cigarette smoking for young adults was lowest for 18-year-olds (20%) and 19- to 20-year-olds (21%). More of those in the 21- to 30-year-old range were current smokers—23% to 25%. Johnston et al. note that smoking rates for people in their early 20s used to be about the same rate as among high school seniors and then those rates would drop with age, because most smokers began using tobacco while they were in high school. Beginning in 2005, however, smoking rates among high school seniors—as well as among high school students in general—dropped.

Johnston et al. examine the trends in current cigarette smoking among college students and other young adults who were one to four years beyond high school. In 2009 other young adults (31%) had a higher rate of current cigarette use than college students (18%), opposite the results of alcohol use described earlier in this chapter. This difference in current cigarette use between college students

and other young adults of the same age has been documented since 1980.

Demographic Factors in Youth Tobacco Use

GENDER, RACIAL, AND ETHNIC DIFFERENCES. In 2009 high school males (29.8%) were much more likely to currently use various tobacco products than females (21.8%). (See Table 5.9.) They were also much more likely to be current cigar smokers (18.6% for males versus 8.8% for females) and current smokeless tobacco users (15% for males versus 2.2% for females). (See Table 5.10.) According to Johnston et al., in *Monitoring the Future National Survey Results on Drug Use, 1975–2009, Volume 1*, there were similar differences in current smokeless tobacco use in 2009 between males and females in grades eight (6.3% for males versus 1.4% for females), 10 (11.1% versus 2%), and 12 (15.8% versus 1.7%).

Looking at current cigarette use alone, Johnston et al. indicate that male rates of cigarette smoking were higher than that of females in all three grades: eighth grade (6.7% for males versus 6% for females), 10th grade (13.7% versus 12.5%), and 12th grade (22.1% versus 17.6%).

Johnston et al. note in *Monitoring the Future National Survey Results on Drug Use, 1975–2009, Volume 2* that in 2009 male college students (20.9%) had a higher rate of current cigarette smoking than females (16%), but it has not always been that way. From 1980 to 1994 female college students were more likely to be current smokers than male college students. In 1994 their current rates of smoking were the same—nearly 24%.

The rates for both increased during the mid- to late 1990s, with males generally leading females, but then both rates dropped to the 1994 level again in 2005, and dropped even further by 2009.

According to Eaton et al., in "Youth Risk Behavior Surveillance—United States, 2009," non-Hispanic white (30.3%) high school students were more likely than Hispanic (20.8%) or non-Hispanic African-American (16.2%) high school students to be current tobacco users in 2009. (See Table 5.9.) This pattern persisted with current smokeless tobacco use (11.9% of non-Hispanic whites, 5.1% of Hispanics, and 3.3% of non-Hispanic African-Americans). (See Table 5.10.) Non-Hispanic white (14.9%) high school students had the highest prevalence of current cigar smoking, but non-Hispanic African-American (12.8%) and Hispanic (12.7%) high school students had about the same prevalence. (See Table 5.9.)

WHERE STUDENTS LIVE. In *Monitoring the Future National Survey Results on Drug Use, 1975–2009, Volume 1*, Johnston et al. look at population density as a factor in student patterns of tobacco use. Eighth, 10th, and 12th graders who lived in the largest cities in the United States in 2009 (large MSAs such as Boston, New York, and Los Angeles) were the least likely to be current smokers. Those who lived in smaller cities (other MSAs) were somewhat more likely to be current smokers, and those who lived in rural areas (non-MSAs) were the most likely to be current smokers. Mark P. Doescher et al. determine in "Prevalence and Trends in Smoking: A National Rural Study" (*Journal of Rural Health*, vol. 22, no. 2, spring 2006) that "the higher prevalence of smoking in rural areas compared to urban areas … can be explained, in part, by lower levels of income and education attainment among rural residents and by the greater likelihood of rural residents being white or American Indian; both groups have high rates of smoking. Additionally, people with lower levels of income and education who reside in rural counties smoke at slightly higher rates than their urban counterparts."

PARENTAL EDUCATION. Johnston et al. note in *Monitoring the Future National Survey Results on Drug Use, 1975–2009, Volume 1* an inverse relationship between current daily cigarette use in eighth and 10th graders and parental education: the less parental education, the more likely eighth and 10th graders were to be current daily smokers in 2009. This relationship did not hold fully for 12th graders. Seniors whose parents were in the three lowest levels of parental education had higher rates of smoking than did seniors with parents in the second-to-highest educational category. Seniors with parents having the highest level of education had the lowest level of smoking. In addition, students in all three grades who had no college plans or had plans to complete less than four years of college were much more likely to be current

smokers and to have used smokeless tobacco than those students who had plans to complete four years of college.

Perception of Harmfulness of Tobacco Use

Figure 5.3 shows results from the *Pride Surveys Questionnaire Report for Grades 6 to 12, National Summary Statistics for 2009–10*. The report reveals that 69.5% of sixth graders perceived the use of tobacco as "very harmful." The perception of tobacco being "very harmful" decreased with increasing grade level to grade nine. Between 63.3% and 65% of ninth, 10th, 11th, and 12th graders perceived tobacco use as being "very harmful." Thus, a much higher percentage of students in grades six to 12 perceived tobacco use as harmful than the percentage who perceived alcohol use as harmful. (See Figure 5.2.) Even though the perception of risk of tobacco use stayed relatively steady in grades nine to 12, the use of tobacco increased in these grades as the grade level increased. (See Table 5.9.) In addition, Table 5.10 shows that as the grade level increased, a higher proportion of students bought cigarettes in a store or gas station.

ILLICIT DRUGS AND YOUTH
Age of First Use

The use of alcohol and tobacco often begins early in life; the initiation data are presented previously in this chapter. Regarding the initiation of other drugs, Johnston et al. reveal in *Monitoring the Future National Survey Results on Drug Use, 1975–2009, Volume 1* that inhalants and marijuana are the drugs next most likely to be initiated early in life. Peak initiation rates for illicit drugs other than marijuana generally do not occur until grades nine to 11 in high school, and initiation rates for cocaine and crack cocaine generally occur in grades 10 to 12. Johnston et al. state:

> Of all 12th graders who reported prior use of any drug, the proportion reporting an initial use of that drug *by the end of grade 9* is presented here. This listing is a good indicator of the order of age initiation:

- inhalants (63%)
- cigarettes (62%)
- alcohol (55%)
- crack (46%)
- marijuana (46%)
- sedatives (barbiturates) (46%)
- smokeless tobacco (45%)
- been drunk (43%)
- daily cigarette smoking (42%)
- heroin (42%)
- amphetamines (39%)
- narcotics other than heroin (35%)

FIGURE 5.3

Harmfulness of tobacco use as perceived by students in grades 6–12, 2009–10

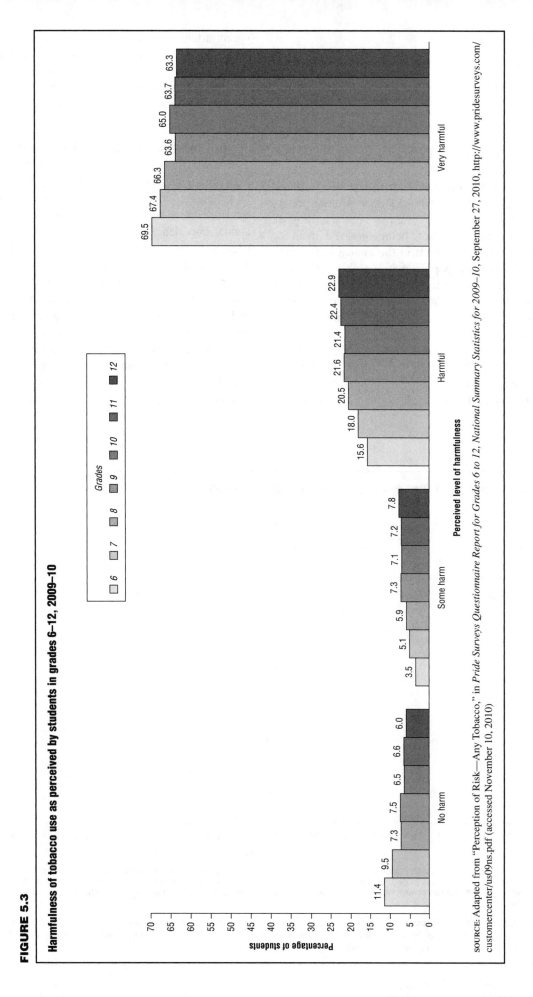

SOURCE: Adapted from "Perception of Risk—Any Tobacco," in *Pride Surveys Questionnaire Report for Grades 6 to 12, National Summary Statistics for 2009–10,* September 27, 2010, http://www.pridesurveys.com/customercenter/us09ns.pdf (accessed November 10, 2010)

- tranquilizers (34%)

- other forms of cocaine (32%)

- cocaine (32%)

- LSD (29%)

- hallucinogens (24%)

- hallucinogens other than LSD (24%)

Trends in Annual Prevalence of Drug Use in Youth

TRENDS ACROSS FIVE POPULATIONS. Annual prevalence means that a person has tried a particular drug at least once during the year before being surveyed about its use. Figure 5.4 compares trends in the annual prevalence of drug use across five populations: eighth-, 10th-, and 12th-grade students, full-time college students aged 19 to 22 years, and all young adults through the age of 28 years who are high school graduates (a group that includes college students). During the early 1980s the rates of drug use decreased, and college students had a higher rate of drug use than high school seniors. By the mid-1980s the annual prevalence of drug use of these two groups was somewhat equivalent. During the late 1980s, when data for young adults were added, the annual prevalence rates of drug use in all three groups declined dramatically. The annual prevalence of drug use by college students and 12th graders was about the same during those years, and the annual prevalence of drug use by young adults was slightly lower.

In 1991 data for eighth and 10th graders were added. The annual prevalence of drug use rose dramatically for high school students for several years, but the increase was less dramatic for college students. The annual prevalence of drug use increase for young adults was minor. Thus, the annual prevalence of drug use for 10th and 12th graders became higher than the annual prevalence for college students and young adults. Around 1998 the annual prevalence of drug use for 12th graders began to slowly drop. It dropped, then rose, then dropped again for 10th graders, and it dropped dramatically for eighth graders. However, the annual prevalence rates continued to slowly climb for young adults and eventually dropped somewhat for college students. In 2005 the annual prevalence rate of drug use was the highest for 12th graders at nearly 40%, followed by college students at about 38%, young adults at about 33%,

FIGURE 5.4

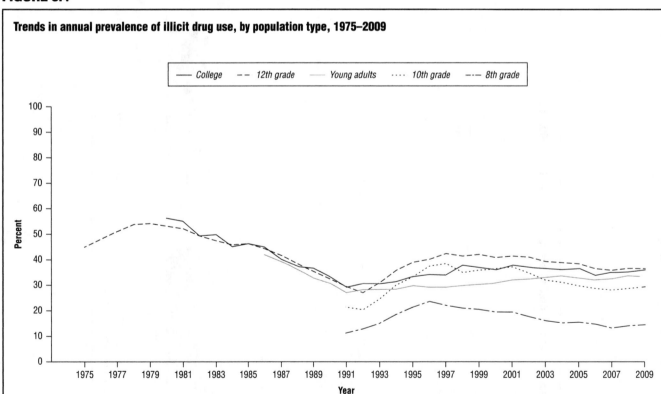

Trends in annual prevalence of illicit drug use, by population type, 1975–2009

Notes: "Illicit drug use index" includes any use of marijuana, LSD, other hallucinogens, crack, other cocaine, or heroin; or any use which is not under a doctor's orders of narcotics other than heroin, stimulants, sedatives (barbiturates), methaqualone (excluded since 1990), or tranquilizers. Beginning in 1982, the question about stimulant use (i.e., amphetamines) was revised to get respondents to exclude the inappropriate reporting of nonprescription stimulants. The prevalence rate dropped slightly as a result of this methodological change.

SOURCE: Lloyd D. Johnston et al., "Figure 2-1. Trends in Annual Prevalence of an Illicit Drug Use Index across 5 Populations," in *Monitoring the Future National Survey Results on Drug Use, 1975–2009: Volume II, College Students and Adults Ages 19–50*, National Institute on Drug Abuse, 2010, http://monitoringthefuture.org/pubs/monographs/vol2_2009.pdf (accessed December 2, 2010).

10th graders at about 30%, and eighth graders at about 17%. By 2009 the rates for all three groups of high school students had dropped somewhat from the 2005 rates, whereas the rates for college students and young adults had increased slightly.

TRENDS IN INHALANT USE IN HIGH SCHOOL STUDENTS. Inhalants have a high early initiation rate. According to Johnston et al., in *Monitoring the Future National Survey Results on Drug Use, 1975–2009, Volume 1*, of all the 12th graders who reported prior use of any drug in 2009, 63% reported an initial use of inhalants by the end of the ninth grade. Inhalants are volatile liquids, such as cleaning fluids, glue, gasoline, paint, and turpentine, the vapors of which are inhaled. Sometimes the sprays of aerosols are inhaled, such as those of spray paints, spray deodorants, hair spray, or fabric protector spray. These products are legal and easily accessible.

Figure 5.5 shows trends in annual prevalence of inhalant use for eighth, 10th, and 12th graders. Since 1991, when data collection began for all three of these grade levels, eighth graders have had the highest annual prevalence of inhalant use, followed by 10th graders and then 12th graders. Between 1991 and 1995 the annual prevalence of inhalant use rose by more than one-third among eighth and 10th graders to reach 12.8% and 9.6%, respectively, and rose by about one-fifth among 12th graders to reach 8%. The annual prevalence rates for inhalant use then fell through 2002 for eighth graders to 7.7%, and through 2003 for 10th and 12th graders to 5.4% and 3.9%, respectively. Rates rose quite steeply for eighth graders from 2002 until 2004, reaching 9.6%, then dropping to 8.1% by 2009. Rates rose less dramatically through 2005 for 10th and 12th graders to 6% and 5%, respectively. Rates stayed relatively steady for 10th graders through 2009 (6.1%), but they dropped for 12th graders to 3.4%.

TRENDS IN MARIJUANA USE IN HIGH SCHOOL STUDENTS. Besides inhalants, marijuana is one of the first drugs tried by high school students. Figure 5.6 shows results from the *Pride Surveys Questionnaire Report for Grades 6 to 12, National Summary Statistics for 2009–10*. The report reveals that between 41.1% and 77.3% of students in all grades perceived the use of marijuana as "very harmful." Only a small proportion of students (between 12.2% and 20%) thought that marijuana use posed "no harm" to the individual. Johnston et al. indicate in *Monitoring the Future National Survey Results on Drug Use, 1975–2009, Volume 1* that even though the perception of risk of illicit drug use was high, of all the 12th graders who reported prior use of any drug in 2009, 46% reported an initial use of marijuana by the end of the ninth grade. Figure 5.6 shows that 57.5% of ninth graders believed marijuana use to be "very harmful."

Figure 5.7 shows trends in annual prevalence rates of marijuana use for eighth, 10th, and 12th graders. Since 1991, when data collection began for all three of these grade levels, 12th graders have had the highest annual

prevalence of marijuana use, followed by 10th graders and then eighth graders. The annual prevalence rate of marijuana use for eighth graders rose from 1991 to 1996, reaching 18.3%. The rate then dropped steadily to 11.8% in 2004 and to 10.3% in 2007 but rose again to 11.8% in 2009. For 10th and 12th graders the annual prevalence rates of marijuana use rose from 1992 to 1997, reaching 34.8% and 38.5%, respectively. The rates for both held relatively steady from 1998 to 2001 and then dropped to the 2007 levels of 24.6% and 31.7%, respectively. In 2009 the rates for 10th and 12th graders rose to 26.7% and 32.8%, respectively.

TRENDS IN TRANQUILIZER USE IN HIGH SCHOOL STUDENTS. In *Monitoring the Future National Survey Results on Drug Use, 1975–2009, Volume 1*, Johnston et al. state that of all the 12th graders who reported prior use of any drug in 2009, 34% reported an initial use of tranquilizers by the end of the ninth grade. Tranquilizers are drugs that are prescribed by a physician to relieve a patient's tension and anxiety. Drugs such as diazepam, chlordiazepoxide, and alprazolam are tranquilizers. This type of illicit drug does not have a high rate of early initiation as inhalants and marijuana do.

Figure 5.8 shows trends in annual prevalence rates of illicit tranquilizer use for eighth, 10th, and 12th graders. Since 1991, when data collection began for all three of these grade levels, 10th and 12th graders have had the highest prevalence of use. Eighth graders have had a lower annual prevalence rate of tranquilizer use. The annual prevalence rate for eighth graders rose slowly from 1.8% in 1991 to 3.3% in 1996. The rate then declined slightly to 2.9% in 1997 and then leveled off. The 2009 annual prevalence rate for tranquilizer use by eighth graders was 2.6%.

For 10th graders the annual prevalence rate remained fairly steady from 1991 to 1994. (See Figure 5.8.) The rate then rose steadily from 3.3% in 1994 to 7.3% in 2001, then declined to 4.8% in 2005. In 2009 the annual prevalence rate of tranquilizer use in 10th graders was 5%. For 12th graders the annual prevalence rate fell from 3.6% in 1991 to 2.8% in 1992. The rate then rose steadily from 1992, reaching 7.7% in 2002. It then declined in 2003, rose in 2004, and declined again in 2005. The 2009 annual prevalence rate of tranquilizer use in 12th graders was 6.3%.

TRENDS IN AMPHETAMINE USE IN HIGH SCHOOL STUDENTS. Johnston et al. explain in *Monitoring the Future National Survey Results on Drug Use, 1975–2009, Volume 1* that of all the 12th graders who reported prior use of any drug in 2009, 39% reported an initial use of amphetamines by the end of the ninth grade. Amphetamines are stimulants (uppers), drugs that produce a sense of euphoria or wakefulness. They are used to increase alertness, boost endurance and productivity, and

FIGURE 5.5

Trends in annual prevalence of inhalant use among eighth, tenth, and twelfth graders, selected years 1975–2009

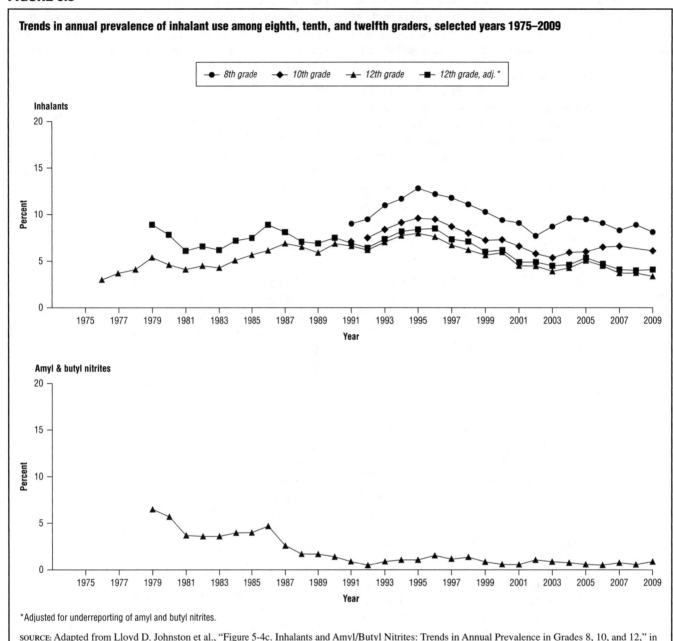

*Adjusted for underreporting of amyl and butyl nitrites.

SOURCE: Adapted from Lloyd D. Johnston et al., "Figure 5-4c. Inhalants and Amyl/Butyl Nitrites: Trends in Annual Prevalence in Grades 8, 10, and 12," in *Monitoring the Future National Survey Results on Drug Use, 1975–2009: Volume 1, Secondary School Students*, National Institute on Drug Abuse, 2010, http://monitoringthefuture.org/pubs/monographs/vol1_2009.pdf (accessed November 9, 2010)

suppress the appetite. Other stimulants include caffeine, nicotine, methamphetamine, and cocaine.

Figure 5.9 shows trends in annual prevalence rates of amphetamine use for eighth, 10th, and 12th graders. Since 1991, when data collection began for all three of these grade levels, 10th and 12th graders have had the highest rate of use. From 1992 to 2001, 10th-grade annual prevalence rates were higher than 12th-grade rates. From 1991 to 2009, eighth-grade annual prevalence rates were consistently lower than those of their older classmates.

The annual prevalence rate for eighth graders rose from 6.2% in 1991 to 9.1% in 1996. (See Figure 5.9.)

The rate then declined to 6.9% in 1999 and then declined in short plateaus to 4.1% in 2009. For 10th graders the annual prevalence rate rose from 8.2% in 1991 to 11.7% in 2001, and then declined to 7.1% in 2009. For 12th graders the annual prevalence rate of amphetamine use generally rose throughout the 1990s and after 2000 in a slight up-and-down fashion, from 8.2% in 1991 to 11.1% in 2002. After 2002 the annual prevalence rate of amphetamine use in 12th graders declined to 6.6% in 2009.

TRENDS IN HALLUCINOGEN USE IN HIGH SCHOOL STUDENTS. In *Monitoring the Future National Survey Results on Drug Use, 1975–2009, Volume 1*, Johnston et al. note that of all the 12th graders who reported prior

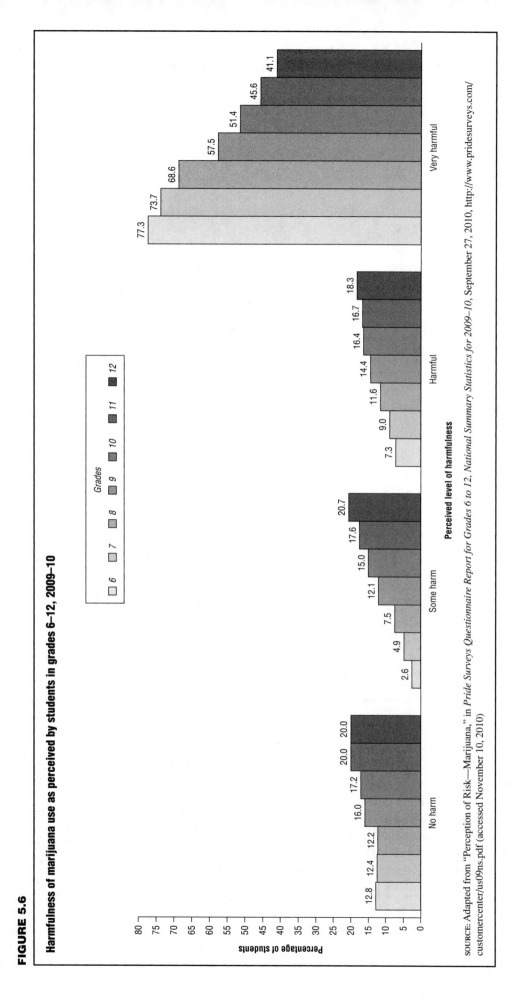

FIGURE 5.6

Harmfulness of marijuana use as perceived by students in grades 6–12, 2009–10

Grades

☐ 6   ☐ 7   ☐ 8   ☐ 9   ☐ 10   ☐ 11   ☐ 12

Percentage of students

Perceived level of harmfulness

No harm: 12.8, 12.4, 12.2, 16.0, 17.2, 20.0, 20.0

Some harm: 2.6, 4.9, 7.5, 12.1, 15.0, 17.6, 20.7

Harmful: 7.3, 9.0, 11.6, 14.4, 16.4, 16.7, 18.3

Very harmful: 77.3, 73.7, 68.6, 57.5, 51.4, 45.6, 41.1

SOURCE: Adapted from "Perception of Risk—Marijuana," in *Pride Surveys Questionnaire Report for Grades 6 to 12, National Summary Statistics for 2009–10*, September 27, 2010, http://www.pridesurveys.com/customercenter/us09ns.pdf (accessed November 10, 2010)

FIGURE 5.7

Trends in annual prevalence of marijuana use among eighth, tenth, and twelfth graders, selected years 1975–2009

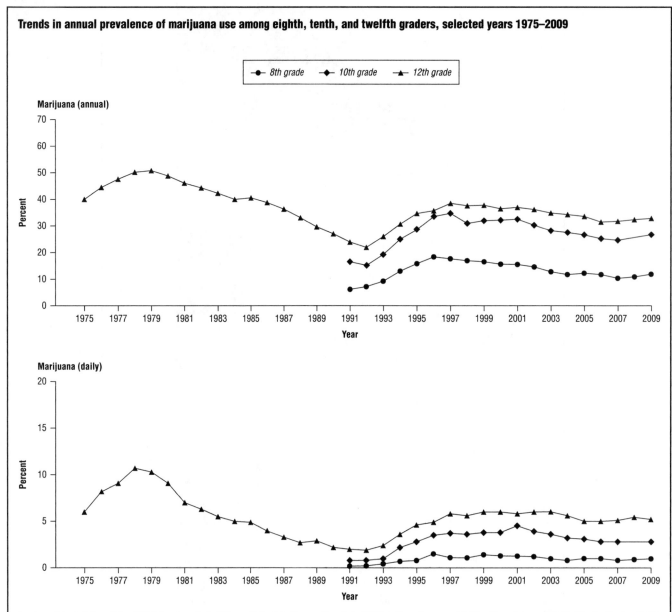

SOURCE: Adapted from Lloyd D. Johnston et al., "Figure 5-4a. Marijuana: Trends in 30-Day Prevalence and 3-Day Prevalence of Daily Use in Grades 8, 10, and 12," in *Monitoring the Future National Survey Results on Drug Use, 1975–2009: Volume 1, Secondary School Students*, National Institute on Drug Abuse, 2010, http://monitoringthefuture.org/pubs/monographs/vol1_2009.pdf (accessed November 9, 2010)

use of any drug in 2009, 24% reported an initial use of hallucinogens by the end of the ninth grade, and 24% the use of hallucinogens other than lysergic acid diethylamide (LSD) by the end of the ninth grade. Hallucinogens, also known as psychedelics, distort the perception of reality. They cause excitation, which can vary from a sense of well-being to severe depression. The experience may be pleasurable or quite frightening. The effects of hallucinogens vary from use to use and cannot be predicted.

Figure 5.10 shows trends in the annual prevalence rates of hallucinogen use for eighth, 10th, and 12th graders. Since 1991, when data collection began for all

three of these grade levels, 12th graders have had the highest annual prevalence of hallucinogen use, followed by 10th graders and then eighth graders.

The annual prevalence rate of hallucinogen use for eighth graders rose from 1.9% in 1991 to 4.1% in 1996. (See Figure 5.10.) The rate declined to 2.2% in 2004 and then slightly rose to 2.4% in 2005. The rate then declined and stabilized from 1.9% to 2.1%, remaining at 1.9% in 2009. The trend patterns of annual prevalence rates of hallucinogen use for 10th and 12th graders were similar to that of eighth graders and to each other. The annual prevalence rates rose from 4% in 1991 to 7.8% in 1996 for 10th graders and from 5.8% in 1991 to 10.1% in 1996

FIGURE 5.8

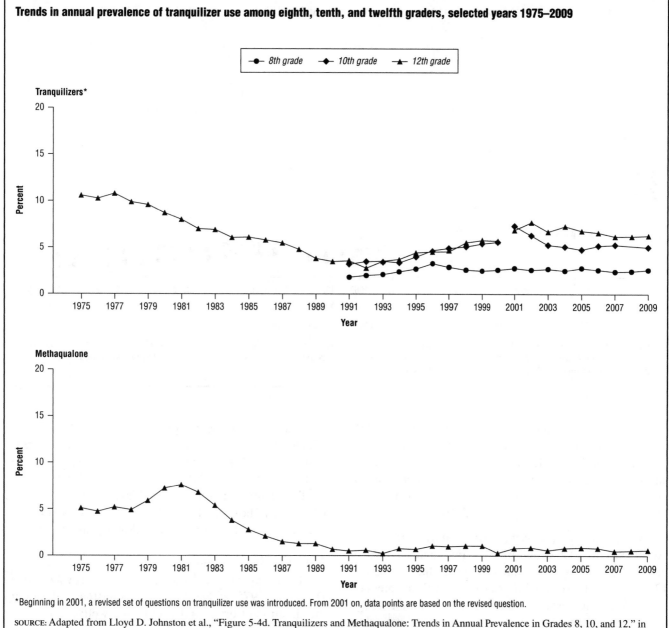

Trends in annual prevalence of tranquilizer use among eighth, tenth, and twelfth graders, selected years 1975–2009

*Beginning in 2001, a revised set of questions on tranquilizer use was introduced. From 2001 on, data points are based on the revised question.

SOURCE: Adapted from Lloyd D. Johnston et al., "Figure 5-4d. Tranquilizers and Methaqualone: Trends in Annual Prevalence in Grades 8, 10, and 12," in *Monitoring the Future National Survey Results on Drug Use, 1975–2009: Volume 1, Secondary School Students*, National Institute on Drug Abuse, 2010, http://monitoringthefuture.org/pubs/monographs/vol1_2009.pdf (accessed November 9, 2010)

for 12th graders. The rates for both grades then declined through 2003 to 4.1% and 5.9%, respectively. For 10th graders the rate stayed relatively steady through 2009. The rate in that year was 4.1%. For 12th graders the rate rose slightly in 2004, dropped through 2006, rose through 2008, and then declined to 4.7% in 2009.

TRENDS IN MDMA USE IN HIGH SCHOOL STUDENTS. MDMA (3,4-methylenedioxy-methamphetamine), or ecstasy, is a mind-altering drug with hallucinogenic properties. It is related to amphetamine and is made in laboratories by making minor modifications in the chemical structure of this drug. Thus, it is called a designer drug and is one of the most popular of this type of drug.

Figure 5.11 shows trends in the annual prevalence rates of ecstasy use for eighth, 10th, and 12th graders. Since 1996, when data collection began for this drug, 12th graders have had the highest annual prevalence of ecstasy use, followed by 10th graders and then eighth graders.

The annual prevalence rate of MDMA use for eighth graders declined initially from 2.3% in 1996 and 1997 to 1.7% in 1999. (See Figure 5.11.) The rate then peaked in 2001 at 3.5% but then dropped significantly through 2006 to 1.4%, and rose to 1.7% in 2008. In 2009 the rate dropped to 1.3%. The trend patterns of annual prevalence rates of MDMA use for 10th and 12th graders were similar to that of eighth graders and to each other, with

FIGURE 5.9

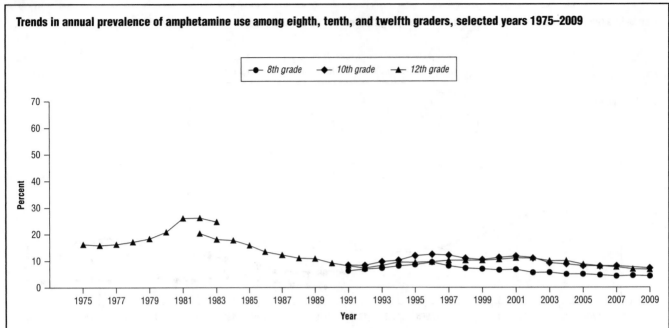

Trends in annual prevalence of amphetamine use among eighth, tenth, and twelfth graders, selected years 1975–2009

Note: Beginning in 1982, the lines connect percentages that result if nonprescription stimulants are excluded.

SOURCE: Lloyd D. Johnston et al., "Figure 5-4b. Amphetamines: Trends in Annual Prevalence in Grades 8, 10, and 12," in *Monitoring the Future National Survey Results on Drug Use, 1975–2009: Volume 1, Secondary School Students*, National Institute on Drug Abuse, 2010, http://monitoringthefuture.org/pubs/monographs/vol1_2009.pdf (accessed November 9, 2010)

an initial drop, a sharp peak in 2001, a drop through 2004 and 2005, and then an increase through 2007. After a drop in 2008, the rate for 10th graders was 3.7% in 2009 and for 12th graders was 4.3%. The peak annual prevalence rate for MDMA use for 10th graders was 6.2% and for 12th graders was 9.2%, both in 2001.

ABUSE OF NONPRESCRIPTION COUGH AND COLD MEDICINES. In 2006 Monitoring the Future added dextromethorphan to its questionnaires for eighth, 10th, and 12th graders. Dextromethorphan is a cough suppressant that is found in over-the-counter (nonprescription) cough and cold remedies. Students were asked how often they took cough or cold medicines to get high. In *Monitoring the Future National Survey Results on Drug Use, 1975–2009, Volume 1*, Johnston et al. note that 4.2% of eighth graders, 5.3% of 10th graders, and 6.9% of 12th graders were current abusers of this drug in 2006. In 2009 the rates were similar, at 3.8%, 6%, and 5.9%, respectively.

Current, Past-Year, and Lifetime Use of Illicit Drugs in Youth

The NSDUH indicates that young people had the highest rate of current illicit drug use in the U.S. population in 2009. The rate of current drug use starting with 12-year-olds increased with age, peaking with 18- to 20-year-olds, who had a current drug use rate of 22.2%. The rate of illicit drug use then generally declined with age.

The NSDUH also compares age groups 12 to 17, 18 to 25, and 26 and older regarding their past-month (current), past-year, and lifetime prevalence of drug use. Those aged 18 to 25 years showed the highest rates of illicit drug use in all categories in both 2008 and 2009. (See Table 4.1 in Chapter 4.) Those aged 12 to 17 years had the next highest prevalence rate for past-month and past-year drug use.

A Youth Phenomenon

In *Monitoring the Future National Survey Results on Drug Use, 1975–20007, Volume 1*, Johnston et al. sum up the situation of drugs and youth quite well:

> Young people are often at the leading edge of social change, and this has been particularly true of drug use. The massive upsurge in illicit drug use during the last 35 to 40 years has proven to be a youth phenomenon, and MTF documented that the relapse in the drug epidemic in the early 1990s initially occurred almost exclusively among adolescents. Adolescents and adults in their 20s fall into the age groups at highest risk for illicit drug use; moreover, for some drug users, use that begins in adolescence continues well into adulthood. The original epidemic of illicit drug use began on the nation's college campuses and then spread downward in age, but the more recent relapse phase first manifested itself among secondary school students and then started moving upward in age as those cohorts matured.

FIGURE 5.10

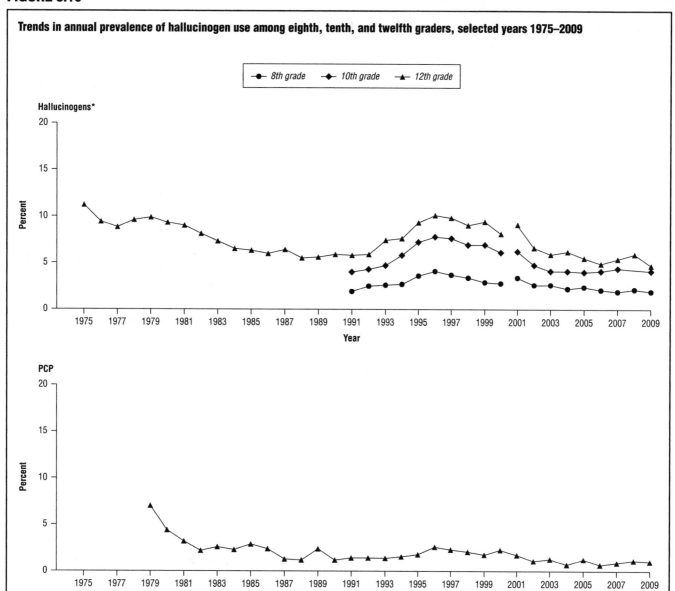

Trends in annual prevalence of hallucinogen use among eighth, tenth, and twelfth graders, selected years 1975–2009

*In 2001, a revised set of questions on other hallucinogen use was introduced. Data for hallucinogens were affected by these changes. From 2001 on, data points are based on the revised questions.

SOURCE: Adapted from Lloyd D. Johnston et al., "Figure 5-4f. Hallucinogens and PCP: Trends in Annual Prevalence in Grades 8, 10, and 12," in *Monitoring the Future National Survey Results on Drug Use, 1975–2009: Volume 1, Secondary School Students*, National Institute on Drug Abuse, 2010, http://monitoringthefuture.org/pubs/monographs/vol1_2009.pdf (accessed November 9, 2010)

FIGURE 5.11

Trends in annual prevalence of ecstasy (MDMA) use among eighth, tenth, and twelfth graders, selected years 1975–2009

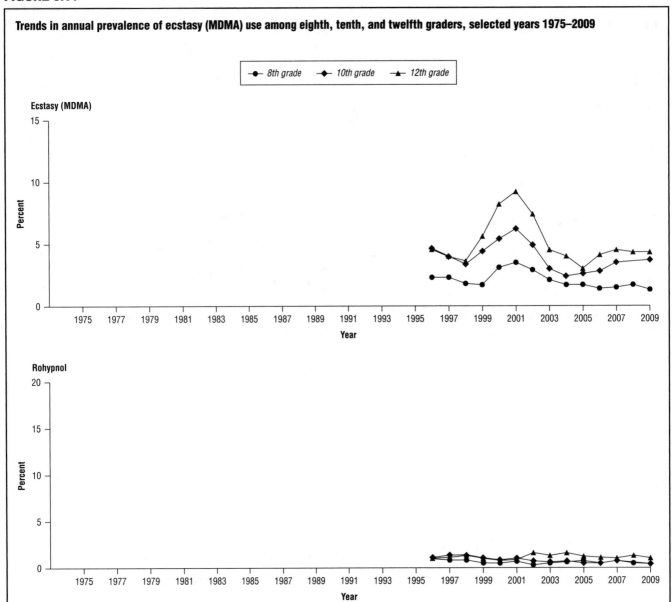

SOURCE: Adapted from Lloyd D. Johnston et al., "Figure 5-4l. Ecstasy (MDMA) and Rohypnol: Trends in Annual Prevalence in Grades 8, 10, and 12," in *Monitoring the Future National Survey Results on Drug Use, 1975–2009: Volume 1, Secondary School Students*, National Institute on Drug Abuse, 2010, http://monitoringthefuture.org/pubs/monographs/vol1_2009.pdf (accessed November 9, 2010)

CHAPTER 6
DRUG TREATMENT

DRUG ABUSE AND ADDICTION
Psychiatric Definition

Even though not all experts agree on a single definition of drug addiction, the American Psychiatric Association's (APA) *Diagnostic and Statistical Manual of Mental Disorders-IV Text Revision* (*DSM-IV-TR*; 2000) is the most widely used reference for diagnosing and treating mental illness and substance-related disorders. In the *DSM-IV-TR*, the APA draws a distinction between the terms *substance abuse* and *substance dependence*. It stresses that these terms should not be used interchangeably.

As mentioned in Chapter 1, the *DSM-IV-TR* requires that at least one of the following conditions be met within the year prior before a person can be diagnosed as a substance abuser:

- The person has repeatedly failed to live up to major obligations, such as on the job, at school, or in the family, because of drug use

- The person has used the substance in dangerous situations, such as before driving

- The person has had multiple legal problems because of drug use

- The person continues to use drugs in the face of interpersonal problems, such as arguments or fights caused by substance use

The *DSM-IV-TR* requires that at least three of the following conditions be met during the previous year before a person can be said to be substance dependent (drug addicted):

- Increased tolerance, withdrawal, loss of control over the quantity or duration of use

- An ongoing wish or inability to decrease use

- Inordinate amounts of time spent procuring or consuming drugs or recovering from substance use

- Important goals or activities given up because of substance use

- Substance use continued despite knowledge experiencing damaging effects

The National Institute on Drug Abuse Definition

In *Drugs, Brains, and Behavior: The Science of Addiction* (February 2008, http://www.drugabuse.gov/Scienceof Addiction/sciofaddiction.pdf), the National Institute on Drug Abuse (NIDA) answers the question "What is drug addiction?" the following way: "Addiction is defined as a chronic, relapsing brain disease that is characterized by compulsive drug seeking and use, despite harmful consequences. It is considered a brain disease because drugs change the brain—they change its structure and how it works. These brain changes can be long lasting, and can lead to the harmful behaviors seen in people who abuse drugs.... Addiction is similar to other diseases, such as heart disease. Both disrupt the normal, healthy functioning of the underlying organ, have serious harmful consequences, are preventable, treatable, and if left untreated, can last a lifetime."

Disease Model of Addiction

Beginning in the 1980s advances in neuroscience led to a new understanding of how people become addicted to drugs and why they stay that way. As reflected in the NIDA definition, most psychiatric and medical researchers espouse the disease model of addiction. Addicts, they say, respond to drugs differently than people who are not addicted. Much of the difference is associated with differences in brain functioning and can be linked to genetic factors. According to George R. Uhl et al., in "Molecular Genetics of Addiction and Related Heritable Phenotypes" (*Annals of the New York Academy of Sciences*, vol. 1141, October 2008), drug addiction is a disease that is linked to the effects of many genes as well as to environmental factors. Approaches to treatment emphasize that addiction must be treated in the same way as other chronic diseases.

In "Evidence-Based Treatments of Addiction" (*Philosophical Transactions of the Royal Society*, vol. 363, no. 1507, October 12, 2008), Charles P. O'Brien of the University of Pennsylvania points out that modern definitions of addiction (such as the NIDA definition) emphasize "uncontrolled drug use rather than tolerance and physiological dependence as essential features of the disorder." He adds that "it is generally recognized that addiction has strong hereditary influences and once established, it behaves as a chronic brain disorder with relapses and remissions over the long term." To help understand this pattern of compulsive behavior and its importance, O'Brien suggests that one only need to think of a friend, relative, or acquaintance who has tried to give up smoking only to relapse at some later time, and probably multiple times, into compulsive smoking behavior while knowing full well the health consequences of his or her actions.

An Integrated Approach to Treatment

The modern approach to treatment has come to reflect the complexity of the drug abuse-addiction spectrum and combines medical approaches, behavior modification, education, and social support functions that are intended to redress imbalances in the patient's total environment. The components of a comprehensive drug treatment approach are shown in Figure 6.1. Arrayed in the center are categories of treatment used alone or in combination and, on the periphery, social service functions that may have to be deployed to solve some of the patient's problems that led to drug use or addiction in the first place.

HOW MANY PEOPLE ARE BEING TREATED?
N-SSATS Data

The Substance Abuse and Mental Health Services Administration (SAMHSA) has been collecting data on substance abuse facilities since 1976. One of its current programs is the National Survey of Substance Abuse Treatment Services (N-SSATS). The N-SSATS numbers represent a snapshot of the treatment units on a particular day and do not indicate how many people are being treated over the course of an entire year.

SAMHSA reports in *National Survey of Substance Abuse Treatment Services (N-SSATS): 2009, Data on*

FIGURE 6.1

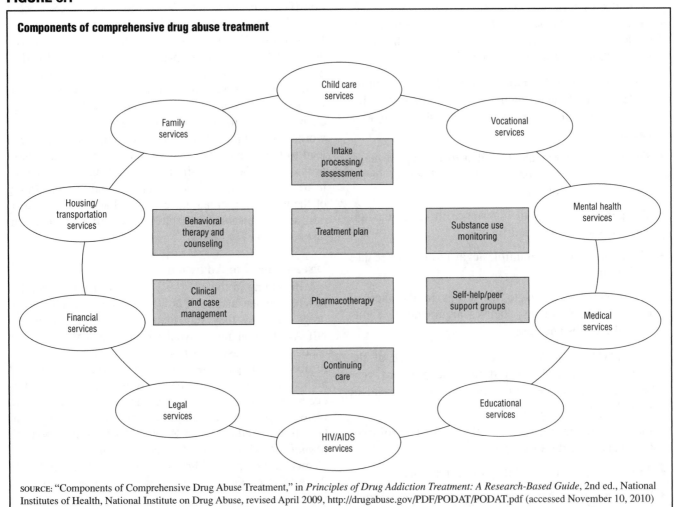

Components of comprehensive drug abuse treatment

SOURCE: "Components of Comprehensive Drug Abuse Treatment," in *Principles of Drug Addiction Treatment: A Research-Based Guide*, 2nd ed., National Institutes of Health, National Institute on Drug Abuse, revised April 2009, http://drugabuse.gov/PDF/PODAT/PODAT.pdf (accessed November 10, 2010)

Substance Abuse Treatment Facilities (June 2010, http://wwwdasis.samhsa.gov/09nssats/nssats2k9web.pdf) that as of March 31, 2009, the number of people in the treatment facilities that responded to the N-SSATS stood at nearly 1.2 million. (See Table 6.1.)

NSDUH Data

To collect data from people who seek and receive substance abuse treatment, SAMHSA included questions about treatment in its 2009 National Survey on Drug Use and Health (NSDUH) and published its findings in *Results from the 2009 National Survey on Drug Use and Health: Volume I. Summary of National Findings* (September 2010, http://www.oas.samhsa.gov/NSDUH/2k9NSDUH/2k9ResultsP.pdf). Figure 6.2 shows the results of asking recipients where they received treatment for substance use in the past year at any location. People could report receiving treatment at more than one location. (This definition of treatment location is different from the specific treatment facilities that reported to SAMHSA for the N-SSATS.) The NSDUH determines that self-help groups, outpatient rehabilitation facilities, inpatient rehabilitation facilities, outpatient mental health centers, and hospital inpatient facilities are where people said they most commonly received treatment in 2009.

The NSDUH also asked substance abusers why they did not receive the treatment they needed. SAMHSA data show that 23.5 million people aged 12 years and older needed treatment in 2009, but only a fraction of those people (2.6 million) received treatment at a specialty facility. Based on 2006–09 combined data, among people who needed but did not receive treatment, most (36.8%) cited financial reasons for not receiving treatment. (See Figure 6.3.) Nearly one-third (30.5%) admitted they were not yet ready to give up drugs.

Treatment Episode Data Set Data

Another source of data for the drug-treatment population comes from SAMHSA's Treatment Episode Data Set (TEDS). This program counts admissions over the period of a year rather than the number of people in treatment on a particular day during the year. When the same person is admitted two or more times during the same year, he or she is counted for each of those admissions, whereas the N-SSATS counts individuals only once. SAMHSA reports in *Treatment Episode Data Set (TEDS) 1998–2008: National Admissions to Substance Abuse Treatment Services* (April 2010, http://wwwdasis.samhsa.gov/teds08/teds2k8natweb.pdf) that there were 1.9 million TEDS admissions in 2008.

CHARACTERISTICS OF THOSE ADMITTED

TEDS data from 1998 to 2008 on admissions by sex, age, race, and ethnicity are presented in Table 6.2 and Table 6.3.

Gender

Males represented most of those who were admitted for drug and/or alcohol treatment, although the percentage of men dropped slightly between 1998 and 2008 (from 70.3% to 67.9%) and that of women increased (from 29.4% to 32.1%). (See Table 6.2.) The number of males admitted for treatment in 2008 was nearly 1.3 million versus 606,503 female admissions. These results and data reflect that a greater proportion of men abuse drugs than women in the United States. According to Table 4.1 in Chapter 4, 9.9% of males were past-month (current) users in 2008 and 10.8% in 2009, compared with 6.3% of females in 2008 and 6.6% in 2009.

Age

In 1998, 35- to 39-year-olds (18.5% of total) accounted for the largest percentage receiving substance abuse treatment, followed by those aged 30 to 34 years (17.1%). (See Table 6.2.) Ten years later the two largest groups receiving treatment were those aged 25 to 29 years (14.8%) and 20 to 24 years (14.4%). Those aged 65 years and older were the least represented, accounting for 0.7% in 1998 and 0.6% in 2008.

Race and Ethnicity

Most of those admitted to substance abuse treatment facilities in 2008 were non-Hispanic white (59.8%), and non-Hispanic whites were admitted in the greatest numbers (1.1 million). (See Table 6.3.) They were followed by non-Hispanic African-Americans at 20.9% (388,363). Compared with data from 1998, non-Hispanic whites increased slightly from 59.5% and increased in number from 1 million, and non-Hispanic African-Americans decreased in percentage, from 24.9%, and in number, from 418,094. Hispanics increased their proportion of admissions to drug treatment facilities from 11.4% (190,886) in 1998 to 13.7% (254,036) in 2008. Native Americans or Alaskan natives dropped in share of those treated from 2.4% (40,303) to 2.3% (42,199) during this period. Asian-Americans or Pacific Islanders increased from 0.7% (11,485) of the total admissions in 1998 to 1% (18,325) in 2008.

TYPES OF TREATMENT

The disease model of addiction described at the beginning of this chapter, which views drug addiction as a chronic disease, views long-term treatment as necessary. O'Brien notes that "as is the case with other chronic diseases, when the treatment is ended, relapse eventually occurs in most cases."

Detoxification is usually a precursor to rehabilitation because that process cannot begin until the individual's body has been cleared of the drug and a certain physiological equilibrium has been established. Drug rehabilitation

TABLE 6.1

Persons admitted into substance abuse treatment, by state or region and type of care received, as of March 31, 2009

State or jurisdiction*	Total	Total out patient	Outpatient Regular	Intensive	Day treatment or partial hospitalization	Detox	Methadone/ buprenorphine maintenance	Total residential	Residential (non-hospital) Short-term	Long-term	Detox	Total hospital inpatient	Hospital inpatient Treatment	Detox
Total	**1,182,077**	**1,064,562**	**598,282**	**147,132**	**23,822**	**10,786**	**284,540**	**103,174**	**25,807**	**71,300**	**6,067**	**14,341**	**7,914**	**6,427**
Alabama	15,820	14,669	3,628	3,984	154	81	6,822	809	231	507	71	342	287	55
Alaska	3,464	3,063	2,162	675	75	8	143	400	200	188	12	1	1	‡
Arizona	29,994	28,495	18,397	4,388	267	366	5,077	1,266	300	880	86	233	140	93
Arkansas	3,721	2,737	1,422	643	108	20	544	949	328	532	89	35	24	11
California	137,960	118,165	69,185	15,429	3,261	2,038	28,252	18,822	2,743	15,081	998	973	536	437
Colorado	39,179	37,713	33,738	2,386	105	121	1,363	1,374	488	739	147	92	60	32
Connecticut	24,831	23,166	8,967	2,230	418	361	11,190	1,320	380	887	53	345	173	172
Delaware	4,117	3,860	1,990	122	79	4	1,665	192	—	178	14	65	30	35
District of Columbia	5,410	5,006	2,414	769	456	66	1,301	383	109	250	24	21	—	21
Fed. of Micronesia	‡	‡	‡	‡	‡	‡	‡	‡	‡	‡	‡	‡	‡	‡
Florida	49,975	43,836	26,768	2,384	1,621	689	12,374	5,344	1,295	3,672	377	795	458	337
Georgia	19,237	16,483	7,791	1,461	891	340	6,000	2,414	549	1,631	234	340	173	167
Guam	183	142	81	50	4	3	4	37	28	3	6	4	—	4
Hawaii	4,458	4,055	2,034	1,298	122	8	593	403	33	352	18	4	2	2
Idaho	4,246	4,026	2,604	1,327	—	35	60	160	90	67	3	60	32	28
Illinois	45,149	41,127	21,987	6,453	570	150	11,967	3,450	1,065	2,255	130	572	88	484
Indiana	31,721	30,715	15,148	6,781	1,229	95	7,462	558	109	414	35	448	198	250
Iowa	7,892	7,331	5,603	1,039	79	7	603	522	320	192	10	39	12	27
Kansas	10,314	9,664	7,118	1,210	2	69	1,265	647	234	347	66	3	3	‡
Kentucky	19,392	17,579	14,411	1,444	90	44	1,590	1,410	232	1,084	94	403	284	119
Louisiana	13,829	11,928	5,978	2,180	103	12	3,655	1,654	532	981	141	247	154	93
Maine	9,553	9,022	4,523	425	88	—	3,986	422	153	252	17	109	36	73
Maryland	42,867	40,412	16,420	6,413	2,218	349	15,012	2,205	407	1,676	122	250	158	92
Massachusetts	36,815	32,759	17,289	2,177	973	1,528	10,792	2,984	747	2,027	210	1,072	275	797
Michigan	40,044	37,461	28,072	2,650	141	522	6,076	2,420	682	1,500	238	163	114	49
Minnesota	14,074	10,828	3,519	3,771	282	24	3,232	3,155	1,143	1,870	142	91	55	36
Mississippi	5,967	4,779	4,193	246	83	17	240	967	258	689	20	221	118	103
Missouri	21,004	18,668	9,672	4,964	886	90	3,056	1,965	1,266	557	142	371	113	258
Montana	3,602	3,324	2,740	460	26	2	96	237	112	118	7	41	24	17
Nebraska	4,864	3,957	2,971	692	50	7	237	902	214	647	41	5	2	3

TABLE 6.1

Persons admitted into substance abuse treatment, by state or region and type of care received, as of March 31, 2009 [CONTINUED]

State or jurisdiction*	Total	Number of clients — Type of care offered												
		Outpatient					Methadone/ buprenorphine maintenance	Residential (non-hospital)				Hospital inpatient		
		Total out patient	Regular	Intensive	Day treatment or partial hospitalization	Detox		Total residential	Short-term	Long-term	Detox	Total hospital inpatient	Treatment	Detox
Nevada	7,004	6,249	4,102	591	28	77	1,451	703	165	468	70	52	27	25
New Hampshire	5,107	4,763	2,645	189	29	146	1,754	307	88	201	18	37	29	8
New Jersey	31,634	28,516	9,933	6,072	980	293	11,238	2,351	500	1,799	52	767	571	196
New Mexico	15,315	14,630	9,485	1,683	39	841	2,582	609	147	367	95	76	57	19
New York	121,527	108,782	53,026	12,636	3,618	251	39,251	10,969	1,725	8,879	365	1,776	1,049	727
North Carolina	28,997	26,394	12,756	2,729	598	291	10,020	2,027	378	1,554	95	576	405	171
North Dakota	2,108	1,756	1,175	319	223	31	8	325	88	234	3	27	16	11
Ohio	35,664	32,823	23,000	4,303	311	198	5,011	2,392	471	1,828	93	449	261	188
Oklahoma	14,929	12,802	9,875	837	64	38	1,988	2,044	599	1,227	218	83	21	62
Oregon	23,136	21,223	13,873	3,685	446	88	3,131	1,793	492	1,180	121	120	105	15
Palau	38	35	35	—	—	—	‡	3	‡	‡		3	‡	3
Pennsylvania	49,528	44,786	21,269	8,034	683	75	14,725	4,346	1,860	2,174	312	396	277	119
Puerto Rico	13,669	9,578	2,542	641	194	143	6,058	3,826	178	3,399	249	265	170	95
Rhode Island	8,623	8,131	4,397	216	101	146	3,271	453	105	329	19	39	4	35
South Carolina	14,187	13,297	8,261	1,820	60	131	3,025	552	177	354	21	338	194	144
South Dakota	3,002	2,480	1,701	705	72	‡	2	433	141	265	27	89	79	10
Tennessee	12,544	10,797	4,491	1,184	180	4	4,938	1,560	656	817	87	187	109	78
Texas	34,503	28,704	13,707	5,639	421	136	8,801	4,895	1,626	3,048	221	904	549	355
Utah	13,492	11,923	8,134	1,361	280	99	2,049	1,538	395	1,046	97	31	18	13
Vermont	4,722	4,521	2,989	669	60	13	790	81	17	56	8	120	88	32
Virgin Islands	83	60	36	‡	‡	‡	24	23	—	23	‡	‡	‡	‡
Virginia	20,846	19,484	12,582	2,247	480	184	3,991	1,176	261	775	140	186	81	105
Washington	42,734	40,694	22,464	11,150	147	217	6,716	1,869	1,009	750	110	171	111	60
West Virginia	10,062	9,679	3,218	390	42	249	5,780	344	91	234	19	39	25	14
Wisconsin	15,526	14,449	9,538	1,244	320	74	3,273	845	250	550	45	232	102	130
Wyoming	3,411	3,036	2,223	737	65	5	6	342	140	167	35	33	16	17

*Facilities operated by federal agencies are included in the states in which the facilities are located.
—Quantity is zero.
‡No facilities in this category.

SOURCE: "Table 6.26a. Clients in Treatment, according to Type of Care Received, by State or Jurisdiction: March 31, 2009, Number," in *National Survey of Substance Abuse Treatment Services (N-SSATS): 2009. Data on Substance Abuse Treatment Facilities*, U.S. Department of Health and Human Services, Substance Abuse and Mental Health Services Administration, Office of Applied Studies, June 2010, http://wwwdasis.samhsa.gov/09nssats/hssats2k9web.pdf (accessed December 2, 2010)

FIGURE 6.2

Where persons aged 12 and over received substance abuse treatment, 2009

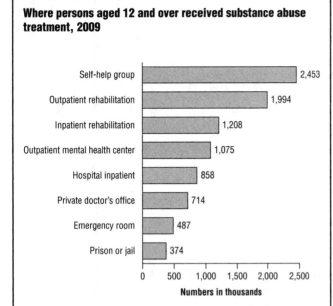

SOURCE: "Figure 7.7. Locations Where Past Year Substance Use Treatment Was Received among Persons Aged 12 or Older: 2009," in *Results from the 2009 National Survey on Drug Use and Health: Volume I. Summary of National Findings*, U.S. Department of Health and Human Services, Substance Abuse and Mental Health Services Administration, Office of Applied Studies, September 2010, http://www.oas.samhsa.gov/NSDUH/2k9NSDUH/2k9ResultsP.pdf (accessed November 8, 2010)

FIGURE 6.3

Reasons persons aged 12 and over gave for not receiving the substance abuse treatment they sought, 2006–09 combined

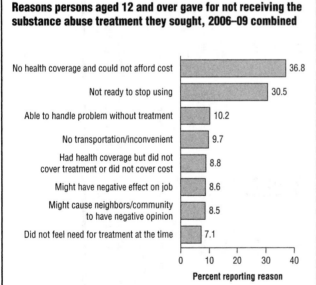

SOURCE: "Figure 7.11. Reasons for Not Receiving Substance Use Treatment among Persons Aged 12 or Older Who Needed and Made an Effort to Get Treatment but Did Not Receive Treatment and Felt They Needed Treatment: 2006–2009 Combined," in *Results from the 2009 National Survey on Drug Use and Health: Volume I. Summary of National Findings*, U.S. Department of Health and Human Services, Substance Abuse and Mental Health Services Administration, Office of Applied Studies, September 2010, http://www.oas.samhsa.gov/NSDUH/2k9NSDUH/2k9ResultsP.pdf (accessed November 8, 2010)

refers to processes that assist a drug-addicted person in discontinuing drug use and returning to a drug-free life.

Detoxification

Drug-addicted individuals must usually undergo medical detoxification (detox) in an outpatient facility, a residential center, or a hospital. Medical help, including sedation, is provided to manage the painful physical and psychological symptoms of withdrawal. The detox of many drugs can be achieved with minimal discomfort by replacing the drug of dependence with a less risky drug in the same pharmacological category (e.g., replacing heroin with methadone) and gradually reducing the dose. People addicted to nicotine can accomplish detox on their own by using gradually decreasing doses of nicotine patches. Rehabilitation usually follows detox.

Rehabilitation

Rehabilitation (rehab) has many forms, but it is always designed to change the behavior of the drug abuser. Changed behavior (achieving independence of drugs or alcohol) requires understanding the circumstances that led to dependence, building the confidence that the individual can succeed, and changing the individual's lifestyle so that the individual avoids occasions that produce drug-using behavior. Individual counseling, interaction with support groups, and formal education are used in combination with close supervision, incentives, and disincentives. Certain individuals require a new socialization that is achieved by living for an extended period in a structured and supportive environment in which new life skills can be acquired. Treatment may involve guiding the individual to seek help from other social agencies to reorder his or her life. (See Figure 6.1.)

Individuals, of course, may be mentally ill and will then receive, as part of drug rehab, mental health services in outpatient or hospital settings. Most treatment takes place in outpatient settings, with the individual reporting daily, weekly, or less frequently for periodic treatment and assessment.

Distribution of Patients

On March 31, 2009, nearly 1.1 million (90.1%) out of 1.2 million patients were receiving outpatient care. (See Table 6.1.) Of the remainder, 103,174 (8.7%) were in residential facilities and 14,341 (1.2%) were receiving hospital inpatient treatment. Of those under outpatient treatment but not in detox, the majority were receiving what SAMHSA calls regular, or nonintensive, treatment.

Of the total treatment population, 23,280 individuals (2% of all patients) were undergoing detox, most in outpatient settings (10,786) and the rest in residential facilities (6,067) and hospitals (6,427). (See Table 6.1.)

TABLE 6.2

Number of persons admitted into substance abuse treatment, by gender and age at admission, 1998–2008

[Based on administrative data reported to Treatment Episode Data Set (TEDS) by all reporting states and jurisdictions, excluding Puerto Rico]

Gender and age at admission	1998	1999	2000	2001	2002	2003	2004	2005	2006	2007	2008
Total	1,704,606	1,715,336	1,750,426	1,767,430	1,885,044	1,857,589	1,815,977	1,884,210	1,918,256	1,866,737	1,890,547
Gender											
Male	1,198,766	1,208,724	1,224,487	1,233,312	1,316,481	1,283,893	1,243,291	1,285,535	1,307,926	1,258,956	1,283,657
Female	500,712	504,806	522,515	531,913	568,040	573,306	571,973	598,189	609,911	607,245	606,503
No. of admissions	1,699,478	1,713,530	1,747,002	1,765,225	1,884,521	1,857,199	1,815,264	1,883,724	1,917,837	1,866,201	1,890,160
Age at admission											
12 to 17 years	139,129	137,596	137,863	145,385	157,748	156,999	147,155	144,592	144,498	140,261	141,645
18 to 19 years	68,513	69,627	72,863	73,460	77,586	76,452	75,963	77,344	76,402	75,149	76,748
20 to 24 years	176,995	188,581	204,846	221,426	245,613	249,291	255,889	270,814	272,117	265,611	272,802
25 to 29 years	226,010	213,835	206,779	201,480	213,889	216,300	225,372	249,628	266,120	268,812	279,064
30 to 34 years	291,287	274,559	266,377	257,679	259,309	244,370	227,056	223,716	216,365	208,511	213,008
35 to 39 years	315,770	314,697	313,288	301,983	304,696	281,832	258,753	256,113	251,838	232,497	220,381
40 to 44 years	233,984	244,952	257,214	262,409	281,654	279,734	269,934	273,664	269,977	248,457	238,017
45 to 49 years	135,198	144,957	155,927	163,565	185,610	188,088	187,603	201,772	215,573	213,742	218,230
50 to 54 years	62,013	68,581	75,126	80,679	92,176	95,735	98,925	110,003	120,395	125,044	134,412
55 to 59 years	30,383	32,101	33,536	33,272	39,213	41,027	41,938	47,106	54,229	56,006	61,778
60 to 64 years	13,713	14,198	14,770	15,073	16,412	16,631	16,570	18,060	19,046	20,777	22,246
65 years and older	11,611	11,652	11,837	11,019	11,138	11,130	10,819	11,398	11,696	11,870	12,216
No. of admissions	1,704,606	1,715,336	1,750,426	1,767,430	1,885,044	1,857,589	1,815,977	1,884,210	1,918,256	1,866,737	1,890,547
Average age at admission	33.5 yrs	33.8 yrs	33.9 yrs	33.8 yrs	33.9 yrs	34.0 yrs	34.0 yrs	34.1 yrs	34.3 yrs	34.4 yrs	34.4 yrs

SOURCE: "Table 1.3a. Admissions Aged 12 and Older by Gender and Age at Admission: TEDS 1998–2008, Number and Average Age at Admission," in *Treatment Episode Data Set (TEDS) 1998–2008. National Admissions to Substance Abuse Treatment Services,* U.S. Department of Health and Human Services, Substance Abuse and Mental Health Services Administration, Office of Applied Studies, April 2010, http://www.dasis.samhsa.gov/teds08/teds2k8natweb.pdf (accessed November 10, 2010)

TABLE 6.3

Number and percentage distribution of persons admitted into substance abuse treatment, by race/ethnicity, 1998–2008

[Based on administrative data reported to Treatment Episode Data Set (TEDS) by all reporting states and jurisdictions, excluding Puerto Rico]

Race/ethnicity	1998	1999	2000	2001	2002	2003	2004	2005	2006	2007	2008	U.S. pop. 2008 (000s)[a]
Total	**1,704,606**	**1,715,336**	**1,750,426**	**1,767,430**	**1,885,044**	**1,857,589**	**1,815,977**	**1,884,210**	**1,918,256**	**1,866,737**	**1,890,547**	
							Number					
White (non-Hispanic)	1,000,795	1,005,135	1,009,585	1,029,321	1,094,208	1,080,658	1,077,090	1,101,653	1,128,856	1,109,607	1,108,789	167,513
Black (non-Hispanic)	418,094	412,171	434,600	431,605	454,520	442,784	410,983	417,329	418,807	382,267	388,363	28,093
Hispanic origin	190,886	202,994	210,699	214,328	240,191	236,752	230,424	254,300	262,053	254,045	254,036	33,718
Mexican	73,131	79,162	80,304	80,766	97,661	95,138	95,437	100,459	105,536	106,744	106,232	n/a
Puerto Rican	72,081	76,465	78,576	82,569	81,935	76,494	69,367	74,135	73,339	65,844	70,005	n/a
Cuban	3,934	4,436	4,633	4,197	5,449	7,069	5,553	9,466	8,158	3,710	3,629	n/a
Other/not specified	41,740	42,931	47,186	46,796	55,146	58,051	60,067	70,240	75,020	77,747	74,170	n/a
Other	71,998	76,760	79,748	77,257	82,491	83,832	85,503	89,649	98,502	101,727	103,638	17,288
American Indian/Alaska Native[2]	40,303	39,874	37,563	37,530	39,274	35,503	35,906	38,877	41,641	42,397	42,199	1,792
Asian/Pacific Islander	11,485	13,565	14,619	14,083	16,427	17,716	16,087	19,016	18,443	17,595	18,325	11,322
Other	20,210	23,321	27,566	25,644	26,790	30,613	33,510	31,756	38,418	41,735	43,114	4,174
No. of admissions	1,681,773	1,697,060	1,734,632	1,752,511	1,871,410	1,844,026	1,804,000	1,862,931	1,908,218	1,847,646	1,854,826	246,613
							Percent distribution					
White (non-Hispanic)	59.5	59.2	58.2	58.7	58.5	58.6	59.7	59.1	59.2	60.1	59.8	67.9
Black (non-Hispanic)	24.9	24.3	25.1	24.6	24.3	24.0	22.8	22.4	21.9	20.7	20.9	11.4
Hispanic origin	11.4	12.0	12.1	12.2	12.8	12.8	12.8	13.7	13.7	13.7	13.7	13.7
Mexican	4.3	4.7	4.6	4.6	5.2	5.2	5.3	5.4	5.5	5.8	5.7	n/a
Puerto Rican	4.3	4.5	4.5	4.7	4.4	4.1	3.8	4.0	3.8	3.6	3.8	n/a
Cuban	0.2	0.3	0.3	0.2	0.3	0.4	0.3	0.5	0.4	0.2	0.2	n/a
Other/not specified	2.5	2.5	2.7	2.7	2.9	3.1	3.3	3.8	3.9	4.2	4.0	n/a
Other	4.3	4.5	4.6	4.4	4.4	4.5	4.7	4.8	5.2	5.5	5.6	7.0
American Indian/Alaska Native[b]	2.4	2.3	2.2	2.1	2.1	1.9	2.0	2.1	2.2	2.3	2.3	0.7
Asian/Pacific Islander	0.7	0.8	0.8	0.8	0.9	1.0	0.9	1.0	1.0	1.0	1.0	4.6
Other	1.2	1.4	1.6	1.5	1.4	1.7	1.9	1.7	2.0	2.3	2.3	1.7
Total	**100.0**	**100.0**	**100.0**	**100.0**	**100.0**	**100.0**	**100.0**	**100.0**	**100.0**	**100.0**	**100.0**	**100.0**

[a]Resident population aged 12 and older; excludes Alaska and Georgia, which did not report TEDS data for 2008.
[b]Alaska did not report TEDS data for 2004–2008.
n/a = Not available.

SOURCE: "Table 1.4. Admissions Aged 12 and Older by Race/Ethnicity: TEDS 1998–2008 and U.S. Population Aged 12 and Older 2008 Number and Percent Distribution," in *Treatment Episode Data Set (TEDS) 1998–2008. National Admissions to Substance Abuse Treatment Services*, U.S. Department of Health and Human Services, Substance Abuse and Mental Health Services Administration, Office of Applied Studies, April 2010, http://www.dasis.samhsa.gov/teds08/teds2k8natweb.pdf (accessed November 10, 2010)

Among all patients under treatment, 284,540 (24.1%) were receiving methadone.

STATISTICS ON ADMITTED PATIENTS

Admissions by Substance

Data on admissions by the primary substance of abuse provided by TEDS for 2008 are shown in Table 6.4. In that year alcohol alone or in combination with a secondary substance accounted for the largest number of people receiving treatment (784,262, or 41.4% of all admissions), followed by opiates (378,586, or 20%, mainly heroin), marijuana (321,648, or 17%), cocaine (213,971, or 11.3%), and methamphetamine/amphetamine (121,485, or 6.4%).

The 2008 admissions for alcohol abuse (either alone or in combination with a secondary substance) of 41.4% were down from 49% reported by TEDS in 1998. Total alcohol-related admissions declined annually through 2005, reaching a low of 39%, largely accounting for the decreasing trend in total admissions. Alcohol-related admissions climbed slightly after 2005.

The category showing the largest growth in admissions is methamphetamine/amphetamine. In 1998 these stimulant drugs accounted for approximately 4% of all admissions, whereas in 2008 they accounted for 6.4%. (See Table 6.4.) Marijuana-related admissions had the second-most rapid growth, representing 17% of cases in 2008, up from 13% in 1998.

Opiate-related admissions have been growing, whereas cocaine-related admissions have been declining. In 1998 opiate-related admissions were 16% and cocaine-related admissions were 15% of the total; 10 years later opiates accounted for 20% and cocaine for 11.3% of admissions. (See Table 6.4.)

Demographics by Substance

A detailed examination of admissions in 2008 is provided in Table 6.4, which shows the distribution of people admitted by major drug categories, gender, race, and ethnicity at admission.

GENDER. As noted previously in this chapter, the total male admissions (67.9%) were higher than the total female admissions (32.1%) in 2008. (See Table 6.2.) This trend held in all but one substance category: sedatives (56.9% females versus 39.6% males; the total does not add to 100% because the "other" category does not show gender). (See Table 6.4.) The tranquilizer category was about equal in 2008: 47.6% females versus 48% males. The greatest male-female differences were noted in alcohol-only admissions (68.1% males versus 25.3% females), alcohol admissions with a secondary drug (68.5% males versus 25.7% females), marijuana-related admissions (68.1% males versus 24.2% females), and heroin (63.2% males versus 30.3% females).

RACE AND ETHNICITY. In 2008 non-Hispanic whites made up 59.7% of the substance abuse treatment admissions; non-Hispanic African-Americans, 20.9%; Hispanics, 9.7%; Native Americans or Alaskan natives, 2.2%; and Asian-Americans or Pacific Islanders, 1%. (See Table 6.4.) Non-Hispanic whites had the highest admission rates for all drug categories except smoked cocaine and phencyclidine (PCP). Non-Hispanic African-Americans had the highest smoked-cocaine admissions (50.2%) and PCP-related admissions (57.6%). Non-Hispanic African-Americans were second in admission rates for alcohol only, alcohol with a secondary drug, heroin, other opiates, cocaine other than smoked, marijuana, sedatives, hallucinogens, and other. Hispanics were second in admission rates for methamphetamine/amphetamine, PCP, and inhalants. It should be noted that the Hispanics category is treated as an ethnicity rather than as a race and includes both white and African-American individuals of Hispanic origin.

It is important, however, to consider these rates of substance abuse treatment by race in the context of the overall racial composition of the United States. The 2008 TEDS data indicate that the total U.S. population consisted of 67.9% non-Hispanic whites, 13.7% Hispanics, and 11.4% non-Hispanic African-Americans in that year. (See Table 6.3.) When substance abuse treatment rates are compared with these population statistics, non-Hispanic whites were underrepresented in treatment (59.8% in treatment versus 67.9% of the U.S. population), the proportion of Hispanics in treatment was comparable to Hispanics in the population (13.7% in treatment versus 13.7% of the U.S. population), and non-Hispanic African-Americans were disproportionately admitted for treatment (20.9% in treatment versus 11.4% of the U.S. population).

AGE AT ADMISSION. The 2008 TEDS data show that 59.1% of people admitted for alcohol-only abuse that year were between the ages of 18 and 44 years. The average age of admission for alcohol-only abuse was 40 years. Crack (smoked) cocaine treatment recipients were primarily aged 35 years and older (71.4%) and had an average age of 40 years. In contrast, 38.6% of those admitted for using inhalants were aged 12 to 17 years and had an average age of 25 years. Those being treated for marijuana abuse were another young group. Nearly three-quarters (72.4%) were between the ages of 15 and 29 years. The marijuana treatment group had an average age of 24 years.

Type of Treatment

In 2008, 62.8% of those admitted to treatment were admitted into ambulatory (nonresidential) treatment facilities; of the remainder, 19.3% went into residential-type (24-hour) detox and 17.9% went into residential facilities. (See Table 6.5.)

Among those going into residential-type detox, the largest percentages were admitted for tranquilizers (33.2%),

TABLE 6.4

Percentage of persons admitted into substance abuse treatment, by gender, ethnicity, and primary substance abused, 2008

[Based on administrative data reported to Treatment Episode Data Set (TEDS) by all reporting states and jurisidictions]

Selected race/ethnicity/ gender/age group	All admissions	Primary substance at admission													
		Alcohol		Opiates		Cocaine		Marijuana/ hashish	Meth-amphetamine/ amphetamine	Tran-quilizers	Sedatives	Hallu-cinogens	PCP	Inhalants	Other/ none specified
		Alcohol only	Secondary drug	Heroin	Other opiates	Smoked cocaine	Other route								
Total	1,893,640	437,204	347,058	267,335	111,251	152,819	61,152	321,648	121,485	11,234	4,416	1,709	3,853	1,224	51,252
White (non-Hisp.) male	39.2	49.0	42.9	35.9	47.6	19.9	31.7	34.9	35.2	40.8	32.6	47.9	9.3	42.8	32.7
White (non-Hisp.) female	20.5	19.9	17.4	19.8	41.0	18.6	20.3	13.9	29.9	43.4	48.5	18.6	6.6	22.9	24.1
Black (non-Hisp.) male	14.8	8.9	17.2	13.5	1.7	30.0	17.1	22.8	2.1	3.1	2.8	12.6	37.0	4.3	19.1
Black (non-Hisp.) female	6.1	2.6	5.3	7.0	1.8	20.2	7.2	7.0	1.1	1.9	3.8	5.9	20.6	2.4	9.6
Mexican-orig. male	4.2	5.2	2.9	3.5	0.9	1.5	4.8	5.6	9.4	0.6	2.7	2.5	4.6	6.3	1.0
Mexican-orig. female	1.6	1.1	1.0	1.2	0.8	1.0	2.7	1.6	6.5	0.5	2.8	0.9	4.0	4.6	0.6
Puerto Rican-orig. male	3.2	1.7	3.0	9.7	0.6	1.8	4.8	2.7	0.3	2.8	0.5	1.5	5.5	1.1	0.9
Puerto Rican-orig. female	0.7	0.3	0.6	1.9	0.3	0.9	1.4	0.8	0.2	1.1	0.3	0.3	2.6	0.3	0.4
American Indian/Alaska Native male*	1.4	2.8	2.0	0.3	0.7	0.3	0.5	1.2	1.0	0.4	0.5	1.1	0.4	3.5	0.9
American Indian/Alaska Native female*	0.8	1.1	1.2	0.3	1.0	0.5	0.4	0.6	1.3	0.5	0.8	0.7	0.4	2.4	0.7
Asian/Pacific Islander male	0.7	0.8	0.5	0.3	0.3	0.4	0.4	0.9	2.1	0.3	0.5	1.1	0.4	0.5	0.4
Asian/Pacific Islander female	0.3	0.3	0.2	0.1	0.2	0.2	0.2	0.3	1.2	0.2	0.7	0.3	0.2	0.7	0.2
All other	6.5	6.4	5.7	6.4	3.0	4.5	8.4	7.8	9.9	4.4	3.5	6.5	8.4	8.2	9.5
Total	100.0	100.0	100.0	100.0	100.0	100.0	100.0	100.0	100.0	100.0	100.0	100.0	100.0	100.0	100.0
No. of admissions	1,857,595	429,583	340,635	264,663	109,755	150,297	60,439	314,610	121,121	11,090	4,370	1,685	3,811	1,186	44,350

*Alaska did not report TEDS data for 2008.

SOURCE: Adapted from "Table 2.3a. Admissions Aged 12 and Older by Selected Race/Ethnicity/Gender/Age Groups, according to Primary Substance of Abuse: TEDS 2008 Column Percent Distribution," in *Treatment Episode Data Set (TEDS) 1998–2008. National Admissions to Substance Abuse Treatment Services*, U.S. Department of Health and Human Services, Substance Abuse and Mental Health Services Administration, Office of Applied Studies, April 2010, http://wwwdasis.samhsa.gov/teds08/teds2k8natweb.pdf (accessed November 10, 2010)

TABLE 6.5

Percentage of persons admitted into substance abuse treatment, by primary substance of abuse and type of care received, 2008

[Based on administrative data reported to Treatment Episode Data Set (TEDS) by all reporting states and jurisdictions]

Type of service and medication-assisted opioid therapy	All admissions	Alcohol		Opiates		Cocaine		Marijuana/ hashish	Meth-amphetamine/ amphetamine	Tran-quilizers	Sedatives	Hallu-cinogens	PCP	Inhalants	Other/ none specified
		Alcohol only	Secondary drug	Heroin	Other opiates	Smoked cocaine	Other route								
Primary substance at admission															
Total	1,893,640	437,204	347,058	267,335	111,251	152,819	61,152	321,648	121,485	11,234	4,416	1,709	3,853	1,224	51,252
Type of service															
Ambulatory	62.8	58.1	59.1	50.5	59.0	54.8	68.3	83.8	66.4	45.1	59.5	65.6	64.6	67.7	82.0
Outpatient	50.1	47.2	46.6	39.5	45.6	41.2	53.7	68.0	54.3	35.3	43.4	48.5	43.9	52.8	67.6
Intensive outpatient	11.5	9.7	11.9	6.9	10.4	13.1	14.3	15.8	12.0	9.3	14.5	16.9	20.6	14.5	14.1
Detoxification	1.2	1.3	0.5	4.1	2.9	0.4	0.3	0.1	0.1	0.5	1.5	0.2	0.1	0.5	0.3
Rehabilitation/residential	17.9	12.9	19.3	17.2	19.1	30.2	23.1	14.1	26.3	21.7	24.0	28.4	28.1	22.5	11.3
Short-term (<31 days)	9.8	8.1	11.6	8.7	12.0	15.4	12.4	7.4	9.4	14.6	16.9	15.2	12.4	12.0	7.7
Long-term (31+ days)	7.8	4.4	7.3	8.2	6.6	14.5	10.5	6.5	16.7	6.5	6.2	12.6	15.6	10.0	3.3
Hospital (non-detox)	0.3	0.4	0.4	0.4	0.5	0.3	0.3	0.1	0.2	0.6	0.9	0.6	0.1	0.6	0.4
Detoxification (24-hour service)	19.3	29.0	21.6	32.3	21.9	15.0	8.6	2.1	7.3	33.2	16.4	6.0	7.3	9.7	6.7
Free-standing residential	15.4	24.1	15.7	23.9	17.8	14.2	7.6	1.9	6.9	21.2	12.8	5.5	6.9	8.6	5.9
Hospital inpatient	3.9	4.9	5.9	8.4	4.1	0.8	1.0	0.2	0.4	12.0	3.6	0.5	0.4	1.1	0.7
Total	100.0	100.0	100.0	100.0	100.0	100.0	100.0	100.0	100.0	100.0	100.0	100.0	100.0	100.0	100.0
No. of admissions	1,893,620	437,200	347,054	267,332	111,249	152,818	61,151	321,643	121,485	11,234	4,416	1,709	3,853	1,224	51,252
Medication-assisted opioid therapy*															
Yes	5.7	0.5	0.6	30.2	19.1	0.6	0.8	0.6	0.3	2.5	3.2	2.2	0.3	1.9	2.6
No	94.3	99.5	99.4	69.8	80.9	99.4	99.2	99.4	99.7	97.5	96.8	97.8	99.7	98.1	97.4
Total	100.0	100.0	100.0	100.0	100.0	100.0	100.0	100.0	100.0	100.0	100.0	100.0	100.0	100.0	100.0
No. of admissions	1,725,376	399,647	317,215	230,918	100,649	145,907	57,249	302,434	111,130	10,020	4,172	1,519	3,724	1,167	39,625

*Therapy with methadone or buprenorphine.

SOURCE: "Table 2.7. Admissions Aged 12 and Older by Type of Service and Medication-Assisted Opioid Therapy, According to Primary Substance of Abuse: TEDS 2008 Percent Distribution," in *Treatment Episode Data Set (TEDS) 1998–2008. National Admissions to Substance Abuse Treatment Services,* U.S. Department of Health and Human Services, Substance Abuse and Mental Health Services Administration, Office of Applied Studies, April 2010, http://wwwdasis.samhsa.gov/teds08/teds2k8natweb.pdf (accessed November 10, 2010) heroin (32.3%), and alcohol only (29%). (See Table 6.5.) Those using marijuana had the highest percentage entering ambulatory care (83.8%). The largest proportion of substance abusers assigned to residential treatment were smoked-cocaine users (53.3%).

Referring Source

Table 6.6 shows the source of referral of patients to substance abuse treatment in 2008. Nearly one-third (32.1%) of all people admitted came to get treatment on their own volition. The largest referral source (sending 37.8% of individuals) was the criminal justice system. Much of the remaining one-third of all referrals came from substance abuse treatment providers and other health care agencies (10.9% and 6.3% of referrals, respectively). Other referrals came from schools, employers, and community agencies.

Regarding the source of referral based on the drug of abuse, most heroin users (55.5%) and other opiate users (50.2%) sought treatment on their own accord. (See Table 6.6.) The criminal justice system sent over half of marijuana users (57%) and methamphetamine/amphetamine users (58.7%), along with nearly half of PCP users (48.4%), to treatment.

HOW EFFECTIVE IS TREATMENT?

During the 1960s there was an opioid epidemic in the United States, and the federal government released substantial funds to substance abuse treatment programs. This funding has continued over the decades and is supplemented by state governments and private sources. According to the Office of National Drug Control Policy, in *National Drug Control Strategy: FY 2011 Budget Summary* (2010, http://www.whitehousedrugpolicy.gov/publications/policy/11budget/fy11budget.pdf), the 2011 federal budget request for drug abuse treatment was $3.2 billion, and the request for treatment research was $674.2 million.

With so much money devoted to substance abuse treatment, there has been considerable research conducted on the effectiveness of the programs. The bulk of this research began during the late 1960s and extended into the 1990s.

In the press release "New Research Documents Success of Drug Abuse Treatments" (December 15, 1997, http://www.nih.gov/news/pr/dec97/nida-15.htm), the National Institutes of Health notes that the first major study of drug-treatment effectiveness was the Drug Abuse Reporting Program (DARP), which studied more than 44,000 clients in 52 treatment centers between 1969 and 1973. Program staff then studied a smaller group of these clients six and 12 years after their treatment. A second important study was the Treatment Outcome Prospective Study (TOPS), which followed 11,000 clients admitted to 41 treatment centers between 1979 and 1981. Both the DARP and the TOPS found major reductions in both drug abuse and criminal activity after treatment.

Services Research Outcomes Study

SAMHSA's Services Research Outcomes Study (SROS; September 1998, http://www.oas.samhsa.gov/sros/toc.htm) confirmed that both drug use and criminal behavior are reduced after drug treatment. Because it conducted a five-year follow-up on initial data in the Drug Services Research Survey (DSRS; http://www.oas.samhsa.gov/dsrs.htm), the SROS provided the first nationally representative data to answer the question: "Does treatment work?" This study, although now over a decade old and reporting on even older data, has not been repeated.

In this nationally representative sample, alcohol use decreased by 14% and drug use declined by 21%. Decreases varied from drug to drug, with heroin use decreasing the least.

Results by type of treatment were variable. On average, the best results for decreasing use of all drugs, especially cocaine and marijuana, were achieved with treatment that lasted six months or more. Long-term drug treatment appears to be necessary due to the chronic nature of addiction and its tendency to recur when treatment is stopped.

The SROS also showed that treatment for substance abuse can significantly reduce crime. Criminal activities such as breaking and entering, drug sales, prostitution, driving under the influence, and theft/larceny decreased between 23% and 38% after drug treatment.

Current Principles of Effective Treatment

The NIDA provides scientific information on principles of effective treatment based on the classic research studies described in this chapter as well as on other research studies. In the fact sheet "Treatment Approaches for Drug Addiction" (September 2009, http://www.nida.nih.gov/PDF/InfoFacts/IF_Treatment_Approaches_2009_to_NIDA_92209.pdf), the NIDA lists key principles and reiterates that adequate time is needed for treatment to be effective. Additionally, the NIDA notes that treatment should be readily available and address issues in a person's life—not just the addiction. According to the NIDA principles, effective treatment should include counseling, behavioral therapies, appropriate medications, and drug use monitoring. Drug-addicted individuals often have other illnesses, such as mental illnesses or infectious diseases that were contracted by needle-sharing or other risky practices, and the NIDA suggests that these illnesses should also be treated. The NIDA adds that one single treatment is not appropriate for everyone and that any drug treatment plan should be periodically reevaluated and adjusted, depending on a patient's progress and needs.

TABLE 6.6

Percentage of persons admitted into substance abuse treatment, by primary substance of abuse and source of referral, 2008

[Based on administrative data reported to Treatment Episode Data Set (TEDS) by all reporting states and jurisdictions]

| Treatment referral source and detailed criminal justice referral* | All admissions | Alcohol | | Opiates | | Cocaine | | Marijuana/ hashish | Meth-amphetamine/ amphetamine | Tran-quilizers | Sedatives | Hallu-cinogens | PCP | Inhalants | Other/ none specified |
		Alcohol only	Secondary drug	Heroin	Other opiates	Smoked cocaine	Other route								
Total	1,893,640	437,204	347,058	267,335	111,251	152,819	61,152	321,648	121,485	11,234	4,416	1,709	3,853	1,224	51,252
Treatment referral source															
Criminal justice/DUI (see detail, below)	37.8	41.9	36.0	14.7	18.0	29.9	39.4	57.0	58.7	21.5	23.9	39.3	48.4	29.1	36.3
Individual	32.1	29.2	31.5	55.5	50.2	34.9	27.1	15.0	19.7	41.9	37.2	29.0	24.7	34.0	32.8
Substance abuse provider	10.9	8.5	12.3	17.5	14.2	15.6	12.2	6.1	6.1	15.0	15.0	11.0	9.5	9.2	5.6
Other health care provider	6.3	8.0	7.6	5.2	8.4	6.0	5.2	4.0	2.7	10.9	9.4	7.3	3.3	10.6	8.7
School (educational)	1.0	0.7	0.7	*	0.2	0.1	0.3	3.4	0.3	0.6	1.4	0.8	0.2	5.6	3.7
Employer/EAP	0.6	0.8	0.6	0.1	0.6	0.3	1.0	0.8	0.3	0.4	0.8	0.1	0.3	0.6	0.6
Other community referral	11.2	11.0	11.2	6.8	8.5	13.3	14.8	13.7	12.3	9.7	12.3	12.5	13.6	11.0	12.3
Total	100.0	100.0	100.0	100.0	100.0	100.0	100.0	100.0	100.0	100.0	100.0	100.0	100.0	100.0	100.0
No. of admissions	1,859,777	430,457	341,424	264,379	109,521	150,620	60,350	316,582	119,669	11,076	4,320	1,671	3,791	1,184	44,733
Detailed criminal justice referral*															
Total	703,807	180,277	122,944	38,889	19,669	45,034	23,785	180,452	70,257	2,381	1,032	656	1,835	344	16,252
Probation/parole	42.7	24.9	39.9	51.4	39.0	49.2	55.0	50.6	54.0	34.1	38.9	46.2	59.5	30.8	31.6
State/Federal court	12.7	12.7	15.3	8.8	18.7	13.0	10.7	13.3	6.4	18.7	16.0	14.5	8.5	23.5	27.5
Formal adjudication	10.9	13.5	11.1	9.4	15.7	9.5	8.1	8.9	11.3	18.8	20.1	9.8	7.2	8.5	12.2
Other legal entity	5.6	5.4	5.3	5.3	4.5	5.1	5.6	7.6	1.9	6.8	4.7	4.0	5.0	10.3	10.1
DUI/DWI	8.3	23.3	11.9	1.3	3.9	0.7	2.0	1.8	0.5	7.5	5.1	2.0	1.1	7.3	2.6
Diversionary program	3.6	1.5	3.2	9.1	6.5	5.8	5.2	4.3	0.4	5.6	3.2	2.9	6.4	2.6	5.7
Prison	2.2	1.1	2.0	4.7	2.7	3.8	3.3	1.7	2.9	2.5	2.7	5.4	3.0	3.0	1.6
Other	14.0	17.4	11.3	9.9	9.1	12.9	10.1	11.8	22.6	6.0	9.4	15.2	9.4	14.1	8.7
Total	100.0	100.0	100.0	100.0	100.0	100.0	100.0	100.0	100.0	100.0	100.0	100.0	100.0	100.0	100.0
No. of admissions	536,120	123,573	91,088	33,994	14,485	36,001	19,000	141,716	61,851	2,010	787	448	1,574	234	9,359

Primary substance at admission

*Detailed criminal justice referral is a supplemental data set item. Supplemental data set items are not reported by all states and jurisdictions.

DUI = Driving under the influence.

DWI = Driving while intoxicated.

SOURCE: "Table 2.6. Admissions Aged 12 and Older by Treatment Referral Source and Detailed Criminal Justice Referral, according to Primary Substance of Abuse: TEDS 2008 Percent Distribution," in *Treatment Episode Data Set (TEDS) 1998–2008. National Admissions to Substance Abuse Treatment Services*, U.S. Department of Health and Human Services, Substance Abuse and Mental Health Services Administration, Office of Applied Studies, April 2010, http://wwwdasis.samhsa.gov/teds08/teds2k8natweb.pdf (accessed November 10, 2010)

The Development of Antidrug Vaccines

Medications can help drug-addicted individuals not only by suppressing drug withdrawal symptoms but also by helping reestablish proper brain function and reducing drug cravings during treatment. Antidrug vaccines, which were under development as of February 2011, may help drug-addicted individuals in the future. In "Anti-drug Vaccines to Treat Substance Abuse" (*Immunology and Cell Biology*, vol. 87, no. 4, May–June 2009), Berma M. Kinsey, David C. Jackson, and Frank M. Orson review the status of the development of these vaccines for treating addictions. The researchers explain that antidrug vaccines work by triggering the development of antibodies against particular drugs in vaccinated individuals. The antibodies bind to the drug in the bloodstream before it is able to get to the brain. Thus, the vaccinated individual receives no drug effects by taking a drug, such as cocaine or methamphetamine; that is, the pleasure centers of the brain are not stimulated because the drug never gets to the brain. Because the person does not experience any "reward" for taking the drug, the craving sensations for the drug eventually subside.

In reality, however, antidrug vaccines do not work perfectly. For example, if an individual's body does not respond well to the vaccine by developing a substantial amount of antibodies, then only some of the drug is bound in the bloodstream and some enters the brain. To get a desired drug effect, a drug addict will have to increase the doses of a drug. Thus, Kinsey, Jackson, and Orson suggest that counseling and behavior therapy will also be needed for antidrug vaccines to be effective.

Kinsey, Jackson, and Orson surmise that antinicotine vaccines are the ones most likely to be available first to the public because their development is the furthest along. Vaccines are also under development for cocaine, morphine, and methamphetamine addictions.

DRUG COURTS

Drug courts are programs that use the court's authority to offer certain drug-addicted offenders to have their charges dismissed or their sentences reduced if they participate in drug court substance abuse treatment programs. Drug court programs vary across the nation, but most programs offer a range of treatment options and generally require one year of commitment from the defendant.

Randall T. Brown of the University of Wisconsin School of Medicine and Public Health describes drug courts and reviews their effect in "Systematic Review of the Impact of Adult Drug-Treatment Courts" (*Translational Research*, vol. 155, no. 6, June 2010). Brown notes that drug courts vary in the number of individuals they serve annually, with the typical range being between 80 and 120. Courts in large urban areas often serve hundreds more. He explains that drug courts use sanctions and rewards to motivate individuals to comply with their treatment. Rewards include praise from the judge, fewer court appearances, and gift cards to local stores. Those who adhere to the rules and remain drug free for a sustained period (48% on average) graduate from treatment and are provided with a ceremony that is attended by family and friends. Sanctions include admonitions from the judge, community service, increased drug screening, and incarceration. Brown's review of the literature on the effect of drug courts "points toward benefit versus traditional adjudication in averting future criminal behavior and in reducing future substance use, at least in the short term."

The National Drug Court Institute (NDCI), which is supported by the Office of National Drug Control Policy and the U.S. Department of Justice's Office of Justice Programs, studied its own drug court system, and its findings were reported by C. West Huddleston III, Douglas B. Marlowe, and Rachel Casebolt in *Painting the Current Picture: A National Report Card on Drug Courts and Other Problem-Solving Court Programs in the United States* (May 2008, http://www.ndci.org/sites/default/files/ndci/PCPII1_web%5B1%5D.pdf). Huddleston, Marlowe, and Casebolt indicate that drug courts decrease criminal recidivism (relapse into criminal activity), save money, increase retention in treatment, and provide affordable treatment.

Figure 6.4 shows the increase in the use of drug courts nationwide between 1989 and 2009. There were almost 2,500 drug courts operating in the United States in 2009, and more were in the planning stages.

WHERE TO GO FOR HELP

Many organizations provide assistance for addicts, their families, and their friends. Most of the self-help groups are based on the Twelve Step program of Alcoholics Anonymous (AA). Whereas AA is a support group for problem drinkers, Al-Anon/Alateen is for friends and families of alcoholics. Families Anonymous provides support for family members and friends who are concerned about a loved one's problems with drugs and/or alcohol. Other organizations include Adult Children of Alcoholics, Cocaine Anonymous, and Narcotics Anonymous. For an addict, many of these organizations can provide immediate help. For families and friends, they can provide knowledge, understanding, and support. For contact information for some of these organizations, see the Important Names and Addresses section at the back of this book.

FIGURE 6.4

Increase in drug courts, 1989–2009

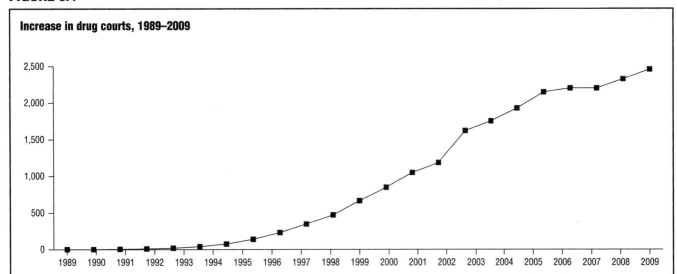

SOURCE: "Figure 13. The Number of Drug Courts Continues to Increase Nationwide (1989–2009)," in *National Drug Control Strategy: 2010*, Executive Office of the President, Office of National Drug Control Policy, 2010, http://www.whitehousedrugpolicy.gov/publications/policy/ndcs10/ndcs2010.pdf (accessed November 10, 2010). Data from the National Drug Court Institute.

HOW ALCOHOL, TOBACCO, AND DRUG USE AFFECT ECONOMICS AND GOVERNMENT

The alcohol and tobacco industries play large roles in the U.S. economy. Both industries not only provide jobs and income for those involved in growing, manufacturing, and selling these products but also contribute significant tax revenues to the federal, state, and local governments. The U.S. economy also feels the effects of alcohol, tobacco, and illicit drug use in other, less beneficial, ways. All these drugs can have significant health consequences, with associated health care costs. There are also costs in the form of loss of productivity—work that was never performed because of poor health, death, or imprisonment. The cost of enforcing drug laws and incarcerating those convicted of breaking such laws are also significant.

U.S. ALCOHOL SALES AND CONSUMPTION

Retail sales of alcoholic beverages are divided into three groups: beer, wine, and distilled spirits. According to the Economic Research Service (ERS; March 23, 2010, http://www.ers.usda.gov/Data/FoodConsumption/spread sheets/beverage.xls), Americans consumed a total of 25.7 gallons (97.3 L) of alcoholic beverages per person in 2008. Of the three alcoholic beverage categories, beer was consumed in the greatest quantity (21.7 gallons [82.1 L] per person in 2008), followed by wine (2.5 gallons [9.5 L] per person) and distilled spirits (1.4 gallons [5.3 L] per person).

Beer

The ERS notes that the per capita (per person) consumption of beer was 18.5 gallons (70 L) in 1970 and rose to a peak per capita consumption of 24.6 gallons (93.1 L) in 1981. It then fell steadily through the 1980s and much of the 1990s. From 1997 on, beer consumption per person remained quite steady, at 21.6 gallons (81.8 L) per person in 1997 and 21.7 gallons (82.1 L) per person more than a decade later in 2008. Even though per capita consumption remained quite steady over those years, the population grew and the total beer consumption grew. According to the Beer Institute, in *Brewer's Almanac 2010* (October 1, 2010,

http://www.beerinstitute.org/statistics.asp?bid=200), there were an estimated 1,679 domestic brewers in the United States in 2008, nearly six times the number in 1990. Microbreweries and brewpubs (specialty brewers) account for this increase.

Wine

The ERS data show that the per capita consumption of wine was 1.3 gallons (4.9 L) in 1970 and rose to 2.4 gallons (9.1 L) in 1984. Per capita consumption held steady through 1987 and then began to decline, reaching a low of 1.7 gallons (6.4 L) in 1995. Consumption remained steady for a few years but in 1996 it began an upward climb again. By 2008 per capita wine consumption was at an all-time high of 2.5 gallons (9.5 L) per person.

The Wine Institute reports in "2009 California Wine Sales" (2010, http://www.wineinstitute.org/resources/sta tistics/article122) that wine sales in the United States grew 2% in 2009 to 767.4 million gallons (2.9 billion L), for a retail sales value of $28.7 billion. Even though volume was up, the retail sales value of the wine was down 4% from 2008 because consumers were buying lower-priced wines due to an ongoing recession. In comparison, a total of 617 million gallons (2.3 billion L) of wine were sold in the United States in 2002, for a retail sales value of $21.8 billion.

According to the Wine Institute, the California wine industry accounted for a 61% share of the U.S. wine market in 2009. Red wines held a 47% market share in 2009, white wines a 40% share, and blush wines a 13% share. Chardonnay was the leading varietal wine (a wine produced from a single variety of grape), followed by cabernet sauvignon, merlot, and white zinfandel, respectively.

Distilled Spirits

The ERS data show that the per capita consumption of distilled spirits was 1.8 gallons (6.8 L) in 1970 and rose to an all-time high of 2 gallons (7.6 L) in 1974. This level of consumption persisted through 1981 and thereafter slowly declined to 1.2 gallons (4.5 L) in 1995. In 2000 the level of consumption began to increase slightly, reaching 1.4 gallons (5.3 L) in 2004 and remaining at that level through 2008.

In *A Decade of Progress: Distilled Spirits Council 2009 Industry Review* (February 2, 2010, http://www.discus.org/pdf/2009IndustryBriefing.pdf), the Distilled Spirits Council of the United States indicates that in 2009 the revenues from distilled spirits (e.g., whiskey, vodka, and rum) were $18.7 billion, an increase of 60% from the revenues in 2000. Each year from 2000 to 2009 industry revenues grew an average of about 2%, although this average included a period of no growth from 2008 to 2009.

How Much Do Individuals and Families Spend on Alcohol?

The Bureau of Labor Statistics (BLS) reports in *Consumer Expenditures in 2009* (October 2010, http://www.bls.gov/cex/2009/Standard/cucomp.pdf) that the average American family (or other consumer unit) spent $511 on alcoholic beverages in 2009. This figure represents 0.8% of the average annual expenditures for the American family.

The amount spent on alcohol varied in 2009, depending on the characteristics of the household. On average, single parents with at least one child under the age of 18 years spent only $177 on alcoholic beverages in 2009, or about 0.5% of their average annual expenditures. Married couples with no children spent $582, which was 1% of their average annual expenditures. The percentage other groups spent on alcohol varied within a range of 0.5% to 0.8%, except for the "single person and other consumer units"

group. This group spent the largest proportion of its average annual expenditures on alcohol: 1.1%.

U.S. TOBACCO PRODUCTION AND CONSUMPTION
Farming Trends

In 1881 James A. Bonsack (1859–1924) invented the cigarette-making machine, which made cigarettes cheaper and faster to manufacture. Thomas Capehart of the ERS notes in "Trends in U.S. Tobacco Farming" (November 2004, http://www.ers.usda.gov/publications/tbs/nov04/tbs25702/tbs25702.pdf) that tobacco production in the United States grew from 300 million pounds (136,000 t) during the mid-1860s to over 1 billion pounds (454,000 t) in 1909. In 1946, at the end of World War II (1939–1945), tobacco production was above 2 billion pounds (907,000 t).

During the 1960s changes in tobacco preparation and the introduction of new machinery increased the amount of tobacco production per acre. Nonetheless, the number of tobacco farms dropped dramatically from about 512,000 in 1954 to 56,977 in 2002. In general, the amount of land devoted to cultivating tobacco, the value of production, and the production of tobacco decreased as well. Table 7.1 shows that the acreage devoted to tobacco declined steadily from 1999 to 2005, but rose slightly in 2006 and 2007. The value of production declined in 2003, rose in 2004, declined again in 2005, and rose between 2006 and 2008. In spite of this increase in the value of production, the overall production of tobacco fell, from 1.3 billion pounds (586,000 t) in 1999 to 800 million pounds (363,000 t) in 2008.

In 2008 North Carolina led in tobacco production, followed by Kentucky, Tennessee, Virginia, South Carolina, and Georgia. (See Table 7.2.) Tobacco plays a major

TABLE 7.1

Tobacco crops by area, yield, production, price, and value, 1999–2008

Year	Area harvested	Yield per acre	Production*	Marketing year average price per pound received by farmers	Value of production
	Acres	*Pounds*	*1,000 pounds*	*Dollars*	*1,000 dollars*
1999	647,160	1,997	1,292,692	1.828	2,356,304
2000	469,420	2,244	1,053,264	1.910	2,001,811
2001	432,490	2,292	991,293	1.956	1,938,892
2002	427,310	2,039	871,122	1.936	1,686,809
2003	411,150	1,952	802,560	1.964	1,576,436
2004	408,050	2,161	881,875	1.984	1,749,856
2005	297,080	2,171	645,015	1.642	1,059,324
2006	339,000	2,146	727,897	1.665	1,211,885
2007	356,000	2,213	787,653	1.693	1,329,235
2008	354,490	2,258	800,504	1.861	1,482,437

*Production figures are on farm-sales-weight basis.

SOURCE: "Table 2-37. Tobacco: Area, Yield, Production, Price, and Value, United States, 1999–2008," in *Agricultural Statistics 2009*, U.S. Department of Agriculture, National Agricultural Statistics Service, 2009, http://www.nass.usda.gov/Publications/Ag_Statistics/2009/chp02.pdf (accessed November 10, 2010)

TABLE 7.2

Area, yield, and production of tobacco, by tobacco-growing state, 2006–08

State	Area harvested			Yield per harvested acre			Production		
	2006	2007	2008[a]	2006	2007	2008[a]	2006	2007	2008[a]
	Acres	Acres	Acres	Pounds	Pounds	Pounds	1,000 pounds	1,000 pounds	1,000 pounds
CT	2,500	2,900	2,600	1,549	1,733	1,352	3,873	5,025	3,516
FL[b]	1,100	—	—	2,600	—	—	2,860	—	—
GA	17,000	18,500	16,000	1,770	2,150	2,100	30,090	39,775	33,600
KY	83,000	89,200	87,800	2,250	2,209	2,345	186,780	197,040	205,850
MA	1,150	1,320	690	1,558	1,725	1,403	1,792	2,277	968
MO	1,500	1,600	1,500	2,250	2,330	2,240	3,375	3,728	3,360
NC	158,900	170,000	174,300	2,080	2,255	2,240	330,580	383,420	390,360
OH	3,500	3,500	3,400	2,000	2,050	2,050	7,000	7,175	6,970
PA	7,900	7,900	7,900	2,125	2,318	2,232	16,240	18,310	17,630
SC	23,000	20,500	19,000	2,100	2,250	2,100	48,300	46,125	39,900
TN	19,800	19,980	21,800	2,482	1,934	2,403	49,135	38,636	52,380
VA	19,650	20,600	19,500	2,408	2,240	2,357	47,322	46,142	45,970
U.S.	339,000	356,000	354,490	2,146	2,213	2,258	727,897	787,653	800,504

[a]Preliminary.
[b]Estimates discontinued in 2007.

SOURCE: "Table 2-38. Tobacco: Area, Yield, and Production, by State, 2006–2008," in *Agricultural Statistics 2009*, U.S. Department of Agriculture, National Agricultural Statistics Service, 2009, http://www.nass.usda.gov/Publications/Ag_Statistics/2009/chp02.pdf (accessed November 10, 2010)

role in the agricultural economies of these leading tobacco-producing states.

Manufacturing

In *Tobacco Outlook* (October 24, 2007, http://usda .mannlib.cornell.edu/usda/ers/TBS//2000s/2007/TBS-10-24-2007.pdf), the ERS estimates that in 2007 U.S. factories produced 471.6 billion cigarettes, of which 108.9 billion were shipped to other countries. Of the available data beginning in 1996, this output was down from a peak of 754.5 billion cigarettes produced by U.S. factories in 1996. Exports were high that year as well: 243.9 billion cigarettes.

Tobacco Consumption

The ERS (January 9, 2008, http://www.ers.usda.gov/ Briefing/Archive/Tobacco/) notes that cigarette smoking in the United States has been dropping almost every year since 1963, when per capita consumption reached a record high of 4,345 cigarettes. A decline began in earnest after the release of the 1964 U.S. surgeon general's report on cigarette smoking that linked this habit to the development of lung cancer and other diseases and conditions. By 2006 the annual per capita consumption of cigarettes for those aged 18 years and older was 1,691. These data are taken from *Tobacco Outlook* by ERS. This was the final report provided by the ERS on this topic because the ERS discontinued this publication, along with another tobacco-related publication, the *Tobacco Briefing Room*, after a tobacco buyout was formalized by the U.S. Department of Agriculture (USDA) in February 2005. The tobacco buyout is part of the Fair and Equitable Tobacco Reform Act of 2004 and is formally known as the Tobacco Transition Payment

Program. Several USDA agencies discontinued their tobacco programs after the buyout. However, the ERS will continue to conduct research on other, less-routine tobacco-related projects.

The ERS finds that the per capita consumption of all tobacco products generally decreased from 1996 to 2006, from 4.8 pounds (2.2 kg) in 1996 to 3.7 pounds (1.7 kg) in 2006. However, the per capita consumption of large cigars by males increased during this period, jumping from 31.9 large cigars and cigarillos (small cigars) per adult male in 1996 to 47.8 in 2006.

Consumer Spending on Tobacco

Table 7.3 shows that the average American family (or other consumer unit) spent $327 on tobacco products and smoking supplies in 2006, $323 in 2007, and $317 in 2008. The BLS reports in *Consumer Expenditures in 2009* that the average American family (or other consumer unit) spent $375 on tobacco products and smoking supplies in 2009. This figure represents 0.6% of the average annual expenditures for the American family.

The amount spent on tobacco products and smoking supplies varied in 2009, depending on the characteristics of the household. On average, married couples with no children spent $335, which was 0.4% of their average annual expenditures. The percentage other groups spent on tobacco and smoking supplies varied within a range of 0.4% to 0.7%, except for the "single person and other consumer units" group, the "other husband and wife consumer units" group, and the "one parent, at least one child under 18" group. These groups spent the largest proportion of their average annual expenditures on tobacco products and smoking supplies: 1.1%, 1.1%, and 0.9%, respectively.

TABLE 7.3

Average annual consumer spending and percent changes, by category, 2006–08

Item	2006	2007	2008	Percent change 2006–07	Percent change 2007–08
Number of consumer units (in thousands)	118,843	120,171	120,770	—	—
Income before taxes	$60,533	$63,091	$63,563	—	—
Averages:				—	—
Age of reference person	48.7	48.8	49.1	—	—
Number of persons in consumer unit	2.5	2.5	2.5	—	—
Number of earners	1.3	1.3	1.3	—	—
Number of vehicles	1.9	1.9	2.0	—	—
Percent homeowner	67	67	66	—	—
Average annual expenditures	$48,398	$49,638	$50,486	2.6	1.7
Food	6,111	6,133	6,443	.4	5.1
Food at home	3,417	3,465	3,744	1.4	8.1
Cereals and bakery products	446	460	507	3.1	10.2
Meats, poultry, fish, and eggs	797	777	846	−2.5	8.9
Dairy products	368	387	430	5.2	11.1
Fruits and vegetables	592	600	657	1.4	9.5
Other food at home	1,212	1,241	1,305	2.4	5.2
Food away from home	2,694	2,668	2,698	−1.0	1.1
Alcoholic beverages	497	457	444	−8.0	−2.8
Housing	16,366	16,920	17,109	3.4	1.1
Shelter	9,673	10,023	10,183	3.6	1.6
Utilities, fuels, and public services	3,397	3,477	3,649	2.4	4.9
Household operations	948	984	998	3.8	1.4
Housekeeping supplies	640	639	654	−.2	2.3
Household furnishings and equipment	1,708	1,797	1,624	5.2	−9.6
Apparel and services	1,874	1,881	1,801	.4	−4.3
Transportation	8,508	8,758	8,604	2.9	−1.8
Vehicle purchases (net outlay)	3,421	3,244	2,755	−5.2	−15.1
Gasoline and motor oil	2,227	2,384	2,715	7.0	13.9
Other vehicle expenses	2,355	2,592	2,621	10.1	1.1
Public transportation	505	538	513	6.5	−4.6
Healthcare	2,766	2,853	2,976	3.1	4.3
Entertainment	2,376	2,698	2,835	13.6	5.1
Personal care products and services	585	588	616	.5	4.8
Reading	117	118	116	.9	−1.7
Education	888	945	1,046	6.4	10.7
Tobacco products and smoking supplies	327	323	317	−1.2	−1.9
Miscellaneous	846	808	840	−4.5	4.0
Cash contributions	1,869	1,821	1,737	−2.6	−4.6
Personal insurance and pensions	5,270	5,336	5,605	1.3	5.0
Life and other personal insurance	322	309	317	−4.0	2.6
Pensions and Social Security	4,948	5,027	5,288	1.6	5.2

SOURCE: "Table A. Average Annual Expenditures of All Consumer Units and Percent Changes, Consumer Expenditure Survey, 2006–08," in *Consumer Expenditures in 2008*, U.S. Department of Labor, U.S. Bureau of Labor Statistics, March 2010, http://www.bls.gov/cex/csxann08.pdf (accessed November 10, 2010)

Exports

The ERS reports in *Tobacco Outlook* that between July 2006 and June 2007, 102 billion cigarettes were exported. Most of the cigarettes exported in 2006–07 went to Japan (76.7 billion), Saudi Arabia (9.1 billion), Lebanon (3.5 billion), Israel (2.1 billion), and Kuwait (2.1 billion). Other major importers of American cigarettes were Hong Kong (1.8 billion) and the United Arab Emirates (1.7 billion). Many of the importers in these countries export these cigarettes to other countries.

WORLD TOBACCO MARKETS

In *Agricultural Statistics, 2005* (2005, http://www.nass.usda.gov/Publications/Ag_Statistics/2005/agstats2005.pdf), the National Agricultural Statistics Service (NASS) estimates the world production of tobacco in 2004 at 7.3 million tons (6.7 million t), down from 7.6 million tons (6.9

million t) in 2000. China produced 36% (about 2.6 million tons [2.4 million t]). Other leading tobacco producers included Brazil (981,608 tons [890,500 t]), India (733,037 tons [665,000 t]), the United States (438,000 tons [397,347 t]), Indonesia (175,157 tons [158,900 t]), Argentina (170,086 tons [154,300 t]), and Turkey (169,480 tons [153,750 t]). As of February 2011, these data were the most recent available because the NASS and the Food and Agriculture Organization of the United Nations, the two agencies that collect and disseminate such information, were no longer doing so.

In *WHO Report on the Global Tobacco Epidemic, 2008: The MPOWER Package* (2008, http://whqlibdoc.who.int/publications/2008/9789241596282_eng.pdf), the World Health Organization (WHO) reveals that in 2008 nearly two-thirds of the world's smokers lived in 10 countries, with China being the top consumer of cigarettes.

About 29% of the world's smokers lived in China, and about 11% lived in India, the world's second-largest consumer of cigarettes. Indonesia, the Russian Federation, and the United States were tied for third place. The remaining top-10 cigarette-consuming countries were Japan, Brazil, Bangladesh, Germany, and Turkey.

World Tobacco Control Treaty

On February 27, 2005, the world's first tobacco control treaty, the WHO Framework Convention on Tobacco Control (2005, http://www.who.int/tobacco/framework/WHO_FCTC_english.pdf), became law in the 40 countries that ratified it (became bound by it). According to the WHO, in "Parties to the WHO Framework Convention on Tobacco Control" (January 20, 2011, http://www.who.int/fctc/signatories_parties/en/index.html), the United States signed the measure in May 2004, but as of January 2011 it had still not ratified the treaty. However, 168 other countries had ratified the treaty by that time. The goal of the treaty is to improve global health by reducing tobacco consumption. Nations that ratified the treaty obligate themselves to raise their taxes on tobacco products, ban tobacco advertising, pass laws requiring smoke-free workplaces and public places, and provide stronger health warnings about the dangers of smoking to their residents. (For further information on this effort and its progress, see Chapter 3.)

ALCOHOL AND TOBACCO ADVERTISING
Alcohol Advertising

The Center for Science in the Public Interest (CSPI) indicates in "Alcoholic-Beverage Advertising Expenditures" (October 2008, http://www.cspinet.org/booze/Fact Sheets/AlcAdExp.pdf), the most recent publication on this topic as of February 2011, that the beer industry spent approximately $978.9 million in 2007 on advertising, down from over $1 billion spent each year between 2002 and 2006. The liquor industry spent $547 million in 2007, up from the $400 million spent each year between 2001 and 2006. The wine industry spent approximately $120.5 million in 2007, which was within its general range of advertising expenditures during the previous decade.

According to the CSPI, in 2007 the beer industry focused most (74%) of its advertising dollars on television. The wine industry targeted print media (magazines, newspapers, and billboards) with 80% of its spending. Wine industry spending for television advertising (15%) was down considerably from the late 1990s. The liquor industry focused its advertising primarily on print media (75%) as well, but its spending on television advertising (22%) rose substantially between 1999 and 2007 as a result of this industry's decision in 1996 to lift its self-imposed ban on advertising on television so that it could compete with the wine and beer industries.

After the liquor industry lifted its ban, the National Broadcasting Company (NBC) also ended its ban on hard liquor advertising and became the first network television station to do so. NBC's 2001 decision was met with nearly universal derision, and a short time later the broadcaster returned to its ban on hard liquor advertisements. As a response, the liquor industry developed guidelines to restrict advertising to publications or television programs with at least 70% of readers or viewers being aged 21 years and older, which resulted in an underage reader or viewer threshold of 30%. In 2003 the wine and beer industries agreed to these guidelines as well.

Stuart Elliott reports in "Thanks to Cable, Liquor Ads Find a TV Audience" (*New York Times*, December 15, 2003) that by the end of 2003 hard liquor was being advertised on two dozen national cable networks, 140 local cable systems, and 420 local broadcast stations. In "In a First, CNN Runs a Liquor Commercial" (*New York Times*, March 2, 2005), Elliott notes that in March 2005 CNN became the first national cable news network to air advertisements for hard liquor with a commercial for Grey Goose vodka. According to Paul J. Chung et al., in "Association between Adolescent Viewership and Alcohol Advertising on Cable Television" (*American Journal of Public Health*, vol. 100, no. 3, March 2010), cable television has become the largest source of alcohol advertisements for youth.

ALCOHOL ADVERTISING AND YOUTH. In "Exposure to Alcohol Advertising and Teen Drinking" (*Preventive Medicine*, vol. 52, no. 2, February 1, 2011), Matthis Morgenstern et al. test whether there is an association between exposure to alcohol advertisements and the use of alcohol in adolescents. The researchers acknowledge that the results of many studies show that exposure to alcohol advertisements encourages youth to drink alcoholic beverages, to drink more if they already drink, and to develop favorable attitudes toward drinking. Morgenstern et al. go a step further, however, by testing whether an association exists between youth drinking and alcohol advertisements in particular, or between youth drinking and any type of advertisements in general. The researchers conclude that a positive association exists between exposure to alcohol advertising and certain youth drinking behaviors, such as current and binge drinking, but that no association exists between these behaviors and advertisements in general. These findings suggest that attempts to reduce youth drinking must involve limiting or changing alcohol advertising to lessen its effect on youth and/or countering alcohol advertising with public health campaigns to reduce youth drinking.

Is alcohol advertising targeted to youth or do young people just happen to watch advertising that is aimed at those aged 21 years and older? Chung et al. research this question and conclude that "across the vast majority of time slots, adolescent viewers, especially girls, were exposed to more beer, spirits, and alcopop [flavored alcoholic beverage] ads on cable television than would be expected through incidental exposure." The researchers comment that "the underage viewership threshold of 30% adopted by the various industries has been ineffective in reducing adolescent exposure to advertisements. Moreover, the wine industry's relative success in reaching young adults while avoiding adolescents suggests that more-careful discrimination between the two groups may be possible."

The Center on Alcohol Marketing and Youth notes in *Youth Exposure to Alcohol Advertising on Television, 2001–2009* (December 15, 2010, http://www.camy.org/bin/u/r/CAMYReport2001_2009.pdf) that "in 2009, 7.5 percent of all alcohol product ad placements (23,718 ads) and 9 percent of all alcohol product ad placements on cable (16,283 ads) were on programming with underage audiences greater than 30 percent." The center also states that "the National Research Council and Institute of Medicine, as well as 20 state attorneys general, have suggested that a 15 percent standard, roughly proportionate to the percentage of the population between the ages of 12 and 20, would be more appropriate."

One effort to reduce alcohol advertising that is seen by youth is the CSPI's Campaign for Alcohol-Free Sports TV. Joshua Robinson observes in "N.C.A.A. Is Criticized for Beer Advertising" (*New York Times*, January 16, 2009) that between 2005 and early 2009, 16 National Collegiate Athletic Association–member athletic conferences and 372 colleges had signed the campaign's pledge to remove beer advertisements from sports games and broadcasts. Signing the pledge does not mean that schools need to take action on the pledge, however. As of January 2009, beer advertisements had been eliminated in the Chick-fil-A Bowl and on the Big Ten Network.

Tobacco Advertising

According to the Federal Trade Commission (FTC), in *Cigarette Report for 2006* (2009, http://www.ftc.gov/os/2009/08/090812cigarettereport.pdf), the most recent report on this topic as of February 2011, cigarette sales fell 2.3% between 2005 and 2006, from 351.6 billion cigarettes to 343.4 billion cigarettes. Advertising expenditures decreased as well, from $13.1 billion in 2005 to $12.5 billion in 2006, a decline of nearly 5%.

The tobacco industry is forbidden by law to advertise on radio, television, and billboards. Where do the industry's advertising dollars go? In 2006 the largest share ($9.2 billion or 74%) of the $12.5 billion spent was used for price discounts, which are paid to cigarette retailers or wholesalers to discount the price of the cigarettes to consumers. About $817.8 million was given to consumers for promotional cigarettes and $625.8 million was used for coupons. These are all considered promotional

activities and are the primary ways in which cigarettes are advertised.

In March 2010 the U.S. Food and Drug Administration (FDA) announced that it would restrict tobacco companies' marketing practices—especially the ones that targeted youth—using the power given it under a new tobacco control law that was passed in 2009. Lyndsey Layton notes in "New FDA Rules Will Greatly Restrict Tobacco Advertising and Sales" (*Washington Post*, March 19, 2010) that tobacco companies will no longer be able to sell cigarettes to people under the age of 18 years; sponsor sporting and entertainment events; give away cigarettes or other items with the purchase of tobacco products, such as tiny purses, wristbands, and cell phone jewelry for women and girls; provide cigarettes in packages fewer than 20, which makes them less affordable and more unlikely to be purchased by youth; and sell cigarettes in vending machines to which young people have access. These new rules went into effect in June 2010.

TOBACCO ADVERTISING AND YOUTH. In *The Role of the Media in Promoting and Reducing Tobacco Use* (June 2008, http://cancercontrol.cancer.gov/tcrb/monographs/19/m19_complete.pdf), the National Cancer Institute (NCI) includes an examination of how the marketing efforts of the tobacco industry affect adolescent tobacco use. The NCI concludes that "much tobacco advertising targets the psychological needs of adolescents, such as popularity, peer acceptance, and positive self-image. Advertising creates the perception that smoking will satisfy these needs." It cites "strong and consistent evidence" that "exposure to cigarette advertising influences nonsmoking adolescents to initiate smoking and to move toward regular smoking." The NCI also discusses cigarette product placement in movies and concludes that seeing people smoke in films can influence attitudes toward smoking in positive ways, not only among adolescents but also among adults. Furthermore, based on a variety of scientific studies, the NCI determines that there is "a causal relationship between exposure to movie smoking depictions and youth smoking initiation."

ALCOHOL AND TOBACCO TAXATION

Taxation is an age-old method by which the government raises money. Alcoholic beverages have been taxed since colonial times, and tobacco products have been taxed since 1863. The alcohol and tobacco industries contribute a great deal of tax money to federal, state, and local governments.

Alcohol Taxes

According to the Distilled Spirits Council of the United States, in "Distilled Spirits Taxes" (2007, http://www.discus.org/issues/taxes.asp), hard liquor is the most highly taxed consumer product in the nation. The council

TABLE 7.4

Federal government tax collections on alcohol and tobacco, October 2008–September 2009

[In thousands of dollars]

REPORTING PERIOD: OCTOBER 2008–SEPTEMBER 2009

Revenue source	1st quarter	2nd quarter	3rd quarter	4th quarter	Cumulative 2009	Cumulative 2008
Excise tax, total	$3,992,141	$3,733,489	$6,491,870	$8,861,831	$23,079,331	$16,965,626
Alcohol tax, total	$2,326,664	$2,025,510	$2,477,984	$2,611,335	$9,441,493	$9,499,27 9
Distilled spirits tax, total	$1,268,593	$997,245	$1,250,255	$1,283,965	$4,800,058	$4,839,774
Domestic	$909,912	$716,776	$974,775	$963,023	$3,564,486	$3,558,562
Imported	$358,681	$280,469	$275,480	$320,942	$1,235,572	$1,281,212
Wine tax, total	$257,725	$199,813	$217,426	$224,086	$899,050	$880,575
Domestic	$171,837	$132,459	$147,635	$157,129	$609,060	$609,791
Imported	$85,888	$67,354	$69,791	$66,957	$289,990	$270,784
Beer tax, total	$800,346	$828,452	$1,010,303	$1,103,284	$3,742,385	$3,778,930
Domestic	$680,188	$727,851	$878,736	$963,389	$3,250,164	$3,252,159
Imported	$120,158	$100,601	$131,567	$139,895	$492,221	$526,771
Tobacco tax, total	$1,571,096	$1,605,708	$3,886,852	$6,120,304	$13,183,960	$7,153,044
Domestic						
Regular	$1,510,317	$1,529,470	$3,739,504	$4,769,563	$11,548,854	$6,851,714
Floor stocks	$0	$0	$20,514	$1,171,863	$1,192,377	$0.080
Imported	$60,779	$76,238	$126,834	$178,878	$442,729	$301,330
Unclassified alcohol and tobacco tax (domestic), total	$647	$377	$23	$139	$1,186	$684
Firearms and ammunition tax, total	$93,734	$101,894	$127,011	$130,053	$452,692	$312,619
Special (occupational) tax, total	$30	$10	$158	$74	$272	$448
Total tax collections	**$3,992,171**	**$3,733,499**	**$6,492,028**	**$8,861,905**	**$23,079,603**	**$16,966,074**

Notes:
1. This is an unofficial report. Official revenue collection figures are stated in the TTB/ATF Chief Financial Officer Annual Report.
2. All "imported" tax collection figures are obtained from U.S. Customs data.
3. Addition of current fiscal year prior quarter figures may not agree with cumulative figures for current fiscal year due to the figures being adjusted to reflect classification of unclassified alcohol and tobacco tax collections previously reported, to reflect collection adjustments for prior tax periods and to reflect rounding adjustments.
4. Source for other tax collection figures on this report is a TTB/ATF database that records tax collection data by tax return period. This data is summarized on this report by the quarter in which an incurred tax liability is satisfied.
5. Unclassified Alcohol and Tobacco Tax is tax collected, but not yet posted to a taxpayer account due to missing Employer Identification Number (EIN), permit number, and/or other taxpayer identity information.
TTB = Alcohol and Tobacco Tax and Trade Bureau (U.S. Department of the Treasury).
ATF = Bureau of Alcohol, Tobacco, Firearms and Explosives (U.S. Department of Justice).

SOURCE: "Tax Collections TTB S 5630-FY-2009 Cumulative Summary Fiscal Year 2009 Final," in *Alcohol and Tobacco Tax and Trade Bureau Statistical Release*, U.S. Department of the Treasury, Alcohol and Tobacco Tax and Trade Bureau, March 25, 2010, http://www.ttb.gov/statistics/final09.pdf (accessed November 11, 2010)

estimates that direct and indirect local, state, and federal taxes and fees account for 59% of the typical bottle price. Even though the beer and wine industries are taxed at lower levels, they still contribute a significant amount of tax revenue.

In fiscal year (FY) 2009 the federal government collected approximately $9.4 billion in excise taxes (monies paid on purchases of specific goods) on alcoholic beverages. (See Table 7.4.) Federal excise taxes on distilled spirits amounted to approximately half that total—about $4.8 billion, which included taxes on both domestic and imported distilled spirits. Distilled spirits are taxed by the proof gallon, which is a standard U.S. gallon of 231 cubic inches (3,785 cubic cm) containing 50% ethyl alcohol by volume, or 100 proof.

Excise taxes on wine and beer make up the other half of the excise taxes that are collected on alcoholic beverages. The calculation of wine taxes depends on several variables, such as alcohol content and the size of the winery. In FY 2009 federal excise taxes on wine totaled $899.1 million. (See Table 7.4.) Total beer excise taxes were much higher, at $3.7 billion. According to the Alcohol and Tobacco Tax and Trade Bureau (TTB), in "Beer" (2011, http://www.ttb.gov/beer/tax.shtml), brewers who produce fewer than 2 million barrels (1 barrel equals 31 gallons [117.3 L]) get a reduced excise tax rate of $7 per barrel on the first 60,000 barrels. Those who produce more than 2 million barrels pay an excise tax of $18 per barrel. According to the TTB, in "Statistical Release: Tax Collections, TTB S 5630-FY-2010" (December 8, 2010, http://www.ttb.gov/statistics/final10.pdf), in FY 2010 the federal government collected a total of $9.5 billion in excise taxes on alcoholic beverages.

Besides the federal excise taxes, the states levy sales taxes on alcohol. In "State Government Tax Collections in 2009" (March 2010, http://www2.census.gov/govs/statetax/2009stcreport.pdf), the U.S. Census Bureau indicates that the state sales tax collected on alcoholic beverages totaled $5.3 billion in 2009. The total state tax collections from alcohol include not only the sales tax but

FIGURE 7.1

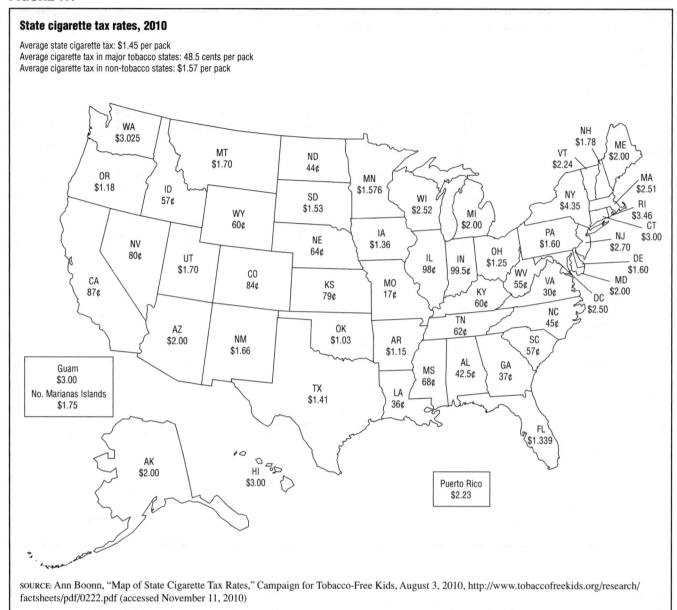

State cigarette tax rates, 2010

Average state cigarette tax: $1.45 per pack
Average cigarette tax in major tobacco states: 48.5 cents per pack
Average cigarette tax in non-tobacco states: $1.57 per pack

WA $3.025
OR $1.18
MT $1.70
ND 44¢
MN $1.576
NH $1.78
ME $2.00
VT $2.24
ID 57¢
SD $1.53
WI $2.52
NY $4.35
MA $2.51
RI $3.46
CT $3.00
WY 60¢
NE 64¢
IA $1.36
MI $2.00
PA $1.60
NJ $2.70
NV 80¢
UT $1.70
CO 84¢
IL 98¢
IN 99.5¢
OH $1.25
WV 55¢
DE $1.60
CA 87¢
KS 79¢
MO 17¢
KY 60¢
VA 30¢
MD $2.00
DC $2.50
AZ $2.00
NM $1.66
OK $1.03
AR $1.15
TN 62¢
NC 45¢
SC 57¢
TX $1.41
MS 68¢
AL 42.5¢
GA 37¢
LA 36¢
FL $1.339

Guam $3.00
No. Marianas Islands $1.75

AK $2.00
HI $3.00

Puerto Rico $2.23

SOURCE: Ann Boonn, "Map of State Cigarette Tax Rates," Campaign for Tobacco-Free Kids, August 3, 2010, http://www.tobaccofreekids.org/research/factsheets/pdf/0222.pdf (accessed November 11, 2010)

also payments for alcoholic beverage licenses. Taxes on alcohol amounted to about 0.7% ($5.3 billion of $715.2 billion) of the total state taxes collected in 2009.

Tobacco Taxes

The Census Bureau reports in "State Government Tax Collections: 2009" that state sales taxes on tobacco products amounted to $16.7 billion in 2009. States have raised their excise taxes on cigarettes to help defray health care costs that are associated with tobacco, to discourage young people from starting to smoke, and to motivate smokers to stop. Figure 7.1 shows state cigarette excise tax rates and rankings in 2010. New York had the highest state excise tax on cigarettes at $4.35 per pack. Rhode Island was second with $3.46 per pack. Missouri had the lowest excise tax of $0.17 per pack. The Campaign for Tobacco-Free Kids indicates in the fact sheet "State Ciga-

rette Excise Tax Rates and Rankings" (August 3, 2010, http://www.tobaccofreekids.org/research/factsheets/pdf/0097.pdf) that Missouri is one of three states that has not increased its cigarette excise tax since 1999 or earlier (the other two states are California and North Dakota). The average tax in the nation in 2010 was $1.45 per pack.

In addition to state taxes on tobacco, the federal government implements taxes on cigarettes and other tobacco products. In February 2009 President Barack Obama (1961–) signed into law the State Children's Health Insurance Plan bill, which includes an increase in the federal tobacco tax. According to the National Conference of State Legislatures, in "2009–2010 Proposed State Legislation for Tobacco Tax Increases" (May 19, 2010, http://www.ncsl.org/programs/health/tobacco_tax_bill09.htm), the federal excise tax on cigarettes increased to $1.01 per pack effective April 1, 2009.

GOVERNMENT REGULATION OF ALCOHOL AND TOBACCO

Besides taxation, the alcohol and tobacco industries are subject to federal and state laws that regulate factors such as sales, advertising, and shipping.

Alcohol Regulation

The best-known pieces of legislation regarding alcohol are the 18th and 21st Amendments to the U.S. Constitution. The 18th Amendment prohibited the manufacture, sale, and importation of alcoholic beverages. Ratified in 1919, it took effect in 1920 and ushered in a period in U.S. history known as Prohibition. After 13 years, during which it failed to stop the manufacture and sale of alcohol, Prohibition was repealed in 1933 by the 21st Amendment.

Most interpretations of the 21st Amendment hold that the amendment gives individual states the power to regulate and control alcoholic beverages within their own borders. Consequently, every state has its own alcohol administration and enforcement agency. "Control states" directly control the sale and distribution of alcoholic beverages within their borders. According to the TTB, in "Alcohol Beverage Control Boards" (2011, http://www.ttb.gov/wine/control_board.shtml), there are 18 control states: Alabama, Idaho, Iowa, Maine, Michigan, Mississippi, Montana, New Hampshire, North Carolina, Ohio, Oregon, Pennsylvania, Utah, Vermont, Virginia, Washington, West Virginia, and Wyoming. Montgomery County in Maryland acts as a control state as well. Some critics of this policy question whether such state monopolies violate antitrust laws. The other 32 states are licensure states and allow only licensed businesses to operate as wholesalers and retailers.

DIRECT SHIPMENTS: RECIPROCITY OR FELONY? A legislative controversy has developed over the direct shipment of alcoholic beverages from one state directly to consumers or retailers in another state. Under the U.S. Constitution's Interstate Commerce Clause, Congress has the power to regulate trade between states. Nevertheless, the 21st Amendment gives states the authority to regulate the sale and distribution of alcoholic beverages. Furthermore, it allows states to set their own laws governing the sale of alcohol within their borders.

Because the laws of the states are not uniform, several states have passed reciprocity legislation that allows specific states to exchange direct shipments, thus eliminating the state-licensed wholesalers from the exchange. Wholesalers and retailers charge that reciprocity and direct shipment are violations of the 21st Amendment. They fear being bypassed in the exchange, as do states that prohibit direct shipments of alcohol. Other stakeholders in this issue are consumers and wine producers who want the right to deal directly with each other.

ALCOHOL SALES AND THE INTERNET. In January 2001 the 21st Amendment Enforcement Act became law.

This legislation makes it difficult for companies to sell alcohol over the Internet or through mail-order services. It allows state attorneys general in states that ban direct alcohol sales to seek a federal injunction against companies that violate their liquor sales laws.

Within a month of the passage of this act, the high-tech community voiced its concern regarding such legislation, suggesting that if states could ban Internet alcohol sales they might restrict other electronic commerce as well. Senator Orrin G. Hatch (1934–; R-UT) said he crafted the bill to take other e-commerce concerns into account and insisted that the measure is narrowly tailored to deal only with alcohol.

In May 2005 the U.S. Supreme Court ruled on three cases that had been consolidated under the name *Granholm v. Heald* (544 U.S. 460). At issue were state laws in Michigan and New York that prohibited out-of-state wineries from selling their products over the Internet directly to Michigan and New York residents, but allowed in-state wineries to make such sales. The Michigan and New York state governments argued that these laws were permissible under the 21st Amendment. A group of wineries and business advocates argued that the state laws were unconstitutional restrictions of interstate trade. In a 5–4 decision, the court agreed that the state laws were unconstitutional, stating, "States have broad power to regulate liquor under §2 of the Twenty-First Amendment. This power, however, does not allow States to ban, or severely limit, the direct shipment of out-of-state wine while simultaneously authorizing direct shipment by in-state producers. If a State chooses to allow direct shipment of wine, it must do so on evenhanded terms." It should be noted that this ruling only applies to state laws that prohibit out-of-state Internet alcohol sales and not to the 21st Amendment Enforcement Act.

Early Tobacco Regulation and Legislation

Federal tobacco legislation has covered everything from unproved advertising claims and warning label requirements to the development of cigarettes and little cigars that are less likely to start fires. In the past the FDA prohibited the claim that Fairfax cigarettes prevented respiratory and other diseases (1953) and denied the claim that tartaric acid, which was added to Trim Reducing-Aid cigarettes, helped promote weight loss (1959).

The FTC has also been given jurisdiction over tobacco issues in several areas. As early as 1942 the FTC issued a cease-and-desist order in reference to Kool cigarettes' claim that smoking Kools gave extra protection against or cured colds. In January 1964 the FTC proposed a rule to strictly regulate cigarette advertisements and to prohibit explicit or implicit health claims by cigarette companies.

The tobacco industry has managed to avoid some federal regulation by being exempted from many federal health and safety laws. In the Hazardous Substances Act of 1960, the term *hazardous substance* does not include tobacco and tobacco products, nor does the term *consumer product* in the Consumer Product Safety Act of 1972. Tobacco is similarly exempted from regulation under the Fair Packaging and Labeling Act of 1966 and the Toxic Substance Control Act of 1976.

Some of the legislation of the late 1980s included requiring four alternating health warnings to be printed on tobacco packaging, prohibiting smokeless tobacco advertising on television and radio, and banning smoking on domestic airline flights. In 1992 the Synar Amendment was passed. The amendment said that states must have laws that ban the sale of tobacco products to people under 18 years of age.

In 1993 the U.S. Environmental Protection Agency released its final risk assessment on secondhand smoke and classified it as a known human carcinogen (cancer-causing agent). In 1994 the Occupational Safety and Health Administration proposed regulations that would prohibit smoking in workplaces, except in smoking rooms that are separately ventilated. As of February 2011, the United States did not have federal smoking control legislation, but many states and municipalities did have legislation that banned smoking in a variety of public places and workplaces. However, the Family Smoking and Tobacco Control Act of 2009 did give the FDA the authority to regulate the production and marketing of tobacco products within limits, such as banning certain flavored cigarettes that appealed to youth and strengthening the warnings on cigarette packages.

TOBACCO SALES AND THE INTERNET. The Internet plays a role in the distribution of tobacco. However, a number of problems began to develop with some of the websites that were operated by the vendors of tobacco products. For example, some vendors did not indicate that sales to minors were prohibited on their site. Many required that the user simply state that he or she was of legal age. In addition, many did not collect and pay cigarette sales taxes.

As a response to these problems, Congress passed the Prevent All Cigarette Trafficking (PACT) Act of 2009. The law affects Internet sales of tobacco products in that it ensures the collection of federal, state, and local taxes on cigarettes and smokeless tobacco by requiring online vendors of tobacco products to register with the states in which their customers reside and by imposing strong penalties against those who do not comply. Paying these taxes are important not only for government revenues but also to keep the price of cigarettes high to discourage their use, especially by youth.

To further safeguard illegal sales to youth, the PACT Act also bars Internet vendors of tobacco products from shipping these products via the U.S. Postal Service (USPS). The USPS does not have the means to verify the age and identification of the person receiving the products. According to the Campaign for Tobacco-Free Kids, in the fact sheet "Preventing Illegal Internet Sales of Cigarettes and Smokeless Tobacco" (March 31, 2010, http://www.tobaccofreekids.org/research/factsheets/pdf/0361.pdf), "the PACT Act will stop such Internet sales of cigarettes and smokeless tobacco to kids by requiring the sellers to verify the age of their customers prior to sale by checking against available government and commercial ID databases, and by requiring sellers to use a method of delivery that will verify the age and ID of the person accepting the final delivery of the cigarettes or smokeless tobacco prior to handing them over."

FDA REGULATION OF TOBACCO PRODUCTS. In 1994 the FDA investigated the tobacco industry to determine whether nicotine is an addictive drug that should be regulated like other addictive drugs. Weeks of testimony before Congress indicated that tobacco companies may have been aware of the addictive effects of nicotine and the likely connection between smoking and cancer as early as the mid-1950s.

In August 1995 the FDA ruled that the nicotine in tobacco products is a drug and, therefore, is liable to FDA regulation. However, the tobacco, advertising, and convenience store industries filed a lawsuit against the FDA, claiming it did not have the authority to regulate tobacco as an addictive drug. After conflicting decisions in the lower courts, the Supreme Court ruled 5–4 in *FDA v. Brown and Williamson Tobacco Corp.* (529 U.S. 120 [2000]) that the FDA lacks this authority. Even though the ruling did not allow the FDA to regulate tobacco, state laws regarding selling cigarettes to minors were not affected.

In March 2005 bipartisan bills were introduced in the U.S. House of Representatives and the U.S. Senate to grant the FDA the authority to regulate tobacco products. The bills never became law during that session of Congress, but similar legislation was introduced again in 2009. The Family Smoking and Tobacco Control Act was passed by the House and the Senate and was subsequently signed into law by President Obama in June 2009. This law gives the FDA the authority to control tobacco advertising and sales to children, require changes in tobacco products to make them less harmful, prohibit health claims that have no scientific backing, and require the contents and health dangers of tobacco products to be listed on the packaging.

ECONOMIC COSTS OF SUBSTANCE USE

Few reports are available on the economic costs of alcohol, tobacco, and drug use, and many are outdated. As of February 2011, the most recent report that calculated the economic costs of alcohol was *Updating Estimates of the Economic Costs of Alcohol Abuse in the United States:*

Estimates, Update Methods, and Data (2000, http://pubs
.niaaa.nih.gov/publications/economic-2000/alcoholcost
.PDF) by the Lewin Group for the National Institute on
Alcohol Abuse and Alcoholism (NIAAA). This report
estimates that national costs related to alcohol abuse and
dependence were approximately $185 billion in 1998.
More research has ensued in the last decade on the costs
of drug abuse and tobacco use.

Economic Costs of Drug Abuse

The Office of National Drug Control Policy
(ONDCP) asked the Lewin Group to develop data on
the costs to society of drug abuse while using data the
group had collected from a previous report for the
ONDCP. The report, *The Economic Costs of Drug Abuse
in the United States, 1992–2002* (December 2004, http://
www.ncjrs.gov/ondcppubs/publications/pdf/economic_co
sts.pdf), does not include the costs of alcohol abuse or
smoking-attributable costs. As of February 2011, it was
the most comprehensive report on this topic.

Figure 7.2 is taken from this report and shows the
progression of the economic costs of drug abuse between
1992 and 2002. The overall cost to society of drug abuse
in 2002 was estimated to be $180.8 billion, rising approx-
imately 5.3% per year between 1992 and 2002. A more
recent estimate of nearly $215 billion per year is provided
by the U.S. Department of Justice's National Drug Intelligence Center in *National Drug Threat Assessment, 2010*
(February 2010, http://www.justice.gov/ndic/pubs38/386
61/38661p.pdf).

The ONDCP report divides the costs of drug abuse
into three major cost components: productivity, health,
and "other." The proportion of each cost component
remained relatively stable between 1992 and 2002.

The largest cost component is productivity. In this
case, productivity means *loss* from productivity. It is an
indirect cost that reflects losses such as work that was
never performed because of poor health, premature death,
or incarceration. Productivity losses due to drug abuse
were estimated to be $128.6 billion in 2002.

The second-largest cost component is "other," which
includes drug-related crime costs such as the operation of
prisons, state and local police protection, and victim
costs. It also includes drug-related costs of the social
welfare system. These costs totaled $36.4 billion in 2002.

The third-largest cost component associated with drug
abuse is health care. Table 7.5 compares the health care
costs between 1992 and 2002 and shows the annual
change. The ONDCP report notes that drug abuse–related
health care costs are considerable. In 2002 the total health
care costs were $15.8 billion, up from $10.7 billion in
1992. The largest share ($3.8 billion) was the cost of
treating human immunodeficiency virus (HIV)/acquired
immunodeficiency syndrome (AIDS) patients who had a
history of injection drug use. Other significant drug abuse–
related health care costs in 2002 were hospital and ambulatory care (outpatient) costs at about $1.5 billion and
federal efforts to prevent drug abuse at $1.2 billion.

In 2009 Rosalie Liccardo Pacula et al. published *Issues
in Estimating the Economic Cost of Drug Abuse in*

FIGURE 7.2

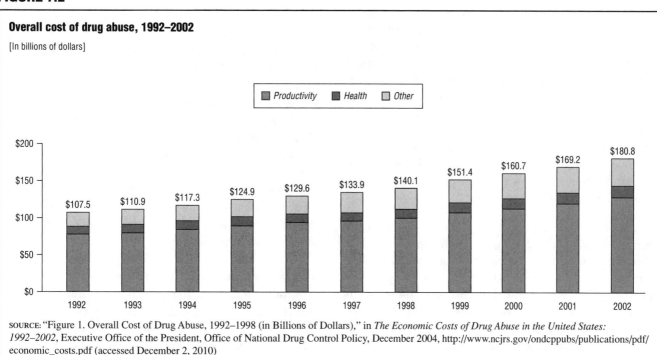

Overall cost of drug abuse, 1992–2002

[In billions of dollars]

■ *Productivity* ■ *Health* □ *Other*

SOURCE: "Figure 1. Overall Cost of Drug Abuse, 1992–1998 (in Billions of Dollars)," in *The Economic Costs of Drug Abuse in the United States:
1992–2002*, Executive Office of the President, Office of National Drug Control Policy, December 2004, http://www.ncjrs.gov/ondcppubs/publications/pdf/
economic_costs.pdf (accessed December 2, 2010)

TABLE 7.5

Health care costs resulting from drug abuse, 1992 and 2002

Detailed cost components	1992	2002	Annual change
Community-based specialty treatment	$3,770	$5,997	4.8%
Federally provided specialty treatment			
Department of Defense	$14	$8	−5.8%
Indian Health Services	$26	$54	7.6%
Bureau of Prisons	$17	$39	8.8%
Department of Veterans Affairs	$113	$116	0.2%
Health infrastructure and support			
Federal prevention	$616	$1,203	6.9%
State and local prevention	$89	$148	5.2%
Training	$49	$69	3.5%
Prevention research	$158	$402	9.8%
Treatment research	$195	$564	11.2%
Insurance administration	$268	$476	5.9%
Medical consequences			
Hospital and ambulatory care costs	$518	$1,454	10.9%
Special disease costs			
Drug-exposed infants	$407	$605	4.0%
Tuberculosis	$30	$19	−4.6%
HIV/AIDS	$3,489	$3,755	0.7%
Hepatitis B and C	$462	$312	−3.9%
Crime victim health care costs	$92	$110	1.8%
Health insurance administration	$340	$513	4.2%
Total	**$10,653**	**$15,844**	**4.1%**

SOURCE: "Table III-1. Health Care Costs, 1992 and 2002 (in Millions of Dollars)," *The Economic Costs of Drug Abuse in the United States: 1992–2002*, Executive Office of the President, Office of National Drug Control Policy, December 2004, http://www.ncjrs.gov/ondcppubs/publications/pdf/economic_costs.pdf (accessed December 2, 2010). Analysis by The Lewin Group, 2004.

Consuming Nations (http://www.rand.org/content/dam/rand/pubs/technical_reports/2009/RAND_TR709.pdf), which was developed for the European Commission by the RAND Corporation. The researchers recognize the ONDCP report as one of "considerable work" like others undertaken in various developed countries to try to quantify the economic costs of drug abuse. Pacula et al. analyze these studies and observe that they use a variety of approaches and methods, which makes it impossible to compare results across countries. The researchers also note that "the pitfalls and assumptions necessary to construct a comparable estimate across countries are quite significant and described in detail throughout this report. We conclude that it is not possible at this time to develop a meaningful comparative estimate of the cost of drug use across countries or to aggregate these costs to the regional or global level."

Likewise, a coalition of drug abuse agencies came together in Canada to develop an international model for estimating the costs of substance abuse, and its findings were published by Eric Single of the University of Toronto in "Why We Should Still Estimate the Costs of Substance Abuse Even If We Needn't Pay Undue Attention to the Bottom Line" (*Drug and Alcohol Review*, vol. 28, no. 2, March 2009). Single indicates that studies carried out in various countries use differing methods,

so they cannot be compared. He also notes that the results of cost studies in general are uncertain due to problems such as incomplete data and "a layering of multiple assumptions." Nonetheless, the coalition promotes the idea of conducting cost studies and improving their methods to help target problems and develop policies, to determine which policies and programs are most effective, and to develop national research agendas.

Economic Costs of Tobacco Use

In 2008 the Centers for Disease Control and Prevention (CDC) published "Smoking-Attributable Mortality, Years of Potential Life Lost, and Productivity Losses—United States, 2000–2004" (*Morbidity and Mortality Weekly Report*, vol. 57, no. 45, November 14, 2008), which included data on the economic costs of tobacco use. As of February 2011, this was the CDC's most recent report on this topic. The CDC estimates the economic cost of smoking-attributable lost productivity at $96.8 billion annually between 2000 and 2004. The CDC suggests, however, that with smoking-attributable health care expenditures added to this figure, the annual economic cost of cigarette smoking was approximately $193 billion per year.

TOBACCO COMPANIES AND RESPONSIBILITY FOR THE COSTS OF TOBACCO USE

Between 1960 and 1988 approximately 300 lawsuits sought damages from tobacco companies for smoking-related illnesses; courts, though, consistently held that people who choose to smoke are responsible for the health consequences of that decision. This changed in 1988, when a tobacco company was ordered to pay damages for the first time. A federal jury in Newark, New Jersey, ordered Liggett Group Inc. to pay $400,000 to the family of Rose Cipollone, a longtime smoker who died of lung cancer in 1984. The case was overturned on appeal, but the Supreme Court ruled in favor of the Cipollone family in *Cipollone v. Liggett Group, Inc.* (505 U.S. 504 [1992]). In a 7–2 ruling, the court broadened a smoker's right to sue cigarette makers in cancer cases. The justices decided that the Federal Cigarette Labeling and Advertising Act of 1965, which required warnings on tobacco products, did not preempt damage suits. Despite the warnings on tobacco packaging, people could still sue on the grounds that tobacco companies purposely concealed information about the risks of smoking.

The Master Settlement Agreement

Following the Supreme Court's decision, the tobacco industry was faced with the possibility of never-ending lawsuits and massive damage awards. Many state governments began lawsuits against major cigarette companies, seeking to recover the costs the states had paid in caring for those with smoking-related health problems. The tobacco industry responded by negotiating with the states and offering money and changes in its business practices in exchange for an end to the lawsuits and protection from future lawsuits.

In November 1998 the attorneys general from 46 states (Florida, Minnesota, Mississippi, and Texas were excluded because they had already concluded previous settlements), five territories, and the District of Columbia signed an agreement with the five largest cigarette companies (Philip Morris, R. J. Reynolds, Brown and Williamson, Lorillard, and Liggett and Myers) to settle all the state lawsuits brought to recover the Medicaid costs of treating smokers. The Master Settlement Agreement (MSA; http://ag.ca.gov/tobacco/msa.php) required the tobacco companies to make annual payments totaling $206 billion over 25 years, beginning in 2000. It also placed restrictions on how the companies could advertise, market, and promote tobacco products. Since the original signing, more than 30 additional tobacco firms have signed the MSA, and Philip Morris has contributed more than half of the payments received by the states under the agreement. Even though the MSA settles all the state and local government lawsuits, the tobacco industry is still subject to class-action and individual lawsuits.

The four states that negotiated their own lawsuit settlements began receiving payments from the tobacco companies in 1998. "Up-front" payments to other states began in 1999, prior to the beginning of the annual payments in 2000. In the fact sheet "Actual Tobacco Settlement Payments Received by the States, 1998–2009" (August 10, 2009, http://www.tobaccofreekids.org/research/factsheets/pdf/0218.pdf), the Campaign for Tobacco-Free Kids details the amount of money that the states received between 1998 and 2009. (See Table 7.6.)

HOW ARE STATES USING THE SETTLEMENT FUNDS?
The MSA did not place any restrictions on how state governments are to use the funds they receive under the agreement. Antismoking and public health organizations argue that the most appropriate use for MSA money is to fund smoking prevention and cessation programs. Since the November 1998 tobacco settlement, the Campaign for Tobacco-Free Kids, the American Lung Association, the American Cancer Society, and the American Heart Association have published an annual report to monitor how states are handling the settlement funds. The FY 2011 report *A Broken Promise to Our Children: The 1998 State Tobacco Settlement 12 Years Later* (November 17, 2010, http://www.tobaccofreekids.org/content/what_we_do/state_local_issues/settlement/FY2011/StateSettlementReport_FY2011_web.pdf) notes that states have fallen far short in their efforts to adequately fund tobacco prevention and cessation programs and that "there is more evidence than ever that tobacco prevention and cessation programs work."

According to the report, in FY 2011 no states were funding tobacco prevention and cessation programs at the minimum levels recommended by the CDC. (See Table 7.7.) Eight states were funding these programs at about half that level or more: Alaska, North Dakota, Hawaii, Montana, Wyoming, Delaware, Maine, and Oklahoma. The remaining 42 states and the District of Columbia funded tobacco prevention and cessation programs at less than half the CDC-recommended amount. Table 7.8 shows each state's tobacco prevention spending versus tobacco company spending for marketing in each state. On average, tobacco companies outspend the states 24.8 to 1 in marketing versus prevention spending.

What have states done with the tobacco settlement funds not allocated to tobacco prevention and cessation programs? The answer to this question varies with each state; in general, states have used settlement monies to fund other health-and youth-related programs, capital projects (e.g., building hospitals), medical research, medical education, enforcement of tobacco control laws, and expansion of health clinics for low-income citizens. Some states also used part of the money to pay down their debt or to help balance their budgets.

TOBACCO QUOTA SYSTEM ENDED

In 1938 federal tobacco marketing quota and price support loan programs were established during the Great Depression under the Agricultural Adjustment Act of 1933. The act provided funding for farmers who left part of their fields unplanted, which reduced crop sizes and crop surpluses and caused prices to rise. This approach helped stabilize crop prices and raise their value so that American farmers would remain or become profitable.

Since the 1930s prices for tobacco have been supported through this system of quotas that limited supply and raised market prices to a federally guaranteed price. If the guaranteed price of tobacco was not reached in the marketplace, tobacco farmers were given the guaranteed price, called a nonrecourse loan price. However, in recent years high-priced American tobacco has been losing market share to less-costly foreign-grown tobacco.

Euromonitor International (2011, http://www.euromonitor.com/), which analyzes tobacco industry markets, shows the production of cigarettes in the United States to have fallen by nearly half from 680 billion cigarettes in 1998 to 385 billion cigarettes in 2009. During the same period cigarette imports rose from 6.4 billion in 1998 to a high of 27.1 billion in 2003, and then dropped to 8 billion in 2009. In addition, exports of U.S.-produced cigarettes to foreign markets plunged from 151.8 billion cigarettes in 1999 to 55 billion in 2009.

In 2004 the Fair and Equitable Tobacco Reform Act ended the quota program and in 2005 established the Tobacco Transition Payment Program, which provided

TABLE 7.6

Tobacco settlement payments, by state, 1998–2009

State	1998	1999	2000	2001	2002	2003	2004	2005	2006	2007	2008	2009	State tobacco prevention*
Alabama	$0.0	$0.0	$163.0	$104.8	$114.4	$92.7	$100.7	$103.0	$94.3	$98.1	$106.1	$116.6	$2.3
Alaska	$0.0	$15.8	$19.6	$20.7	$23.7	$19.6	$21.2	$21.8	$19.9	$20.7	$34.7	$37.3	$9.2
Arizona	$0.0	$0.0	$148.9	$90.2	$105.4	$85.8	$91.6	$94.0	$86.0	$89.5	$115.6	$125.6	$21.3
Arkansas	$0.0	$0.0	$0.0	$140.1	$57.4	$47.5	$51.5	$52.8	$48.3	$50.3	$57.3	$62.7	$16.9
California	$0.0	$589.7	$688.6	$773.5	$912.7	$743.4	$793.5	$813.7	$744.5	$774.8	$832.1	$914.4	$78.1
Colorado	$0.0	$63.3	$78.9	$83.3	$95.0	$78.6	$85.2	$87.4	$80.0	$83.2	$103.6	$112.8	$27.5
Connecticut	$0.0	$85.8	$100.2	$112.5	$132.7	$108.1	$115.4	$118.4	$108.3	$112.7	$141.3	$153.8	$8.3
Delaware	$0.0	$18.3	$21.3	$24.0	$28.3	$23.0	$24.6	$25.2	$23.1	$24.0	$30.5	$33.2	$11.3
DC	$0.0	$28.0	$34.9	$36.9	$42.1	$34.8	$37.7	$38.7	$35.4	$36.9	$43.6	$47.6	$4.0
Florida	$562.5	$531.0	$640.9	$743.4	$765.7	$546.4	$363.9	$416.7	$389.7	$396.4	$398.0	$388.0	$60.2
Georgia	$0.0	$60.6	$141.2	$149.1	$170.0	$140.7	$152.6	$156.5	$143.2	$149.0	$159.5	$175.4	$3.2
Hawaii	$0.0	$14.9	$32.5	$36.5	$43.0	$35.1	$37.4	$38.4	$35.1	$36.5	$56.1	$60.4	$11.3
Idaho	$0.0	$9.0	$20.9	$22.1	$25.2	$20.8	$22.6	$23.2	$21.2	$22.1	$28.5	$31.0	$2.6
Illinois	$0.0	$114.9	$267.8	$282.7	$322.4	$266.9	$289.3	$296.7	$271.5	$282.5	$310.0	$340.2	$9.5
Indiana	$0.0	$50.4	$117.4	$123.9	$141.3	$117.0	$126.8	$130.0	$119.0	$123.8	$147.4	$161.0	$16.0
Iowa	$0.0	$21.5	$50.0	$52.8	$60.2	$49.9	$54.1	$55.4	$50.7	$52.8	$75.5	$81.6	$11.2
Kansas	$0.0	$20.6	$48.0	$50.6	$57.7	$47.8	$51.8	$53.1	$48.6	$50.6	$66.3	$72.0	$2.0
Kentucky	$0.0	$43.5	$95.0	$106.7	$125.9	$102.6	$109.5	$112.3	$102.7	$106.9	$115.1	$126.5	$3.7
Louisiana	$0.0	$55.7	$129.8	$137.0	$156.2	$129.3	$140.2	$143.8	$131.5	$136.9	$160.6	$175.5	$8.5
Maine	$0.0	$19.0	$44.3	$46.7	$53.3	$44.1	$47.8	$49.0	$44.9	$46.7	$58.2	$63.4	$11.7
Maryland	$0.0	$55.8	$130.0	$137.4	$156.6	$129.6	$140.5	$144.1	$131.8	$137.2	$166.2	$181.2	$20.6
Massachusetts	$0.0	$99.7	$217.9	$244.8	$288.8	$235.2	$251.1	$257.5	$235.6	$245.2	$288.5	$315.2	$13.5
Michigan	$0.0	$107.5	$234.8	$263.7	$311.2	$253.5	$270.5	$277.4	$253.8	$264.2	$290.2	$318.4	$5.1
Minnesota	$0.0	$220.8	$326.7	$351.5	$377.9	$260.2	$168.5	$175.5	$180.8	$183.9	$182.0	$179.9	$21.5
Mississippi	$232.1	$109.8	$199.5	$231.1	$229.0	$169.6	$112.5	$116.9	$120.5	$122.6	$121.3	$120.1	$10.7
Missouri	$0.0	$0.0	$0.0	$387.8	$159.6	$130.4	$141.4	$145.0	$132.7	$138.1	$153.3	$168.1	$2.7
Montana	$0.0	$10.5	$24.4	$25.8	$29.4	$24.4	$26.4	$27.1	$24.7	$25.8	$34.6	$37.5	$9.3
Nebraska	$0.0	$14.7	$34.2	$36.1	$41.2	$34.1	$37.0	$37.9	$34.7	$36.1	$42.9	$46.8	$4.0
Nevada	$0.0	$15.1	$35.1	$37.0	$42.3	$35.0	$37.9	$38.9	$35.6	$37.0	$46.0	$50.1	$4.1
New Hampshire	$0.0	$16.4	$38.3	$40.4	$46.1	$38.2	$41.4	$42.5	$38.8	$40.4	$48.4	$52.8	$1.1
New Jersey	$0.0	$0.0	$402.5	$235.8	$267.9	$221.7	$240.4	$246.5	$225.5	$234.7	$262.2	$287.4	$10.2
New Mexico	$0.0	$14.7	$34.3	$36.2	$41.3	$34.2	$37.1	$38.0	$34.8	$36.2	$44.9	$48.9	$10.5
New York	$0.0	$315.1	$688.5	$773.4	$912.5	$743.3	$793.4	$813.6	$744.4	$774.7	$834.5	$916.8	$81.9
North Carolina	$0.0	$57.6	$125.8	$141.3	$166.8	$135.8	$145.0	$148.7	$136.0	$141.6	$160.0	$175.2	$18.5
North Dakota	$0.0	$9.0	$21.0	$22.2	$25.4	$21.0	$22.8	$23.3	$21.3	$22.2	$36.5	$39.2	$4.1
Ohio	$0.0	$124.4	$289.8	$306.0	$348.9	$288.8	$313.1	$321.1	$293.8	$305.8	$334.3	$366.9	$7.1

Alcohol, Tobacco, and Illicit Drugs

TABLE 7.6

Tobacco settlement payments, by state, 1998–2009 [CONTINUED]

State	1998	1999	2000	2001	2002	2003	2004	2005	2006	2007	2008	2009	State tobacco prevention*
Oklahoma	$0.0	$25.6	$59.6	$62.9	$71.8	$59.4	$64.4	$66.1	$60.4	$62.9	$89.0	$96.2	$19.1
Oregon	$0.0	$28.3	$61.9	$69.5	$82.1	$66.8	$71.3	$73.2	$66.9	$69.7	$90.3	$98.1	$9.1
Pennsylvania	$0.0	$0.0	$452.3	$348.5	$410.9	$334.7	$357.3	$366.4	$335.2	$348.8	$382.0	$419.2	$33.2
Rhode Island	$0.0	$17.7	$41.4	$43.7	$49.8	$41.2	$44.7	$45.8	$41.9	$43.6	$53.2	$58.0	$1.9
South Carolina	$0.0	$29.0	$67.7	$71.5	$81.5	$67.4	$73.1	$76.0	$68.6	$71.4	$83.5	$91.2	$1.0
South Dakota	$0.0	$8.6	$20.1	$21.2	$24.2	$20.0	$21.7	$22.2	$20.4	$21.2	$27.6	$30.0	$5.8
Tennessee	$0.0	$0.0	$256.4	$150.4	$169.1	$140.0	$151.7	$155.6	$142.4	$148.2	$157.3	$173.0	$6.1
Texas	$378.0	$1,018.9	$839.8	$974.2	$1,004.5	$719.0	$479.9	$498.6	$516.1	$524.4	$525.2	$512.6	$12.6
Utah	$0.0	$11.0	$25.6	$27.0	$30.8	$25.5	$27.7	$28.4	$25.9	$27.0	$42.1	$45.2	$8.2
Vermont	$0.0	$10.2	$22.2	$24.9	$29.4	$23.9	$25.6	$26.2	$24.0	$25.0	$39.9	$42.9	$6.1
Virginia	$0.0	$50.5	$117.6	$124.2	$141.6	$117.2	$127.1	$130.4	$119.3	$124.1	$132.7	$145.9	$13.6
Washington	$0.0	$50.7	$118.1	$124.7	$142.2	$117.7	$127.6	$130.9	$119.8	$124.6	$173.0	$187.2	$28.4
West Virginia	$0.0	$21.9	$51.0	$53.8	$61.4	$50.8	$55.1	$56.5	$51.7	$53.8	$73.0	$79.1	$6.7
Wisconsin	$0.0	$51.2	$111.8	$125.6	$148.2	$120.7	$128.8	$132.1	$120.9	$125.8	$149.2	$162.9	$16.3
Wyoming	$0.0	$6.1	$13.4	$15.0	$17.8	$14.5	$15.4	$15.8	$14.5	$15.1	$21.4	$23.1	$6.9
Am. Samoa	$0.0	$0.4	$0.8	$0.9	$1.1	$0.9	$0.9	$1.0	$0.89	$0.9	$2.4	$2.5	NA
Guam	$0.0	$0.5	$1.2	$1.3	$1.6	$1.3	$1.4	$1.4	$1.28	$1.3	$2.8	$3.0	NA
No. Mariana	$0.0	$0.2	$0.5	$0.3	$0.4	$0.6	$0.5	$0.5	$0.49	$0.5	$2.0	$2.0	NA
Puerto Rico	$0.0	$27.7	$60.5	$46.2	$54.6	$83.9	$70.0	$71.5	$65.4	$68.1	$82.6	$90.1	NA
Virgin Islands	$0.0	$0.4	$0.9	$0.7	$0.8	$1.3	$1.1	$1.1	$1.10	$1.1	$2.5	$2.7	NA
MSA total	$0.0	$2.4 bill.	$6.0 bill.	$6.4 bill.	$7.0 bill.	$5.8 bill.	$6.2 bill.	$6.4 bill.	$5.8 bill.	$6.1 bill.	$7.0 bill.	$7.6 bill.	$0.6 bill.
Ind. State total	$1.4 bill.	$1.9 bill.	$2.0 bill.	$2.3 bill.	$2.4 bill.	$1.7 bill.	$1.1 bill.	$1.2 bill.	$1.2 bill.	$1.2 bill.	$1.2 bill.	$1.2 bill.	$0.1 bill.
National total	**$1.4 bill.**	**$4.3 bill.**	**$8.0 bill.**	**$8.7 bill.**	**$9.4 bill.**	**$7.5 bill.**	**$7.3 bill.**	**$7.6 bill.**	**$7.0 bill.**	**$7.3 bill.**	**$8.2 bill.**	**$8.8 bill.**	**$0.7 bill.**

MSA = Master Settlement Agreement.

*State tobacco prevention spending includes state and federal funds.

SOURCE: "Actual Tobacco Settlement Payments Received by the States, 1998–2009," Campaign for Tobacco-Free Kids, August 10, 2009, http://www.tobaccofreekids.org/research/factsheets/pdf/0218.pdf (accessed November 10, 2010)

TABLE 7.7

Rankings of funding for state tobacco prevention programs, fiscal year 2011

State	Fiscal year 2011 current annual funding ($millions)	CDC annual recommendation (millions)	Fiscal year percent of CDC's recommendation	Current rank
Alaska*	$9.8	$10.7	92.0%	1
North Dakota*	$8.2	$9.3	88.1%	2
Hawaii	$9.3	$15.2	61.1%	3
Montana	$8.4	$13.9	60.4%	4
Wyoming	$5.4	$9.0	60.0%	5
Delaware	$8.3	$13.9	59.5%	6
Maine	$9.9	$18.5	53.5%	7
Oklahoma	$21.7	$45.0	48.2%	8
Vermont	$4.5	$10.4	43.4%	9
Minnesota	$19.6	$58.4	33.6%	10
Arkansas	$11.8	$36.4	32.4%	11
South Dakota	$3.5	$11.3	31.0%	12
Utah	$7.1	$23.6	30.2%	13
New Mexico	$7.0	$23.4	29.8%	14
Florida	$61.6	$210.9	29.2%	15
Arizona	$19.8	$68.1	29.1%	16
Mississippi	$9.9	$39.2	25.3%	17
New York	$58.4	$254.3	23.0%	18
West Virginia	$5.7	$27.8	20.4%	19
Iowa	$7.3	$36.7	20.0%	20
Washington	$13.4	$67.3	19.8%	21
North Carolina	$18.3	$106.8	17.1%	22
California	$75.0	$441.9	17.0%	23
Louisiana	$9.0	$53.5	16.9%	24
Oregon	$7.1	$43.0	16.6%	25
Nebraska	$2.9	$21.5	13.3%	26
Colorado	$7.0	$54.4	12.9%	27
Indiana	$9.2	$78.8	11.7%	28
Wisconsin	$6.9	$64.3	10.7%	29
Pennsylvania	$14.7	$155.5	9.5%	30
Virginia	$9.4	$103.2	9.1%	31
Idaho	$1.5	$16.9	8.9%	32
South Carolina	$5.0	$62.2	8.0%	33
Maryland	$4.3	$63.3	6.9%	34
Illinois	$9.5	$157.0	6.1%	35
District of Columbia	$569,000	$10.5	5.4%	36
Massachusetts	$4.5	$90.0	5.0%	37
Rhode Island	$735,095	$15.2	4.8%	38
Kentucky	$2.6	$57.2	4.5%	39
Texas	$11.4	$266.3	4.3%	40
Kansas	$1.0	$32.1	3.1%	41
Michigan	$2.6	$121.2	2.1%	42
Georgia	$2.0	$116.5	1.8%	43
Alabama	$860,000	$56.7	1.5%	44
Connecticut	$400,000	$43.9	0.9%	45
New Jersey	$600,000	$119.8	0.5%	46
Tennessee	$222,268	$71.7	0.3%	47
Missouri	$60,000	$73.2	0.1%	48
Nevada	$0	$32.5	0.0%	51
New Hampshire	$0	$19.2	0.0%	51
Ohio	$0	$145.0	0.0%	51

*Alaska and North Dakota currently fund tobacco prevention programs at the CDC-recommended levels if both state and federal funding is counted.
CDC = Center for Disease Control.

SOURCE: "FY2011 Rankings of Funding for State Tobacco Prevention Programs," in *A Broken Promise to Our Children: The 1998 State Tobacco Settlement 12 Years Later*, Campaign for Tobacco-Free Kids, November 17, 2010, http://www.tobaccofreekids.org/reports/settlements/FY2011/StateSettlementReport_FY2011_web.pdf (accessed December 2, 2010)

10 years of transitional payments to farmers previously holding quota contracts. The USDA's Farm Service Program reports in "Tobacco Transition Payment Program" (2011, http://www.fsa.usda.gov/FSA/webapp?area=home &subject=toba&topic=landing) that "payments are funded through assessments of approximately $10 billion on tobacco product manufacturers and importers." Since the termination of the federal tobacco program with the 2005 crop, the USDA Economic Research Service (ERS) no longer maintains an active tobacco market analysis program. Thus, many annual tobacco-related publications are no longer being produced.

TABLE 7.8

Tobacco prevention spending, fiscal year 2011, vs. tobacco company marketing, 2006, by state

State	Annual smoking caused health costs in state	Fiscal year 2011 total tobacco prevention spending	2006 tobacco company marketing in state	Percentage of tobacco company marketing that state spends on tobacco prevention	Ratio of tobacco company marketing to state tobacco prevention spending
Total	$96.7 bill.	$517.9	$12.8 bill.	4.0%	24.8 to 1
Alabama	$1.49 bill.	$860,000	$261.6	0.3%	304.1 to 1
Alaska	$169	$9.8	$24.9	39.5%	2.5 to 1
Arizona	$1.3 bill.	$19.8	$172.8	11.5%	8.7 to 1
Arkansas	$812	$11.8	$155.7	7.6%	13.2 to 1
California	$9.14 bill.	$75.0	$819.5	9.2%	10.9 to 1
Colorado	$1.31 bill.	$7.0	$170.7	4.1%	24.4 to 1
Connecticut	$1.63 bill.	$400,000	$123.0	0.3%	307.5 to 1
Delaware	$284	$8.3	$106.7	7.8%	12.9 to 1
DC	$243	$569,000	$16.0	3.6%	28.1 to 1
Florida	$6.32 bill.	$61.6	$881.4	7.0%	14.3 to 1
Georgia	$2.25 bill.	$2.0	$426.4	0.5%	209.0 to 1
Hawaii	$336	$9.3	$42.1	22.1%	4.5 to 1
Idaho	$319	$1.5	$57.9	2.6%	38.6 to 1
Illinois	$4.10 bill.	$9.5	$452.4	2.1%	47.6 to 1
Indiana	$2.08 bill.	$9.2	$426.2	2.2%	46.3 to 1
Iowa	$1.01 bill.	$7.3	$174.2	4.2%	23.7 to 1
Kansas	$927	$1.0	$104.6	1.0%	104.6 to 1
Kentucky	$1.50 bill.	$2.6	$417.5	0.6%	161.6 to 1
Louisiana	$1.47 bill.	$9.0	$241.0	3.8%	26.7 to 1
Maine	$602	$9.9	$59.0	16.8%	6.0 to 1
Maryland	$1.96 bill.	$4.3	$188.8	2.3%	43.4 to 1
Massachusetts	$3.54 bill.	$4.5	$194.6	2.3%	43.4 to 1
Michigan	$3.40 bill.	$2.6	$393.6	0.7%	151.5 to 1
Minnesota	$2.06 bill.	$19.6	$196.6	10.0%	10.0 to 1
Mississippi	$719	$9.9	$185.5	5.3%	18.7 to 1
Missouri	$2.13 bill.	$60,000	$419.9	0.0%	6,998.1 to 1
Montana	$277	$8.4	$33.3	25.2%	4.0 to 1
Nebraska	$537	$2.9	$72.1	4.0%	25.2 to 1
Nevada	$565	$0	$113.8	0.0%	NA
New Hampshire	$564	$0	$122.2	0.0%	NA
New Jersey	$3.17 bill.	$600,000	$226.3	0.3%	377.2 to 1
New Mexico	$461	$7.0	$47.0	14.9%	6.7 to 1
New York	$8.17 bill.	$58.4	$429.6	13.6%	7.4 to 1
North Carolina	$2.46 bill.	$18.3	$535.9	3.4%	29.3 to 1
North Dakota	$247	$8.2	$32.3	25.4%	3.9 to 1
Ohio	$4.37 bill.	$0	$556.7	0.0%	NA to 1
Oklahoma	$1.16 bill.	$21.7	$213.1	10.2%	9.8 to 1
Oregon	$1.11 bill.	$7.1	$137.0	5.2%	19.2 to 1
Pennsylvania	$5.19 bill.	$14.7	$533.9	2.8%	36.3 to 1
Rhode Island	$506	$735,095	$35.1	2.1%	47.7 to 1
South Carolina	$1.09 bill.	$5.0	$282.6	1.8%	56.5 to 1
South Dakota	$274	$3.5	$37.0	9.5%	10.6 to 1
Tennessee	$2.16 bill.	$222,268	$405.5	0.1%	1,824.3 to 1
Texas	$5.83 bill.	$11.4	$854.2	1.3%	74.9 to 1
Utah	$345	$7.1	$58.7	12.1%	8.2 to 1
Vermont	$233	$4.5	$27.4	16.5%	6.1 to 1
Virginia	$2.08 bill.	$9.4	$411.3	2.3%	43.9 to 1
Washington	$1.95 bill.	$13.4	$146.0	9.1%	10.9 to 1
West Virginia	$690	$5.7	$140.4	4.0%	24.8 to 1
Wisconsin	$2.02 bill.	$6.9	$274.0	2.5%	40.0 to 1
Wyoming	$136	$5.4	$27.6	19.6%	5.1 to 1

SOURCE: "Spending vs. Tobacco Company Marketing," in *A Broken Promise to Our Children: The 1998 State Tobacco Settlement 12 Years Later,* Campaign for Tobacco-Free Kids, November 17, 2010, http://www.tobaccofreekids.org/reports/settlements/FY2011/StateSettlementReport_FY2011_web.pdf (accessed December 2, 2010)

CHAPTER 8
DRUG TRAFFICKING

Trafficking in drugs refers to commercial activity: the buying and selling of illegal and controlled substances without a permit to do so—a permit that, for example, a physician, pharmacist, or researcher would have. Illegal drugs are those with no currently accepted medical use in the United States, such as heroin, lysergic acid diethylamide (LSD), and marijuana. It is illegal to buy, sell, possess, and use these drugs except for research purposes. (Some states and local jurisdictions have decriminalized certain uses of specific amounts of marijuana, but federal laws supersede these state and local marijuana decriminalization laws. For a more detailed discussion on the legalization of marijuana, see Chapter 9.)

Legal drugs are those whose sale, possession, and use as intended are not forbidden by law. However, the use of legal psychoactive (mood- or mind-altering) drugs, which have the potential for abuse, is restricted. These drugs, which include narcotics, depressants, and stimulants, are available only with a prescription. They are called controlled substances. Drug trafficking includes all commercial activities that are integral to the buying and selling of illegal and controlled substances, including their manufacture, production, preparation, importation, exportation, supply, distribution, or transportation.

CRIMINAL PENALTIES FOR TRAFFICKING
Federal Penalties

The Controlled Substances Act of 1970 provides penalties for the unlawful trafficking in controlled substances, based on the schedule (rank) of the drug or substance. (For definitions of the schedules, see Table 1.2 in Chapter 1.) Generally, the more dangerous the drug and the larger the quantity involved, the stiffer the penalty. The trafficking of heroin, cocaine, LSD, and phencyclidine (PCP), all Schedule I or II drugs, includes mandatory jail time and fines. For example, a person caught selling at least 18 ounces (500 g) but less than 11 pounds (5 kg) of cocaine powder will receive a minimum of five years in prison and may be fined up to $2 million for a first offense. (See Table 8.1.) The same penalty is imposed for the sale of 0.2 to 1.7 of an ounce (5 to 49 g) of cocaine base (crack). Six plain M&Ms candies weigh 0.2 of an ounce (5 g), and a bag of M&Ms candies (about 60 M&Ms) weighs 1.6 of an ounce (47.9 g). Legislators have imposed the high penalty for selling crack in an effort to curb the use of this drug.

Following the second offense, penalties double to a minimum of 10 years in prison and up to $4 million in fines. When higher quantities are involved (11 or more pounds [5 or more kg] of cocaine powder, 1.8 of an ounce or more [50 g or more] of crack, and so on), penalties for the first offense are a minimum of 10 years in prison and fines up to $4 million may be levied. For the second offense, a minimum of 20 years and up to $8 million in fines are given, and the third offense results in mandatory life imprisonment. These examples are for an individual. Higher penalties apply if an organized group is involved or if a death or injury is associated with the arrest event.

These penalties also apply to the sale of fentanyl (a powerful painkiller medicine) or similar-acting drugs, heroin, LSD, methamphetamine, and PCP. The smallest amount, which can earn someone a minimum sentence of five years in prison and a fine of up to $2 million, involves trafficking in LSD, in which an amount of 0.03 of an ounce (1 g) carries a five-year-minimum sentence in prison.

Punishments for marijuana, hashish, and hashish oil are shown in Table 8.2. Special penalties exist for marijuana trafficking because it may be traded in large quantities or grown in substantial amounts. The lower the amounts sold or the fewer the plants grown, the lower the sentence. A person cultivating 1 to 49 plants or selling less than 110 pounds (50 kg) of marijuana mixture, 22 pounds (10 kg) or less of hashish, or 2.2 pounds (1 kg) or less of hashish oil may get a maximum sentence of five years in prison and a maximum fine of $250,000. Sentences for second offenses

TABLE 8.1

Federal drug trafficking penalties, excluding marijuana

Drug/Schedule	Quantity	Penalties	Quantity	Penalties
Cocaine (Schedule II)	500–4,999 gms mixture	**First offense:** Not less than 5 yrs, and not more than 40 yrs. If death or serious injury, not less than 20 or more than life. Fine of not more than $2 million if an individual, $5 million if not an individual. **Second offense:** Not less than 10 yrs, and not more than life. If death or serious injury, life imprisonment. Fine of not more than $4 million if an individual, $10 million if not an individual.	5 kgs or more mixture	**First offense:** Not less than 10 yrs, and not more than life. If death or serious injury, not less than 20 or more than life. Fine of not more than $4 million if an individual, $10 million if not an individual. **Second offense:** Not less than 20 yrs, and not more than life. If death or serious injury, life imprisonment. Fine of not more than $8 million if an individual, $20 million if not an individual. **2 or more prior offenses:** Life imprisonment.
Cocaine base (Schedule II)	5–49 gms mixture		50 gms or more mixture	
Fentanyl (Schedule II)	40–399 gms mixture		400 gms or more mixture	
Fentanyl Analogue (Schedule I)	10–99 gms mixture		100 gms or more mixture	
Heroin (Schedule I)	100–999 gms mixture		1 kg or more mixture	
LSD (Schedule I)	1–9 gms mixture		10 gms or more mixture	
Methamphetamine (Schedule II)	5–49 gms pure or 50–499 gms mixture		50 gms or more pure or 500 gms or more mixture	
PCP (Schedule II)	10–99 gms pure or 100–999 gms mixture		100 gms or more pure or 1 kg or more mixture	
Other Schedule I & II drugs (and any drug product containing Gamma Hydroxybutyric Acid)	Any amount	**First offense:** Not more that 20 yrs. If death or serious injury, not less than 20 yrs, or more than life. Fine $1 million if an individual, $5 million if not an individual. **Second offense:** Not more than 30 yrs. If death or serious injury, not less than life. Fine $2 million if an individual, $10 million if not an individual.		
Flunitrazepam (Schedule IV)	1 gm or more			
Other Schedule III drugs	Any amount	**First offense:** Not more than 5 years. Fine not more than $250,000 if an individual, $1 million if not an individual. **Second offense:** Not more than 10 yrs. Fine not more than $500,000 if an individual, $2 million if not an individual.		
Flunitrazepam (Schedule IV)	30 to 999 mgs			
All other Schedule IV drugs	Any amount	**First offense:** Not more than 3 years. Fine not more than $250,000 if an individual, $1 million if not an individual. **Second offense:** Not more than 6 yrs. Fine not more than $500,000 if an individual, $2 million if not an individual.		
Flunitrazepam (Schedule IV)	Less than 30 mgs			
All Schedule V drugs	Any amount	**First offense:** Not more than 1 yr. Fine not more than $100,000 if an individual, $250,000 if not an individual. **Second offense:** Not more than 2 yrs. Fine not more than $200,000 if an individual, $500,000 if not an individual.		

gms = grams
kg = kilograms
mgs = milligrams

SOURCE: Adapted from "Federal Trafficking Penalties," U.S. Department of Justice, U.S. Drug Enforcement Administration, undated, http://www.usdoj.gov/dea/agency/penalties.pdf (accessed November 11, 2010)

TABLE 8.2

Federal marijuana trafficking penalties

Drug	Quantity	First offense	Second offense
Marijuana	1,000 kg or more mixture; or 1,000 or more plants	• Not less than 10 years, not more than life • If death or serious injury, not less than 20 years, not more than life • Fine not more than $4 million if an individual, $10 million if other than an individual	• Not less than 20 years, not more than life • If death or serious injury, mandatory life • Fine not more than $8 million if an individual, $20 million if other than an individual
Marijuana	100 kg to 999 kg mixture; or 100 to 999 plants	• Not less than 5 years, not more than 40 years • If death or serous injury, not less than 20 years, not more than life • Fine not more than $2 million if an individual, $5 million if other than an individual	• Not less than 10 years, not more than life • If death or serious injury, mandatory life • Fine not more than $4 million if an individual, $10 million if other than an individual
Marijuana	More than 10 kg hashish; 50 to 99 kg mixture More than 1 kg of hashish oil; 50 to 99 plants	• Not more than 20 years • If death or serious injury, not less than 20 years, not more than life • Fine $1 million if an individual, $5 million if other than an individual	• Not more than 30 years • If death or serious injury, mandatory life • Fine $2 million if an individual, $10 million if other than individual
Marijuana	1 to 49 plants; less than 50 kg mixture	• Not more than 5 years • Fine not more than $250,000, $1 million other than individual	• Not more than 10 years • Fine $500,000 if an individual, $2 million if other than individual
Hashish	10 kg or less		
Hashish oil	1 kg or less		

SOURCE: Adapted from "Federal Trafficking Penalties—Marijuana," U.S. Department of Justice, U.S. Drug Enforcement Administration, undated, http://www.usdoj.gov/dea/agency/penalties.pdf (accessed November 11, 2010)

involving large amounts of marijuana may earn the trafficker up to life imprisonment.

State Laws

States have the discretionary power to make their own drug laws. The possession of marijuana may be a misdemeanor in one state but a felony in another. Prison sentences can also vary for the same charges in different states—the distribution of 18 ounces (500 g) of cocaine as a Class C felony may specify 10 to 50 years in one state and 24 to 40 years in another. Most states follow the model of the Controlled Substances Act and enforce laws that facilitate the seizure of drug trafficking profits, specify greater penalties for trafficking, and promote user accountability by punishing drug users.

IS THE PROFIT WORTH THE RISK?

Despite the possibility of long prison terms (up to life imprisonment), many drug dealers evidently consider the enormous potential profits of drug trafficking worth the risk. The media often report drug busts and indictments of people involved in multimillion- or billion-dollar operations. Paying fines of hundreds of thousands of dollars, or even millions of dollars, becomes part of doing business when the profits are so high.

THE WORLD'S POPULATION AND ILLICIT DRUGS

The United Nations Office on Drugs and Crime estimates in *World Drug Report 2010* (June 2010, http://www.unodc.org/documents/wdr/WDR_2010/World_Drug_Report_2010_lo-res.pdf) that between 155 million and 250 million people (3.5% to 5.7% of the world's population aged 15 to 64 years) were users of illicit drugs in 2008. Between 16 million and 38 million people were addicted to drugs. In 2008, 129 million to 190 million people used cannabis, 13.7 million to 52.9 million people used amphetamine-type stimulants, 15 million to 19.3 million people used cocaine, and 12.8 million to 21.8 million people used opiates.

WORLD PRODUCTION OF PLANT-DERIVED (ORGANIC) DRUGS

In *International Narcotics Control Strategy Report: Volume I, Drug and Chemical Control* (March 2010, http://www.state.gov/documents/organization/138548.pdf), the Bureau of International Narcotics and Law Enforcement Affairs (INL), an element of the U.S. Department of State, provides data on the amount of land that is cultivated to raise opium poppy, the source of heroin and other opioids; coca leaf, from which cocaine is derived; and cannabis, the hemp plant from which marijuana and hashish are derived.

According to the INL, the largest amount of cultivated land was dedicated to the production of opium poppy, followed by coca leaf and cannabis. (See Table 8.3.) In 2008, the most recent year for which data are complete, 485,300 acres (196,400 ha) of land were used to grow opium poppy, a decrease from 2007. The largest producer was Afghanistan. Coca was cultivated on 474,400 acres (192,000 ha), which was also a decrease from the previous year. The largest producer was Colombia. Cannabis

TABLE 8.3

Illicit drug production worldwide, by crop and country, 2005–09

[All figures in hectares]

	2005	2006	2007	2008	2009
Poppy					
Afghanistan	107,400	172,600	202,000	157,000	131,000
Burma	40,000	21,000	21,700	22,500	17,000
Colombia[a]		2,300	1,000		in process
Guatemala	100				
Laos[b]	5,600	1,700	1,100	1,900	1,000
Mexico	3,300	5,000	6,900	15,000	in process
Pakistan[c]					
Total poppy	**156,400**	**202,600**	**232,700**	**196,400**	**149,000**
Coca					
Bolivia	26,500	25,800	29,500	32,000	in process
Colombia	144,000	157,200	167,000	119,000	in process
Peru[d]	34,000	42,000	36,000	41,000	in process
Total coca	**204,500**	**225,000**	**232,500**	**192,000**	**0**
Cannabis					
Mexico	5,600	8,600	8,900	12,000	in process
Total cannabis	**5,600**	**8,600**	**8,900**	**12,000**	**0**

Note: Survey areas were expanded in 2005. USG = United States Government.
[a]Partial survey in 2009 due to cloud cover. No survey was conducted in 2008. Partial survey in 2007 due to cloud cover. The 2005 survey could not be conducted due to cloud cover.
[b]A partial survey of only the Phongsali growing area was conducted in 2009.
[c]There are no valid USG countrywide numbers for Pakistan.
[d]In the 2006 survey, the Cusco growing area could not be completed; the value for that area is an average of the 2005 and 2007 estimates.

SOURCE: "Worldwide Illicit Drug Cultivation: 2005–2009 (All Figures in Hectares)," in *International Narcotics Control Strategy Report: Volume I, Drug and Chemical Control*, U.S. Department of State, Bureau of International Narcotics and Law Enforcement Affairs, March 2010, http://www.state.gov/documents/organization/138548.pdf (accessed November 11, 2010)

cultivation, which excludes what is grown in the United States in this tabulation, took place on 29,700 acres (12,000 ha) in 2008. Over the four-year period from 2005 to 2009, coca leaf cultivation was higher than poppy cultivation in 2005 and 2006, but lower than poppy cultivation in 2007 and 2008. Cannabis cultivation is a distant third, reflecting the much lower value of marijuana than of opium, cocaine, and their derivatives.

Table 8.4 provides data on the production of opium, coca leaf, and cannabis between 2005 and 2009. The largest tonnage of drug material is coca leaf, followed by cannabis and opium. In 2008, the most recent year for which data are complete, 192,400 tons (174,500 t) of coca leaf, 23,700 tons (21,500 t) of cannabis, and 6,814 tons (6,182 t) of opium were produced. Leading producer countries were Colombia for coca leaf, Mexico for cannabis, and Afghanistan for opium.

ILLICIT DRUG MOVEMENT INTO AND WITHIN THE UNITED STATES

Worldwide illicit drug cultivation takes place primarily outside the United States. Even though each drug type has its own method and route of entering the United States, the overall method is overland smuggling and subsequent transportation via the interstate highway system. The National Drug Intelligence Center (NDIC) provides in *National Drug Threat Assessment, 2010* (February 2010,

http://www.justice.gov/ndic/pubs38/38661/38661p.pdf) data on the seizures of drugs in transit within the United States. Of the 1,792 tons (1,626 t) of illegal drugs that moved into the United States in 2009, 98% (3.5 million pounds [1.6 million kg]) was smuggled over land, entering via the southwest border with Mexico or the northern border with Canada. (See Figure 8.1.) Only 1.5% (54,536 pounds [24,737 kg]) was smuggled via maritime (ocean) routes and 0.8% (27,366 pounds [12,413 kg]) via air routes.

Table 8.5 shows drug seizures along the southwest and northern borders of the United States between 2005 and 2009. These seizures are an indication of the relative quantity of the flow of drugs along these borders; they also indicate that most drugs enter the United States across the southwest border, with the exception of MDMA (3,4-methylenedioxy-methamphetamine), which arrives primarily across the northern border.

After illicit drugs enter the United States, they travel along eight principal drug corridors to major drug markets. Figure 8.2 shows these corridors, labeled A to H. Corridors A and B are the drug traffickers' most important routes. Corridor A is a primary route for transporting large quantities of drugs from entry points along the southwest border to major drug markets in the east and northeast. Corridor B traverses the middle of the country and is used to move methamphetamine and marijuana that is produced in California and Mexico to the central and eastern states.

TABLE 8.4

Potential illicit drug production worldwide, by crop and country, 2005–09

[All figures in metric tons]

	2005	2006	2007	2008	2009
Opium					
Afghanistan	4,475	5,644	8,000	5,500	5,300
Burma	380	230	270	340	250
Colombia[a]		37	15		in process
Guatemala	4				
Laos[c]	28	8.5	5.5	17	10.6
Mexico	71	108	149	325	in process
Pakistan[b]					
Total opium	**4,958**	**6,027.5**	**8,439.5**	**6,182**	**5,560.6**
Coca leaf					
Bolivia[d]	36,000	37,000	38,500	43,500	in process
Colombia[e]	151,000	158,000	150,000	87,500	in process
Peru[f]	52,000	54,500	43,500	43,500	in process
Total coca leaf	**239,000**	**249,500**	**232,000**	**174,500**	**0**
Potential pure cocaine					
Bolivia	115	115	120	195	in process
Colombia	525	550	535	295	in process
Peru	250	265	210	215	in process
Total potential pure cocaine	**890**	**930**	**865**	**705**	**0**
Cannabis					
Mexico (marijuana)	10,100	15,500	15,800	21,500	in process
Total cannabis	**10,100**	**15,500**	**15,800**	**21,500**	**0**

CNC = Crime and Narcotics Center. USG = United States Government.
[a]Partial survey in 2009 due to cloud cover. No survey was conducted in 2008. Partial survey in 2007 due to cloud cover. The 2005 survey could not be conducted due to cloud cover.
[b]There are no valid USG countrywide numbers for Pakistan.
[c]A partial survey of only the Phongsali growing area was conducted in 2009.
[d]In 2006, CNC revised the 2002–05 values due to new yield information.
[e]New research in 2007 led to revised leaf and cocaine production figures for 2003–2006. Survey areas were expanded greatly in 2005, and to a lesser extent in 2006 and 2007.
[f]In the 2006 survey, the Cusco growing area could not be completed; the value for that area is an average of the 2005 and 2007 estimates. Survey areas were expanded in 2005. The 2001–2005 values were revised in 2007 to reflect new yield numbers for immature fields.

SOURCE: "Potential Worldwide Illicit Drug Production: 2005–2009 (All Figures in Metric Tons)," in *International Narcotics Control Strategy Report: Volume I, Drug and Chemical Control*, U.S. Department of State, Bureau of International Narcotics and Law Enforcement Affairs, March 2010, http://www.state.gov/documents/organization/138548.pdf (accessed November 11, 2010)

Greatest Drug Threat

The NDIC surveyed state and local law enforcement agencies nationwide in 2009 to determine what they believed to be the greatest drug threat in the United States. Approximately 37% of these agencies identified cocaine (powder or crack) as the drug that poses the greatest threat to their area. (See Figure 8.3.) Methamphetamine was identified by 27.6% as the greatest threat, followed far behind by heroin (12.9%), marijuana (12.1%), and illicitly trafficked pharmaceuticals (9.8%).

The NDIC notes that methamphetamine was identified as the greatest threat most often in the western portion of the United States, whereas cocaine was more frequently identified in the eastern portion. Figure 8.4 shows the greatest drug threat by region for 2009.

METHAMPHETAMINE

Methamphetamine (meth) is made in laboratories from precursor drugs rather than directly from plant material. The drug was first synthesized in 1919 and has been a factor on the drug market since the 1960s. The Substance Abuse

and Mental Health Services Administration (SAMHSA) reveals in *Results from the 2009 National Survey on Drug Use and Health: Volume I. Summary of National Findings* (September 2010, http://www.oas.samhsa.gov/NSDUH/2k9NSDUH/2k9ResultsP.pdf) that 502,000 people were current users of methamphetamine in 2009. In addition, 154,000 people aged 12 years and older were first-time users of methamphetamine.

Methamphetamine Production

Like other synthetics, such as LSD or MDMA, methamphetamine appeals to small and large criminal enterprises alike because it frees them from dependence on vulnerable crops such as coca or opium poppy. Even a small organization can control the whole process, from manufacture to sale on the street, of methamphetamine. The drug can be made almost anywhere and can generate large profit margins.

Clandestine methamphetamine laboratories in the United States are usually operated as temporary facilities. Drug producers make a batch, tear down the lab, and either store the lab and equipment for later use or rebuild it at another site. This constant assembling and disassembling of laboratories is necessary to avoid detection by law enforcement authorities.

FIGURE 8.1

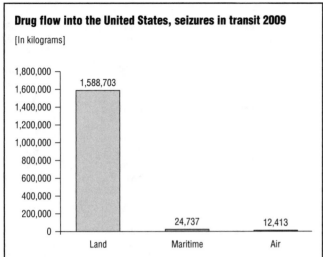

Drug flow into the United States, seizures in transit 2009

[In kilograms]

Note: Data as of December 1, 2009; graph includes seizures of cocaine, methamphetamine, marijuana, heroin, and MDMA (Ecstasy).

SOURCE: "Figure 1. Seizures of Drugs in Transit, within the United States in Kilograms, 2009," in *National Drug Threat Assessment, 2010*, U.S. Department of Justice, National Drug Intelligence Center, February 2010 (updated May 25, 2010), http://www.justice.gov/ndic/pubs38/38661/38661p.pdf (accessed November 11, 2010)

The ingredients for making methamphetamine are lithium from batteries, acetone from paint thinner, lye, and ephedrine/pseudoephedrine. Anhydrous ammonia, which is used as a fertilizer, can be used to dry the drug and cut the production cycle by 10 hours. According to the NDIC, in *National Drug Threat Assessment, 2010*, this process produces 5 to 7 pounds (2.3 to 3.2 kg) of toxic waste products for every pound of methamphetamine. Making methamphetamine creates a horrible odor, forcing producers into remote areas to avoid arousing the suspicion of those living downwind; explosions and fires are also common.

Ephedrine, a stimulant, appetite suppressant, and decongestant, is the key ingredient for making methamphetamine. In 1989 the Chemical Diversion and Trafficking Act gave the U.S. Drug Enforcement Administration (DEA) authority to regulate bulk sales of ephedrine, but over-the-counter (without a prescription) sales were not included. As a result, manufacturers simply bought ephedrine at drugstores and then used it to manufacture methamphetamine.

The passage of the Domestic Chemical Diversion Control Act of 1993 made it illegal to sell ephedrine over the counter as well, but pseudoephedrine, a substitute, was not included in the ban. The Comprehensive Methamphetamine Control Act of 1996 made it illegal to knowingly possess ephedrine and pseudoephedrine (called precursor

TABLE 8.5

Drug seizures along the southwest and northern borders, in kilograms, 2005–09

	2005	2006	2007	2008	2009
Cocaine					
Southwest border	22,653	28,284	22,656	16,755	17,085
Northern border	>1	2	>1	>1	18
Total	**22,654**	**28,286**	**22,657**	**16,756**	**17,103**
Heroin					
Southwest border	228	489	404	556	642
Northern border	3	2	<1	<1	28
Total	**231**	**491**	**405**	**557**	**670**
Marijuana					
Southwest border	1,034,102	1,146,687	1,472,536	1,253,054	1,489,673
Northern border	10,447	4,177	2,791	3,184	3,423
Total	**1,044,549**	**1,150,864**	**1,475,327**	**1,256,238**	**1,493,096**
MDMA					
Southwest border	23	16	39	92	54
Northern border	479	351	240	616	303
Total	**502**	**367**	**279**	**708**	**357**
Methamphetamine					
Southwest border	2,918	2,798	1,860	2,201	3,478
Northern border	>1	>1	136	>1	10
Total	**2,919**	**2,799**	**1,996**	**2,202**	**3,488**

Note: Data as of December 1, 2009; totals are rounded to the nearest kilogram.
MDMA = Methylenedioxymethamphetamine/Ecstasy.

SOURCE: "Table 1. Drug Seizures along the Southwest and Northern Borders in Kilograms, 2005–2009," in *National Drug Threat Assessment, 2010*, U.S. Department of Justice, National Drug Intelligence Center, February 2010 (updated May 25, 2010), http://www.justice.gov/ndic/pubs38/38661/38661p.pdf (accessed November 11, 2010)

FIGURE 8.2

Regional drug transportation corridors, 2009

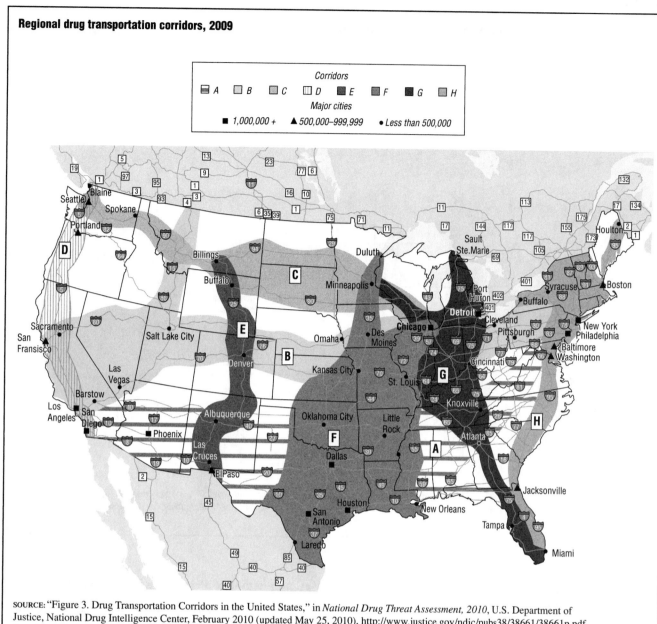

SOURCE: "Figure 3. Drug Transportation Corridors in the United States," in *National Drug Threat Assessment, 2010*, U.S. Department of Justice, National Drug Intelligence Center, February 2010 (updated May 25, 2010), http://www.justice.gov/ndic/pubs38/38661/38661p.pdf (accessed November 11, 2010)

chemicals) and doubled the possible penalty for manufacturing and/or distributing methamphetamine from 10 to 20 years. The Methamphetamine Trafficking Penalty Enhancement Act of 1998 further increased penalties for trafficking in methamphetamine. The Combat Methamphetamine Epidemic Act of 2005 placed restrictions on the amount of ephedrine, pseudoephedrine, and phenylpropanolamine (another precursor drug to methamphetamine) that can be sold in one day and over a 30-day period to an individual, required vendors to verify the identity of purchasers of these drugs, and required vendors to keep these products inaccessible to customers without vendor help. Because of these restrictions on the purchase and sale of ephedrine and pseudoephedrine, the drug ephedra is often used as a substitute. Ephedra, also known as

ma huang in traditional Chinese medicine, contains both ephedrine and pseudoephedrine. In addition, drug traffickers circumvent the law on restrictive sales by having many individuals purchase the drugs up to the daily and monthly limit, a practice that is called "smurfing."

Importation of Methamphetamine and Its Precursors

When the precursors ephedrine and pseudoephedrine became difficult to get in large quantities in the United States due to restrictive laws, methamphetamine and its precursors flowed into the United States from other countries, primarily Mexico. According to the NDIC, in *National Drug Threat Assessment, 2009* (December 2008, http://www.usdoj.gov/ndic/pubs31/31379/31379p.pdf), methamphetamine production in the United States

FIGURE 8.3

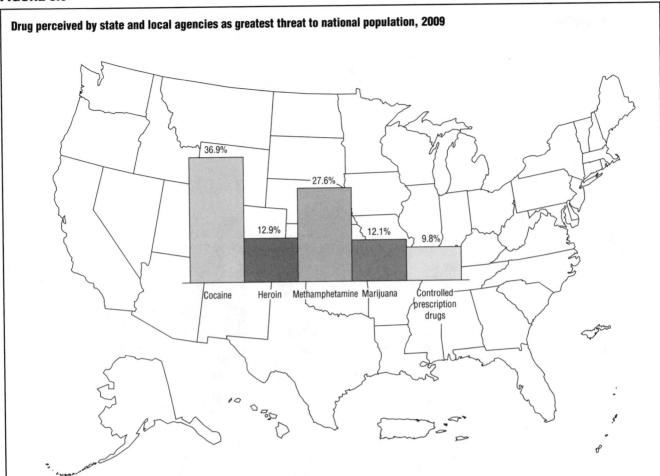

Drug perceived by state and local agencies as greatest threat to national population, 2009

SOURCE: "Map A6. 2009 Greatest Drug Threat, As Reported by State and Local Agencies," in *National Drug Threat Assessment, 2010*, U.S. Department of Justice, National Drug Intelligence Center, February 2010 (updated May 25, 2010), http://www.justice.gov/ndic/pubs38/38661/38661p.pdf (accessed November 11, 2010)

decreased each year from 2003 to 2007, but as this downturn occurred, the synthesis of methamphetamine in Mexico increased, and the drug was smuggled into the United States. However, Mexico implemented prohibitions on the importation of ephedrine and pseudoephedrine in 2005 and instituted a complete importation ban in 2008. That same year Mexico banned all cold medications that used these drugs. As a result of these importation restrictions and bans, along with the destruction of methamphetamine laboratories by trained law enforcement officials, methamphetamine production in Mexico declined in 2007 and 2008 as did its flow into the United States. The NDIC notes in *National Drug Threat Assessment, 2010* that in 2008 production increased in the United States as methamphetamine traffickers circumvented laws by smurfing. By late 2008 Mexican drug trafficking organizations also adapted their operating procedures in several ways to circumvent laws and law enforcement officials, and the flow of methamphetamine into the United States subsequently increased. Production in the United States continued as well.

Methamphetamine Prices, Purities, and Supply

The prices and purity of illicit drugs play an important role in understanding and analyzing drug markets. The purity of a drug refers to the extent to which it is diluted (mixed) with other substances. Determining the prices and purities of illicit drugs accurately is challenging because illicit drugs are not sold in standard quantities and are generally sold at varying purities. In addition, data can be collected only from seizures and purchases by undercover agents. Thus, the data gleaned from the samples collected must be used to estimate these factors for the total drug supply for that year.

Figure 8.5 shows the average price and purity of methamphetamine between January 2006 and September 2009. Drug prices fluctuate with supply and demand. As with other products, when supply outpaces demand, the price drops. Conversely, when the demand outpaces supply, the price rises. In addition, the purity of drugs may drop if demand outpaces supply; it is a way for drug traffickers to stretch the drug resources they have.

FIGURE 8.4

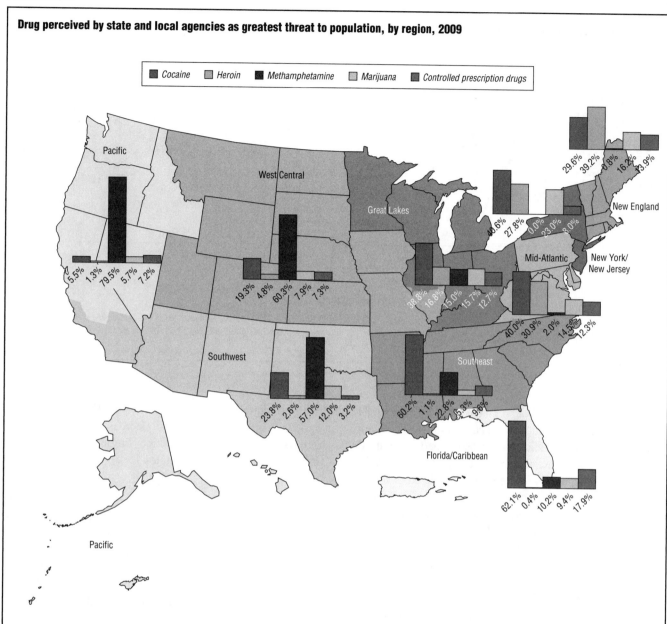

Drug perceived by state and local agencies as greatest threat to population, by region, 2009

SOURCE: "Map A5. 2009 Greatest Drug Threat by Region, As Reported by State and Local Agencies," in *National Drug Threat Assessment, 2010*, U.S. Department of Justice, National Drug Intelligence Center, February 2010 (updated May 25, 2010), http://www.justice.gov/ndic/pubs38/38661/38661p.pdf (accessed November 11, 2010)

The price per gram of methamphetamine plummeted in 2006, rose in 2007, and declined throughout most of 2008 and 2009 as production increased in both Mexico and the United States. (See Figure 8.5.) The highest price was $278.97 per gram in 2007, which was more than twice the price per gram in 2009 of $127.28. In addition, as the price of methamphetamine rose in early 2006 and 2007, its purity declined. A rise in price of the drug with a concurrent drop in purity is evidence of its decreased availability.

Distribution of Methamphetamine

In *National Drug Threat Assessment, 2009*, the NDIC explains that Mexican drug trafficking organizations (DTOs) control most of the wholesale distribution

of both the powder and ice forms of methamphetamine in the United States and are the greatest organized crime threat to this country. Mexican DTOs exist throughout the United States. These groups, which are often Mexican criminal groups as well, supply midlevel distributors in at least 230 U.S. cities. Table 8.5 shows that nearly all the methamphetamine that is smuggled across U.S. borders enters along the southwest border.

COCAINE

Production and Distribution

The coca plant, from which cocaine is produced, is grown primarily in the Andean region of Colombia, Peru,

FIGURE 8.5

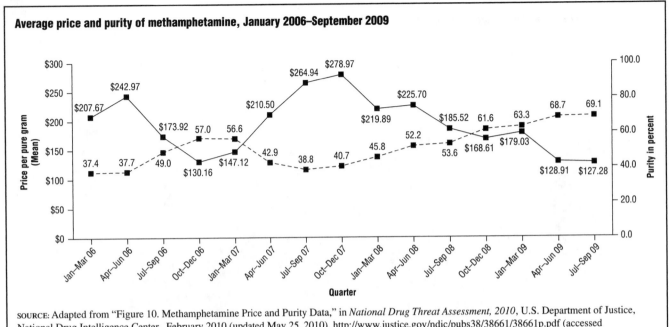

Average price and purity of methamphetamine, January 2006–September 2009

SOURCE: Adapted from "Figure 10. Methamphetamine Price and Purity Data," in *National Drug Threat Assessment, 2010*, U.S. Department of Justice, National Drug Intelligence Center, February 2010 (updated May 25, 2010), http://www.justice.gov/ndic/pubs38/38661/38661p.pdf (accessed November 11, 2010)

and Bolivia, with Colombia being the largest producer. The first step in the production of cocaine is to mix the coca leaves with sulfuric acid in a plastic-lined hole in the ground. The leaves are then pounded to create an acidic juice. When this juice is filtered and neutralized, it forms a paste. The paste is purified into cocaine base by the addition of more chemicals and filtering. This cocaine base includes coca paste, freebase cocaine, and crack cocaine. It is transported from the jungles of Bolivia and Peru to southern Colombia, where it is processed into cocaine hydrochloride (white powder) at clandestine drug laboratories. Small, independent Bolivian and Peruvian trafficking groups also process some cocaine. It takes 661 to 1,102 pounds (300 to 500 kg) of coca leaf to make 2.2 pounds (1 kg) of cocaine.

After processing, cocaine is shipped to the United States and Europe. Caribbean and Central American countries serve as transit countries for the shipment of drugs into the United States. Drug traffickers shift routes according to law enforcement and interdiction pressures. (Interdiction is the interception of smuggled drugs.) Cocaine is one drug that often enters the country via maritime routes in the eastern Pacific.

Cocaine Prices, Purities, and Supply

According to the NDIC, in *National Drug Threat Assessment, 2010*, the availability of cocaine in the United States has decreased since 2006. The NDIC states that "although no single factor for the decline in cocaine availability can be identified, a combination of factors, including increased law enforcement efforts in Mexico and the transit zones, decreased cocaine production in Colombia, high

levels of cartel violence, and cocaine flow to non-U.S. markets likely contributed to decreased amounts being transported to the U.S.–Mexico border for subsequent smuggling into the United States."

Figure 8.6 shows the average price and purity of cocaine between January 2006 and September 2009. The average price per gram of cocaine increased by 75% ($99.24 to $174.03) between January 2007 and September 2009. Similarly, the average purity decreased by 31.5% (67.4% to 46.2% pure) over the same period. As mentioned earlier, a rise in price of a drug with a concurrent drop in purity is evidence of its decreased availability.

MARIJUANA
Production, Availability, and Distribution

Marijuana is made from the flowering tops and leaves of the cannabis plant; these are collected, trimmed, dried, and then smoked in a pipe or as a cigarette. Many users smoke "blunts," named after the inexpensive blunt cigars from which they are made. Blunt cigars are approximately 5 inches (12.7 cm) long and can be purchased at any store that sells tobacco products. A marijuana blunt is made from the emptied cigar casing, which is then stuffed with marijuana or a marijuana-tobacco mixture. A blunt may contain as much marijuana as six regular marijuana cigarettes. In some cases blunt users add crack cocaine or PCP to the mixture to make it more potent.

According to the NDIC, in *National Drug Threat Assessment, 2010*, marijuana was widely available in the United States in 2009. Marijuana production in Mexico

FIGURE 8.6

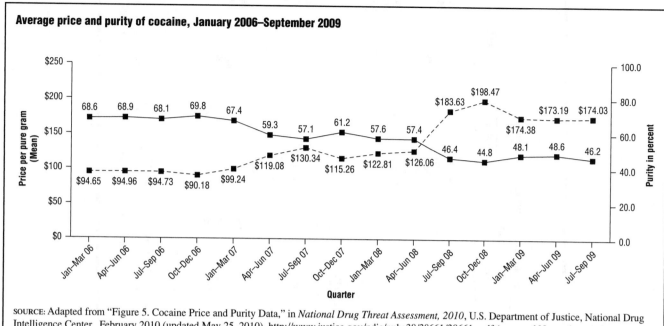

Average price and purity of cocaine, January 2006–September 2009

SOURCE: Adapted from "Figure 5. Cocaine Price and Purity Data," in *National Drug Threat Assessment, 2010*, U.S. Department of Justice, National Drug Intelligence Center, February 2010 (updated May 25, 2010), http://www.justice.gov/ndic/pubs38/38661/38661p.pdf (accessed November 11, 2010)

increased by 59% between 2003 and 2008 and eradication decreased by 48% between 2006 and 2008. In addition, Mexican drug traffickers have begun to cultivate marijuana in the United States to avoid border seizure of the drug and transportation costs. One favored type of location for growing marijuana is public land that is out of the way. Some growers cultivate the plant indoors to avoid detection and to benefit from year-round, easily controlled growing conditions. Growers may cultivate a dozen or so plants in a closet or operate elaborate, specially constructed (sometimes underground) greenhouses where thousands of plants grow under intense electric lighting or in sunlight. Indoor cultivators often use hydroponics, in which the plants are grown in nutrient solution rather than in soil. The NDIC notes that indoor cannabis cultivation is increasing in the United States, particularly in the western states, Florida, and Georgia.

Nondomestically grown marijuana arrives in the continental United States via the southwest border with Mexico and the northern border with Canada. (See Table 8.5.) Mexican DTOs control most of the wholesale distribution of marijuana throughout the United States, and marijuana has become their primary source of income. Mexican DTOs make more money from trafficking in marijuana alone than they do from trafficking in heroin, methamphetamine, and cocaine combined.

Mexican criminal groups control most of the distribution of marijuana in the United States; however, Asian criminal groups (primarily Chinese and Vietnamese) are beginning to control distribution of the Canadian-grown drug and to grow significant quantities of the crop

indoors in the United States. Asian DTOs are distributed across the United States, but few are in the western and west-central portions of the country, except for a concentration on the West Coast.

THC Content and Price

The active ingredient in marijuana is THC (delta-9-tetrahydrocannabinol), which is mostly concentrated in the flowering tops (colas or buds) of the cannabis plant. The flowering tops of female plants that have not yet been pollinated and, therefore, have not yet produced seeds, have the highest THC content. This plant part is called sinsemilla (literally, "without seed"). In contrast, feral hemp, commonly called ditchweed, contains a low THC content and is generally not a product drug users want.

The ONDCP notes in *National Drug Control Strategy: Data Supplement 2010* (2010, http://www.whitehousedrugpolicy.gov/publications/policy/ndcs10/ndcs10_data_supl/10datasupplement.pdf) that between 1985 and 1995 the THC content of marijuana in federal seizure samples averaged less than 4% and in state and local eradication samples less than 3%. (See Table 8.6.) The potency found in federal seizure samples increased dramatically as the years went on; by 2007 the THC content in these samples was 7.2% and was nearly that in 2008. Even though the THC content in state and local eradication samples increased to 3.9% in 2000, it then began to decrease. In 2008 the THC content in these samples was 1.8%.

In 1996 the THC content for sinsemilla in federal seizure samples was 11.3%, peaking at 14.4% in 2002.

TABLE 8.6

Marijuana potency, 1985–2008

	Non-domestic samples (federal seizures)								Domestic samples (state and local eradication)							
	Type of cannabis								Type of cannabis							
	Ditchweed		Marijuana		Sinsemilla		All types[a]		Ditchweed		Marijuana		Sinsemilla		All types[a]	
Year	Potency[b]	Number[c]	Potency[b]	Number[c]	Potency[b]	Number[c]	Potency[b]	Number[c]	Potency[b]	Number[c]	Potency[b]	Number[c]	Potency[b]	Number[c]	Potency[b]	Number[c]
1985	0.30%	9	3.44%	745	7.95%	12	3.48%	767	0.50%	102	2.19%	703	7.07%	40	2.22%	845
1986	0.30%	23	2.75%	711	8.78%	14	2.80%	753	0.32%	124	1.95%	661	8.16%	18	1.84%	803
1987	0.35%	17	3.16%	1,110	8.29%	17	3.20%	1,147	0.34%	86	2.46%	441	7.69%	26	2.38%	553
1988	0.39%	13	3.62%	1,127	8.30%	29	3.70%	1,171	0.40%	69	2.20%	513	7.33%	69	2.56%	651
1989	0.30%	7	3.68%	725	7.13%	29	3.78%	761	0.29%	104	1.71%	350	6.86%	57	2.00%	511
1990	0.33%	15	3.78%	756	9.59%	16	3.82%	788	0.33%	78	2.09%	352	10.29%	45	2.58%	475
1991	0.35%	37	3.18%	1,498	11.20%	29	3.26%	1,564	0.31%	246	2.90%	651	10.10%	46	2.57%	943
1992	0.27%	21	3.09%	2,461	9.67%	33	3.16%	2,515	0.31%	107	3.05%	875	7.72%	43	2.96%	1,025
1993	0.35%	11	3.67%	1,994	4.64%	5	3.65%	2,010	0.37%	189	2.83%	1,039	5.82%	118	2.75%	1,346
1994	0.32%	12	3.76%	2,052	6.92%	10	3.75%	2,074	0.39%	136	2.95%	980	7.55%	94	3.02%	1,210
1995	0.44%	14	3.95%	3,729	9.64%	17	3.96%	3,762	0.41%	149	2.55%	701	7.26%	147	2.93%	997
1996	0.62%	3	4.40%	1,385	11.30%	22	4.50%	1,410	0.37%	115	2.90%	762	8.92%	147	3.48%	1,024
1997	0.57%	3	4.92%	1,315	11.62%	19	5.00%	1,337	0.48%	57	3.34%	958	11.61%	102	3.95%	1,117
1998	0.18%	6	4.71%	1,300	11.88%	37	4.89%	1,343	0.40%	81	3.38%	775	12.58%	64	3.76%	920
1999	0.56%	13	4.34%	1,759	13.49%	55	4.59%	1,827	0.33%	59	3.76%	691	13.31%	81	4.45%	831
2000	0.54%	4	5.10%	1,862	12.87%	62	5.34%	1,928	0.34%	69	3.94%	1,066	12.71%	51	4.10%	1,186
2001	0.53%	4	5.77%	1,590	12.05%	95	6.11%	1,689	0.42%	59	3.56%	808	7.86%	140	3.98%	1,007
2002	0.30%	8	5.66%	1,381	14.41%	302	7.19%	1,691	0.41%	67	3.28%	408	7.29%	226	4.30%	701
2003	0.34%	9	5.63%	1,516	14.00%	347	7.15%	1,872	0.35%	57	2.35%	377	7.21%	191	3.65%	625
2004	0.43%	9	6.17%	1,420	14.06%	485	8.14%	1,914	0.37%	53	2.55%	395	7.67%	246	4.20%	694
2005	0.79%	4	5.91%	1,610	13.04%	681	8.01%	2,295	0.34%	52	2.25%	354	7.81%	251	4.23%	657
2006	0.50%	4	6.50%	1,409	13.60%	666	8.76%	2,079	0.28%	49	1.99%	363	6.83%	366	4.16%	778
2007	0.62%	7	7.20%	1,299	13.42%	831	9.60%	2,137	0.35%	40	1.92%	340	7.21%	503	4.86%	883
2008	0.43%	5	7.17%	1,045	13.09%	941	9.95%	1,991	0.46%	27	1.79%	299	7.55%	366	4.78%	692

[a]All tested samples include a small number of Thai sticks.

[b]These percentages, indicating potency, are based on simple arithmetic means calculated by dividing the sum of the delta-9THC concentrations of each sample by the number of seizures and are not normalized by weight of seizure.

[c]Number of tested samples that yield the potency in prior column.

SOURCE: "Table 56. Potency of Tested Cannabis from Federal Seizure and State and Local Eradication Samples, by Type, 1985–2008 (Percent Delta-9 THC Concentrations and Number of Samples Tested)," in *National Drug Control Strategy: Data Supplement 2010*, Executive Office of the President, Office of National Drug Control Policy, 2010, http://www.whitehousedrugpolicy.gov/publications/policy/ndcs10/ndcs10_data_supl/ds_list_of_tables.pdf (accessed November 12, 2010). Data from University of Mississippi, National Center for Natural Products Research, *Quarterly Report, Potency Monitoring Project Report 107, September 16, 2009 thru December 15, 2009*, January 12, 2010.

TABLE 8.7

Average price of marijuana, 1981–2007

Year	Purchases of 10 grams or less[a]	Purchases greater than 10 but less than 100 grams[b]
	Price per gram ($)	Price per gram ($)
1981	5.97	3.91
1982	6.49	5.58
1983	8.29	9.50
1984	8.39	4.95
1985	7.81	6.94
1986	16.78	10.78
1987	15.44	7.76
1988	14.30	8.90
1989	15.62	9.03
1990	15.87	11.08
1991	17.57	12.35
1992	16.41	8.34
1993	15.04	12.45
1994	12.67	12.03
1995	9.79	8.41
1996	8.83	7.28
1997	8.21	5.40
1998	7.87	6.79
1999	8.87	9.61
2000	8.25	6.02
2001	9.04	6.57
2002	10.83	10.18
2003	11.54	9.34
2004	10.44	7.15
2005	10.38	8.82
2006	10.55	10.26
2007	10.41	10.03

[a]Quantities purchased at the "retail" level.
[b]Quantities purchased at the "dealer" level.

SOURCE: "Table 55. Average Price of Marijuana in the United States, 1981–2007 (2007 Dollars)," in *National Drug Control Strategy: Data Supplement 2010*, Executive Office of the President, Office of National Drug Control Policy, 2010, http://www.whitehousedrugpolicy.gov/publications/policy/ndcs10/ndcs10_data_supl/ds_list_of_tables.pdf (accessed November 12, 2010)

(See Table 8.6.) By 2008 the THC content had dropped to 13.1%, but this level was still considered high. The THC content of state and local eradication samples of sinsemilla in 2008 was 7.6%.

The average price of marijuana at the retail level rose from $5.97 per gram in 1981 to $17.57 per gram in 1991. (See Table 8.7.) The price then fell to $7.87 per gram in 1998, rose to $11.54 per gram in 2003, and then stabilized at about $10.50 per gram. The average price of marijuana at the retail level in 2007 was $10.41 per gram.

In *National Drug Threat Assessment, 2010*, the NDIC notes that in 2009 the levels of use for marijuana in the United States were higher than for any other drug. (See Figure 4.2 in Chapter 4.) However, the NDIC also indicates that use among adolescents is decreasing. (See Figure 5.7 in Chapter 5.)

HEROIN

Heroin users represent the smallest group using a major drug. According to SAMHSA, in *Results from the 2009 National Survey on Drug Use and Health*, there were 200,000 current heroin users in the United States in 2009. (See Figure 4.2 in Chapter 4.)

Heroin Production and Distribution

PRODUCTION PROCESS. The source of heroin is the opium poppy. After the leaves of the poppy fall off, only the round poppy pods remain. Heroin production begins by scoring the poppy pod with a knife. A gummy substance begins to ooze out. This opium gum is scraped off and collected. The rest of the process is explained by the Central Intelligence Agency (CIA) in "From Flowers to Heroin" (April 23, 2009, http://www.erowid.org/plants/poppy/poppy_article2.shtml):

> Once the opium gum is transported to a refinery, it is converted into morphine, an intermediate product. This conversion is achieved primarily by chemical processes and requires several basic elements and implements. Boiling water is used to dissolve opium gum; 55-gallon drums are used for boiling vessels; and burlap sacks are used to filter and strain liquids. When dried, the morphine resulting from this initial process is pressed into bricks. The conversion of morphine bricks into heroin is also primarily a chemical process. The main chemical used is acetic anhydride, along with sodium carbonate, activated charcoal, chloroform, ethyl alcohol, ether, and acetone. The two most commonly produced heroin varieties are No. 3 heroin, or smoking heroin, and No. 4 heroin, or injectable heroin.

The CIA explains that this generic process produces heroin that may be 90% pure. Variations in the process are introduced as the heroin is diluted to increase its bulk and profits. The pure heroin is mixed with various substances including caffeine, baking soda, powdered milk, and quinine.

OVERVIEW OF THE TRADE. Opium poppies are intensely cultivated in four regions of the world: Southeast Asia, Southwest Asia, Mexico, and South America. In 2008 Afghanistan accounted for approximately 89% of known opium gum production. (See Table 8.4.) In 2001 Afghanistan's production dropped as a consequence of steps that were taken by the Taliban to suppress the trade. However, when the Taliban fell in 2002, production began to increase again. In 2005 production was at 4,900 tons (4,475 t) and it nearly doubled to 8,800 tons (8,000 t) by 2007. Production decreased to 6,100 tons (5,500 t) in 2008 and then again slightly to 5,800 tons (5,300 t) in 2009.

Figure 8.7 shows the pattern of opium poppy cultivation in Afghanistan in 2008 along with the security risk of each area. Most provinces in the northern and eastern portions of Afghanistan were no longer growing poppies. The bulk of the opium poppy crop was grown in the southern provinces of Afghanistan, with the largest areas of poppy cultivation located in the Helmand, Kandahar, and Farah provinces. The security risk was extreme in

FIGURE 8.7

Opium poppy cultivation in Afghanistan, 2008

SOURCE: "Figure 18. Security Map with Opium Poppy Cultivation in Afghanistan, 2008," in *National Drug Control Strategy: 2009 Annual Report*, Executive Office of the President, Office of National Drug Control Policy, 2009, http://www.whitehousedrugpolicy.gov/publications/policy/ndcs09/ 2009ndcs.pdf (accessed November 12, 2010). Data on security from United Nations Department of Safety and Security as of July 12, 2008.

Helmand and Kandahar and high in Farah, which impeded counternarcotics operations.

The DEA conducts the Heroin Signature Program. The name of the program comes from the fact that each producing region uses a unique process for deriving heroin from opium, thus the heroin has a unique signature. Under this program heroin seized by federal authorities is analyzed to determine the purity of the heroin and its origin. In *National Drug Threat Assessment, 2010*, the NDIC indicates that 58% of all heroin seized in 2008 came from South America and 39% came from Mexico, making up

97% of the heroin in the United States. Relatively little heroin produced in Afghanistan is distributed in the United States because it is sold, instead, in Asia and Europe. In addition, Colombian and Dominican criminal groups control most of the distribution of heroin in the United States, and they distribute drugs produced in Central and South America.

Mexico produces a variety of heroin called black tar because it looks like roofing tar. It was once considered inferior to Colombian and Asian heroin, but it has reached a level of purity high enough so that it can be snorted or smoked. Mexican heroin is targeted almost exclusively to the U.S. market. The long U.S.-Mexican land border provides many opportunities for drug smugglers to cross. Female couriers are used more frequently than male couriers. Mexican heroin is smuggled in cars, trucks, and buses and may also be hidden on or in the body of the smuggler. Many smugglers send their drugs by overnight-package express services.

The bulk of heroin from South America comes from Colombia. Many Colombian coca traffickers have been requiring their dealers to accept a small amount of heroin along with their normal deliveries of coca. This has allowed the Colombian producers to use an existing network to introduce a pure grade of heroin into the U.S. market. Much of the increasing Colombian heroin production is sent through Central America and Mexico by smugglers traveling on commercial airline flights into the United States. These smugglers hide the drugs in false-sided luggage, clothing, hollowed-out shoe soles, or inside their bodies. The Colombian-based heroin traffickers have established distribution outlets throughout the eastern half of the United States.

Purity and Price

According to the NDIC, in *National Drug Threat Assessment, 2010*, the purity of South American heroin has decreased and the purity of Mexican heroin has increased in recent years. In *National Drug Threat Assessment, 2009*, the NDIC notes that in 2001 South American heroin purity was 49.7%, whereas Mexican heroin purity was 21%. The NDIC indicates in *National Drug Threat Assessment, 2010* that the purity of South American heroin decreased through 2006, but then rose and stabilized at 57% by 2008. Whereas the purity of South American heroin had decreased through 2006, the purity of Mexican heroin had

risen to 47% in 2005. However, by 2008 the purity of Mexican heroin fell to 40%, putting the purity of South American heroin above that of Mexican heroin once again.

Purity is important to heroin addicts because low-purity heroin must be injected to get the most out of the drug. Many people feel uncomfortable using needles and fear contracting the human immunodeficiency virus (HIV), which can be spread by sharing a needle with an infected user. Higher purity heroin can be smoked or snorted, which makes heroin more attractive to potential users who do not want to use needles. Despite these so-called advantages of higher purity heroin, an estimated three out of five heroin users continue to inject the drug no matter what its purity.

PHARMACEUTICALS

According to the NDIC, in both *National Drug Threat Assessment, 2009* and *National Drug Threat Assessment, 2010*, even though the abuse of prescription narcotics, depressants, stimulants, and painkillers exists in the United States, there is little trafficking in these drugs by DTOs. The NDIC notes that people who abuse pharmaceuticals obtain their Schedule II controlled prescription drugs (such as oxycodone, methylphenidate, and dextroamphetamine) primarily through theft, forged prescriptions, doctor shopping (seeking out different doctors to prescribe more medications), and fraudulent practices of some physicians and pharmacists. Abusers generally obtain Schedules III and IV controlled prescription drugs (such as acetaminophen with codeine, hydrocodone with acetaminophen, Valium, and Darvon) through the Internet, although many sites have been shut down. However, the involvement of street gangs and outlaw motorcycle gangs in the distribution of prescription drugs increased between 2004 and 2009.

CHAPTER 9
ANTIDRUG EFFORTS AND THEIR CRITICISMS

The Harrison Narcotic Act of 1914, which outlawed opiates and cocaine, was the first legislation aimed at prohibiting the possession and use of mood-altering drugs. Following that act, laws were passed or amended at intervals, but the war on drugs did not begin in earnest until the early 1970s with the Comprehensive Drug Abuse Prevention and Control Act of 1970. The phrase "War on Drugs" was coined in 1971 during the first administration of Richard M. Nixon (1913–1994). A national effort was launched after that to bring illicit drug use under control, and it is still very much under way in the 21st century.

Not everyone agrees with governmental efforts to control or prohibit the use of mood-altering substances. Prohibition came to an end because of massive public disobedience. (See Chapter 1.) Data from the 2009 National Survey on Drug Use and Health (NSDUH), which are published in *Results from the 2009 National Survey on Drug Use and Health: Volume I. Summary of National Findings* (September 2010, http://www.oas.samhsa.gov/NSDUH/2k9NSDUH/2k9ResultsP.pdf) by the Substance Abuse and Mental Health Services Administration (SAMHSA), suggest a similar public response to laws that prohibit the use of drugs. For example, SAMHSA (September 2010, http://www.oas.samhsa.gov/NSDUH/2k9NSDUH/tabs/Sect1peTabs1to46.htm#Tab1.1A) notes that in 2009, 47.1% of people aged 12 years and older (118.7 million people) had used an illicit drug at some point during their life. Approximately 15% (38 million) had done so in the past 12 months and 8.7% (21.8 million) had used an illicit drug during the past 30 days. According to SAMHSA (February 5, 2009, http://www.oas.samhsa.gov/nhsda/PE1996/artab007.htm#E8E11), the percentage of lifetime users increased during the preceding three decades; in 1979, 31.3% of people aged 12 years and older reported using an illicit drug at some point during their life.

One criticism leveled at governmental efforts to control or prohibit the use of mood-altering substances is that they appear to be inconsistent with the public health issues they raise. Tobacco and alcohol, both legal substances, cause many more deaths per year than drugs do. In the fact sheet "Health Effects of Cigarette Smoking" (October 29, 2010, http://www.cdc.gov/tobacco/data_statistics/fact_sheets/health_effects/effects_cig_smoking/), the Centers for Disease Control and Prevention (CDC) estimates that 443,000 premature deaths occur each year as a result of smoking and exposure to secondhand smoke. Arialdi M. Miniño, Jiaquan Xu, and Kenneth D. Kochanek report in "Deaths: Preliminary Data for 2008" (*National Vital Statistics Reports*, vol. 59, no. 2, December 9, 2010) that 24,081 people died of alcohol-related causes in 2008. The National Highway Traffic Safety Administration reports in "Traffic Safety Facts, 2009 Data: Alcohol-Impaired Driving" (December 2010, http://www-nrd.nhtsa.dot.gov/Pubs/811385.pdf) that in 2009, 10,839 people died from car crashes that were alcohol related. In comparison, drug abuse produced 31,785 deaths in 2007, according to the Office of National Drug Control Policy, in *National Drug Control Strategy: Data Supplement 2010* (2010, http://www.whitehousedrugpolicy.gov/publications/policy/ndcs10/ndcs10_data_supl/10datasupplement.pdf). SAMHSA shows in *Drug Abuse Warning Network, 2008: Area Profiles of Drug-Related Mortality* (May 2010, http://dawninfo.samhsa.gov/files/ME2008/ME08_Complete.pdf) that marijuana, which is preponderantly the drug used by most of those classified as illicit drug users, causes few fatalities and virtually none by itself.

NATIONAL DRUG CONTROL STRATEGY

The Anti-drug Abuse Act of 1988 established the creation of a drug-free nation as a U.S. policy goal. As part of this initiative, Congress created the Office of National Drug Control Policy (ONDCP; http://www.whitehousedrugpolicy.gov/about/index.html) "to establish policies, priorities, and objectives for the Nation's drug control program. The goals of the program are to reduce illicit drug use, manufacturing, and trafficking, drug-related crime and violence, and drug-related health consequences." The ONDCP director develops the National Drug Control Strategy annually, which describes the nation's antidrug program and puts forth the proposed budget of the ONDCP.

The first National Drug Control Strategy was prepared by William J. Bennett (1943–), the first ONDCP director, and submitted to Congress by President George H. W. Bush (1924–) in 1989. Demand reduction was a priority, and has remained such over the years. The strategy also called for directing efforts at countries where cocaine originated, improving the targeting of interdiction (the interception of smuggled drugs), increasing the capacity of treatment providers, accelerating the efforts aimed at drug prevention, and focusing on the education of youth. In its details, the drug strategy laid emphasis on law enforcement activities and the expansion of the criminal justice system.

Since that time the basic building blocks of the National Drug Control Strategy have remained the same, but the specific emphases taken by different administrations, or by the same administration in different years, have changed. Some presidents lean more toward enforcement, others more toward fighting drug traffickers, and yet others more toward treatment and prevention. Whatever the model, all strategies to date have had the same components: prevention and treatment (together constituting demand reduction); and law enforcement, interdiction,

and international efforts (together constituting supply disruption). The emphasis given to each of these components has been reflected in federal budgets.

In January 2009 President Barack Obama (1961–) appointed Edward H. Jurith, the former general counsel of the ONDCP, as the office's acting director. As early as the spring of 2009, only a few months into his presidency, Obama had given indications of the direction his administration would take in the War on Drugs, including nominating a "drug czar" who favored treatment over incarceration and developing a major initiative to curtail violent drug trafficking on the U.S.-Mexican border. (See Chapter 1.) In May 2009 Gil Kerlikowske (1949–) was sworn in as director of the ONDCP and shortly thereafter the phrase "War on Drugs" was dropped.

THE FEDERAL DRUG BUDGET

The national drug control budget is shown in Table 9.1. The data span fiscal year (FY) 2002 to the budget request for FY 2011. The federal fiscal year begins October 1 and ends September 30, so that FY 2009 dollars, for example, include funding for the last quarter of 2008 and the first three quarters of 2009. The drug control budget has grown from $10.8 billion in FY 2002 to $15.6 billion in FY 2011, an increase of 44%. The budgets for FYs 2002 through 2009 were determined during the administration of George W. Bush (1946–). The budgets for FYs 2010 and 2011 were determined during the Obama administration. The 44%

TABLE 9.1

Distribution of federal drug control spending, by function, fiscal years 2002–11

[In millions]

Functions	Fiscal year 2002 Final	Fiscal year 2003 Final	Fiscal year 2004 Final	Fiscal year 2005 Final	Fiscal year 2006 Final	Fiscal year 2007 Final	Fiscal year 2008 Final	Fiscal year 2009 Final	Fiscal year 2010 Enacted	Fiscal year 2011 Requested
Demand reduction										
Drug abuse treatment	2,358.3	2,387.7	2,545.5	2,556.9	2,470.4	2,465.1	2,647.2	2,747.3	3,092.3	3,208.3
Treatment research	547.8	611.4	607.2	621.2	600.3	600.8	608.0	814.7	653.2	674.2
Total treatment	**2,906.1**	**2,999.1**	**3,152.7**	**3,178.1**	**3,070.7**	**3,065.9**	**3,255.2**	**3,561.9**	**3,745.5**	**3,882.5**
Drug abuse prevention	1,642.5	1,567.2	1,557.3	1,544.0	1,465.4	1,423.4	1,334.7	1,358.0	1,090.2	1,279.8
Prevention research	367.4	382.9	412.4	422.0	411.5	413.4	415.6	496.7	424.1	437.9
Total prevention	**2,009.9**	**1,950.1**	**1,969.7**	**1,966.0**	**1,876.9**	**1,836.8**	**1,750.3**	**1,854.7**	**1,514.3**	**1,717.7**
Total demand reduction	**4,916.0**	**4,949.2**	**5,122.4**	**5,144.1**	**4,947.6**	**4,902.7**	**5,005.5**	**5,416.6**	**5,259.9**	**5,600.2**
Percentage	45.6%	44.1%	42.7%	40.2%	37.6%	35.4%	37.7%	35.5%	35.0%	36.0%
Supply reduction										
Domestic law enforcement	2,867.2	3,018.3	3,189.8	3,318.1	3,475.0	3,715.3	3,544.8	3,869.4	3,843.5	3,917.3
Interdiction	1,913.7	2,147.5	2,534.1	2,928.7	3,287.0	3,175.9	2,901.4	3,910.2	3,640.1	3,727.0
International	1,084.5	1,105.1	1,159.3	1,393.3	1,434.5	2,050.2	1,824.6	2,082.2	2,288.0	2,308.1
Total supply reduction	**5,865.4**	**6,270.9**	**6,883.2**	**7,640.1**	**8,196.5**	**8,941.4**	**8,270.8**	**9,861.8**	**9,771.6**	**9,952.4**
Percentage	54.4%	55.9%	57.3%	59.8%	62.4%	64.6%	62.3%	64.5%	65.0%	64.0%
Totals	**10,781.4**	**11,220.1**	**12,005.6**	**12,784.2**	**13,144.1**	**13,844.1**	**13,276.3**	**15,278.4**	**15,031.5**	**15,552.5**

Note: Detail may not add due to rounding.

SOURCE: "Table 3. Historical Drug Control Funding by Function, FY 2002–FY 2010 (Budget Authority in Millions)," in *National Drug Control Strategy: FY 2011 Budget Summary*, Executive Office of the President, Office of National Drug Control Policy, 2010, http://www.whitehousedrugpolicy.gov/publications/policy/11budget/fy11budget.pdf (accessed November 12, 2010)

TABLE 9.2

Federal drug control spending, by function, fiscal years 2009–11

[In millions]

Function	Fiscal year 2009 Final	Fiscal year 2010 Enacted	Fiscal year 2011 Request	10–11 change Dollars	Percent
Treatment	3,561.9	3,745.5	3,882.5	136.9	3.7%
Percent	23.3%	24.9%	25.0%		
Prevention	1,854.7	1,514.3	1,717.7	203.3	13.4%
Percent	12.1%	10.1%	11.0%		
Domestic law enforcement	3,869.4	3,843.5	3,917.3	73.8	1.9%
Percent	25.3%	25.6%	25.2%		
Interdiction	3,910.2	3,640.1	3,727.0	86.9	2.4%
Percent	25.6%	24.2%	24.0%		
International	2,082.2	2,288.0	2,308.1	20.1	0.9%
Percent	13.6%	15.2%	14.8%		
Total	**$15,278.4**	**$15,031.5**	**$15,552.5**	**$521.1**	**3.5%**
Supply/demand					
Demand reduction	5,416.6	5,259.9	5,600.2	340.3	6.5%
Percent	35.5%	35.0%	36.0%		
Supply reduction	9,861.8	9,771.6	9,952.4	180.8	1.9%
Percent	64.5%	65.0%	64.0%		
Total	**$15,278.4**	**$15,031.5**	**$15,552.5**	**$521.1**	**3.5%**

Note: Detail may not add due to rounding.

SOURCE: "Table 1. Federal Drug Control Spending by Function, FY 2009–FY 2011 (Budget Authority in Millions)," in *National Drug Control Strategy: FY 2011 Budget Summary*, Executive Office of the President, Office of National Drug Control Policy, 2010, http://www.whitehousedrugpolicy.gov/publications/policy/11budget/fy11budget.pdf (accessed November 12, 2010)

increase in the budget took place primarily during the Bush years; the budgets during the Obama administration show a slight drop in FY 2010 and then a slight rise in FY 2011.

The budget is divided into two broad components: reducing the demand for drugs and disrupting their supply. Reducing the demand for drugs supports research and programs that help communities work toward a drug-free environment and encourage young people to reject drug use. In Table 9.1 these funding categories are "Drug abuse prevention" and "Prevention research." Reducing the demand for drugs also supports research and treatment for drug abuse and abusers. In Table 9.1 these funding categories are "Drug abuse treatment" and "Treatment research." Funding to disrupt the supply of drugs supports efforts to keep individuals and organizations from profiting from trafficking in illicit drugs, both domestically and internationally. In Table 9.1 these funding categories are "Domestic law enforcement," "Interdiction," and "International."

Some budgetary fluctuation over time has been associated with international programs. Funds ranged from 10% of the total budget in FY 2002 to 15% in FYs 2007, 2010, and 2011. (See Table 9.1.) Significant portions of the international budget are spent on supporting international eradication efforts that, in turn, depend on the cooperation of other countries and on the U.S. drug certification program, which may temporarily deny funding to certain regimes.

Table 9.2 shows the overall supply and demand proportions from FY 2009 to FY 2011. Approximately 35% to 36% of drug control spending each year is allocated to reducing the demand for drugs. A much larger proportion—approximately 64% to 65%—is allocated to disrupting the drug supply.

Table 9.3 summarizes the drug control budget by agency. The agencies that work to reduce the demand for drugs are the ONDCP; the U.S. Departments of Education, Health and Human Services, Interior, Transportation, and Veterans Affairs; and the U.S. Small Business Administration. The agencies that work to disrupt the drug supply are the U.S. Departments of Defense, Homeland Security, Justice, State, and the Treasury.

Most domestic law enforcement funds are spent by the U.S. Department of Justice, or on its behalf, and underwrite the operations of the U.S. Drug Enforcement Administration (DEA), the chief domestic drug control agency. Interdiction funds are managed by the U.S. Department of Homeland Security, which now oversees all border-control functions and the U.S. Coast Guard. International funds are divided roughly equally between the U.S. Departments of State and Defense. The Department of State's Bureau of International Narcotics and Law Enforcement Affairs (INL) is the lead agency that manages international programs. The Department of Defense is involved in supporting anti-insurgency programs in the Andean region and

TABLE 9.3

Distribution of federal drug control spending, by agency, fiscal years 2009–11

[In millions]

	Fiscal year 2009 Final	Fiscal year 2010 Enacted	Fiscal year 2011 Request
Department of Defense	1,405.1	1,598.8	1,588.5
Department of Education	429.8	175.8	283.1
Department of Health and Human Services			
Centers of Medicare and Medicaid Services	215.0	430.0	400.0
Substance Abuse and Mental Health Services Administration	2,494.1	2,557.4	2,688.2
National Institutes of Health—National Institute on Drug Abuse	1,293.6	1,059.0	1,094.1
Indian Health Service	91.5	96.0	103.1
Total, Health and Human Services	**4,094.2**	**4,142.8**	**4,285.4**
Department of Homeland Security			
Customs and Border Protection	2,101.0	2,108.6	2,086.1
Immigration and Customs Enforcement	437.1	477.7	499.8
United States Coast Guard	1,096.9	1,162.3	1,208.1
Office of Counternarcotics Enforcement	3.7	3.6	3.9
Total, Homeland Security	**3,638.7**	**3,752.2**	**3,797.9**
Department of the Interior			
Bureau of Indian Affairs	6.3	10.0	10.0
Department of Justice			
Bureau of Prisons	79.2	87.6	93.5
Drug Enforcement Administration	2,203.5	2,271.5	2,421.9
Organized Crime Drug Enforcement Task Force Program	515.0	528.6	579.3
Office of Justice Programs	397.5	288.4	307.6
National Drug Intelligence Center	44.0	44.0	44.6
Total, Justice	**3,239.2**	**3,220.1**	**3,446.9**
Office of National Drug Control Policy			
Counterdrug Technology Assessment Center	3.0	5.0	0.0
High Intensity Drug Trafficking Areas	234.0	239.0	210.0
Other Federal Drug Control Programs	174.7	154.4	165.3
Salaries and Expenses	27.2	29.6	26.2
Total, Office of National Drug Control Policy	**438.9**	**428.0**	**401.4**
Department of State			
Bureau of International Narcotics and Law Enforcement Affairs	1,150.4	870.7	892.0
United States Agency for International Development	418.6	365.1	365.1
Total, State	**1,569.0**	**1,235.9**	**1,257.1**
Department of Transportation			
National Highway Traffic Safety Administration	2.7	2.7	2.7
Department of the Treasury			
Internal Revenue Service	60.6	59.2	60.3
Department of Veterans Affairs			
Veterans Health Administration	392.8	405.0	418.0
Small Business Administration	1.0	1.0	1.0
	15,278.4	**15,031.5**	**15,552.5**

Note: Detail may not add due to rounding.

SOURCE: "Table 2. Federal Drug Control Spending by Agency (Budget Authority in Millions)," in *National Drug Control Strategy: FY 2011 Budget Summary*, Executive Office of the President, Office of National Drug Control Policy, 2010, http://www.whitehousedrugpolicy.gov/publications/policy/11budget/fy11budget.pdf (accessed November 12, 2010)

elsewhere. (Insurgencies are organized, armed rebellions against governments.)

INTERNATIONAL WAR ON DRUGS

The linkages among drugs, organized crime, and insurgencies outside the United States have long been known. A connection to terrorism is a contemporary emphasis that arose in the aftermath of the September 11, 2001 (9/11),

terrorist attacks against the United States. In *Fiscal Year 2004 Budget: Congressional Justification* (May 20, 2003, http://www.state.gov/documents/organization/22061.pdf), the INL made a case for the convergence between the War on Drugs and the War on Terror:

The September 11 attacks and their aftermath highlight the close connections and overlap among terrorists, drug traffickers, and organized crime groups. The nexus is far-reaching. In many instances, such as Colombia, the groups are the same. Drug traffickers benefit from terrorists' military skills, weapons supply, and access to clandestine organizations. Terrorists gain a source of revenue and expertise in the illicit transfer and laundering of money for their operations. All three groups seek out weak states with feeble justice and regulatory sectors where they can corrupt and even dominate the government. September 11 demonstrated graphically the direct threat to the United States by a narcoterrorist state such as Afghanistan where such groups once operated with impunity. Although the political and security situation in Colombia is different from the Taliban period in Afghanistan—the central government is not allied with such groups but rather is engaged in a major effort to destroy them—the narco-terrorist linkage there poses perhaps the single greatest threat to the stability of Latin America and the Western Hemisphere and potentially threatens the security of the United States in the event of a victory by the insurgent groups. The bottom line is that such groups invariably jeopardize international peace and freedom, undermine the rule of law, menace local and regional stability, and threaten both the United States and our friends and allies.

The key to the international War on Drugs is disruption of the drug supply. The ONDCP states in *National Drug Control Strategy, 2006* (February 2006, http://www.usdoj.gov/olp/pdf/ndcs06.pdf) that market disruption "contributes to the Global War on Terrorism, severing the links between drug traffickers and terrorist organizations in countries such as Afghanistan and Colombia, among others. It renders support to allies such as the courageous administration of President Alvaro Uribe [1952–] in Colombia. Market disruption initiatives remove some of the most violent criminals from society, from kingpins such as the remnants of the Cali Cartel to common thugs such as the vicious MS-13 street gang."

In *National Drug Control Strategy, 2009* (January 2009, http://www.whitehousedrugpolicy.gov/publications/policy/ndcs09/2009ndcs.pdf), President George W. Bush summarizes his administration's approach to the United States' drug problem in the following way: "From community coalitions to international partnerships, we pursued a balanced strategy that emphasized stopping initiation, reducing drug abuse and addiction, and disrupting drug markets." The Obama administration's first National Drug Control Strategy report, *National Drug Control Strategy, 2010* (April 2010, http://www.whitehousedrugpolicy.gov/publications/policy/ndcs10/ndcs2010.pdf), appears not to agree that the Bush administration's approach was balanced, and opens its report with the following statement by President Obama: "I am committed to restoring balance in our efforts to combat the drug problems that plague our communities. While I remain steadfast in my commitment to continue our strong enforcement efforts, especially along the southwest bor-

der, I directed the Office of National Drug Control Policy to reengage in efforts to prevent drug use and addiction and to make treatment available for those who seek recovery. This new, balanced approach will expand efforts for the three critical ways that we can address the drug problem: prevention, treatment, and law enforcement." Nonetheless, whether the United States' approach to its drug problem is considered "balanced" or not, it still involves disrupting the drug supply as part of its efforts.

DISRUPTING THE DRUG SUPPLY

Internationally, the federal effort is concentrated on what the INL calls the Andean ridge, the northwestern part of South America where Colombia, Ecuador, and Peru, running north to south, touch the Pacific and where land-locked Bolivia lies east of Peru. In *International Narcotics Control Strategy Report: Volume I Drug and Chemical Control* (March 2009, http://www.state.gov/documents/organization/120054.pdf), the INL estimates that 90% of all cocaine entering the United States comes from Colombia. The remaining cocaine comes from Bolivia and Peru. Besides focusing on Colombia, the INL also concentrates on Mexico because the country is a major transmission route of drugs to the United States and because it is a significant source of heroin, marijuana, and methamphetamine.

The centerpiece of the effort is the eradication of coca and poppy by providing airplanes and funds for spraying herbicides that kill the plants. Efforts also include assisting foreign law enforcement agencies and foreign governments with counternarcotics and anticorruption activities, and providing financial support through the U.S. Agency for International Development (USAID) for the planting of legal crops and improving infrastructure (roads and bridges) so that farm goods can be delivered to market. The latter measures are necessary because many of the people who are involved in cultivating drug-producing plants live in remote and undeveloped regions and this is the only source of income. The USAID programs are intended to give them alternatives.

Elsewhere, the INL is concentrating on Afghanistan and Pakistan. In all, INL programs extend to about 150 countries and involve assistance in law enforcement and in the fight against money laundering (making illegally acquired cash seem as though it was legally acquired). What follows is a brief encapsulation of the INL strategy in selected high-focus areas.

Colombia

The primary effort to disrupt the drug supply in Colombia is coca eradication. The coca tree (*Erythroxylon coca*) is a densely leafed plant that is native to the eastern slopes of the Andes mountains and is heavily cultivated in Colombia.

TABLE 9.4

TABLE 9.5

Amount of coca leaf cultivated, 1986–2008

Amount of coca leaf eradicated, 1987–2009

[In hectares]

Year	Net coca cultivation (hectares)			
	Total	**Bolivia**	**Colombia**	**Peru**
1986	162,500	37,800	18,700	106,000
1987	175,700	41,300	25,600	108,800
1988	193,300	48,900	34,000	110,400
1989	215,700	52,900	42,400	120,400
1990	211,700	50,300	40,100	121,300
1991	206,200	47,900	37,500	120,800
1992	211,700	45,500	37,100	129,100
1993	195,700	47,200	39,700	108,800
1994	201,700	48,100	45,000	108,600
1995	203,900	48,600	50,900	104,400
1996	201,700	48,100	67,200	86,400
1997	187,100	45,800	79,500	61,800
1998	185,500	38,000	101,800	45,700
1999	179,900	21,800	122,500	34,700
2000	187,500	19,600	136,200	31,700
2001	221,800	19,900	169,800	32,100
2002	200,750	21,600	144,450	34,700
2003	166,300	23,200	113,850	29,250
2004	166,200	24,600	114,100	27,500
2005	204,500	26,500	144,000	34,000
2006	224,800	25,800	157,000	42,000
2007	232,500	29,500	167,000	36,000
2008	192,000	32,000	119,000	41,000

SOURCE: Adapted from "Table 108. Andean Net Coca Cultivation and Potential Cocaine Hydrochloride Production, 1986–2008," in *National Drug Control Strategy: Data Supplement 2010*, Executive Office of the President, Office of National Drug Control Policy, 2010, http://www .whitehousedrugpolicy.gov/publications/policy/ndcs10/ndcs10_data_supl/ds_ list_of_tables.pdf (accessed November 12, 2010)

Year	Eradicated		
	Bolivia	**Colombia**	**Peru**
1987	1,040	460	355
1988	1,475	230	5,130
1989	2,500	640	1,285
1990	8,100	900	NA
1991	5,486	972	NA
1992	3,152	959	NA
1993	2,397	793	0
1994	1,058	541*	0
1995	5,493	3,243*	0
1996	7,512	15,407*	1,259
1997	7,026	31,663*	3,462
1998	11,621	49,641*	7,825
1999	16,999	39,113*	13,800
2000	7,653	42,283*	6,200
2001	NA	77,165*	3,900
2002	11,839	102,225*	7,000
2003	10,000	132,817*	7,022
2004	8,437	136,555*	7,605
2005	6,073	138,775*	8,966
2006	5,070	171,613*	10,137
2007	6,269	153,133*	11,057
2008	5,484	133,496*	10,143
2009	6,314	104,772*	10,025

NA = Data not available.
Note: Beginning in 2001, (USG) United States Government surveys of Bolivian coca take place over the period June to June.
*Colombian figures pertain to aerial eradication from 1994 to 2009.

SOURCE: "Table 109. Amount of Coca Leaf Eradicated, 1987–2009 (Hectares)," in *National Drug Control Strategy: Data Supplement 2010*, Executive Office of the President, Office of National Drug Control Policy, 2010, http://www.whitehousedrugpolicy.gov/publications/policy/ndcs10/ ndcs10_data_supl/ds_list_of_tables.pdf (accessed November 12, 2010). Data for Colombian eradication for 1999–2002 from the Policia Nacional de Colombia (CNP)/US Department of State INL Air Wing.

Table 9.4 shows the amount of coca leaf that was cultivated between 1986 and 2008, and Table 9.5 shows the amount of coca leaf that was eradicated between 1987 and 2009. The area cultivated in Colombia increased from 1986 to 2001 about ninefold, from 46,200 acres (18,700 ha) to 419,600 acres (169,800 ha). The area of cultivation then declined through 2003, rose again through 2007 to near-2001 levels, and then dropped dramatically in 2008 to 294,100 acres (119,000 ha). U.S. eradication efforts increased dramatically, from 104,484 acres (42,283 ha) in 2000, during the Clinton administration, to a high of 424,065 acres (171,613 ha) in 2006, during the Bush administration. This was a fourfold increase in eradication. Eradication declined from 2006 to 2009, with 258,897 acres (104,772 ha) eradicated in 2009.

When the source of a drug such as cocaine is diminished, two things happen: the purity of the finished product (the drug) declines and the price of it rises. There is a lag time, however, between the eradication of source plants and the detection of the decline in purity and the rise in price of the drug in the United States. Figure 8.6 in Chapter 8 shows the decline in purity and the rise in price of cocaine beginning in the first quarter of 2007, reflecting the results of coca eradication from years prior.

Poppy eradication takes place in Colombia as well, because this country supplies a great deal of the heroin entering the United States. Table 9.6 shows there was a 76% increase in Colombian opium poppy eradication between 2001 and 2004. In 2001 eradication efforts removed 6,383 acres (2,583 ha) of the plants and in 2004 they removed 11,261 acres (4,557 ha). Eradication then fell by about half in 2005 and 2006, and then fell to extremely low levels in 2007, 2008, and 2009 as aerial eradication of poppies was discontinued to focus on the aerial eradication of coca. Additionally, Colombian cultivation of opium poppy declined from 16,062 acres (6,500 ha) in 2001 to only 2,471 acres (1,000 ha) in 2007; no data were available for 2008 and 2009.

Along with the eradication of coca and poppy in Colombia, USAID has been conducting the Alternative Livelihoods Program, which is aimed at providing farmers who are involved in cultivating coca and poppy with alternative crops. USAID began operations in Colombia late in 2000, although this idea started in some areas more than 30 years earlier.

Besides Colombia's aggressive seizure of drugs within its borders, the country is working with the United States in

TABLE 9.6

Amount of opium poppy cultivated and eradicated, 1990–2009

[In hectares]

Year	Afghanistan	Pakistan	Burma	Laos	Thailand	Colombia	Guatemala	Mexico[a]
Cultivated								
1990	12,370	8,220	150,100	30,580	3,435	NA	845	5,450
1991	17,190	8,205	160,000	29,625	3,000	1,160	1,145	3,765
1992	19,470	8,170	153,700	25,610	2,050	NA	NA	730
1993	21,080	6,280	146,600	18,520	2,110	NA	440	438
1994	29,180	7,270	154,070	19,650	2,110	NA	NA	50
1995	38,740	6,950	154,070	19,650	1,750	6,540	150	5,050
1996	37,950	3,400	163,100	25,250	2,170	6,300	90	5,100
1997	39,150	4,100	155,150	28,150	1,650	6,600	NA	4,000
1998	41,720	3,030	130,300	26,100	1,350	6,100	NA	5,500
1999	51,500	1,570	89,500	21,800	835	7,500	NA	3,600
2000	64,510	515	108,700	23,150	890	7,500	NA	1,900
2001	1,685	213	105,000	22,000	820	6,500	NA	4,400
2002	30,750	213	77,700	23,200	750	4,900	NA	2,700
2003	61,000	1,714	47,130	18,900	NA	4,400	NA	4,800
2004	206,700	NA	36,000	10,000	NA	2,100	NA	3,500
2005	107,400	NA	40,000	5,600	NA	NA	330	3,300
2006	172,600	NA	21,000	1,700	NA	2,300	100	5,000
2007	202,000	NA	21,700	1,100	NA	1,000	NA	6,900
2008	157,000	NA	22,500	1,900	NA	NA	NA	15,000
2009	131,000	NA	17,000	1,000	NA	NA	NA	NA
Eradicated								
1990	NA	185	NA	0	720	NA	1,085	4,650
1991	NA	440	1,012	0	1,200	1,156	576	6,545
1992	NA	977	1,215	0	1,580	12,858	470	11,583
1993	NA	856	604	0	0	9,821	426	13,015
1994	NA	463	3,345	0	0	3,906	150	11,036
1995	NA	0	0	0	580	3,760	86	15,389
1996	NA	867	0	0	880	6,028	12	14,671
1997	NA	654	10,501	0	1,050	6,972	3	17,732
1998	NA	2,194	16,194	NA	715	NA	5	17,449
1999	NA	1,197	9,800	NA	808	NA	1	15,469
2000	NA	1,704	0	NA	757	9,254[b]	1	15,300
2001	NA	1,484	9,317	NA	832	2,583[b]	1	19,115
2002	NA	NA	25,862	NA	507	3,371[b]	1	19,157
2003	NA	3,641	683	18,900	767	2,994[b]	1	20,034
2004	NA	4,426	NA	NA	NA	4,557[b]	NA	15,925
2005	NA	707	NA	NA	NA	2,121[b]	NA	21,609
2006	NA	363	NA	NA	NA	2,161[b]	NA	16,889
2007	NA	614	NA	NA	NA	375[b]	NA	11,046
2008	NA	0	NA	NA	NA	381[b]	NA	NA
2009	NA	NA	NA	NA	NA	586[b]	NA	NA

NA = Data not available.

[a] The eradication figures shown for 1992–2001 are derived from data supplied by Mexican authorities to the International Narcotics Control Strategy Report (INCSR). The effective eradication figure is an estimate of the actual amount of crop destroyed—factoring in replanting, repeated spraying of one area, and other factors.

[b] Eradication figures shown for Colombia represent aerial eradication from 2000 to 2003; combined aerial and manual form 2004 to 2006; and manual eradication since 2007 after aerial eradication was discontinued in April 2006 to put all aerial assets against coca cultiviation.

SOURCE: "Table 104. Amount of Opium Poppy Cultivated and Eradicated, 1990–2009 (Hectares)," in *National Drug Control Strategy: Data Supplement 2010*, Executive Office of the President, Office of National Drug Control Policy, 2010, http://www.whitehousedrugpolicy.gov/publications/policy/ndcs10/ndcs10_data_supl/ds_list_of_tables.pdf (accessed November 12, 2010)

the resumption of the Air Bridge Denial (ABD) program. The ABD program works by forcing or shooting down aircraft that appear to be taking part in drug trafficking activities. The program was halted in 2001, when a civilian aircraft was downed in Peru and two U.S. citizens were killed. It was resumed in 2003. According to the INL, in *International Narcotics Control Strategy Report*, by the end of 2008 the ABD program was instrumental in decreasing illegal flights over Colombia to less than 50, so the focus of the personnel and equipment was shifted to maritime patrols.

Colombia, however, illustrates some of the fundamental dilemmas of interdiction. The drug trade there has been one symptom of a festering civil war. Through the 1990s and into the first decade of the 21st century antigovernment insurgent groups and illegal paramilitary groups were heavily funded by the drug trade. However, the Central Intelligence Agency notes in *World Factbook: Colombia* (February 11, 2011, https://www.cia.gov/library/publications/the-world-factbook/geos/co.html) that "more than 31,000 former paramilitaries had demobilized by the end of 2006 and the United Self Defense Forces of Colombia

(AUC) as a formal organization had ceased to function. In the wake of the paramilitary demobilization, emerging criminal groups arose, whose members include some former paramilitaries. The Colombian Government has stepped up efforts to reassert government control throughout the country, and now has a presence in every one of its administrative departments."

In "Colombian Paramilitaries' Successors Called a Threat" (*New York Times*, February 3, 2010), Simon Romero reports that as of early 2010 the Colombian security policy was not working as well as expected to thwart the paramilitaries. Romero notes that the group Human Rights Watch issued a report explaining that these groups were massacring, raping, and displacing Colombians while continuing to be funded by the drug trade. The largest of the insurgent groups is the Fuerzas Armadas Revolucionarios de Colombia (FARC; Revolutionary Armed Forces of Colombia). However, Romero indicates in "Rebels' Second in Command Has Been Killed, Colombia Says" (*New York Times*, September 23, 2010) that in September 2010 government security forces killed Mono Jojoy, the FARC's second in command, and 20 other FARC members during a bombing raid. This attack on the FARC was a major setback to the insurgent group.

With an internal conflict that has lasted more than 40 years, quite some time may pass before civil order is totally restored in Colombia and economic development has advanced enough to make coca and poppy cultivation unattractive.

Bolivia and Peru

According to the INL, in *International Narcotics Control Strategy Report*, Bolivia is the third-largest producer of cocaine and "is a significant transit zone for Peruvian-origin cocaine." Bolivia is poor and has had an unsettled history (nearly 200 coups since its independence in 1825). The country has been under democratic rule since the 1980s, but successive governments have been reluctant to support eradication programs energetically because coca cultivation (but not cocaine production) is legal in Bolivia. Coca is a traditional crop in this country, and the coca leaf is chewed by the inhabitants; eradication has resulted in a popular antiestablishment movement.

Table 9.5 shows the amount of coca leaf that has been eradicated in Bolivia, from 29,255 acres (11,839 ha) in 2002 to 15,602 acres (6,314 ha) in 2009. These eradication efforts are offset by replanting, and eradication is sometimes violently opposed by the population. As a result, the amount of coca leaf that was cultivated in Bolivia increased 48% during this period, from 53,375 acres (21,600 ha) in 2002 to 79,074 acres (32,000 ha) in 2008. (See Table 9.4.)

The INL explains that Peru is the second-largest producer of cocaine in the world and a major importer of cocaine precursor chemicals. However, unlike the Bolivian

government, the Peruvian government is committed to counternarcotics activities. Regardless, the government's actions are hampered by organized bodies of *cocaleros* (coca growers), who enjoy sufficient popular support. Thus, in Peru as in Bolivia, replanting frequently follows eradication efforts. Nonetheless, Table 9.4 shows that the cultivation of coca leaf in Peru decreased dramatically from a peak of 319,013 acres (129,100 ha) in 1992 to a low of 67,954 acres (27,500 ha) in 2004. Data are unavailable for many years, but eradication increased sixfold between 1996 and 2004, from 3,110 acres (1,259 ha) to 18,792 acres (7,605 ha). Cultivation rose after 2004 to 101,313 acres (41,000 ha) in 2008, but eradication increased as well, to 24,772 acres (10,025 ha) in 2009.

Mexico

Mexico is one of the principal producers of marijuana, methamphetamine, and heroin that enter the United States. It also serves as a thoroughfare for cocaine, which is produced in South America and sent north to the United States.

From 2000 to 2006 the Mexican president Vicente Fox (1942–) and the Mexican government were energetic both in the eradication of the marijuana and poppy crops and in the arrest and prosecution of the members of drug cartels, even though efforts were hampered by severe budget constraints, corruption, and inefficiencies within law enforcement and criminal justice institutions. In 2006 Felipe Calderón (1962–) succeeded Fox. According to the INL, in *International Narcotics Control Strategy Report*, during the first two years of the Calderón administration significant progress was made in attacking drug trafficking and consumption. In October 2008 Presidents Bush and Calderón announced the Merida Initiative, a plan to achieve stronger law enforcement cooperation between the United States and Mexico. In March 2009 President Obama expanded the initiative, and in March 2010 the initiative was developed even further. The new expansion focused on training Mexican police and supporting programs that would strengthen communities in an effort to divert young people from criminal activity. However, Elisabeth Malkin and Randal C. Archibold indicate in "U.S. Withholds Millions in Mexico Antidrug Aid" (*New York Times*, September 3, 2010) that by September 2010 the United States was withholding some funds from Mexico "because of concerns that the country has not done enough to protect its people from police and military abuse."

Table 9.7 shows that marijuana cultivation in Mexico decreased ninefold from 86,610 acres (35,050 ha) in 1990 to 9,637 acres (3,900 ha) in 2000. After 2000 it began to increase, reaching 21,992 acres (8,900 ha) in 2008. The table also shows that eradication of marijuana crops in Mexico increased from 16,680 acres (6,750 ha) in 1990 to a high of 90,404 acres (36,585 ha) in 2003. Eradication

TABLE 9.7

Amount of cannabis cultivated and eradicated by foreign countries, 1990–2008

[In hectares]

Year	Cultivated				Eradicated		
	Mexico*	Jamaica	Colombia		Mexico	Jamaica	Colombia
1990	35,050	1,220	1,500		6,750	1,030	500
1991	17,915	950	2,000		10,795	833	0
1992	16,420	398	2,000		16,872	811	49
1993	21,190	1,200	5,050		16,645	456	50
1994	19,045	1,000	5,000		14,227	692	14
1995	18,650	1,000	5,000		21,573	695	20
1996	18,700	1,000	5,000		22,961	473	NA
1997	15,300	1,060	5,000		23,576	743	NA
1998	4,600	NA	5,000		23,928	705	NA
1999	3,700	NA	5,000		33,583	894	NA
2000	3,900	NA	5,000		33,000	517	NA
2001	4,100	NA	5,000		28,699	332	NA
2002	7,900	NA	5,000		30,775	80	NA
2003	7,500	NA	5,000		36,585	445	NA
2004	5,800	NA	5,000		30,851	NA	NA
2005	5,600	NA	NA		30,842	NA	NA
2006	8,600	NA	NA		30,162	NA	NA
2007	NA	NA	NA		22,348	NA	NA
2008	8,900	NA	NA		15,756	NA	NA

NA = Data not available.

*The eradication figures shown for 1992–2001 are derived from data supplied by Mexican authorities to the International Narcotics Control Strategy Report (INCSR). The effective eradication figure is an estimate of the actual amount of crop destroyed—factoring in replanting, repeated spraying of one area, and other factors. Reported cultivation is described as harvestable/net production.

SOURCE: "Table 112. Amount of Cannabis Cultivated and Eradicated by Foreign Countries, 1990–2008 (Hectares)," in *National Drug Control Strategy: Data Supplement 2010*, Executive Office of the President, Office of National Drug Control Policy, 2010, http://www.whitehousedrugpolicy.gov/publications/policy/ndcs10/ndcs10_data_supl/ds_list_of_tables.pdf (accessed November 12, 2010)

leveled out at about 74,000 acres (30,000 ha) through 2006, but fell to 38,934 acres (15,756 ha) in 2008.

Table 9.6 shows the eradication of 39,352 acres (15,925 ha) of the Mexican opium poppy crop in 2004 and 27,295 acres (11,046 ha) in 2007. No data were available for 2008 and 2009. In spite of eradication efforts, poppy cultivation was higher in 2007 than in all previous years shown on the table, and in 2008 poppy cultivation more than doubled to 37,066 acres (15,000 ha) for an all-time high.

Along with marijuana and heroin, one of the drugs that comes to the United States over the U.S.-Mexican border is methamphetamine, a synthetic drug that is made in illegal laboratories. This drug has become an increasing problem in the United States. (See Chapter 4.) U.S. law enforcement agencies have done much to combat the spread of this drug domestically, but they are also active in stopping the flow of methamphetamine and its precursors (other substances that are used to make methamphetamine) into the country. In general, increased production of methamphetamine within Mexico is indicated by increased seizures at the U.S. southwest border. Table 8.5 in Chapter 8 shows that methamphetamine seizures were up in 2005 and 2006, dropped significantly in 2007, and rose again in 2008 and 2009.

Afghanistan

In *International Narcotics Control Strategy Report*, the INL indicates that trafficking in opium provided over one-fifth of Afghanistan's gross domestic product in 2008. This country is the world's largest supplier of opium. When Afghanistan was under the control of the fanatically religious and conservative Taliban regime, cultivated poppy acreage dropped precipitously, from 159,408 acres (64,510 ha) in 2000 to 4,164 acres (1,685 ha) in 2001. (See Table 9.6.) The United States invaded Afghanistan in 2001, in a response to the 9/11 terrorist attacks, and the Taliban was driven from power. An unintended consequence of this was that poppy cultivation resumed, rising to 75,985 acres (30,750 ha) in 2002. By 2004 poppy cultivation reached a staggering 510,767 acres (206,700 ha) but then dropped by nearly half to 265,391 acres (107,400 ha) in 2005. The recultivation of poppy was in part a response to a continuing drought in the region: opium poppy is hardy and can grow under adverse conditions, supplying income to farmers. By 2007 poppy cultivation in Afghanistan had nearly reached 2004 levels at 499,153 acres (202,000 ha), but by 2009 it had dropped to 323,708 acres (131,000 ha).

Afghanistan's post-9/11 government officially banned opium poppy cultivation and has pressured its regional governors to suppress the drug trade. Despite these efforts, the situation in Afghanistan was, in the immediate post-Taliban era, similar to the situation in Colombia, with a weak central government unable to assert itself in areas where autonomous warlords hold de facto (virtual) power. Other countries and organizations have tried to help. For example, USAID has been active in establishing alternative development programs. The United Kingdom has conducted some eradication efforts and established a counter-narcotics mobile force; Germany has provided training and equipment to establish an Afghan security force; and Italy has been involved in strengthening the country's judicial system.

The DEA developed the Foreign-Deployed Advisory Support Teams program in Afghanistan to identify, target, investigate, and disrupt or dismantle transnational drug trafficking operations in the region. A major goal of this program is to help develop Afghanistan's antidrug abilities. Training began in 2004 and operations began in 2005. Even though results were initially positive, the INL indicates in *International Narcotics Control Strategy Report* that "although opium poppy cultivation is largely confined to insecure provinces in the south, Afghanistan's narcotics industry continues to threaten efforts to establish security, governance, and a licit economy throughout the country."

FOSTERING INTERNATIONAL COOPERATION: THE DRUG CERTIFICATION PROCESS

The United States uses a drug certification process to promote international cooperation in controlling drug production and trafficking. Section 490 of the Foreign Assistance Act of 1961 requires the president to annually submit to Congress a list of major drug-producing and drug-transiting countries. The president must also assess each country's performance in battling narcotics trade and trafficking based on the goals and objectives of the 1988 United Nations Convention against Illicit Traffic in Narcotic Drugs and Psychotropic Substances. Countries that have fully cooperated with the United States or that have taken adequate steps to reach the goals and objectives of the United Nations convention are "certified" by the president. U.S. aid is withheld to countries that are not certified. Many countries resent the process, but most work toward certification.

TRANSIT-ZONE AGREEMENTS

Other countries not on the list are frequently reluctant to cooperate with the United States to stop drug traffickers. The Caribbean basin, for example, is a major transit zone for drug trafficking. The Caribbean basin countries are those that border, or lie in, the Gulf of Mexico and the Caribbean Sea, such as the island nations of the West Indies, Mexico, Central American nations, and northern South American nations. Bermuda is also included, even though it is in the Atlantic Ocean. Most of the islands have bilateral agreements with the United States, but these agreements are limited to maritime matters that permit U.S. ships to seize traffickers in the territorial waters of particular Caribbean islands. Few transit-zone countries permit U.S. planes to fly in their airspace to force suspected traffickers

to land. Some transit-zone countries have no maritime agreements with the United States.

DOMESTIC DRUG SEIZURES

The DEA is also at work within the United States to disrupt the drug supply. Table 9.8 shows drug seizures across the United States between 1989 and 2008. Seizures of cocaine, heroin, methamphetamine, and marijuana vary during the time span shown but, in general, have risen. For example, seizures of cocaine ranged from a low of 211,831 pounds (96,085 kg) in 1990 to a high of 385,101 pounds (174,679 kg) in 2005. Table 9.9 shows domestic seizures of MDMA between 2000 and 2008. These seizures varied widely as well. The year in which domestic seizures were the greatest was 2001 with 10.7 million dosage units; the year in which domestic seizures were the lowest was 2003 with 1.9 million dosage units.

In 2006 the Combat Methamphetamine Epidemic Act was signed into law, establishing stricter national controls for the over-the-counter (nonprescription) sale of products containing the methamphetamine precursor drugs ephedrine and pseudoephedrine. Before this act, many states had imposed restrictions on the retail sale of pseudoephedrine. These state and national restrictions have resulted in a significant decline in methamphetamine laboratory seizures, because without these precursor drugs the laboratories cannot manufacture methamphetamine. Table 9.10 shows that the number of superlab seizures (laboratories that are capable of producing more than 10 pounds [4.5 kg] of methamphetamine per production run) has decreased as well. The table shows that 246 superlabs were seized in 2001, compared with 11 in 2007 and 17 in 2008.

MARIJUANA LEGALIZATION MOVEMENT

In the United States the legalization of drugs almost invariably refers to the legalization of marijuana rather than, for instance, heroin and cocaine. The use of "hard drugs" such as these is relatively limited, and most Americans consider them to be highly addictive and damaging to one's physical and mental health. Marijuana's situation is different. According to SAMHSA, in *Results from the 2009 National Survey on Drug Use and Health*, 76.6% of all current drug users in 2009 were using marijuana, and 58% of all current drug users used only marijuana and no other drugs. Some studies suggest significant harm from marijuana use, including effects on the heart, lungs, brain, and social and learning capabilities. Other studies find little or no harm from moderate marijuana use. Regardless of what the research says, marijuana is generally thought of as a relatively mild drug, an opinion that is supported in Canada by those who introduced repeated initiatives to decriminalize marijuana possession and in the Netherlands, where marijuana sales are tolerated in coffee shops.

TABLE 9.8

Cocaine, heroin, methamphetamine, and cannabis seizures, 1989–2008

[In kilograms]

Year	Cocaine	Heroin	Metham- phetamine	Cannabis	
				Marijuana	Hashish
1989	114,903	1,311	NA	393,276	23,043
1990	96,085	687	NA	233,478	7,683
1991	128,247	1,448	NA	224,603	79,110
1992	120,175	1,251	NA	344,899	111
1993	121,215	1,502	7	409,922	11,396
1994	129,378	1,285	178	474,856	561
1995	111,031	1,543	369	627,776	14,470
1996	128,555	1,362	136	638,863	37,851
1997	101,495	1,624	1,099	698,799	756
1998	118,436	1,458	2,559	827,149	241
1999	132,063	1,151	2,779	1,075,154	797
2000	106,619	1,674	3,470	1,235,938	10,867
2001	105,748	2,496	4,051	1,214,188	161
2002	102,515	2,773	2,477	1,101,459	621
2003	117,024	2,381	3,853	1,229,615	155
2004	172,804	2,116	3,899	1,180,688	166
2005	174,679	1,692	4,772	1,117,189	388
2006	152,726	1,779	4,716	1,141,735	178
2007	142,174	2,514	2,836	1,456,855	338
2008	97,764	1,776	4,209	1,587,322	289

NA = Data not available.

SOURCE: "Table 57. Federal-Wide Cocaine, Heroin, Methamphetamine, and Cannabis Seizures, 1989–2008 (Kilograms)," in *National Drug Control Strategy: Data Supplement 2010*, Executive Office of the President, Office of National Drug Control Policy, 2010, http://www.whitehousedrugpolicy.gov/publications/policy/ndcs10/ndcs10_data_supl/ds_list_of_tables.pdf (accessed November 12, 2010).

TABLE 9.9

MDMA (ecstasy) seizures, 2000–08

Year	Reported in dosage units	Reported in kilograms
2000	8,289,023	0
2001	10,710,509	80
2002	4,715,098	1,056
2003	1,888,475	484
2004	2,326,434	107
2005	4,357,631	242
2006	6,792,366	477
2007	5,721,730	450
2008	6,633,329	268

SOURCE: "Table 60. Domestic Seizures of MDMA, 2000–2008," in *National Drug Control Strategy: Data Supplement 2010*, Executive Office of the President, Office of National Drug Control Policy, 2010, http://www.whitehousedrugpolicy.gov/publications/policy/ndcs10/ndcs10_data_supl/ds_list_of_tables.pdf (accessed November 12, 2010).

Public Opinion

The polling data that the Gallup Organization gathered for selected years between 1969 and 2010 show public opinion increasingly favoring the legalization of marijuana. (See Figure 9.1.) In 1969, 84% of the public opposed legalization and 12% favored it. By 2010 those opposed had declined to 50% of the public, whereas 46% were in favor.

It is with the support of this population that a number of initiatives and referenda attempting to legalize marijuana for medical purposes or to decriminalize possession of modest quantities have appeared on state ballots. Many states and local jurisdictions *have* decriminalized certain uses of specific amounts of marijuana. Decriminalization means that the state or local jurisdiction no longer considers uses of marijuana in the amounts and manners it specifies as illegal, but the jurisdiction may still consider these uses as civil infractions and may impose civil fines, drug education, or drug treatment. Nevertheless, the possession and use of marijuana is still illegal under federal law, and this law supersedes state and local marijuana decriminalization laws. Therefore, a person residing in a state that has decriminalized the possession and use of marijuana can still be arrested and prosecuted by federal officials under federal law.

California provides an example of a state in which this dichotomy would have been played out had a 2010 ballot initiative passed. Proposition 19 would have allowed those over the age of 21 years to possess up to 1 ounce (28 g) of marijuana and would have allowed local officials to tax the drug. Even though Proposition 19 did not garner a majority vote, it did receive 46.5% of the vote and came close to creating a situation in which state and federal laws would have been in opposition.

Arguments for and against Legalization

FOR LEGALIZATION. Most of those who favor legalization in some form (for medical use, decriminalization, or regulation) use two arguments in combination. The first argument is that an approach to drugs based on

TABLE 9.10

Methamphetamine superlab seizures by state, 2000–08

State	2000	2001	2002	2003	2004	2005	2006	2007	2008
Alabama	0	0	1	0	0	0	0	0	0
Arizona	0	0	1	0	0	0	0	0	0
Arkansas	0	0	2	0	0	0	0	0	0
California	122	224	125	125	42	28	14	10	15
Colorado	0	0	2	0	0	0	0	0	0
Georgia	0	0	0	0	0	1	1	0	1
Illinois	0	0	0	2	0	0	0	0	0
Indiana	0	0	1	0	0	0	0	0	0
Louisiana	0	0	1	0	0	0	0	0	0
Missouri	0	0	0	1	1	1	1	1	0
Montana	0	0	0	0	0	0	0	0	1
Nevada	0	3	1	0	0	0	0	0	0
North Dakota	0	0	1	0	0	0	0	0	0
Ohio	0	0	0	0	1	0	2	0	0
Oklahoma	1	0	2	0	1	2	0	0	0
Oregon	3	5	2	1	4	1	0	0	0
South Carolina	0	0	0	0	1	0	0	0	0
Tennessee	0	0	0	1	0	0	0	0	0
Texas	3	9	2	0	2	0	0	0	0
Utah	0	0	0	0	0	1	0	0	0
Washington	1	5	2	0	1	0	0	0	0
West Virginia	0	0	1	0	0	0	0	0	0
Wisconsin	0	0	0	0	1	0	0	0	0
Total	**131**	**246**	**144**	**130**	**54**	**34**	**18**	**11**	**17**

Note: Super lab capacity is 10 pounds or more.

SOURCE: "Table 82. States with Methamphetamine Seizures of Super Labs by State, 2000–2008," in *National Drug Control Strategy: Data Supplement 2010*, Executive Office of the President, Office of National Drug Control Policy, 2010, http://www.whitehousedrugpolicy.gov/publications/policy/ndcs10/ndcs10_data_supl/ds_list_of_tables.pdf (accessed November 12, 2010)

FIGURE 9.1

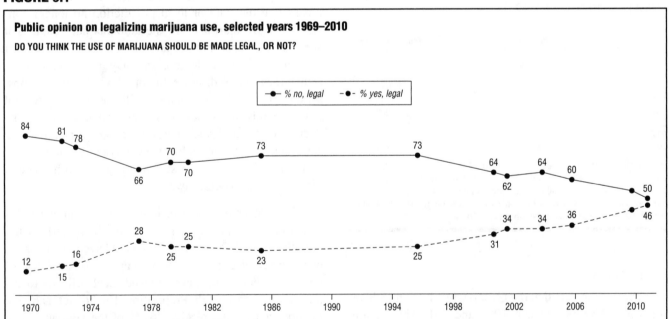

Public opinion on legalizing marijuana use, selected years 1969–2010

DO YOU THINK THE USE OF MARIJUANA SHOULD BE MADE LEGAL, OR NOT?

SOURCE: Elizabeth Mendes, "Support for Making Use of Marijuana Legal," in *New High of 46% of Americans Support Legalizing Marijuana*, The Gallup Organization, October 28, 2010, http://www.gallup.com/poll/144086/New-High-Americans-Support-Legalizing-Marijuana.aspx (accessed November 13, 2010). Copyright © 2010 by The Gallup Organization. Reproduced by permission of The Gallup Organization.

prohibition and criminalization does not work, produces excessive rates of incarceration, and costs a lot of money that could be more productively spent on treatment and prevention. The second argument is that drug use is an activity arbitrarily called a crime. It is imposed by law on some drugs and not on others, and can be seen as criminal at one time but perhaps not at another. Murder, rape, and robbery have always been considered inherently criminal acts, but drug use is just a consumption of substances; its control is arbitrary and follows fashions. For example, alcohol consumption was once prohibited but is now legal. Likewise, during the early 1900s opiates were sold in pharmacies and the soft-drink Coca-Cola contained small quantities of cocaine.

Some who advocate the legalization of drugs believe the government has no right telling people what they may and may not ingest. However, most legalization proponents recognize that many drugs can be harmful (though many dispute the degree), but they do not see this as a reason to make their use illegal. They point out that tobacco use and alcohol abuse are harmful—possibly more harmful or addictive than some drugs that are illicit—but their use is legal. The policy these legalization advocates recommend is based on educational and public health approaches such as those that are used for tobacco and alcohol. They feel that a greater harm is imposed on society by prohibiting such substances, as evidenced by the consequences of the Prohibition period of the early 20th century, during which alcohol was banned and crime, racketeering, and homicide rates soared.

Many proponents argue that legalization will result in decreased harm and crime from trafficking, gang wars, and crimes committed to obtain drugs; lower incarceration rates and associated cost savings; and more funds available for treatment from savings and from taxes on legally distributed drugs. Legalization of drugs is also seen as making available marijuana in medical applications, such as relieving the suffering of cancer and acquired immunodeficiency syndrome (AIDS) patients.

AGAINST LEGALIZATION. The federal government's case against legalization is summarized by the DEA in the brochure *Speaking out against Drug Legalization* (2010, http://www.justice.gov/dea/demand/speakout/speak _out_101210.pdf). The 10 arguments presented by the DEA are shown in Table 9.11.

Like legalization proponents, the DEA's position is organized around the concept of harm. Certain drugs are illegal or controlled because they cause harm. In the DEA's view, the legalization of drugs—even if only marijuana— will increase the harm already suffered by the drug-using public by spreading use to ever larger numbers of people. The agency makes the point that drugs are much more addictive than alcohol and invites the public to contemplate a situation in which commercial interests might be enabled to promote the sale of presently illicit substances.

Would legalization reduce crime? The DEA does not believe it would. Under a regulated drug-use system, age restrictions would apply. A criminal enterprise would continue to supply those under age. If marijuana were legalized, trade in heroin and cocaine would continue. If all three of the major drugs were permitted to be sold legally,

TABLE 9.11

Top ten facts on legalization of drugs cited by the Drug Enforcement Administration (DEA), 2010

Fact 1: Significant progress has been made in fighting drug use and drug trafficking in America.

Fact 2: A balanced approach of prevention, enforcement, and treatment are the keys in the fight against drug abuse.

Fact 3: Drug use is regulated and access to drugs is controlled because drugs can be harmful.

Fact 4: Smoked marijuana has never been and will never be scientifically approved medicine.

Fact 5: Drug control spending is a minor portion of the U.S. budget. Compared to the social costs of drug abuse and addiction, government spending on drug control is minimal.

Fact 6: Legalization of drugs will lead to increased use and increased levels of addiction.

Fact 7: Crime, violence, and drug use go hand-in-hand.

Fact 8: Alcohol and tobacco have caused significant health, social, and crime problems, and legalized drugs would only make the situation worse.

Fact 9: Europe's more liberal drug policies are not the right model for America.

Fact 10: Most non-violent drug users get treatment, not jail time.

SOURCE: Adapted from "Summary of the Top Ten Facts on Legalization," in *Speaking out against Drug Legalization*, U.S. Department of Justice, Drug Enforcement Administration, 2010, http://www.justice.gov/dea/demand/ speakout/speak_out_101210.pdf (accessed November 13, 2010)

other substances, such as phencyclidine and methamphetamine, would still support a criminal trade. The DEA does not envision that a black market in drugs could be eliminated entirely, because health authorities would never permit potent drugs to be sold freely on the open market.

For all these reasons, the DEA advocates the continuation of a balanced approach to the control of drugs including prevention, enforcement, and treatment.

MEDICAL MARIJUANA

The medicinal value of THC (delta-9-tetrahydrocannabinol), the active ingredient in marijuana, has long been known to the medical community. The drug has been shown to alleviate the nausea and vomiting caused by chemotherapy, which is used to treat many forms of cancer. Marijuana has also been found useful in alleviating pressure on the eye in glaucoma patients. Furthermore, the drug has been found effective in helping to fight the physical wasting that usually accompanies AIDS. AIDS patients lose their appetite and can slowly waste away because they do not eat. Complicating matters, many of the newer AIDS remedies must be taken on a full stomach. Marijuana has been found effective in restoring the appetite of some AIDS patients. This is not to say that all scientists agree that marijuana is healthy or useful. For example, some studies find that marijuana suppresses the immune system and contains a number of lung-damaging chemicals. Still, the potentially beneficial uses of marijuana as a medicine have led to a movement for it to be made legally available by prescription.

Opponents of the medical legalization of marijuana often point to Marinol (a laboratory-made form of THC found in marijuana) as a superior alternative. Marinol provides a standardized THC content and does not contain impurities, such as leaves, mold spores, and bacteria, which are generally found in marijuana. However, many patients do not respond to Marinol, and the determination of the right dosage is variable from patient to patient. Nonresponding patients claim that smoking marijuana or eating it incorporated into foods such as brownies allows them to control the dosage that they need.

Marijuana has been used illegally by an unknown number of cancer, glaucoma, and AIDS patients on the recommendation of their doctors. Nonetheless, the medical use of marijuana is not without risk. The primary negative effect is diminished control over movement. In some cases users may experience unpleasant emotional states or feelings. In addition, the usefulness of medicinal marijuana is limited by the harmful effects of smoking, which can increase a person's risk of cancer, lung damage, and problems with pregnancies (such as low birth weight). However, these risks are usually not important for terminally ill patients or those with debilitating symptoms. Also, the drug can be eaten to be effective.

Some states and local jurisdictions have decriminalized the cultivation of marijuana for personal medical use. As mentioned previously, however, the cultivation of marijuana is still illegal under federal law, which supersedes state and local marijuana decriminalization laws. In addition, such state and local rulings do not necessarily establish that the use of marijuana is medically appropriate. That issue is hotly debated in the media and among Americans, but no nationally recognized medical organization—including the American Medical Association, the American Cancer Society, or the American Academy of Pediatrics—has endorsed the medical use of smoked marijuana.

IMPORTANT NAMES AND ADDRESSES

AAA Foundation for Traffic Safety
607 14th St. NW, Ste. 201
Washington, DC 20005
(202) 638-5944
FAX: (202) 638-5943
E-mail: info@aaafoundation.org
URL: http://www.aaafoundation.org/

Action on Smoking and Health
701 Fourth St. NW
Washington, DC 20001
(202) 659-4310
URL: http://www.ash.org/

Adult Children of Alcoholics
PO Box 3216
Torrance, CA 90510
(562) 595-7831
URL: http://www.adultchildren.org/

**Al-Anon Family
Group Headquarters**
1600 Corporate Landing Pkwy.
Virginia Beach, VA 23454-5617
(757) 563-1600
FAX: (757) 563-1655
E-mail: wso@al-anon.org
URL: http://www.al-anon
.alateen.org/

**Alcoholics Anonymous
World Services**
PO Box 459
New York, NY 10163
(212) 870-3400
URL: http://www.aa.org/

Beer Institute
122 C St. NW, Ste. 350
Washington, DC 20001
(202) 737-2337
1-800-379-2739
FAX: (202) 737-7004
E-mail: info@beerinstitute.org
URL: http://www.beerinstitute.org/

**Bureau of International Narcotics and
Law Enforcement Affairs
U.S. Department of State**
2201 C St. NW
Washington, DC 20520
(202) 647-4000
URL: http://www.state.gov/p/inl

Campaign for Tobacco-Free Kids
1400 Eye St., Ste. 1200
Washington, DC 20005
(202) 296-5469
URL: http://www.tobaccofreekids.org/
index.php

Cocaine Anonymous World Services
PO Box 492000
Los Angeles, CA 90049-8000
(310) 559-5833
FAX: (310) 559-2554
E-mail: cawso@ca.org
URL: http://www.ca.org/

**Distilled Spirits Council of the
United States**
1250 Eye St. NW, Ste. 400
Washington, DC 20005
(202) 628-3544
URL: http://www.discus.org/

Drug Policy Alliance Network
70 W. 36th St., 16th Floor
New York, NY 10018
(212) 613-8020
FAX: (212) 613-8021
E-mail: nyc@drugpolicy.org
URL: http://www.dpf.org/

Nar-Anon Family Group Headquarters
22527 Crenshaw Blvd., Ste. 200B
Torrance, CA 90505
(310) 534-8188
1-800-477-6291
FAX: (310) 534-8688
E-mail: wso@nar-anon.org

URL: http://nar-anon.org/Nar-Anon/Nar-
Anon_Home.html

**Narcotics Anonymous
World Services**
PO Box 9999
Van Nuys, CA 91409
(818) 773-9999
FAX: (818) 700-0700
URL: http://www.na.org/

**National Council on Alcoholism and Drug
Dependence**
244 E. 58th St., Fourth Floor
New York, NY 10022
(212) 269-7797
FAX: (212) 269-7510
E-mail: national@ncadd.org
URL: http://www.ncadd.org/

**National Drug and Alcohol Treatment
Referral Routing Service**
1-800-662-4357

**National Institute on Alcohol Abuse and
Alcoholism**
5635 Fishers Ln., MSC 9304
Bethesda, MD 20892-9304
(301) 443-3860
URL: http://www.niaaa.nih.gov/

National Institute on Drug Abuse
6001 Executive Blvd., Rm. 5213
Bethesda, MD 20892-9561
(301) 443-1124
E-mail: information@nida.nih.gov
URL: http://www.nida.nih.gov/

**National Organization for the Reform of
Marijuana Laws**
1600 K St. NW, Ste. 501
Washington, DC 20006-2832
(202) 483-5500
FAX: (202) 483-0057

E-mail: norml@norml.org
URL: http://www.norml.org/

Office of National Drug Control Policy
Drug Policy Information
Clearinghouse
PO Box 6000
Rockville, MD 20849-6000
1-800-666-3332
FAX: (301) 519-5212
URL: http://www.whitehousedrugpolicy.gov/

Office of Safe and Drug-Free
Schools
U.S. Department
of Education
400 Maryland Ave. SW
Washington, DC 20202
(202) 401-2000
1-800-872-5327
URL: http://www.ed.gov/about/
offices/list/osdfs

Office on Smoking and Health
Centers for Disease Control and
Prevention
4770 Buford Hwy., MS K-50
Atlanta, GA 30341-3717
1-800-232-4636
E-mail: tobaccoinfo@cdc.gov
URL: http://www.cdc.gov/tobacco/

SAMHSA's Health Information Network
PO Box 2345
Rockville, MD 20847-2345
(240) 221-4036?
1-877-726-4727?
FAX: (240) 221-4292
URL: http://www.healthfinder.gov/orgs/
HR0027.htm

Substance Abuse and Mental Health
Services Administration
One Choke Cherry Rd.
Rockville, MD 20857

1-877-726-4727
FAX: 1-800-729-6686
URL: http://www.samhsa.gov/

U.S. Drug Enforcement
Administration
Office of Diversion Control
8701 Morrissette Dr.
Springfield, VA 22152
(202) 307-1000
1-800-882-9539
URL: http://www.usdoj.gov/dea/

Wine Institute
425 Market St., Ste. 1000
San Francisco, CA 94105
(415) 512-0151
FAX: (415) 356-7569
URL: http://www.wineinstitute.org/

RESOURCES

The various agencies of the U.S. Department of Health and Human Services (HHS) produce important publications on the consumption of alcohol, tobacco, and illicit drugs in the United States and their health effects. Reports of the U.S. surgeon general and special reports to Congress are published through this office.

The Substance Abuse and Mental Health Services Administration (SAMHSA) produces the annual National Survey on Drug Use and Health. SAMHSA also tracks treatment services. The most recent report is *National Survey of Substance Abuse Treatment Services (N-SSATS): 2009, Data on Substance Abuse Treatment Facilities* (June 2010). SAMHSA also tracks reported episodes of drug abuse; the most recent published results are in *Treatment Episode Data Set (TEDS) 1998–2008: National Admissions to Substance Abuse Treatment Services* (April 2010). The agency also operates the Drug Abuse Warning Network, which collects data from emergency departments.

The HHS also publishes the bimonthly *Public Health Reports*, the official journal of the U.S. Public Health Service. The journal is a helpful resource on health problems, including those that are caused by alcohol and tobacco. The Association of Schools of Public Health has been a partner in the publication of *Public Health Reports* since 1999.

The National Institute on Alcohol Abuse and Alcoholism (NIAAA) publishes the journal *Alcohol Research and Health*. The journal contains current scholarly research on alcohol addiction issues. The NIAAA also publishes the quarterly bulletin *Alcohol Alert*, which disseminates research findings on alcohol abuse and alcoholism.

The National Center for Health Statistics, in its annual *Health, United States*, reports on all aspects of the nation's health, including tobacco- and alcohol-related illnesses and deaths. The *Morbidity and Mortality Weekly Report* is published by the Centers for Disease Control and Prevention (CDC), which also publishes many studies on the trends and health risks of smoking and drinking. Additionally, the American Cancer Society and the American Lung Association provide many facts on cancer and heart disease.

The U.S. Department of Agriculture (USDA) was responsible for several helpful reports concerning tobacco up until 2005. Its publications *Tobacco Outlook* and *Tobacco Briefing Room* monitored tobacco production, consumption, sales, exports, and imports. These publications were discontinued in 2005 after the government ended the decades-old tobacco quota system. (See Chapter 7.) The USDA still publishes the annual *Agricultural Statistics*, which provides valuable information about farming, and *Food Consumption, Prices, and Expenditures*, which compiles data on how the nation spends its consumer dollars. Other useful information is provided by the Economic Research Service of the USDA and the U.S. Department of Labor's Bureau of Labor Statistics, which examines how people spend their income, including spending on cigarettes and alcohol.

The National Highway Traffic Safety Administration of the U.S. Department of Transportation produces the annual *Traffic Safety Facts*, which includes data on alcohol-related accidents.

The Bureau of Justice Statistics monitors crime in the United States and focuses on criminal prosecutions, prisons, sentencing, and related subjects. Particularly helpful are *Drug Use and Dependence, State and Federal Prisoners, 2004* (Christopher J. Mumola and Jennifer C. Karberg, October 2006), *Drugs and Crime Facts* (Tina L. Dorsey and Priscilla Middleton, 2011), and the annual publications *Compendium of Federal Justice Statistics* and *Sourcebook of Criminal Justice Statistics*. The Federal Bureau of Investigation's annual *Crime in the United States* provides arrest statistics for the United States. The U.S. Department of the Treasury's Alcohol and Tobacco Tax and Trade Bureau provides alcohol and tobacco tax information.

Other important annual surveys of alcohol, tobacco, and illicit drug use in the United States are conducted by both public and private organizations. The CDC's Youth Risk Behavior Surveillance monitors not only alcohol, tobacco, and illicit drug use but also other risk behaviors, such as teenage sexual activity and weapons possession. The Monitoring the Future survey of substance abuse among students from middle school through college is conducted by the National Institute on Drug Abuse and the University of Michigan Institute for Social Research. The most recent reports are *Monitoring the Future: National Survey Results on Drug Use, 1975–2009, Volume I: Secondary School Students* (Lloyd D. Johnston et al., September 2010) and *Monitoring the Future National Survey Results on Drug Use, 1975–2009, Volume 2: College Students and Adults Ages 19–50* (Lloyd D. Johnston et al., November 2010). The *Pride Surveys Questionnaire Report for Grades 6 to 12, National Summary Statistics for 2009–10* (September 2010), which is based on a survey of youth and parents, is produced by the Pride Survey.

The Wine Institute, the Distilled Spirits Council of the United States, and the Beer Institute are private trade organizations that track alcoholic beverage sales and consumption, as well as political and regulatory issues. Action on Smoking and Health publishes reviews that are concerned with the problems of smoking and the rights of nonsmokers. The Campaign for Tobacco-Free Kids provides information on tobacco-related federal, state, and global initiatives; cigarette taxes; tobacco advertisements; tobacco and smoking statistics; and tobacco-related special reports.

The Gallup Organization provides important information about the attitudes and behaviors of the American public.

The national policy on combating drug abuse is centered in the Office of National Drug Control Policy (ONDCP). The ONDCP, which prepares a drug control policy each year for the president and coordinates efforts across the federal bureaucracy, is an excellent source for statistics that are collected from many other agencies. Publications consulted for this volume include *National Drug Control Strategy: Data Supplement 2010* (2010), *National Drug Control Strategy: FY 2011 Budget Summary* (2010), *National Drug Control Strategy, 2010* (April 2010), and earlier reports.

Domestic law enforcement and interdiction activities fall under the U.S. Department of Justice. The U.S. Drug Enforcement Administration (DEA) oversees all domestic drug control activities. The DEA publishes *Drugs of Abuse* (2005), a resource tool that educates the public about drug facts and the inherent dangers of illegal drugs.

The effort to control drugs beyond the nation's borders is largely under the supervision of the U.S. Department of State. The agency within the Department of State in charge of the drug control effort is the Bureau of International Narcotics and Law Enforcement Affairs. An excellent source of information is the bureau's annual *International Narcotics Control Strategy Report*.

Gale, Cengage Learning sincerely thanks all the organizations listed here for the valuable information they provide.

INDEX

Page references in italics refer to photographs. References with the letter t *following them indicate the presence of a table. The letter* f *indicates a figure. If more than one table or figure appears on a particular page, the exact item number for the table or figure being referenced is provided.*

A

AA (Alcoholics Anonymous), 100, 151

AAA Foundation for Traffic Safety, 151

Abuse, substance

    admissions for treatment by substances abuse, 95

    deaths related to, 137

    drug, 8*f*

    economic costs of, 112–114

    five categories of, 2

    overall cost of, 113*f*

    overview of, 2–7

    persons admitted into drug treatment by substances abused, 96*t*

    persons admitted into substance abuse treatment, by primary substance of abuse/care received, 97*t*

    persons admitted into substance abuse treatment by/source of referral, 99*t*

    substances abused, demographics by, 95, 98

    See also Addiction; Alcohol abuse; Drug abuse; Drug treatment

ABD (Air Bridge Denial) program, 142–143

Acquired immunodeficiency syndrome (AIDS), 14, 149

Action on Smoking and Health, 151

"Actual Tobacco Settlement Payments Received by the States, 1998–2009 (Campaign for Tobacco-Free Kids), 115

ADAM (Arrestee Drug Abuse Monitoring) Program, 61

ADAM II 2009 Annual Report (National Institute of Justice), 61

Adan, Ana, 25

Addiction

    to cocaine, 55

    as defined by APA, 87

    disease model of addiction, 87–88

    drug addiction, risk factors for, 66*f*

    heroin addicts, numbers in U.S., 133

    to nicotine, 35, 37–38

    overview of, 2–7

    risk/protective factors, 65–66

    to tranquilizers, 53

    See also Dependence

Admissions, for treatment, 89

Adolescents. *See* High school students; Youth

Adult Children of Alcoholics, 151

Adults

    smokers, current adult, by age group/ gender, 36(*f*3.4)

    smokers, current adult, by ethnicity, 37*f*

    smoking among adults, current, 36(*f*3.2)

    smoking status of adults, by gender, 36(*f*3.3)

Advertising

    alcohol, 107–108

    tobacco, 108

    of tobacco products to youth, 73, 74

    tobacco, regulation of, 111

Advisory Committee to the Surgeon General, 40

Afghanistan

    opium poppy cultivation in, 123, 133–134, 134*f*

    terrorism in, links with illegal drugs, 140–141

African-Americans

    arrestee drug use, 61

    cigarette smokers, 34, 35

    current illicit drug users, 47

    drug offense convictions, 62

    drug use by prisoners, 64

    early use of alcohol, tobacco, marijuana, 65–66

    pain relievers, current users of, 52

    youth alcohol use, 71

    youth tobacco use, 76

After the War on Drugs: Blueprint for Regulation (Transform Drug Policy Foundation), 15

Age

    alcohol, age of first use, 66

    alcohol use in high school students by, 67

    binge drinking and, 18

    of cigarette smokers, 34, 35

    cocaine use by, 55, 56*f*

    of current illicit drug users, 47

    drug use by prisoners by, 64

    early use of alcohol, tobacco, marijuana, 65–66

    of first tobacco use, 73–74

    hallucinogens use among persons aged 18–50, by time of use/age group, 58*f*

    illicit drugs, age of first use, 76, 78

    illicit drugs and youth, 84

    of licensed drivers/alcohol-related fatalities, 30

    marijuana, high school students who tried before age 13, by gender, ethnicity, grade, 67*t*

    marijuana, new users of, over age 12, mean age at first use among those aged 12–49, 51(*f*4.5)

    marijuana use among persons aged 18–50, by time of use/age group, 51(*f*4.4)

    marijuana use by, 50

    methamphetamine use and, 54

    past-month illicit drug use among persons aged 12 or older, by age group, 48*f*

    persons admitted into drug treatment by, 93*t*

drunkenness, binge drinking, 69–70

early use of alcohol, tobacco, marijuana, 65–66

ecstasy (MDMA) use, trends in annual prevalence of, among eighth, tenth, twelfth graders, 86*f*

illicit drugs and, 76, 78–80, 81–84

inhalant use among eighth, tenth, twelfth graders, 80*f*

marijuana, harmfulness of, as perceived by students in 6–12, 81*f*

marijuana, students who tried before age 13, by gender, ethnicity, grade, 67*t*

marijuana use, trends in annual prevalence of, among eighth, tenth, twelfth graders, 82*f*

MDMA use by, 57

methamphetamine use by, 54

narcotics use by, 52

sedatives use by, 55

steroid use by, 59

tobacco, students who used smokeless tobacco/who usually bought cigarettes at store or gas station, by gender, ethnicity, grade, 75*t*

tobacco and, 73–76

tobacco use, harmfulness of, as perceived by students in grades 6–12, 77*f*

tranquilizer use, trends in annual prevalence of, among eighth, tenth, twelfth graders, 83*f*

tranquilizer use by, 53

who drank alcohol/smoked cigarettes before age 13, by gender, ethnicity, grade, 66*t*

youth alcohol use, demographic factors, 71

Hirayama, Takeshi, 41

Hispanics

arrestee drug use, 61

binge drinking and, 18

cigarette smokers, 34, 35

drug use by prisoners, 64

early use of alcohol, tobacco, marijuana, 65–66

youth alcohol use, 71

youth tobacco use, 76

HIV (human immunodeficiency virus), 14

Ho, M. K., 37

Hommer, Daniel W., 23

Hoover, Herbert, 13

How Tobacco Smoke Causes Disease: The Biology and Behavioral Basis for Smoking-Attributable Disease: A Report of the Surgeon General (Benjamin)

on deaths from tobacco use, 41

on health consequences of tobacco use, 39

on quitting smoking, 45

on secondhand smoke, 42

HRW (Human Rights Watch), 62

Huddleston, C. West, III, 100

Human immunodeficiency virus (HIV), 14

Human Rights Watch (HRW), 62

Hydrocodone, 52

Hydrogen cyanide, 38

Hypertension, 25

I

Illegal drugs, definition of, 1

Illicit drugs

amphetamine use, trends in annual prevalence of, among eighth, tenth, twelfth graders, 84*f*

anabolic steroids, 59

arrestee drug use, 61

cannabis/marijuana, 49–50

cocaine, 55

cocaine use among persons aged 18–50, by time of use/age group, 56*f*

conviction/sentencing trends, 61–62

crime and, 62–64

definition of, 1, 47

drug abuse arrests, 60

drug addiction, risk factors for, 66*f*

drug arrests, 61(*f*4.10)

drug use among state/federal prisoners in month before their offense, 64(*t*4.6)

drug users, 47

drug-related deaths, 49

drugs, impact of on state prison populations, 61(*f*4.11)

drugs of choice for past-month users aged 12/over, 49(*f*4.2)

ecstasy (MDMA) use, trends in annual prevalence of, among eighth, tenth, twelfth graders, 86*f*

federal budget for control of, 138–140

hallucinogens, 55–57

hallucinogens use among persons aged 18–50, by time of use/age group, 58*f*

heroin, 58–59

inhalant use among eighth, tenth, twelfth graders, 80*f*

inhalants, 57

legalization of, DEA facts regarding, 149*t*

marijuana, early use of, 65–66

marijuana, harmfulness of, as perceived by students in grades 6–12, 81*f*

marijuana, high school students who tried before age 13, by gender, ethnicity, grade, 67*t*

marijuana, new users of, over age 12, mean age at first use among those aged 12–49, 51(*f*4.5)

marijuana use among persons aged 18–50, by time of use/age group, 51(*f*4.4)

marijuana use, trends in annual prevalence of, among eighth, tenth, twelfth graders, 82*f*

methamphetamine, new users of, over age 12, mean age at first use among those aged 12–49, 54(*f*4.6)

methamphetamine use among persons aged 18–30, by time of use/age group, 54(*f*4.7)

pain relievers, nonmedical use of, among persons aged 12 and older, by time of use, demographic characteristics, 52*t*

past-month illicit drug use among females aged 15–44, by pregnancy status, 60*t*

past-month illicit drug use among persons aged 12 or older, by age group, 48*f*

past-month use of illicit drugs among persons aged 12 or older, 49(*f*4.3)

pregnancy, illicit drug use during, 59–60

psychotherapeutics, 50–55

sentenced offenders in state prisons, number of, by race, gender, and offense, 62*t*

sentences for violation of drugs laws, by type/length of sentence, U.S. District Courts, 63*t*–64*t*

tranquilizer use, trends in annual prevalence of, among eighth, tenth, twelfth graders, 83*f*

trends in use of, 6(*f*1.2)

use, trends in annual prevalence of, by population type, 78*f*

use of among persons aged 12/older, by time of use/demographic characteristics, 48*t*

used most frequently, 47, 49

War on Terror and, 140–141

youth and, 76, 78–80, 82–84

See also Antidrug efforts/criticisms

Importation, of methamphetamine into U.S., 127–128

Impotence, alcohol and, 26

"In a First, CNN Runs a Liquor Commercial" (Elliott), 107

Incarceration

conviction/sentencing trends for drug offenses, 61–62

drug abuse arrests and race, 61

drug use among state/federal prisoners in month before their offense, 64(*t*4.6)

drugs, impact of on state prison populations, 61(*f*4.11)

sentenced offenders in state prisons, number of, by race, gender, and offense, 62*t*

Inhalants

age of first use, 76

drugs of choice for past-month users aged 12 and over, 49(*f*4.2)

high school students, trends in use of, 79

inhalant use among eighth, tenth, twelfth graders, 80*f*

overview of, 57

N

morphine, 53

oxycodone/hydrocodone, 52–53

use, early history of, 10–11

use of, 19th century and beyond, 12–15

Narcotics Anonymous World Services, 151

NASS (National Agricultural Statistics Service), 106

National Agricultural Statistics Service (NASS), 106

National Association of Children of Alcoholics (NACoA), 23

National Broadcasting Company (NBC), 107

National Cancer Institute (NCI)

definition of secondhand smoke, 41

on health consequences of tobacco use, 39

The Role of the Media in Promoting and Reducing Tobacco Use, 108

National Center for Chronic Disease Prevention and Health Promotion, 10

National Center for Health Statistics, 34–35

National Center on Addiction and Substance Abuse (CASA)

on alcohol, ways adolescents obtain, 67

on alcohol use, age of first, 66

on teenagers and drugs, 65

National Council on Alcoholism and Drug Dependence, 151

National Drug and Alcohol Treatment Referral Routing Service, 151

National Drug Control Strategy, 2006 (ONDCP), 141

National Drug Control Strategy, 2009 (ONDCP), 141

National Drug Control Strategy, 2010 (ONDCP), 141

National Drug Control Strategy: Data Supplement 2010 (ONDCP), 131, 133

The National Drug Control Strategy, FY 2004 Budget Summary (ONDCP), 14

National Drug Control Strategy: FY 2009 Budget Summary (ONDCP), 14

National Drug Control Strategy: FY 2011 Budget Summary (Office of National Drug Control Policy), 98

National Drug Court Institute (NDCI), 100

National Drug Intelligence Center (NDIC)

on cocaine availability in U.S., 130

on heroin, purity of, 135

on marijuana availability in U.S., 130–131

on marijuana use in U.S., 133

on methamphetamine distribution, 129

on methamphetamine importation, 127–128

on methamphetamine production, 126

National Drug Threat Assessment 2010, 113, 124

on origin of seized heroin, 134

pharmaceuticals, trafficking of, 135

National Drug Threat Assessment 2009 (National Drug Intelligence Center), 127–128

National Drug Threat Assessment 2010 (National Drug Intelligence Center)

on cocaine availability in U.S., 130

on economic costs of drug abuse, 113

on heroin, purity of, 135

on marijuana availability in U.S., 130–131

on marijuana use in U.S., 133

on methamphetamine distribution, 129

on methamphetamine importation, 128

on methamphetamine production, 126

on origin of seized heroin, 134

pharmaceuticals, trafficking of, 135

on trafficking in U.S., 124

National Health Interview Survey (NHIS), 34–35

National Highway Traffic Safety Administration (NHTSA)

on drinking and young drivers, 73

Traffic Safety Facts, 2008, 9, 29

National Institute of Justice, ADAM Program, 61

National Institute on Alcohol Abuse and Alcoholism (NIAAA)

on binge drinking, 70

contact information, 151

creation of, 9

on economic costs of alcohol abuse, 112–113

Five Year Strategic Plan FY09–14, 20

National Institute on Drug Abuse (NIDA)

on addictive nature of nicotine, 37

contact information, 151

on craving for nicotine, 38

creation of, 13

Drugs, Brains, and Behavior: The Science of Addiction, 87

on marijuana, 50

on risk factors for addiction, 65

on treatment, principles of, 98, 100

National Institutes of Health, 98

National Organization for the Reform of Marijuana Laws, 151–152

National Survey of American Attitudes on Substance Abuse XV: Teens and Parents (National Center on Addiction and Substance Abuse)

on alcohol, ways adolescents obtain, 67

on alcohol use, age of first, 66

on teenagers and drugs, 65

National Survey of Substance Abuse Treatment Services (N-SSATS), 88–89

National Survey of Substance Abuse Treatment Services (N-SSATS): 2009, Data on Substance Abuse Treatment Facilities (SAMHSA), 88–89

National Survey on Drug Use and Health (NSDUH)

alcohol, age of first use, 66

on alcohol consumption, 18

on alcohol use among college students/ other young adults, 69

on alcohol use by high school students, 67

on cigarette smokers, 34

on drug users, 47

on hallucinogen use, 55, 57

on illicit drug use during pregnancy, 59–60

on illicit drugs and youth, 84

on oxycodone users, 52

on pregnancy and smoking, 45

on psychotherapeutics, 50

on tobacco use by high school students, 74

on treatment facilities/persons using, 89

on use of tobacco products, 35

National Survey on Drug Use and Health: Volume I. Summary of National Findings (SAMHSA), 89

"The National Tobacco Control Program" (Centers for Disease Control and Prevention), 33

Native Americans and Alaskan Natives

current illicit drug users, 47

early explorers and, 9

pain relievers, current users of, 52

use of hallucinogens, 12

use of mescaline/peyote, 56

NBC (National Broadcasting Company), 107

"N.C.A.A. Is Criticized for Beer Advertising" (Robinson), 108

NCI. *See* National Cancer Institute

NDCI (National Drug Court Institute), 100

NDIC. *See* National Drug Intelligence Center

"Neurobiological Consequences of Maternal Cannabis on Human Fetal Development and Its Neuropsychiatric Outcome" (Justras-Aswad et al.), 59–60

"New FDA Rules Will Greatly Restrict Tobacco Advertising and Sales" (Layton), 108

"New Research Documents Success of Drug Abuse Treatments" (National Institutes of Health), 98

New York City, New York, smoking ban in, 43

NHIS (National Health Interview Survey), 34–35

NHTSA. *See* National Highway Traffic Safety Administration

NIAAA. *See* National Institute on Alcohol Abuse and Alcoholism

Nicotine

addictive nature of, 35, 37–38

FDA regulation of, 112

physical properties of, 33

premature aging from smoking, 39

withdrawal from quitting smoking, 45

Robiquet, Pierre-Jean, 11
Roche, 53
Rodriguez, Alex, 59
Rohypnol (date rape drug), 53
The Role of the Media in Promoting and Reducing Tobacco Use (NCI), 108
Romero, Simon, 144
Room, Robin, 25–26
Rural areas, 76
Rush, Benjamin, 8

S

SAMHSA. *See* Substance Abuse and Mental Health Services Administration
San Luis Obispo, California, 43
Sánchez-Turet, Miquel, 25
Schools, alcohol use and, 66
Schuckit, Marc A., 21
Secondhand smoke
    dangers of, 40
    public opinion on harmfulness of, 42f
    studies on effects of, 41–42
"Secondhand Smoke and Cancer" (National Cancer Institute), 41
Sedatives
    overview of, 54–55
    use of, 50
Seizures
    cocaine/heroin/methamphetamine/cannabis, 147(t9.8)
    domestic drug, 146
    of drugs along southwest/northern borders, 126t
    of drugs flowing into U.S., 126f
    illicit drug, 124
    MDMA, 147(t9.9)
    methamphetamine superlab by state, 148t
Sentencing
    prison sentences, for drug trafficking, 121, 123
    sentenced offenders in state prisons, number of, by race, gender, and offense, 62t
    sentences for violation of drugs laws, by type/length of sentence, U.S. District Courts, 63t–64t
    trends for drug offenses, 61–62
September 11, 2001, terrorist attacks, 140–141
Sertürner, Friedrich, 10–11
Services Research Outcomes Study (SROS) (SAMHSA), 98
Sex, effects of alcohol on, 23, 26–28
"Sex Difference in Alcoholism: Who Is at a Greater Risk for Development of Alcoholic Complication?" (Ceylan-Isik, McBride, & Ren), 22
Sexual assault, alcohol and, 22–23
Shaw, Charles, 15
Shipments, direct, 111

Single, Eric, 114
Sinsemilla, 49–50, 131
Skin, 39
Smith, Robert G., 40
Smokeless tobacco
    age of first use, 73–74
    early use of, 73
    health consequences of, 39
    use by high school students, 74, 75t
    users of, 35
    youth tobacco use, demographic factors, 75
Smoking
    boom in U.S., early twentieth century, 10
    cancers/chronic diseases causally linked to smoking, 39f
    deaths from, 41
    early antismoking efforts in U.S., 10
    health consequences of tobacco use, 38–40
    interactions with other drugs, 40
    movement to ban, 43
    public health and, 40–41
    public opinion on harmfulness of smoking, 34f
    public support for banning smoking in public places, 43f
    secondhand smoke, 41–42
    secondhand smoke, public opinion on harmfulness of, 42f
    smokers, current adult, by age group/gender, 36(f3.4)
    smokers, current adult, by ethnicity, 37f
    smokers, states with highest/lowest percentages of, 37t
    smoking among adults, current, 36(f3.2)
    smoking status of adults, by gender, 36(f3.3)
    stopping, 43–46
    Surgeon General's reports on smoking/health, 40t
    thirdhand smoke, 42–43
    See also Tobacco
Smoking and Health: Report of the Advisory Committee to the Surgeon General of the Public Health Service (Surgeon General's Advisory Committee), 10, 33, 40
"Smoking (Premature Aging)" (University of Alabama Health System), 39
"Smoking-Attributable Mortality, Years of Potential Life Lost, and Productivity Losses—United States, 2000–2004" (CDC), 114
Smuggling. *See* Trafficking, drug
Smurfing, 127
Snuff, 9
Sobering up, 25
Social sanctions, alcohol consumption and, 22

Sociocultural factors, affecting substance use, 4–5
Southwest border, drug seizures along, 126t
Speaking out against Drug Legalization (DEA), 149
Sports, 59
SROS (Services Research Outcomes Study) (SAMHSA), 98
Star-Ledger (newspaper), 59
State Children's Health Insurance Plan, 110
"State Cigarette Excise Tax Rates and Rankings" (Campaign for Tobacco-Free Kids), 110
"State Government Tax Collections in 2009" (Census Bureau), 109–110
State prisons
    drug use among state/federal prisoners in month before their offense, 64(t4.6)
    drug use by prisoners, 62–64
    drugs, impact of on state prison populations, 61(f4.11)
    sentenced offenders in state prisons, number of, by race, gender, and offense, 62t
States
    cigarette tax rates, 110f
    drug laws, 123
    marijuana laws, 147, 150
    persons admitted into drug treatment by, 90t–91t
    smokers, states with highest/lowest percentages of, 35, 37t
    tobacco prevention programs, funding for, 118t
    tobacco producing, 104–105
    tobacco settlement payments by, 116t–117t
Statistical information
    alcohol, annual prevalence of use by full-time college students vs. other young adults 1–4 years beyond high school, by sex, 69(t5.5)
    alcohol, high school students who drank, by gender, ethnicity, grade, 68(t5.3)
    alcohol, high school students who had five or more drinks in a row/who usually obtained alcohol by someone giving to them, 70(t5.8)
    alcohol, past-month use of, by eighth, tenth, twelfth graders, 68(t5.4)
    alcohol, per capita consumption of beer/wine/distilled spirits, 18t
    alcohol use, binge alcohol use, heavy alcohol use among drinkers aged 12/older, 19t
    alcohol use, harmfulness of, as perceived by students in grades 6–12, 72f
    alcohol use, trends in, 6(f1.3)
    alcohol use among college students 1–4 years beyond high school, trends in lifetime prevalence of, 70(t5.7)
    alcohol use among pregnant females, 28(t2.9)